States of Knowledge

In the past twenty years, the field of science and technology studies (S&TS) has made considerable progress toward illuminating the relationship between scientific knowledge and political power. These insights are now ready to be synthesized and presented in forms that systematically highlight the connections between S&TS and other social sciences. This timely collection of essays by some of the leading scholars in the field seeks to meet that challenge. The book develops the theme of 'co-production', showing how scientific knowledge both embeds and is embedded in social identities, institutions, representations and discourses. Accordingly, the authors argue, ways of knowing the world are inseparably linked to the ways in which people seek to organize and control it. Through studies of emerging knowledges, research practices and political institutions, the authors demonstrate that the idiom of co-production importantly extends the vocabulary of the traditional social sciences, offering fresh analytic perspectives on the nexus of science, power and culture.

Sheila Jasanoff is Pforzheimer Professor of Science and Technology Studies at Harvad University.

International Library of Sociology
Founded by Karl Mannheim
Editor: John Urry
Lancaster University

Recent publications in this series include:

Crime and Punishment in Contemporary Culture
Claire Valier

Consuming the Caribbean: From Arwaks to Zombies
Mimi Sheller

Adorno on Popular Culture
Robert R Witkin

Risk and Technological Culture: Towards a Sociology of Virulence
Joost Van Loon

Reconnecting Culture, Technology and Nature: From Society to Heterogeneity
Mike Michael

Mobilising Modernity: The Nuclear Moment
Ian Welsh

Sociology Beyond Societies: Mobilities for the twenty-First Century
John Urry

Property, Bureaucracy and Culture: Middle Class Formation in Contemporary Britain
Mike Savage, James Barlow, Peter Dickens and Tony Fielding

States of Knowledge

The co-production of science and social order

Edited by Sheila Jasanoff

London and New York

First published 2004 by Routledge
2 Park Square, Milton Park, Abingdon, Oxon OX14 4RN

Simultaneously published in the USA and Canada
by Routledge
270 Madison Ave, New York, NY 10016

New in paperback 2006

Routledge is an imprint of the Taylor & Francis Group

© 2004, 2006 Sheila Jasanoff

Transferred to Digital Printing 2006

British Library Cataloguing in Publication Data
A catalogue record for this book is available from the British Library

Library of Congress Cataloging in Publication Data

ISBN 0-415-40329-4 (pbk)
ISBN 0-415-33361-X (hbk)

Contents

Contributors

Michel Callon is Professor at the Ecole des Mines de Paris and researcher at the Centre for the Sociology of Innovation. He has recently published with Pierre Lascoumes and Yannick Barthe *Agir dans un monde incertain. Essai sur la démocratie technique* (Paris, Le Seuil, 2001) and is the editor of *The Laws of the Markets* (Blackwell, Oxford, 1998). He is currently finishing a study with Vololona Rabeharisoa of French patients' organizations. His other main areas of interest are the anthropology of markets and the study of technical democracy.

John Carson is Assistant Professor of history at the University of Michigan, where he teaches courses in U.S. intellectual history and the history of science. His publications include "Army Alpha, Army Brass, and the Search for Army Intelligence," *Isis* 84 (1993); "Minding Matter/Mattering Mind: Knowledge and the Subject in Nineteenth-Century Psychology," *Studies in the History and Philosophy of the Biological and Biomedical Sciences* 30 (1999); and "Differentiating a Republican Citizenry: Talents, Human Science, and Enlightenment Theories of Governance," *Osiris*, 17 (2002): *Science and Civil Society*. He is finishing a book manuscript under contract to Princeton University Press, tentatively entitled *Making Intelligence Matter: Cultural Constructions of Human Difference, 1750–1940*.

Peter Dear is Professor of history and of science and technology studies at Cornell University. He is the author of, *inter alia*, *Revolutionizing the Sciences: European Knowledge and Its Ambitions, 1500–1700* (Palgrave, 2001; Princeton University Press, 2001) and *Discipline and Experience: the Mathematical Way in the Scientific Revolution* (University of Chicago Press, 1995).

Michael Aaron Dennis is a historian of science and technology whose research interests are in the history of American physical sciences in the 20th century. He has been a member of Cornell University's Department of Science and Technology Studies. His book, *A Change of State: Political culture, technical practice and the origins of Cold War America* will appear with Johns Hopkins Press in 2004.

Yaron Ezrahi is Professor of political science at The Hebrew University of Jerusalem. He has published extensively in the areas of science and politics and democratic theory and practice. Among his books are *The Descent of Icarus: Science and the Transformation of Contemporary Democracy* (Harvard University Press,

1990), and *Rubber Bullets: Power and Conscience in Modern Israel* (University of California Press, 1998). He is currently working on a book on the structure of the democratic political imagination since late modernity.

Stephen Hilgartner is Associate Professor in the Department of Science and Technology Studies at Cornell University. He specializes in social studies of science and technology, especially contemporary biology and biotechnology. His book, *Science on Stage: Expert Advice as Public Drama* (Stanford 2000), won the Rachel Carson Prize from the Society for Social Studies of Science in 2002. He is currently completing a book on genome research in the 1990s.

Sheila Jasanoff is Pforzheimer Professor of science and technology studies at Harvard University's John F. Kennedy School of Government. Her research centers on the role of science and technology in democratic governance, with a focus on the production and use of science in legal and political decisionmaking. Her books include *The Fifth Branch: Science Advisers as Policymakers* (Harvard University Press, 1990) and *Science at the Bar: Law Science and Technology in America* (Harvard University Press, 1995). Her forthcoming book, *Designs on Nature*, on the politics of biotechnology in Britain, Germany and the United States will appear with Princeton University Press in 2004.

Michael Lynch is Professor in the Department of Science and Technology Studies at Cornell University. He has a background in sociology, and specializes in studies of the organization of day-to-day laboratory practices. He has also studied the organization of courtroom testimony, and is currently studying the intersection of law and science in criminal investigations involving DNA profiling. His books include, *Scientific Practice and Ordinary Action* (Cambridge University Press, 1993), and (with David Bogen), *The Spectacle of History: Speech, Text, and Memory at the Iran-Contra Hearings* (Duke University Press, 1996). He is Editor of *Social Studies of Science*, an international journal on the social dimensions of science and technology.

Clark A. Miller is Assistant Professor in the Robert M. La Follette School of Public Affairs and the Robert and Jean Holtz Center for Science and Technology Studies at the University of Wisconsin-Madison. His research explores the globalization of science and technology, with particular emphasis on the politics of Earth systems science and the institutionalization of expertise in emerging arrangements for global governance. He is co-editor of *Changing the Atmosphere: Expert Knowledge and Environmental Governance* (with Paul Edwards, MIT Press, 2001).

Vololona Rabeharisoa is Senior Lecturer in sociology at the Ecole Nationale Supérieure des Mines de Paris, France. Her main research interest is in sociology of medicine. She is investigating new modes of production of knowledge and practices in biomedicine related to different categories of diseases (orphan diseases, psychiatric disorders). She is co-author, with Michel Callon, of *Le Pouvoir des malades. L'Association française contre les myopathies & la recherche* (Paris, Les Presses de l'Ecole des mines, 1999).

William K. Storey is Assistant Professor of history at Millsaps College in Jackson, Mississippi, where he teaches British history, South African history, and world history, with special interests in the environment and technology. He is the author of *Science and Power in Colonial Mauritius* (University of Rochester Press, 1997) and *Writing History: A Guide for Students* (Oxford University Press, 1998; 2nd edn, 2003).

Charis Thompson is Assistant Professor of rhetoric and women's studies at the University of California at Berkeley. Her book *Ontological Choreography: Reproductive Technologies, Their Subjectivities and Their Economies* is forthcoming with MIT Press. A collection of essays, *Charismatic Megafauna: Essays in Selective Pronatalism*, is near completion.

Claire Waterton is Lecturer in environment and social policy in the Institute for Environment, Philosophy and Public Policy at Lancaster University. Her teaching and research concern the relationships between scientific knowledge and policymaking. Her current projects include the use of ethnographic methods to investigate commercialization in plant genetics and citizen participation in biodiversity policy. She is co-editor (with Bronislaw Szerszynski and Wallace Heim) of *Nature Performed: environment, culture and performance*, (Blackwell, Sociological Review Monograph Series, 2003).

Brian Wynne is Professor of science studies and deputy director of the UK ESRC Centre for the Social and Economic Aspects of Genomics at Lancaster University. Since the 1970s, he has been involved in research on scientific knowledge as constructed and deployed in public arenas like technology, environment and risk. He is the author of *Rationality and Ritual* (1982), a study of the discourses and rituals of rationality which defined the public inquiry into the controversial THORP nuclear reprocessing plant at Sellafield. He was a member of the European Environment Agency Management Board and Scientific Committee from 1995 to 2000. He acted as special adviser to the UK House of Lords Select Committee on Science and Technology *Inquiry* and *Report on Science and Society*, published in March 2000.

Acknowledgements

Any long academic project owes debts of many kinds, and this one perhaps more than most. Thanks are due, first and foremost, to the National Science Foundation, whose generous support to the Department of Science and Technology Studies at Cornell University (under NSF grant nos. DIR 9017187 to Cornell and SBR 9996124 to Harvard) made possible the interdisciplinary reflection and synthesis that inspired this volume. As the responsible program officers, Rachelle Hollander and Ron Overmann provided constant help and encouragement that went far beyond their formal administrative duties.

I would like to thank Routledge, and particularly James McNally and Mari Shullaw, for their confidence in and support of a collection that is avowedly academic and theoretical. As series editor, John Urry provided crucial and most welcome intellectual backing. In addition, three anonymous reviewers for the press strongly recommended publication. We are indebted to all of them for their support and guidance.

The ideas presented in this book were worked out in significant respects in my graduate seminar on "Science, Power and Politics," first taught at Cornell and continued at Harvard after 1998. I owe an enormous debt to the many talented students and fellows who attended that seminar over the years and who helped sharpen my thinking on the theme of co-production. Several of them have already begun to make their own original contributions to the literature of co-production, showing by example the rich possibilities of a research program couched in this theoretical idiom. Not all of these young scholars can be acknowledged by name, but I would like to thank a few whose intelligent and creative use of the co-production framework has reconfirmed my confidence in the significance of this project: Samer Alatout, Arthur Daemmrich, Robert Doubleday, Saul Halfon, Alastair Iles, Marybeth Long Martello, Shobita Parthasarathy, Jennifer Reardon, Jessie Saul, Kaushik Sunder Rajan, and Mariachiara Tallacchini. My debt to three other remarkable colleagues – Pablo Boczkowski, Martin Kusch and Stefan Sperling – is of a different order. All three read and commented in detail on my chapters in this volume; their perceptive, sympathetic, yet always challenging criticism greatly improved the clarity of the text. I am deeply grateful to them all; any remaining flaws and infelicities are, of course, my own responsibility.

At Harvard, my able assistants Seth Kirshenbaum and Constance Kowtna kept track of manuscript flow and provided invaluable help in the final editing and compilation of the texts. Their dedication and meticulous attention to detail made the final stages of a complex process seem unexpectedly easy.

My gratitude to the colleagues who contributed to the volume is almost beyond words, but it is important to note that their efforts are only partly reflected in the chapters they have written. Invisible but all-important intellectual work was done over many years while we collectively deliberated how to tackle the problem of science and social order in ways that would bring science and technology studies into productive dialogue with more traditional analyses of power and culture. Through corridor conversations and informal email exchanges, workshop meetings and, eventually, formal papers, we managed to overcome our disciplinary divisions and to create a discourse that was rigorous enough to give us shared analytic ground rules, yet flexible enough to accommodate highly varied, personal choices of topic, period, style and method.

Several institutions contributed to the success of the project at key stages, and each deserves acknowledgement. As already stated, Cornell University provided not just the physical but the spiritual home in which the ideas presented here were able to take root and flower. Harvard University's John F. Kennedy School of Government hosted, in November 1998, a workshop at which early drafts of many of the chapters were presented and discussed. Kyoto University, in the summer of 1999, offered a quiet haven for composing the first draft of the introductory chapters. Finally, in 2001–2002, the Wissenschaftskolleg zu Berlin made available the time and space for editorial reflection, without which our efforts could not have reached a successful conclusion. We hope this volume adequately expresses our thanks for all this invaluable support.

Sheila Jasanoff
Cambridge MA, May 2003

1   The idiom of co-production

Sheila Jasanoff

Science and technology permeate the culture and politics of modernity. On any day, the headline news provides crude but telling indicators of their influence. A Martian ethnographer visiting planet Earth in the first few years of the third millennium would have encountered a bewildering array of stories whose only discernible connection would have been the pervasive – though perversely inconsistent – role of science and technology in human affairs. The millennium opened with false fears of the so-called Y2K bug that might have made computer systems throughout the world crash at midnight, when 1999 rotated into 2000. In 2001, the seemingly well regulated technological system of American civil aviation was ferociously turned upon itself by young Islamic militants, who not only destroyed New York's tallest buildings, the twin towers of the World Trade Center, but used planes to expose unsuspected vulnerabilities at the heart of US domestic security. In retaliation, the United States launched two militarily successful wars in Afghanistan and Iraq, demonstrating that the advent of "smart weapons" had radically altered the dynamics of battle since the Vietnam era; by the official end of the Iraq invasion, some US observers even wondered (in a luxury permitted only to winners) whether modern warfare any longer needed human bodies on the front lines. Early 2003 also saw the loss of the US space shuttle Columbia with seven crew members, underlining again the fragility of manned space exploration. Behind the dramatic disasters and the violence of terrorism and war, ordinary human attempts to master nature proceeded at slower rhythms, as societies debated how to manage global climate change, AIDS, and other epidemic diseases; how to solve problems of clean water and renewable energy; how to improve crop yields without endangering farmers' livelihoods; how to treat the ancient infirmities of aging, infertility, mental illness, and disease; and how to stave off death itself.

Yet, in analyzing many of the defining phenomena of human history – those arising at the nexus of science, technology, culture and power – large segments of the social sciences seem almost to retreat into a conspiracy of silence. In a world increasingly driven by the market's logic, and by the discovery of knowledge as a resource, neoclassical economics and rational choice models have sought to explain why firms innovate and how governments can steer research and development for higher productivity (Branscomb and Keller 1998; also see Rosenberg

1994; Mowery and Rosenberg 1989). But these approaches provide at best schematic accounts of the varied human responses to climate change, biological weapons, mammalian cloning, genetically modified foods, new reproductive technologies, emerging diseases, loss of biodiversity, techniques of miniaturization, and the growth of the internet. Entailing prolonged, contested interactions among people, ideas, institutions and material objects, the recognition and uptake of these phenomena challenge many of the most basic categories of social thought — such as structure and agency, nature and culture, science and politics, state and society. The dominant discourses of economics, sociology and political science lack vocabularies to make sense of the untidy, uneven processes through which the production of science and technology becomes entangled with social norms and hierarchies. Still less do these conceptual frameworks allow us to evaluate how sociotechnical formations loop back to change the very terms in which we human beings think about ourselves and our positions in the world (Hacking 1999; 1992; Foucault 1972). Anthropology, with its focus on thick description (Geertz 1973) and its growing attentiveness to modern, non-exotic cultures, does better at the project of sense-making, but at the risk of losing historicity, overemphasizing locality, and sacrificing some of the abstracting and generalizing capacities of the other social sciences (but see, for example, Gingrich and Fox 2002).

By contrast, the emerging field of science and technology studies (S&TS) has adopted as its foundational concern the investigation of knowledge societies in all their complexity: their structures and practices, their ideas and material products, and their trajectories of change. Growing from many disciplinary roots — including history, philosophy, sociology, politics, law, economics and anthropology — S&TS today encompasses a rich tapestry of theoretical and methodological perspectives, all specifically directed toward investigating the place of science and technology in society (Jasanoff *et al.* 1995). Conversations between S&TS and neighboring fields about the links between knowledge, culture and power are therefore urgently needed and could be enormously fruitful. To further these discussions, however, disciplinary divisions within S&TS must be bridged, and more explicit efforts made to link the field's predominant concerns with those of the traditional social sciences. This book takes on both tasks by elaborating the concept of *co-production*, which has recently gained ground in diverse domains of S&TS research.

The book's main argument is that, in broad areas of both present and past human activity, we gain explanatory power by thinking of natural and social orders as being produced together. The texture of any historical period, and perhaps modernity most of all, as well as of particular cultural and political formations, can be properly appreciated only if we take this co-production into account. Briefly stated, co-production is shorthand for the proposition that the ways in which we know and represent the world (both nature and society) are inseparable from the ways in which we choose to live in it. Knowledge and its material embodiments are at once products of social work and constitutive of forms of social life; society cannot function without knowledge any more than knowledge can exist without appropriate social supports. Scientific knowledge, in particular, is not a transcendent mirror of reality. It both embeds and is embedded in social practices, identities, norms, conventions, discourses, instruments and institutions – in short, in all the building blocks of what we term the *social*. The same can be said even more forcefully of technology.

Co-productionist accounts, conceived in this way, avoid the charges of both natural and social determinism that have featured in recent academic debates around the field of science and technology studies, including the infamous "science wars" of the 1990s (Sokal and Bricmont 1998; Koertge 1998; Gross and Levitt 1994). Science, in the co-productionist framework, is understood as neither a simple reflection of the truth about nature nor an epiphenomenon of social and political interests. Rather, co-production is symmetrical in that it calls attention to the social dimensions of cognitive commitments and understandings, while at the same time underscoring the epistemic and material correlates of social formations. Co-production can therefore be seen as a critique of the realist ideology that persistently separates the domains of nature, facts, objectivity, reason and policy from those of culture, values, subjectivity, emotion and politics. However, co-production, in the view of contributors to this volume, should not be advanced as a fully fledged theory, claiming lawlike consistency and predictive power. It is far more an idiom – a way of interpreting and accounting for complex phenomena so as to avoid the strategic deletions and omissions of most other approaches in the social sciences.

The essays in this collection, then, endeavor to address audiences within S&TS and in neighboring social sciences, as well as interested readers in the humanities, sciences and policy institutions. As is implied by the book's title, *States of Knowledge*, a significant aim of several of the contributors is to explore how knowledge-making is incorporated into practices of state-making, or of governance more broadly, and, in reverse, how practices of governance influence the making and use of knowledge. States, we may say, are made of knowledge, just as knowledge is constituted by states. But the title also plays on the theme of co-production at additional levels. Knowledge, in particular, is seen as crystallizing in certain ontological states – organizational, material, embodied – that become objects of study in their own right.[1]

The authors seek to illuminate some shared concerns as well as some possible tensions between S&TS and more established fields. In pursuing these objectives, the book attempts to synthesize findings from the various subfields of science and technology studies (e.g. history of science, technology studies, sociology of scientific knowledge, feminist and cultural studies of science and technology, science and law, and science policy studies). Not all of the synthesis, however, is internalist, working exclusively within the core of S&TS. Once we approach the interconnectivity of nature and society with a co-productionist vision, we find echoes of and parallels to the concerns of science studies in other interpretive social sciences, from anthropology to political theory. Exploring some of these convergences is as much a project of this book as theorizing across S&TS. Indeed, the book makes explicit efforts to link literatures that have not previously been in conversation, revealing connections that should not only interest S&TS researchers but reverberate throughout the social sciences.

That said, a major purpose of the synthesis offered here is to highlight some cross-cutting theoretical assumptions in S&TS scholarship, as well as their normative implications, showing why S&TS methods and findings are indispensable for the analysis of power, culture and social change. Coming from disciplinary backgrounds in history, politics, sociology, law, anthropology, physics and science studies, the contributing authors vary in their research focus and methodological preferences; yet they epitomize the common orientations of many S&TS scholars toward the relationship between knowledge and social order. In jointly presenting their views on co-production, the authors emphasize the analytic achievements of S&TS as a whole in relation to other areas of current humanistic and social thought. They also help contradict certain frequent but unfounded criticisms of S&TS scholarship: that it is too micro-focused to speak convincingly to social theory; too internalist in its focus on science and technology to hold interest for students of other social phenomena; and too lacking in normative bite to be sufficiently critical (Woodhouse *et al.* 2002; Scott *et al.* 1990).

The idiom of co-production speaks to the agendas of the traditional social sciences (and to some extent the humanities) in a number of ways. It fits most comfortably with the interpretive turn in the social sciences, emphasizing dimensions of meaning, discourse and textuality. This approach addresses and complements a number of specific disciplinary lines of thought. To political scientists, particularly those working in post-structuralist frameworks, co-production offers new ways of thinking about power, highlighting the often invisible role of knowledges, expertise, technical practices and material objects in shaping, sustaining, subverting or transforming relations of authority. To sociologists and social theorists, the co-production framework presents more varied and dynamic ways of conceptualizing social structures and categories, stressing the interconnections between the macro and the micro, between emergence and stabilization, and between knowledge and practice. To anthropologists, it offers further tools for analyzing problems of essentialism and stereotypic reproduction, showing how the cultural capacity to produce and validate knowledges and artifacts can account for long-term stability, as well as creativity and change. Finally, co-productionist accounts take on the normative concerns of political theory and moral philosophy by revealing unsuspected dimensions of ethics, values, lawfulness and power within the epistemic, material and social formations that constitute science and technology.

In all these respects, the co-productionist approach in S&TS is entirely compatible with projects in the history of science and technology. It is hardly surprising, then, that several contributors to this volume are historians by training (Carson, Dear, Dennis, Storey). An important value of the co-production idiom is that it may encourage more fruitful dialogue between historical and contemporary studies of science and technology, denying temporality the right to operate as a preordained conceptual and methodological barrier within S&TS. As co-productionist studies make clear, investigations of current science and technology stand to benefit immeasurably from greater historical depth, just as historical work may gain profundity and relevance through more explicit attention to questions of power, culture and normativity.

Research elaborating on the idea of co-production has condensed around a number of shared theoretical questions and their methodological consequences. At what levels of social aggregation (laboratories, communities, cultures, the nation, the state, all of humanity), and in what kinds of institutional spaces or structures does it make sense to look for co-production? Put differently, what is it that gets co-produced in nature and society? Are the most useful insights about co-production to be discovered at the level of science, power and culture writ large? Or is it more illuminating to trace in fine-grained detail how particular concepts for classifying or ordering social worlds – for example, selfhood, national identity, illness or wellness, professional standing, expertise, citizenship – gain, or have gained, stability and coherence, along with equally particular expressions of knowledge – for example, genetic markers, measures of human intelligence, climate change, agricultural science, or the scarcity of elephants? The essays in this volume demonstrate that there is no necessary unanimity about these matters in current research in the co-productionist framework; rather, the very open-endedness of the authors' methodological choices, along with the diversity of their substantive topics, gives this turn in S&TS scholarship some of its undeniable exuberance. At whichever scale individual studies are framed, though, the findings help to clarify how power originates, where it gets lodged, who wields it, by what means, and with what effect within the complex networks of contemporary societies.

Several recurrent and partially overlapping preoccupations in S&TS scholarship offer a means of organizing (and, in the future, fostering) work in the co-productionist idiom. The first has to do with the *emergence and stabilization* of new objects or phenomena: how people recognize them, name them, investigate them, and assign meaning to them; and how they mark them off from other existing entities, creating new languages in which to speak of them and new ways of visually representing them (Daston 2000; Dear 1995; Pickering 1995; Latour 1993; 1988a). The second concerns the framing and resolution of *controversy*. Under this heading, a large body of S&TS research has looked at the practices and processes by which one set of ideas gains supremacy over competing, possibly better established ones, or fails to do so (Richards and Martin 1995; Shapin and Schaffer 1985; Collins 1985). The third important line of research centers on the *intelligibility and portability* of the products of science and technology across time, place and institutional contexts. Topics under this heading range from the standardization of measures and analytic tools to the formation of new communities of practice, such as expert witnesses, who are capable of endowing claims with credibility as they are transported across different cultures of production and interpretation (Bowker and Star 1999; Jasanoff 1995; Shapin 1994; Porter 1992; Latour 1987; Kuhn 1962). The fourth significant tradition examines the *cultural practices* of science and technology in contexts that endow them with legitimacy and meaning. Work in this vein has asked how the supposed universality of facts and artifacts fares in disparate political and cultural settings, as well as how different domains of research and development acquire and retain particular cultural characteristics (Knorr-Cetina 1999; Rabinow 1996; Traweek 1988).

In each of these four focal areas – the emergence of new phenomena, the resolution of conflicts, the standardization of knowledge or technology, and the enculturation of scientific practices – work in the co-productionist idiom stresses the constant intertwining of the cognitive, the material, the social and the normative. Co-production is not about ideas alone; it is equally about concrete, physical things. It is not only about how people organize or express themselves, but also about what they value and how they assume responsibility for their inventions. Equally to the point, co-production occurs neither at random nor contingently, but along certain well documented pathways. Four sites of co-production are repeatedly investigated by the contributors to this volume: making *identities*, making *institutions*, making *discourses* and making *representations*. These provide an important bridge between the S&TS literature and many of the core productions of traditional political and social analysis, which also revolve around these basic analytic categories.

Essays in co-production

As an interpretive framework, co-production begs for illustration rather than proof. The chapters that follow display the idiom's breadth and plasticity, but in working out co-productionist ideas through detailed empirical studies, they also demonstrate the framework's practical uses and limits. In the next chapter, I make the theoretical case for co-production as an analytically useful concept by delineating the spaces it seeks to fill between dominant frames of analysis espoused by the social sciences. The chapter provides a detailed review of the S&TS literature that underwrites work in the co-productionist idiom. Here, we encounter two streams of thought: one focused broadly on the constitution of new technoscientific cultures, often around emergent ideas and objects; the other on solving problems of disorder within established cultures. I refer to these as the constitutive and interactional strands, respectively; they correspond broadly to well documented S&TS engagements with metaphysics and epistemology – or, as Hacking phrases it, "what there is and how we find out about it" (1999: 169). The chapter next outlines the programmatic aims of research on the theme of co-production and elaborates on the pathways by which co-production most often occurs. I conclude with reflections on how co-productionist ideas may help connect S&TS work to ongoing intellectual projects in other fields of social analysis.

The remaining chapters are grouped under three sets of thematic as well as topical headings. The first group – by Miller, Thompson, Waterton and Wynne, and Storey – looks at evolving perceptions of the environment and nature as sites of co-production; all these authors centrally engage with the simultaneous emergence of new knowledges, institutions and identities related to environmental change. The second group, consisting of chapters by Hilgartner, Rabeharisoa and Callon, Lynch, and in part Carson, investigates co-production as related to developments in the human and life sciences, especially the practices of research communities in genetics, clinical medicine and forensic science. These chapters bring to the fore issues of intelligibility and portability of knowledge, linked to the formation of new social identities and expert discourses. The third group, by Carson, Dear, Dennis, and Ezrahi, addresses a complex of issues centering on the macro-politics of knowledge; they focus on institutional conflicts among cognitive, moral and political authority, the mediating presence of experts, and the role of science and technology at times of significant political change. The connections between scientific knowledge-making and other authoritative cultural practices (religion, military, media) figure importantly in these chapters, which also deal with conflicts between alternative institutionalized knowledge-power formations. In short, these chapters play upon the book's title – states of knowledge – in its most open and obvious meaning.

With these groupings in mind, let us turn to a more detailed review of the individual contributions. The theme of institutional and epistemic emergence, as already mentioned, is especially prominent in the chapters dealing with the construction and deployment of environmental knowledge and the building of transnational political orders. Clark Miller addresses these issues on a planetary, or global, scale. Creating environmental knowledge about the biosphere involves, he suggests, not only new sciences and technologies, such as satellite data, general circulation models and integrated assessments, but also the fabrication of new institutions whose authority can credibly span the globe. Globalization, on Miller's account, is not simply the result of pre-stabilized knowledges, beliefs, products and social identities traveling around the world. Rather, it requires the manufacture of a newly imagined global political order that both links and tran-scends earlier nation-based centers of knowledge and power. Miller shows how the framing of climate change as a global issue, replacing the earlier view of climate as an aggregation of local weather problems, supplied a rationale for creating global institutions with claims to both scientific and political legitimacy. Previewing several succeeding chapters, Miller also shows that the attempt to supersede existing political orders produces its own tensions, exposing disagree-ments about the nature of "good science" as well as "good politics" on a supranational scale.

In her account of elephant protection in Africa, Charis Thompson examines co-production from the standpoint of international environmental regimes. She questions the presumption that knowledge must be consolidated in particular places before it can travel freely to other locations. Thompson argues that the shift in the elephant's status from "endangered" to "manageable" was not due to a context-specific, scientific determination of elephant biology, but went hand-in-hand with the emergence of a pan-African identity that could support multi-sited management practices. Originally forced to accept an absolutist scientific discourse of endangerment, African nations were enabled, through successive rounds of international negotiation, to put forward their view that elephants could be both hunted and protected in a regime of sustainable development. This "African" position, which merged ethics with science and made space for regional variation, successfully countered the monolithic bureaucratic rationality of some Western environmentalists. It produced, in effect, an authentically "African" elephant, unshackled by global discourse. A North–South dialogue that reopened divisions between lay and expert, and science and politics, led to the creation of a new moral economy around the elephant – thus making it possible to defend a new ontology for this most charismatic of all large animal species.

Claire Waterton and Brian Wynne also situate their study in the international arena as they examine how institutions and identities are bound up in processes of new knowledge formation. Their focus is on the European Environment Agency (EEA), a body that has been called upon to imagine and project a vision of Europe while at the same time shaping its own identity as a provider of objective, useful environmental knowledge to European policymakers. The agency sits at what one of its own analysts eloquently describes as "the eye of the hurricane" of European integration. The dilemma that Waterton and Wynne explore is that the EEA in a sense presupposes a full-blown European identity in order to legitimate its knowledge-producing activities; yet, in the very act of knowledge-making, the EEA participates in enacting Europe's nascent political order, choosing between models not yet set in stone. The evaluation of genetically modified (GM) crops and environmental chemicals illustrates the practical working out of this tension. The EEA, as Waterton and Wynne argue, recognizes that environmental uncertainty and risk demand new forms of deliberation and a critical approach to the existing centralized and officially sanctioned policy processes. At the same time, for its own legitimacy, as well as for the sake of the imagined, Platonic Europe that is aborning, the EEA cannot wholly let go of older assumptions of universal science and expert rationality. The EEA's experience in this respect is all about the messy and contested emergence of alternatives to the rationalizing, high-modernist state.

William Storey provides a historical counterpoint to the contemporary cases in his account of the foundation of the Imperial Department of Agriculture for the West Indies in 1898. The Department represented an institutional solution to a complex and overlapping set of problems: ecological and economic crisis in Britain's sugar-producing colonies; the unreliability of colonial science; Britain's changing imperial objectives and policies; and the urge to remedy, with the aid of science, perceived social problems that were deemed to be natural. As Storey observes, this was no simple case of science influencing politics or politics influencing science; rather, each set of practices – scientific and political – provided a rationale for the other. This interplay produced a powerful institutional form that was copied in agriculture departments throughout the world and provided a template for an emerging imperial politics.

The human and life sciences are particularly rewarding sites for co-productionist accounts because they are so often implicated in all of the important manifestations of this process discussed above: emergence, contestation, standardization and enculturation. The second group of chapters engages with these dynamics, and the associated roles of several non-state actors, such as scientists, patient groups and litigating parties. Stephen Hilgartner usefully reminds us that the institutions involved in co-production need not be those of the state. Practices for creating and contesting ownership, Hilgartner demonstrates, are deeply embedded in laboratories, where they shape both the internal workings of science and science's relations with the outside world. In his study, the laboratory becomes a site in which the institutions of property and ownership are redefined. Appropriation practices in genome laboratories thus constitute an inseparable part of their technological structure, moral order and everyday operation. Hilgartner's genome scientists challenge essentialist understandings of some basic social science categories. Their discourse blurs the contrast between micro and macro, and they remake the notions of "public" and "private" science through situated debates about who owns what in the laboratory.

Rabeharisoa and Callon also discuss a new kind of non-state institution, the "reflexive organization", which cuts across accepted divisions between lay and expert actors, and facilitates inquiry in a domain that increasingly demands the participation of the patient as an active research collaborator as well as a traditional research subject. Their investigation of the Association of French Muscular Dystrophy Patients shows lay individuals negotiating details of research and practice that are ordinarily thought to be the monopoly of specialist clinicians and scientists. The incorporation of a genetic disease as an element of their identity empowers muscular dystrophy patients and their families to participate in both knowledge-making and political action. Appearing, as it were, on both sides of scientific practice – as researchers and researched – the patients negate the conventional distinction between subject and object that has animated the work of science; only by acting as subjects can patients provide their partners, the orthodox scientific investigators, with a viable object of study. Further, by shaping novel discursive and organizational practices, they reorder many widely held assumptions about how biomedical science should be done in the contemporary world.

Michael Lynch directs his analysis toward the co-production of expert and non-expert knowledges in the context of US common law trials in the late twentieth century. This process, Lynch argues, does not consist simply of drawing a boundary between the two domains. Rather, it requires definition of the very category of expert and the assignment of particular individuals to that category. His analysis of cross-examination shows that the expert's identity is founded not on an individual's control of recognized knowledge and skills, but through mundane conversations and humdrum instruments, such as courtroom presentation of the professional résumé. Like Hilgartner, Lynch problematizes the easy distinction between micro- and macro-analytic categories. Courts engaging with forensic scientific evidence, he argues, are oblivious to such theoretical distinctions. In examining the credentials of a forensic DNA expert, for example, the court problematizes the "macro" categories of "science" and "expert" by enabling micro-, context-specific, adversarial dialogues to occur between witnesses and cross-examining attorneys. Lynch's "grammatical perspective" shows how the use of ordinary words allows courts to shift between two registers: on the one hand, paying homage to science's transcendence by seeming to honor the categories that set science apart; on the other hand, remaking the distinctions between science and common sense through case-centered decisionmaking. Courts in this way perform some of the essential political work of liberal democracies, by invoking and continually reproducing through their own practices the boundary between science and non-science.

John Carson turns his eye on a core problem of contemporary democracy, the fair distribution of scarce resources such as access to educational opportunities. Comparing the genesis of intelligence testing in early-twentieth-century France and the United States, he displays how one of the most taken-for-granted aspects of human identity – *intelligence* – has been configured in different ways in two different democratic cultures. Both intelligence and tests of it are emergent scientific objects, constituted through evolving expert discourses; but, going beyond normal accounts of science in the making, Carson's chapter compellingly delineates the *political* work done by these characterizations of human competence. Variations in the definition and measurement of intelligence between France and the United States can be attributed, he argues, to divergent understandings of equality in the two countries. In France, the democratic challenge is to represent existing social hierarchies as potentially open to all citizens. This has correlated with the assessment of merit through a standardized, state-administered educational system, in which performance according to collectively defined standards – not birth nor heredity – is the putative guarantor of success. In the United States, by contrast, hierarchies of merit are publicly disavowed, education is highly decentralized, and the federal role in rearing educated citizens is both constitutionally and ideologically circumscribed. The peculiarly American commitment to standardized, quantified and privately administered intelligence testing has taken root in this context as an objective, "scientific" instrument for sorting and classifying citizens – yet one which, given its power to produce inequality, remains essentially contested.

How the authority of science conflicts with or warrants other forms of authority, particularly the authority to govern at times of pronounced social change, is the central theme of the three remaining chapters; in these studies, co-production comes into focus as different forms of authority are constituted, embodied, challenged and restabilized. Peter Dear reflects on the interdependence of civil and epistemological authority in seventeenth-century Europe, as natural philosophers wrestled with the sources of legitimate expertise. The political theory underpinning absolutist ideologies of "mystery of state" applied, he suggests, to the establishment of knowledge-claims made through new kinds of experimental procedures resting on observations of nature. The credibility of such demonstrations could not be fully broken down into reasons, or analyzable components, that did not depend, at some irreducible core, on the reliability of the experimenter. For experimental results to be authoritative, experts thus needed recourse to some shared domain of unquestioned moral authority where further explanation was no longer felt to be necessary. In early modernity, Dear proposes, the rituals of absolute monarchy, including display to aristocratic audiences, provided natural philosophers with one such resource for establishing their own claims of transcendent expertise.

Michael Dennis' chapter focuses on the postwar confrontation in the United States between a science profoundly dependent on military funding and the state's defensive interests and the vision of science entertained by Michael Polanyi (1962) and others as an autonomous republic of free-thinking citizens. Vannevar Bush, a contemporary of Robert Oppenheimer and key presidential science adviser, embodies the precarious effort to resolve these contradictions. Dennis' portrayal of Bush uses a suggestive image – Bush's head surrounded by a crown of destructive weaponry – to symbolize the unresolved tensions between the sin of overdependence on a military agenda and redemption, through basic research, in postwar American science. Although Bush is widely identified as the chief architect of the National Science Foundation and author of American society's "contract with science", he is here revealed as a tragic figure, unable to rein in the momentum of militarization and state patronage unleashed by the war. In a personal defeat, this relic of an earlier, more gentlemanly era of independent expertise is sidelined in the less civil, more resource-hungry order of knowledge and power that he did so much to bring into being.

Yaron Ezrahi's essay deals with the most fundamental kind of political crisis – a change in the very foundations of contemporary democracy. Departing from his earlier magisterial work on modern science as legitimator and model for liberal democratic politics (Ezrahi 1990), Ezrahi notes that in today's world the representations of reality produced by science, and shared by a democratic citizenry, fight for space in the public mind with the onrush of images created and disseminated worldwide by the mass media. In contrast to the esoteric knowledge and information produced at great expense by science, media representations, which Ezrahi suggestively calls "outformations", are generally much more accessible to publics. They require less time, effort, knowledge and skills to interpret than does the information generated by science. However expensive they are to produce, media representations, once created, can be accessed by widely dispersed consumers and publics at relatively little additional cost. Media representations also contravene some of the most basic assumptions of scientific reality: that emotion, ambiguity, subjectivity and the inner self have to be bounded out of the space in which we perceive what is truly real. In these respects, they are more appealing to ordinary citizens. Increasingly, Ezrahi argues, the relatively high-cost, high-entry-barrier reality of science has had to distance itself from everyday human experience; lower-cost, more accessible media realities to some extent fill the imaginative void left by the retreat of science. Like other authors in this collection, Ezrahi is careful to note that he is not describing the overthrow of a hegemonic Enlightenment tradition by one that is equally totalizing in its fragmentation of human perceptions. What he describes is far more an emergence of competing claims on the democratic political imagination, whose implications for liberty and order we are not yet in a position to assess.

Finally, in a brief Afterword, I pull together and reiterate the thematic connections among the chapters, noting that they collectively make a strong case against linear, unidirectional causal explanations for complex social phenomena; they also reinforce the need to integrate studies of knowledge-making and technology-production with the analysis of human identities, institutions, discourses and representations. I conclude with some observations on the possible implications of co-production as a cognitive frame that itself gets picked up into newer cycles of world-making.

Note

1   I am especially grateful to Pablo Boczkowski for helping me to articulate the multiple meanings of the title of this volume.

2 Ordering knowledge, ordering society

Sheila Jasanoff

Science in culture and politics

Science and technology account for many of the signature characteristics of contemporary societies: the uncertainty, unaccountability and speed that contribute, at the level of personal experience, to feelings of being perpetually off balance; the reduction of individuals to standard classifications that demarcate the normal from the deviant and authorize varieties of social control; the skepticism, alienation and distrust that threaten the legitimacy of public action; and the oscillation between visions of doom and visions of progress that destabilize the future. Both doing and being, whether in the high citadels of modernity or its distant outposts, play out in territories shaped by scientific and technological invention. Our methods of understanding and manipulating the world curve back and reorder our collective experience along unforeseen pathways, like the seemingly domesticated chlorofluorocarbons released from spray cans and air conditioners that silently ate away at the earth's stratospheric ozone layer. Just as environmental scientists are hard put to find on earth an ecological system that has not been affected by human activity, so it is difficult for social scientists to locate forms of human organization or behavior anywhere in the world whose structure and function have not been affected, to some extent, by science and technology.

Take culture, in particular, or more accurately cultures. Although science and technology are present everywhere, the rambunctious storyline of modernity refuses to conform to any singular narrative of enlightenment or progress. The familiar ingredients of modern life continually rearrange themselves in unpredicted patterns, creating rupture, violence and difference alongside the sense of increasing liberation, convergence and control. The terrorist attacks in the United States on 11 September 2001 acted out in brutal reality and on global television screens many contradictions that were already seething below the surface. On a clear, sparkling day in early fall, nineteen young Muslim militants hijacked four civilian aircraft and rammed them into the World Trade Center's twin towers in New York, the Pentagon in Washington, and a field outside Pittsburgh, Pennsylvania. This was suicidal violence on a previously unimagined scale. The pyres on which the hijackers immolated themselves killed more than 3,000 innocent people who had left home for a normal day at work. The shockwaves broke America's late-twentieth-century dream of inviolability, and hastened the birth, some said, of a new empire dominated by American military might. US-led wars in Afghanistan and Iraq toppled regimes and fundamentally altered the legal and political order of the post-Cold War world.

Yet, at the threshold of a new millennium, this 11 September and its violent aftershocks only dramatized in horrific form much that was already known. Industrial societies, despite their many commonalities, articulate their needs and desires in different voices. Despite the ubiquity of CNN, Microsoft and the Coca-Cola can (Barber 1995) – and the global homogeneity they signal – the din of multivocality rises rapidly as one leaves the havens of the industrial West. Politicians and citizens in Washington, Paris, Tokyo and Baghdad have met the challenges and dislocations of the present with disparate resources and divergent criteria of what makes life worth living. The world is not a single place, and even "the West" accommodates technological innovations such as computers and genetically modified foods with divided expectations and multiple rationalities. Cultural specificity survives with astonishing resilience in the face of the leveling forces of modernity. Not only the sameness but also the diversity of contemporary cultures derive, it seems, from specific, contingent accommodations that societies make with their scientific and technological capabilities.

The dynamics of politics and power, like those of culture, seem impossible to tease apart from the broad currents of scientific and technological change. It is through systematic engagement with the natural world and the manufactured, physical environment that modern polities define and refine the meanings of citizenship and civic responsibility, the solidarities of nationhood and interest groups, the boundaries of the public and the private, the possibilities of freedom, and the necessity for control. What we know about the world is intimately linked to our sense of what can we can do about it, as well as to the felt legitimacy of specific actors, instruments and courses of action. Whether power is conceived in classical terms, as the power of the hegemon to govern the subject, or in the terms most eloquently proposed by Michel Foucault, as a disciplining force dispersed throughout society and implemented by many kinds of institutions, science and technology are indispensable to the expression and exercise of power. Science and technology operate, in short, as *political* agents. It would not be utterly foolhardy to write the political history of the twentieth century in terms of its most salient technoscientific achievements: the discoveries of the atom and the bomb, the gene and its manipulation, radio communication, television, powered flight, computers, microcircuitry, and scientific medicine.

In what conceptual terms, then, should we discuss the relationships between the ordering of *nature* through knowledge and technology and the ordering of *society* through power and culture? How should we characterize the connections between the human capacity to produce facts and artifacts that reconfigure nature, and the equally human ability to produce devices that order or reorder society, such as laws, regulations, experts, bureaucracies, financial instruments, interest groups, political campaigns, media representations or professional ethics?

Does it any longer make sense for those concerned with the study of power to assume that scientific knowledge comes into being independent of political thought and action, or that social institutions passively rearrange themselves to meet technology's insistent demands? Established disciplinary languages fail us in grappling with these questions; disciplinary scholars find themselves at a loss for words, almost as if a Wall Street banker were asked to interpret a Balinese cock fight or a Bangladeshi rice farmer to comment on DNA typing in the O. J. Simpson murder trial. To fill this void, we draw in this book on several decades of detailed scholarship on the workings of science and technology within society. More specifically, we elaborate on the concept of *co-production*, which has recently gained ground in the emerging field of science and technology studies (S&TS).

In this chapter, I begin to make the case for co-production by first delineating the gap it seeks to fill between frames of analysis espoused by the traditional social sciences. This is followed by a review of the literature in science and technology studies that underwrites work in the co-productionist idiom. To clarify the analytic aims of this literature, I delineate two broad streams of thought – the constitutive and the interactional – that deal, respectively, with the emergence of new socio-technical formations and with conflicts within existing formations. The next section elaborates on the patterned pathways by which co-production occurs, identifying four major research programs that have developed around this theme. The chapter concludes by recapitulating the implications of the co-productionist idiom for future work in S&TS. In the interests of cross-disciplinary engagement, the chapter points throughout to connections between work in contemporary science studies and theoretically compatible work in other related disciplines.

A language for hybrids

The need for a generative discourse for discussing the role of science and technology in society is abundantly clear. What happens in science and technology today is interwoven with issues of meaning, values, and power in ways that demand sustained critical inquiry. Consider, for example, the transformation of a sheep named Dolly, born of a virgin mother in an obscure laboratory near Edinburgh, Scotland, into a universally recognized symbol[1] – of progress for some and moral transgression for others. Cloning was hardly the kind of event that could be counted on to set in motion the machinery of high politics. The scientific claims of the Edinburgh researchers had not been tested or replicated when they captured headlines round the world; the implications of the research remained distant and speculative (Wilmut *et al.* 1997). Dolly was a product of biomedical, not military, science. Her materialization posed no immediate threat to people's livelihood or security. Yet presidents and prime ministers reacted in haste to the news of Dolly's cloning, recognizing as if by some inarticulate sixth sense that this was an event for which politicians as well as scientists would be held accountable. Similarly, on 9 August 2001, a still unseasoned President George W. Bush devoted his first ever televised news conference to his government's policies for research with embryonic stem cells. Notably, too, the rush to find the right frames within which to fit Dolly or stem cells – in science, politics, morality or law – led to results that were far from uniform across liberal democratic societies (Jasanoff forthcoming a).

Such complicated choreography is not uniquely associated with the life sciences. In little more than a decade, a formless entity called the internet, whose organization and governance remain a mystery to most of its users, became a player in countless contemporary social transactions. In exploring its possibilities, millions of people began to alter not only the architecture of the internet but also, in diverse ways, their own preconceptions of what it means to belong to social units such as the family, community, workplace, firm or nation. The sum of their interactions has changed the nature of commerce and capital, producing integration and disruption on global scales. Sometimes with a bang, as in the work of the Al-Qaeda terrorist network and its violent aftermath, and at other times in incremental whimpers, notions of ownership, privacy, security, nation and governance are all being transformed. In the computer age, it is increasingly difficult to pin down with certainty the places where politically salient events originate, let alone to determine who controls the levers of power. Similar fragmentation and dispersal of authority have also been noted by sociologists of risk. Not without cause has the German sociologist Ulrich Beck (1998) called the politics of risk "a form of organized irresponsibility" (see also Beck 1992).

To be sure, the idea that the gene or the computer chip can reshape society around its inbuilt logic has lost its cachet in the world of scholarship, even though determinist arguments still predominate in much popular writing about technological developments. Unlike Athena sprung full-grown from brow of Zeus, social and political arrangements for exploiting, resisting or quite simply accommodating technological change do not emerge, intact and fully formed, in response to innovation and discovery. Technology does not, when all is said and done, "drive history" (Smith and Marx 1994). Legal and political institutions lead, as much as they are led by, society's investments in science and technology. The material and cultural resources with which human actors bring new natural phenomena into view, or seek to domesticate unfamiliar inventions, often exist before the "discovery" of the objects themselves. The design of technology is likewise seldom accidental; it reflects the imaginative faculties, cultural preferences and economic or political resources of their makers and users (Bijker 1997; Bijker *et al.* 1987). In engagements with the physical world, we are not mere spectators whose responses and destinies are ineluctably transformed by the growth of knowledge and the acquisition of novel technological capability. At the same time, when we tune into the rhythms of everyday life, even at times of exceptionally rapid technoscientific change (as arguably in the late twentieth century), we experience more often the steady hum of continuity than the sense of disequilibrium. In short, the ways in which we take note of new phenomena in the world are tied at all points – like the muscles on a skeleton or the springs on a cot frame – to the ways in which we have already chosen to live in it. Yet, astonishingly, most theoretical explorations of how social worlds evolve only imperfectly reflect the complicated interplay of the cognitive, the institutional, the material and the normative dimensions of society.

That traditional disciplinary discourses fall short in this way should not be taken as a sign of lack of progress in understanding the intersections of science and technology with politics and culture. To the contrary, several decades of research in science and technology studies have done much to illuminate how orderings of nature and society reinforce each other, creating conditions of stability as well as change, and consolidating as well as diversifying the forms of social life. A compelling body of scholarship has demonstrated that science and technology can be fruitfully studied as social practices geared to the establishment of varied kinds of structure and authority (Biagioli 1999; Jasanoff *et al.* 1995; Pickering 1995; Clarke and Fujimura 1992; Bijker *et al.* 1987; Barnes and Edge 1982). So viewed, the workings of science and technology cease to be a thing apart from other forms of social activity, but are integrated instead as indispensable elements in the process of societal evolution. Science, made social in this way, can be compared and contrasted with other exercises in the production of power (Latour 1999; 1988a; 1987). Increasingly, the realities of human experience emerge as the joint achievements of scientific, technical and social enterprise: science and society, in a word, are *co-produced*, each underwriting the other's existence.

But where does this insight lead political and social analysis? Does the idea of co-production represent anything more than the intuitively obvious point that ideas of nature, no less than ideas of society, are constructed by human endeavor – that both science and technology are fundamentally human achievements? If that were all, it would be cold comfort. A theoretical enterprise that seeks to explain why the world is ordered in certain ways has to promise more than the line from the popular children's song, "Everything hangs together because it's all one piece". Does co-production as we have defined it in Chapter 1 yield better, more complete descriptions of natural and social phenomena than are to be found in more orthodox accounts? Can co-production serve the explanatory purposes that we have come to expect of theories in the social sciences? Can it provide normative guidance, or at least facilitate our critical interpretation of the diverse ways in which societies constitute, or reconstitute, themselves around changes in their apprehension of the natural world? Can the co-productionist approach ever predict?

Recent work in science and technology studies strongly suggests that these questions can be answered in the affirmative, although modestly, especially with regard to prediction, and with due regard for persistent disciplinary divisions within the field that have tended to obscure some of its most general insights. There has been a dearth of scholarship that integrates salient theoretical currents within S&TS, largely emanating from sociological, political and cultural studies of science, with its rich store of empirical findings, the latter deriving most importantly from the history of science and technology, but augmented lately by a growing body of work using disciplines ranging from anthropology to law. A relatively narrow focus on the particularities of scientific and technological production is also partly to blame.

Scientific biographies and studies of specific theories, artifacts or institutions have not always made explicit the connections between the mundane practices of science and those of politics and culture. Feminist theorists are an obvious exception (Haraway 1989; Keller 1985), and a handful of other authors have explicitly addressed state–science relations from an S&TS perspective (for example, Jasanoff 1992; 1990; Ezrahi 1990; Mukerji 1989; Shapin and Schaffer 1985). For the rest, research on science and technology has not sought to build systematic connections between the micro-worlds of scientific practice and the macro-categories of political and social thought. Sociology and political theory, for their part, have tended on the whole to leave science, and only slightly less so technology, out of their analytic programs — again with notable exceptions (Bourdieu 1980; Habermas 1975; Merton 1973). To date, the knowledge-making and knowledge-implementing faculties of human societies have received considerably less critical attention than such staple objects of social theory as race, class, gender, ideology, interests and power.

Among social theorists, the one who perhaps most consistently sought to bring together the analysis of knowledge and power is Michel Foucault (1971; 1972; 1973; 1979), whose work has exercised growing influence on research in S&TS. Foucault's imprint is particularly apparent in work, including contributions to this volume, that deals with classification, standardization, and the accrual of power by institutions that have the capacity to discipline people's bodies, minds and forms of life. His monumental legacy, however, is less well suited to exploring how diversity keeps reappearing and reasserting itself, even in the most entrenched institutions of modernity, such as expert bureaucracies. Some of the chapters in this volume address this problematic.

With the other contributors to this volume, I suggest that we have now arrived at a point at which we can usefully begin to pull together what has been learned in S&TS about the interpenetration of science and technology with cultural expressions and social authority. While it may be premature to propound anything so ambitious as a theory of co-production, it is not too soon to begin with more circumscribed steps. We can ask, in particular, what aspects of the role of science and technology in society may most appropriately be couched in the idiom of co-production: for instance, what sorts of scientific entities or technological arrangements can usefully be regarded as being co-produced with which elements of social order; what are the principal pathways by which such co-production occurs; how do processes of co-production relate to more orthodox accounts of technical or political change in S&TS and other disciplines; and what methods and approaches are best suited to investigating instances of co-production?

In addressing these questions, it is helpful to separate the relevant S&TS literature into two strands that have sought in disparate though closely connected ways to theorize the interplay of society, science and technology. We may call these, for ease of reference, the *constitutive* and the *interactional*. The former is primarily concerned with the ways in which stability is created and maintained, particularly for emergent phenomena, whether in a particular site where knowledge is made, such as a research laboratory, hospital or legal proceeding, or around a novel technoscientific object, such as the human genome or a periodic table for chemicals. At the most basic level, the constitutive strain in S&TS seeks to account for how people perceive elements of nature and society, and how they go about relegating part of their experience and observation to a reality that is seen as immutable, set apart from politics and culture. This body of work is most closely related to metaphysical concerns in the philosophy of science, because one cannot discuss the constitution of nature or society without resolving questions about what it means to be natural or social, human or non-human. Co-productionist accounts, however, are not content simply to ask what *is*; they seek to understand how particular states of knowledge are arrived at and held in place, or abandoned.

The interactional approach, by contrast, is less overtly concerned with metaphysics and more so with epistemology — or less with what is and more with how we know about it (Hacking 1999: 169). This line of work takes for granted that, in most exercises of world-making, neither science nor society begins with a clean slate but operates always against the backdrop of an extant order, in which people already "know" in pragmatic terms what counts as nature or science and what as society or culture. Nonetheless, boundary conflicts about where these domains begin and end continually arise and call for resolution (Gieryn 1999). As well, the recognition of new phenomena often entails confrontation between competing epistemologies. Work in the interactional mode probes how human beings organize, and periodically reorganize, their ideas about reality under these circumstances. It seeks to elucidate the myriad mutual accommodations between social and scientific practices that occur within existing socio-technical dispensations during times of conflict and change. If constitutive analysis focuses in the main on the emergence of new facts, things and systems of thought, then the interactional strain concerns itself more with knowledge conflicts within worlds that have already been demarcated, for practical purposes, into the natural and the social.

Varieties of co-production

Since scientific knowledge first came to be seen as constituted by social practices (Collins 1985; Latour and Woolgar 1979; Bloor 1976; Kuhn 1962), S&TS researchers have realized that the fruits of their labors are at best imperfectly captured by the dictum that scientific knowledge is socially constructed. This formulation gives rise to two unresolvable problems, one theoretical and the other pragmatic. The first is that it confers a kind of causal primacy upon the "social" that careful work in S&TS, broadly conceived, has consistently denied (Knorr-Cetina 1999; Collins 1998; Pickering 1995; Woolgar 1988).[2] Constructivism does not imply that social reality is ontologically prior to natural reality, nor that social factors alone determine the workings of nature; yet the rubric "social construction" carries just such connotations (Hacking 1999). The second and more practical difficulty is that the discourse of social construction tends to inhibit the symmetrical probing of the constitutive elements of both society and science that forms the essence of the S&TS research agenda. One or another aspect of the "social" — be it "interests", "capital", "gender", "state" or "the market" — risks being black-boxed, treated as fundamental, granted agency, and so exempted from further analysis.[3] The suspicion that social constructivists are arrogating to themselves an Archimedean point from which to deconstruct science has provoked criticism of S&TS as insufficiently reflexive (Woolgar 1988). It is also this reductionist reading of the "social" that has allowed defenders of the transcendental nature of science to rail at the idea of science as a social construct; in the so-called science wars of the 1990s, attackers of science studies frequently charged the field with misrepresenting scientific knowledge as "merely" social or political (Sokal and Bricmont 1998; Koertge 1998; Gross and Levitt 1994). Of course, no adequately social representation of science could ever be dismissed with the label "merely".

With greater maturity, science studies as a field has moved to show that what counts as "social" about science is itself a subject of unsuspected depth and complexity. For example, early efforts to explain how controversies end, in both science and technology (Richards and Martin 1995; Nelkin 1992; Bijker *et al.* 1987; Barnes 1977), often represented closure as a negotiated sorting out of competing social interests. Such work assumed, along with mainstream scholarship in economics and political science, that society can be unproblematically conceptualized as composed of interest groups with clearly articulated (exogenous) positions and preferences. These interests, or stakes, were then invoked to explain the positions taken by different actors concerning knowledge claims and their technological embodiments. Newer work recognizes the inadequacy of interests as a primary explanatory category. Interests themselves have a social history: how they arise and are sustained are matters to be investigated, not taken for granted. The results of such investigation include, *inter alia*, a greatly increased concern with the standardization of scientific and social practices (Bowker and Star 1999), a sensitivity to the place of material agents in the production of stable knowledge (Galison 1996; 1987; Pickering 1995; 1992), a focus on the techniques of scientific representation (Hilgartner 2000; Lynch and Woolgar 1990), a growing appreciation of the influence of language (Dear 1995; 1991; Keller 1985), a preoccupation with the bases of trust in science (Irwin and Wynne 1994; Porter 1995; Shapin 1994), and heightened sensitivity to the ways in which knowledge achieves practical universality in widely divergent socio-political settings (Jasanoff and Wynne 1998; Jasanoff 1986).

Perhaps the most important by-product of all this inquiry is the recognition that the production of order in nature and society has to be discussed in an idiom that does not, even accidentally and without intent, give primacy to either. The term *co-production* reflects this self-conscious desire to avoid both social and technoscientific determinism in S&TS accounts of the world. The concept has by now acquired a respectable ancestry within the field, although there are varying schools of thought on exactly how to define and employ it. Barnes (1988) came close to a co-productionist position in talking about the nature of power; the same human capacities for learning, responding to and transmitting knowledge, he noted, are responsible for the creation of natural and social order. His two orderings are more interactional than mutually constitutive in the sense implied by other observers of co-production, and the role of material objects in constituting order is left vague at best. By contrast, Daston (2000), introducing a collection of essays on the "coming into being" of scientific objects, calls attention to their ability not only to focus scientific inquiry but also to crystallize emergent and socially salient features of their cultural contexts. These objects, like people, have "biographies"; they are "not inert" but quite often changeable and "attain their heightened ontological status by producing results, implications, surprises, connections, manipulations, explanations, applications" (Daston 2000: 10). They are for all practical purposes not only scientific objects but also social objects, produced in indiscriminate acts of synthesis out of a society's epistemological, esthetic and instrumental strivings. All this is quite consistent with the standpoint of co-production represented in this volume, but Daston's commitment in the end is to the *history* of science's objects of study; neither power nor culture is explicitly an issue in her account, although the categories of state and society figure in the contributions of some authors. The making of science is also *political*, we argue; indeed, a central claim of our collection is that there cannot be a proper history of scientific things independent of power and culture.

Pursuing this line of thought, some S&TS scholars see co-production as a process that is as foundational as constitution-making or state-making in political theory, because it responds to people's deepest metaphysical concerns. It does so, in part, by continually reinscribing the boundary between the social and the natural, the world created by us and the world we imagine to exist beyond our control. "Science" and "politics" can then be treated as separate and distinct forms of activity rather than as strands of a single, tightly woven cultural enterprise through which human beings seek to make sense of their condition. Others working in a co-productionist vein are less concerned with metaphysics and more interested in the practical accommodation of new knowledge within existing forms of life. For them, there is nothing inherently problematic about seeing the world as organized, at any given moment, into clearly demarcated domains of "science" and "politics". Ideas and objects are simply obliged to undergo a kind of parallel processing in order for problems to be solved in either domain: that is, nothing significant happens in science without concurrent adjustments in society, politics or culture; similarly, intransigent social problems seldom yield to resolution without changes in existing structures of knowledge. Fitting technology into this picture makes for further quandaries, since humanity's material productions affect both what we know and how we behave. S&TS scholars have differed importantly in how they view the role of the material and the inanimate in constituting social order, and the degree of agency that they are prepared to grant to non-humans (Hacking 1999; Latour 1996; Collins and Yearley 1992; Callon and Latour 1992).

As we shall see in subsequent chapters, there is no univocal position on these matters in current work in the co-productionist idiom. Instead, the authors show from varied perspectives that the co-productionist idiom can shed light on the constitution of varied social orders, such as international regimes, imperial or comparative politics, science and democracy, and the boundary between public and private property; equally, this approach can illuminate situated interactions between scientific and other forms of life, in settings ranging from laboratory conversations and patients' discourses to the courtroom. Similarly, the co-productionist approach can address the formation of widely varied elements of natural order: for example, climate change, human intelligence, endangered species or sugar cane propagation.

Constitutive co-production

For the constitutive tradition in co-productionist work, we turn first and foremost to Bruno Latour, who formally introduced the term in his influential essay-monograph, *We Have Never Been Modern* (Latour 1993). Here, he explicitly linked constructivist themes from S&TS with themes of political philosophy, repeatedly asserting that the nature–culture divide is a creation of human (or, more specifi-cally, Western) ingenuity. It is the mechanism by which Western societies sort the multitudes of hybrid networks that constitute their cognitive and material exis-tence into seemingly autonomous worlds of nature and culture. So basic is the resulting duality in "modern" thought that Latour regards it as a constitutional dispensation: it underwrites all other ways of grasping the world. An appealing aspect of this view is that it genuinely is about *co*-production – that is, it does not presuppose any *a priori* demarcations of the world before that world is worked upon by human imagination and labor: "But Society, as we now know, is no less constructed than Nature, since it is the dual result of one single stabilization process" (1993: 94). The analyst's task is to make visible the connections that co-production renders invisible, so that both "natural" objects, such as the cloned sheep Dolly or the ozone hole, and "social" objects, such as experts or govern-ments, can be seen as linked together in *actor-networks* whose heterogeneous constituents criss-cross the constitutional divide.

Latour's take on co-production is more material and less idealistic than that of many Anglo-American scholars writing outside the Marxist tradition, including most adherents of the Edinburgh school of the sociology of scientific knowledge. In exposing the constructed character of the nature–culture boundary, Latour calls attention to the role of material objects as well as human institutions in assigning hybrids to one or the other of his two constitu-tional domains. His program grants agency to humans as well as non-humans, although mechanical agents in Latour's accounts (as contrasted, say, with biological ones like Pasteur's yeast) often seem to operate as surrogates for human actors, homunculi to whom humans have chosen to delegate some part of their own agency. Embroidering on these ideas over many years, Latour has made telling observations about the pervasive interdependence of the natural, the social and the material: thus "nature" is the result, not the cause, of solving social controversies (1987); the laboratory is a microcosm of larger aggrega-tions of power (1988a); material objects and artifacts, such as door locks or speed bumps ("sleeping policemen"), incorporate and effectuate social norms (1992); big social institutions, such as capitalism or markets, are built (paralleling Barnes 1988) by the same means that scientists use in making persuasive representations of nature (1990); and the essence of modernity lies in its dedication to "purifying" the hybrid networks of nature and culture (1993). Representation plays a key role in holding the networks together. Scientific representations, in particular, are products of multiple translations of form and meaning between the observer, the observed, and the means of observation across the network.

For Latour, the power and stability of actor-networks is largely a matter of size; in an oddly realist bow toward bigness, he observes that it takes more resources to put together an ozone-hole network than, let us say, one around a discredited scientific theory such as cold fusion or parapsychology. Correspondingly, it takes more resources to destabilize larger networks than smaller ones. Power is not uniformly distributed throughout a network, even though many local contestations ("trials of strength") may take place between particular contiguous elements within it while the structure is taking shape. Power tends to concentrate, rather, in "centers of calculation" (Latour 1990), which control the instrumentalities – printing presses, statistical formulas, maps, charts, and every manner of scientific "inscription device" (Latour 1987) – by which dominant perceptions of the world are rendered into conveniently portable representations.

While all this is exceptionally rich and provocative, Latour's networks exercise power while displaying curiously little of the moral and political conflicts that normally accompany the creation and maintenance of systems of governance. He has little to say, for instance, about why the organization of technological practices or the credibility of scientific claims varies across cultures; why some actor-networks remain contested and unstable for long periods while others settle quickly; why work at some nodes stabilizes a network more effectively than at others; or what role memories, beliefs, values and ideologies play in sustaining some representations of nature and the social world at the expense of others.[4] Some later work in actor-network theory has gone further than Latour's in acknowledging the fluidity of meanings and ontologies across networks, but the very foregrounding of multiplicity in these stories stands in tension with conventional political analysis that deals with clearly distinguished haves and have-nots (Law 2002; Mol and Law 1994). Put differently, when actor-network theory confronts the nature of power, as it often does, it side-steps the very questions about people, institutions, ideas and preferences that are of greatest political concern. Who loses and who wins through the constitution of networks? How are benefits and burdens (re)distributed by or across them? How willing or unwilling are participants to change their behavior or beliefs because of their enrollment into networks? By downplaying such issues, actor-network theory's welcome attempt to reinvigorate the place of the non-human and the material in accounts of power entails substantial costs with respect to the treatment of human agency and human values.

Andrew Pickering, in *The Mangle of Practice* (1995) directly addresses the normative asymmetry between the human and the non-human. He sets out to rectify what he sees as a major flaw in the classical actor-network approach, observing that, when all is said and done, there are important differences between human minds and bodies and non-human agents such as the weather, television sets or particle accelerators. There are things that machines and devices can do that no thinkable combination of human actors could accomplish without technological enhancement. Similarly, there are things that human actors can do and machines (as yet) cannot, such as form intentions and goals or exercise normative judgments, within the constraints of a world partially fixed or predisciplined by existing cultural commitments. The two kinds of actors nevertheless depend on one another at every phase of scientific practice – and, Pickering argues, also in cultural practices more broadly. Accordingly, what should be posited between human and material agents, he says, is not an exact equivalence, as for instance in the case of Latour's speed bumps and real traffic policemen, but rather *parallels* in their forms of action and an *intertwining* in their constitution of each other (1995: 15).

Speaking very much in a co-productionist idiom, Pickering encapsulates his ontological argument as follows: "The world makes us in one and the same process as we make the world" (1995: 26). The "world" that is the subject of this sentence is not the ultimate reality to which philosophical realists pay homage, but rather any of the many possible worlds that can be constructed through the dialectical interplay of human and non-human agencies (see Hacking 1999: 68–74 for a critique of this account). To spell out in more detail the mechanics of this process of co-production, or as he calls it "interactive stabilization", Pickering introduces the metaphor of the "mangle", a now obsolete machine designed for wringing the water out of wet washing. Scientific work, he says, can be thought of as feeding into the mangle a combination of human goals and practices and material potentialities. What comes out at the other end is a somewhat unpredictable transformation of both inputs, reconfigured into a newly stabilized field of action for further "dances of agency" between humans and machines.

Astute as Pickering is in observing the real-time interplay of human and mechanical agency in scientific practice, the notion of the mangle disconcertingly undercuts the very ideas of human intentionality that he wants to resurrect. There is, to begin with, an immovable, physical obduracy about the concept of the mangle. What is its own ontological status? Is this strange device part of the world it acts on or is it alone exempted from the flurry of actions, both human and material, that constitute the worlds we know? If it acts autonomously, whence does it derive its godlike imperviousness to the contingencies of worldmaking? Is the mangle's operation unpredictable because, in another guise, it is simply the realist's world lurking beyond the analyst's field of vision, ready to bite back upon human curiosity in ways that our comprehension cannot, as yet, absorb? And how thoroughgoing anyway is the unpredictability of mangling? Pickering acknowledges, after all, that "culture" has something to say about the possibilities that confront the scientific entrepreneur, that all ways forward are never equally open, and that the worlds we have already constructed loop back on our efforts to construct new ones (Hacking 1999). Is there nothing, then, that we can usefully generalize about these constraints?

To pursue these questions further, we may usefully contrast Latour's and Pickering's views with those of authors from neighboring areas of philosophy and political theory. One informative contrast is with Philip Kitcher, the philosopher of biology, who also deals with the social nature of science in his monograph, *Science, Truth, and Democracy* (Kitcher 2001). Like Pickering, Kitcher is prepared to grant that science reveals, through human enterprise, only some of the many possible realities that nature in principle holds in store. The actual paths of discovery, according to Kitcher, follow socially ordained "significance graphs" that lead investigators to pursue some lines of inquiry in preference to others. Unlike Pickering's mangle, though, Kitcher's significance graphs do make room for human agency, but as I have suggested elsewhere (Jasanoff forthcoming b), Kitcher's account suffers from inattention to the role of power, resource imbalances and global inequality in privileging some significance judgments over others.

A second illuminating contrast comes from setting actor-network theory beside the work of two political scientists, Benedict Anderson and James C. Scott, who have also written influentially about the role of representational practices in constituting political power. For these authors, however, the power of representation lies not so much in the resources invested in creating them (though these are not irrelevant) as in the resources used to disseminate them, so that they alter the behavior or command the belief of masses of sentient human actors. If Latour and Pickering focus primarily on the production end of representing the world, Anderson and Scott are concerned as much or more with reception: in their case, the uptake of the results of such representations by powerful, and for Scott (1985) also powerless, agents in society. In particular, both political analysts are interested in the resistances that arise when particular grand representations of reality are employed to win the allegiance of large aggregates of people. The ensuing struggles of belief render their work quite explicitly political.

In *Imagined Communities*, his acclaimed account of the rise of the modern nation-state, Anderson (1991) broke with the standard definition of the nation-state as an autonomous entity wielding sovereign rights over a geographically bounded territory and the citizens inhabiting it. Concerned with the phenomenon of *nationhood*, he turned an anthropologist's eye on what makes people believe that they belong to something so nebulous and ill defined as a nation. From this starting point, Anderson defined the nation simply as "an imagined political community – and imagined as both inherently limited and sovereign" (1991: 6). By emphasizing the citizen's imagination, Anderson underscored the reciprocity of nation-making. A state may be, or may become, little more than an empty shell, though possibly one with brutal and oppressive instruments at its command, unless its citizens are willing to invest it with their own dreams of shared identity. Mere accumulation of the hard indices of power – guns, laws, armies, revenues – may not be sufficient to build or maintain a robust dominion unless the state also has the means to exert a continuous, centripetal pull on its citizens' imaginations. The unexpected dissolution of the Soviet Union and of former Yugoslavia in the 1990s, the sudden crumbling of Afghanistan's Taliban regime under US bombardment in 2001, and the collapse of Saddam Hussein's Iraqi regime in 2003, again under US attack, can all be seen in this light as massive breakdowns in the capacity of those states to hold on to just such loyalties of the imagination.

In Anderson's account, nation-making crucially depends on deploying persuasive representations of the symbols that signify nationhood. The instru-mentalities, or technologies, that figure most prominently for him are those that have the power to discipline people's imaginations by making them receptive to shared conceptions of nationalism. Anderson particularly emphasizes the role of print capitalism. National newspapers were among the earliest of his instru-mental devices, simultaneously disseminating the same communal stories to every part of a country and so weaving together their readers in an invisible web of common narrative experience. Other instruments for standardizing national identities include, as Anderson specifies in later editions of his book, the map, the museum and the census (he might, after 2001, have dwelt longer on national flags). With their aid, even so culturally and spatially disjointed a state as Indonesia was able to create in its citizens' minds the sense of being Indonesian, of belonging to a politically integrated community. Any nation so conceived can certainly be seen, in S&TS terms, as a network that is partly held together by circulating technologies of representation and communication. But the dura-bility of this network depends on more than the sum total of its variously functioning parts. A successful nation has to be able to produce the *idea* of nationhood as an emergent, intersubjective property; without this connection of belief, it remains a hollow construct, ruling without assent, and hence unstably.

James Scott (1998), like Latour, is specifically concerned with the texture of modernity, and his state, like Anderson's nation and Latour's science, wields power by making authoritative representations. In *Seeing like a State*, Scott describes how the modern planning state not only conceived of the world in certain recurrent, oversimplified categories, but also imposed its ways of seeing on people's lives. The name of the game was to bind citizens' whole existence, not just their imaginations, to the service of the state's grid-like vision. Through chilling accounts of such disastrous initiatives as scientific forestry in Europe, city planning in Brazil, collective farming in Russia, and villagization in Tanzania, Scott relates how various "high modernist" planners first created idealized, stripped-down images of social order and then ruthlessly redesigned millions of lives to match their reductive visions. The purpose of these grand plans was to make citizens and their economic productions more "legible", that is easier to count, survey, order, exploit and control. Small-scale, diversified, shifting or densely settled patterns of human life were eliminated in favor of large collec-tives, rigidly disciplined spaces, rectilinear orderings of dwellings, croplands and forests. Like Cinderella's stepsisters mutilating their feet to satisfy the glass slipper's cruel dictates of beauty, Scott's planners cropped and purged their citizenry to meet the demands of legibility and centralized control.

These immense feats of natural and social engineering were driven, in Scott's view, as much by an esthetic predilection for clean, transparently governable spaces as by the planners' thirst for domination. He thus adds a normative and cultural element to the quest for power that one vainly looks for in actor-network theory. Moreover, if size alone conferred power on networks, or upon their centers of calculation, then Scott's planners should have been quintessentially powerful. The standardized units and measures that they created, and often forcibly imposed, subjugated vast populations to their templates of control. Yet most of these utopian ventures ultimately failed. Even their temporary successes must be attributed, Scott suggests, to the shadow politics of subversion and resistance played out in and around the peripheries of the governing vision. Squeezed out of planners' designs, "real" life found ways of resurfacing in the unwritten adaptations and accommodations of the powerless. When asked to draw a picture of "home", nine-year-old children living in Brasília's soulless superquadra did not draw "an apartment building of any kind. All drew, instead, a traditional freestanding house with windows, a central door, and a pitched roof" (Scott 1998: 127).[5] More to the point – and playing out a script that Scott (1985) also detailed in his earlier classic study, *Weapons of the Weak* – an entire unplanned Brasília grew up side-by-side with the planned one in order to accommodate the construction workers and their families, illicit and invisible citizens, who had not been provided for in the monumental center that housed the city's bureaucratic elite. In the end neither half of the real Brasília, starkly segregated by wealth and class, conformed to the animating vision of the ideal, modern city that had prompted their joint creation.

Scott's notion of legibility rings changes upon the theme of standardization which many postwar social theorists have identified as perhaps *the* constitutive feature of modernity (Bauman 1991; Foucault 1979). Concerned as he is with measurement, Scott explicitly acknowledges the resonances between his work and that of well known S&TS scholars such as Ian Hacking (1990) and Theodore Porter (1995), who have also called attention to the simplifying moves that are needed to convert the messy realities of people's personal attributes and behaviors into the objective, tractable language of numbers. More recently, he might have included, too, Bowker and Star's (1999) study of classification practices in large social service organizations. But there are two dimensions to Scott's argument that render his work at once more and less compelling than similar studies in the social history of statistics and enumeration. On the one hand, Scott emphasizes the inequality of means between the state and those it wishes to render legible. Not every actor can see "like a state" because the wherewithal to impose such simplifying order on complex masses of humanity lies, for better or worse, outside the competence of most social actors. On the other hand, Scott's monolithic formation of legibility, modernity and the state lacks the nuance and situatedness that characterize the best S&TS work on the ambiguities and discontents of modernity. Legibility, after all, has not been the exclusive prerogative of modernity, as is well illustrated by the highly legible caste systems of ancient India, medieval Europe or feudal Japan (Benedict 1989).[6] Institutions other than the state, such as Foucault's clinics and schools as well as his prisons, and still more recently commercial institutions such as credit card companies and internet marketers, also have the power to create new ways of "reading" people;[7] and these forms of power are diffused through society by micro-processes of clinical observation and diagnosis rather than imposed from above by the mailed hand of the state (also see Bowker and Star 1999). Modernity itself, finally, cannot be taken as a blanket state of affairs, a social *a priori* that is not itself embedded in the shifting sands of history. As historians of science have shown, even the objectivity of representation that Scott and others see as a defining achievement of modernity comes in different flavors at different times and in different socio-cultural settings (Daston and Galison 1992; Porter 1992).

I have suggested thus far that there are important family resemblances between the actor-network approach to thinking about power in constitutive, co-productionist terms and newer approaches in state theory, such as Anderson's and Scott's, that focus on the role of representation, visualization and standardization in constructing political regimes. Juxtaposing the two lines of analysis, however, reveals problems in each. Generally, S&TS work has been less successful than political science in finding places for human beliefs and imagination, and in accounting for significant economic, technological and social disparities in the practices of world-making; nor has science studies paid much attention to what happens when particular epistemic and material constructions of the world circulate through societies configured by very different historical and material constraints. Work in political science, by the same token, has tended to black-box or take for granted the primary units of political analysis, such as "high modernity" or the "state", and has paid insufficient heed to the interplay of social with natural order. Can the co-productionist idiom do better? Before returning to this question, we must consider the second major tributary in the literature on co-production – the interactional strand that takes as its primary object of study the accommodations between scientific and other forms of social life at moments of manifest conflict and change.

Interactions of science and politics

Just as constitutive co-production usefully takes the metaphysics of Latour and the French school of actor-network theory as its point of departure, so the interactionist strand can be grounded, to start with, in the epistemologically oriented Edinburgh school of sociology of scientific knowledge. In *Leviathan and the Air-Pump* (1985), their important study of science and politics in early modern England, Steven Shapin and Simon Schaffer undertook to explain an intriguing – and, for us, instructive – historical puzzle. Casting back to two of Restoration England's most influential thinkers, Thomas Hobbes and Robert Boyle, Shapin and Schaffer observed that the pursuits of these two intellectual giants were not so easily classified in their own time as they have since become. Hobbes today serves as a staple of political theory, whereas Boyle retains his status as one of the founders of modern science. In the seventeenth century, however, both men navigated rather more freely on either side of the science–society boundary, Hobbes pronouncing on natural philosophy and Boyle on politics and power. Where did the divisions come from that later put each man so unambiguously in his place? And does the historical record say anything more general about the origins of the separation between the natural and the social that citizens of the modern world tend to take for granted?

The disputes between Hobbes and Boyle centered in the first instance on the credibility of the latter's experimental method. Hobbes played the skeptic to Boyle's famous air pump experiments, arguing, much in the deconstructive style of a contemporary sociologist of scientific knowledge, that the experimenter's own authority was crucial to establishing the authority of the experiment (Collins 1985). Boyle, as Shapin and Schaffer ingeniously demonstrate, invented a complex technology of validation – including a depersonalized rhetoric of objectivity – to persuade critics like Hobbes of the reliability of his experimental knowledge. The heart of *Leviathan*'s co-productionist argument, however, has to do with the relationship of the debate between these two men and the wider political conflicts of the disordered era in which that debate was taking place. At stake, Shapin and Schaffer propose, was not only the nature of the knowledge that would be deemed reliable in the post-Restoration polity, but also, simultaneously, questions about what kinds of people would be allowed to lay claim to power through the trustworthiness of their knowledge. These observations underwrite what is for our purposes the authors' most significant conclusion: "Solutions to the problem of knowledge are solutions to the problem of social order. That is why the materials in this book are contributions to political history as well as to the history of science" (Shapin and Schaffer 1985: 332).

In this view of co-production, human beings seeking to ascertain facts about the natural world are confronted, necessarily and perpetually, by problems of social authority and credibility. Whose testimony should be trusted, and on what basis, become central issues for people seeking reliable information about the state of a world in which all the relevant facts can never be at any single person's fingertips. At times of significant change, such as those we tend to call "scientific revolutions" (Shapin 1996; Kuhn 1962), it may not be possible to address questions of the facticity and credibility of knowledge claims without, in effect, redrafting the rules of social order pertaining to the trustworthiness and authority of individuals and institutions (witness the new technologies of persuasion created by Boyle and his fellow experimentalists to convince skeptics and absent colleagues). Only by solving social problems in this way can satisfactory warrants be produced for radically new orderings of nature. Doing science merges, in other words, into doing politics. Shapin and Schaffer concluded that there are, in practice, three senses in which the history of science occupies the same terrain as the history of politics. First, scientific practitioners have created, selected, and maintained a polity within which they operate and make their intellectual product; second, the intellectual product made within that polity has become an element in political activity in that state; third, there is a conditional relationship between the nature of the polity occupied by scientific intellectuals and the nature of the wider polity.

(1985: 332)

Although this statement assumes the separate existence of science and politics, the authors are careful not to posit unidirectional causal arrows running from one domain to the other. Natural order does not shape social order, nor vice-versa. Rather, there is, as Pickering also implies, a necessary *parallelism* between goings on in these two spheres of human activity.

Each of the three "senses" of co-production identified by Shapin and Schaffer has respectable resonances elsewhere in writings about the politics of science and technology, and some comparisons with those works let us recognize as well how radically co-productionist ideas and related work in S&TS break with earlier traditions. So, we find in two classic mid-century articles by Michael Polanyi (1962) and Robert K. Merton (1973 [1942]) — on the republic of science and the normative structure of science, respectively — the notion of science as a model polity.[8] Both men saw scientific activity as governed by norms, such as disinterestedness for Merton and the absence of hierarchical authority for Polanyi, that were well adapted to serve the needs of open, democratic discourse. Shapin and Schaffer question the taken-for-granted character of such norms, suggesting that experimental science's claims of reliability and truth had to be sustained through elaborate and carefully designed social practices (see also Shapin 1994). (Ironically, they are less skeptical toward the political order of Restoration England, which they largely take for granted, rather than seeing it too as contingent, contested and stabilized through practice.) Other work in the sociology of scientific knowledge, such as Collins (1985) on "core sets" and Gieryn (1999) on "boundary work", has amplified these ideas, underlining the role of mundane practices in stabilizing and delimiting the polities of science and in defining scientists' ultimate forms of life. The import of such studies has been to challenge the assumption of science as an autonomous sphere whose norms are constituted independently of other forms of social activity. Rather, the resolution of any significantly new problems in science is seen as requiring situated and specific (re)structurings of social order, without which scientific authority itself would be put in jeopardy. Observers of the changing norms of scientific practice at the end of the twentieth century have reached similar conclusions about our own period of transformation (Nowotny *et al.* 2001; Gibbons *et al.* 1994).

The idea of intellectual product becoming "an element in political activity", the second kind of interaction between science and society proposed by Shapin and Schaffer, is reminiscent of work on the politics of technology by David

Noble (1984) and Langdon Winner (1986). Winner, in particular, argued for the "inherently political" nature of technology in somewhat the same language that Shapin and Schaffer used for science:

> [T]here are two basic ways of stating the case. One version claims that the adoption of a given technical system actually requires the creation and maintenance of a particular set of social conditions as the operating environment of that system....A second, somewhat weaker version of the argument holds that a given kind of technology is strongly compatible with, but does not strictly require, social and political relationships of a particular stripe.
>
> (1986: 32)

Technology in these terms is a "solution" to political order in the sense that it sustains particular structures of established power, as in Winner's heuristically useful (though historically problematic[9]) example of highway overpasses in New York designed purposefully too low to allow buses carrying the urban poor to travel into wealthy suburbs. Similarly, in his account of the adoption of numerical control in the machine tool industry, Noble argued that the new technology enabled shop-floor managers to deskill and thus maintain control over potentially fractious workers. Complex technological systems such as nuclear power may embody or necessitate opaque and illiberal forms of political organization, a theme advanced by Winner and echoed by Richard Sclove (1995) in his call for the democratization of technology. While all of these authors are sensitive to the interpenetration of material and social structures, they deviate from the co-productionist thrust in S&TS by taking for granted certain social "facts", such as the necessity of the alliance between economic and political power and the ordering of society according to well defined interests. Hence, in their writing, social formations such as capital or class are held to be off limits for analysis and not available for reconfiguration in new attempts to solve "problems of knowledge". Instead, like James Scott's all-powerful state, they are seen as repeatedly reinscribing themselves in the products of technoscience: highways, power plants and machine tools, for example.

Even the hegemonic forces of capital or colonialism, however, do not maintain themselves static and unchanging for all time. William Storey (1997: 141–149) offers an elegant illustration in his history of colonial-era sugar manufacturing in Mauritius. During the 1920s and 1930s, small planters on the island established a thriving market in Uba canes, a high-yielding variety cultivated by local growers. The canes were profitable at first because sugar factories paid the planters for them by weight rather than yield. The factory owners did not especially care for this arrangement because the Uba variety yielded less sucrose than the standard varieties grown by large plantation owners. Factories continued to accept the canes, however, until low sugar prices and the depression of the 1930s caused them to retreat from this policy. An announcement in 1937 that the sugar factories would pay 15 per cent less for Uba canes caused the small planters to riot and brought the Mauritian economy to a standstill. The British government solved the problem by providing the rioters with new, hybrid canes, which yielded so well that they pre-empted the dispute between planters and factory owners. A radical problem of social order was resolved in this way by changing the accompanying natural order: the switch from "local" Uba to "colonist" or "metropolitan" hybrid canes, and associated changes in the distribution of the knowledge of sugar cane cultivation and in tax policies. The disorder of the riots disclosed, albeit fleetingly, how the very composition of the dominant cane varieties embodied complex accommodations between nature and society. The Uba cane and its hybrid successor stabilized – indeed naturalized – different regimes of colonial knowledge and power, whose rules they at once incorporated and made invisible.[10]

Finally, with respect to possible "conditional relationships" between science and politics – Shapin and Schaffer's third site of interaction – both Polanyi (1962) and more recently Yaron Ezrahi (1990) have argued for the strong case that modern science provides the template for a particular form of politics: liberal democracy. Polanyi's vision, however, was anything but co-productionist. His highly idealized republic of science developed its own rules of the game essentially uncontaminated by power or politics; these rules, Polanyi suggested, are suited to democratic governance because they deny any authority except that which is constituted from below by the self-critical and equally positioned "peers" of the scientific polity.

Ezrahi, by contrast, builds sophisticatedly on Shapin and Schaffer's observations about Boyle's construction of an experimental space whose credibility could be vouched for by distant virtual witnesses. Ezrahi found in the rise of experimental science and the decay of the alchemist's or the absolute monarch's privileged vision a historical antecedent for the creation of authority in democratic polities. Politics after the scientific revolution became, he argues, an extended "experimental space", in which the modern, liberal state could use science and technology for instrumental ends to gain the assent of its witnessing ("attestive") publics. Unlike Polanyi's curiously unsocial republic of virtue, Ezrahi's democracy is constituted through continual pragmatic adjustments between the state and its citizens: the state exercises power only by maintaining a commitment to transparency, while citizens accept rule by the few only because the state's instrumental actions are continually visible, and so available for public review. Importantly, Ezrahi's account of the rise of democracy focuses not only on the state's instrumental strategies, but also on the emergence of a particular kind of knowledgeable citizen, the liberal individual who is capable of attesting, as an informed and reasoning witness, to the legitimacy of the state's technological actions.[11]

To underline the co-productionist well-springs of Ezrahi's thinking about science and the state, it is helpful to contrast his views with Chandra Mukerji's (1989) interesting ethnographic study of a community of oceanographers who owe their existence to state support and funding. Mukerji describes her scientists as a "reserve labor force" for the state, which shores up its authority and serves its eventual security needs by sponsoring their research. The scientists enjoy the illusion of autonomy, while the state produces knowledge to suit its own purposes. In this world, the instrumental state and the science it sponsors are separated by an impermeable wall (it is methodologically telling, for example, that Mukerji does not interview her "state" representatives); the images the scientists produce of the world appear to be of no concern to the state, let alone to loop back in any way on the state's relationship with its citizens. As Noble and Winner black-box the power of capital, so Mukerji takes the power of the state as primary. It is not problematized nor seen to be in continual need of relegitimation with the aid of science and technology, as in Ezrahi's or Storey's accounts of democratic and colonial political orders, respectively.

A more contingent set of "conditional relationships" can be observed in the case of the human and social sciences, whose growth and importance have been closely linked to the rise of the modern managerial state. Foucault's descriptions of the normalization of mental illness and sexuality provide the most influential point of departure for this line of research. The medicalization of insanity (Foucault 1973), the definitions of normal and abnormal sexuality (Foucault 1978), the rise of statistics (Porter 1995; Hacking 1990; Daston 1988), the standardization of intelligence (Carson 1993), the creation of "legible" cadastral maps (Scott 1998), and the sorting activities of health and welfare organizations (Bowker and Star 1999) are among the examples of the social sciences emerging to serve – and shape – the modern state's desire for specific forms of order, control and reassurance.

This literature displays a certain ambivalence about the ways in which the construction of social knowledge relates to the production and exercise of power. Who is empowered through knowledge, and to what ends? Foucault's early writings present a compelling and pessimistic vision of social classification serving the state's need for order and surveillance, leaving citizens more or less powerless to resist. Foucault's state looks through a one-way mirror; his model is Jeremy Bentham's Panopticon, the ingenious circular penal structure in which the centrally positioned guard can look out at all the inmates, but never be seen in return. This is a far cry from Ezrahi's transparent and vulnerable liberal democratic state, which is destined always to deploy science and technology in full view of its citizens, and therefore must continually construct demonstrations – in war and peace – to persuade citizens that it is acting for their collective benefit.

Helga Nowotny (1990) and others (Wagner *et al.* 1991) also suggest a relatively benign reason for the growth of the social sciences in modernity: one of the modern state's necessities is to provide reassurance to citizens against the uncertainties of poverty, crime, unemployment, and more recently environmental and technological risk. Of course, the risks themselves are historically and culturally contingent, and the analytic tools that any society musters for their management reflect a preoccupation with the collective fears or problems that arise in particular times and places. Hacking (1999; 1995; 1992) persuasively describes how the American legal and policy processes created the new "social kinds" of child abuse and "recovered memory" in response to specific cultural anxieties of the

1980s – and, in the process, went about generating "objective" evidence of these phenomena on a scale unparalleled in other Western societies. Other developments in the social sciences that have responded to public demands for reducing uncertainty include mortality tables, actuarial systems, risk assessment, and varied indicators of socio-economic performance (Daston 1988; Porter 1995; Jasanoff 1992; 1986; Hacking 1990; Wynne 1989; Daston 2000; among others). With these we could also range an emerging body of environmental sciences – with names like sustainability science, vulnerability science, integrated assessment – which display similar properties but have not yet been studied in detail. These classifying instruments often have the effect of disciplining people in a Foucauldian sense, but in subjugating prevalent uncertainties, they also create a promise of control, and thus in some instances liberate people to act more freely; whether advisedly so or not is a very different question.

A related strand of the co-production literature deals with notions of objectivity, reliability and expertise that apply not only to the legitimation of science and technology, but also to the constitution of democratically accountable political regimes. The very idea of objectivity implies the existence of a shared reality against which free men and women can test the performance of their governmental representatives. Objectivity, of course, has been an important theme in the philosophy of knowledge (Rorty 1991), but S&TS research has devoted more punctilious attention to this notion's social history and cultural specificity. How objectivity is understood and institutionally embedded in a given political system has enormous implications for the sponsorship of science by the state: it influences the kinds of work that are deemed appropriate for public funding (projects that provoked spirited debates about science's objectivity and neutrality at the turn of the twenty-first century include cloning and stem cell research, the Human Genome Project, climate modeling, DNA typing, and sampling techniques for birds, fish, biodiversity, and racial groups), as well as the organization of scientific research. For example, in sponsoring closer university–industry relations so as to speed technology transfer, states had to take note of, and guard against, charges of conflict of interest (Guston 2001). In turn, concepts of objectivity and reliability affect the uptake of science and technology by state institutions: how the results of research are construed in public domains (for example, as persuasive, biased, irrelevant or inconclusive); how they are factored into the framing and "solution" of public problems; how new technical discourses are constructed to legitimate policy; and so forth. Well entrenched habits of skepticism in American politics, for example, have been linked to a recurrent, utopian search for neutral approaches to conflict resolution, framed by objective, quantitative decisionmaking techniques, such as vulnerability assessment, risk assessment and cost-benefit analysis (Jasanoff 1995; 1986; see also Porter 1995).

Much of the work reviewed thus far concerns itself directly and centrally with relationships between science, technology and governmental power, or its close correlate, economic power – that is, the power of rulers over the ruled. Feminist and cultural studies of science, by contrast, have dealt with the intersections of knowledge, technology and power without necessarily implicating the authority of the state. Thus, in her pathbreaking essays on gender and science, Evelyn Fox Keller (1985) set out to show how concepts central to the practice of science, such as objectivity, came to be gendered as "masculine" through centuries of rhetorical usage. In a passage that is especially germane to this discussion, Keller argued that the concept of "laws of nature" is "indelibly marked by its political origins" (1985: 131). Once cast as a search for law, scientific research orients itself toward monocausal, hierarchical explanations in which nature is controlled by deterministic forces that dominate lower-order variables much in the manner of an authoritarian, centralized state ruling its subservient citizens. Such an understanding of nature, in Keller's view, is anything but gender-neutral. She suggests that "order" rather than "law" would provide a richer (and presumably less masculine) framework for scientific inquiry, because the former term "wider than law, and free from its coercive, hierarchical, and centralizing implications, has the potential to expand our conception of science" (1985: 132).

Keller restricts herself to speaking about natural order, but her argument could easily be extended to show, as the authors in this collection do, that the expansive notion of "order" provides an equally hospitable idiom for enlarging on the interactive, mutually constitutive relations between nature and society. This is a route that Keller herself leaves mostly unexplored; for instance, while she illuminatingly tracks the influence of gender in scientific language and praxis, she does not, in a fully symmetrical, co-productionist move, consider the construction of "gender" itself as a powerful ordering category within the varied knowledge cultures of modernity. An analysis of the cognitive, social, symbolic and even material resources with which the concept of gender is stabilized, would have told us a lot about what is at stake in the politics of femaleness in various socio-cultural settings.

Where Keller's historical explorations focus largely on gender in the conceptual structure of the biological sciences, Donna Haraway (2000; 1991; 1989) provocatively traces the study of gender into the material artifacts through which human societies embody their understandings of nature. In her widely admired history of primate displays in the American Museum of Natural History, Haraway argued that these representations encode deeply engrained cultural attitudes toward gender, its place in human nature, and its varied social manifestations, as for example in accepted understandings of the family. Haraway also led the way in arguing that the dominant paternalistic order of Western societies is engineered into the very design of technological systems. She, like Latour, is intensely aware of the hybrid constructions – *cyborgs*, in her language – that populate modern societies, but her aim in displaying the interconnectedness of things, norms and institutions has a more overtly political edge, inviting and celebrating female engagement through a wild inventiveness of language and association that makes traditional work in actor-network theory look almost businesslike by comparison.

Gender, though intensively studied, is not the only cultural category that can be absorbed into scientific practice, naturalized, and made invisible in everyday routines of research. Race, colonial relations and social class have all been sustained by work in the human and life sciences, from anthropology to medicine and genetics (Reardon 2001; Stepan 1982). As yet, however, studies of science and technology have only begun to look for the often subtle incorporation of other cultural categories in the practice and content of scientific knowledge-making. That cultural features can enter into the life world of scientists is recognized in the work of anthropologists of science, such as Sharon Traweek's (1988) sensitive portrayal of high-energy physics communities in Japan and the United States and Rabinow's (1999) account of a dispute over genetic patrimony in France. More controversial, but of potentially greater interest to politics as well as science, are the efforts of some historians to show how culture may condition the processes of scientific inquiry, producing different styles of research on the "same" problems of knowledge (Harwood 1993).

Perhaps the most important question raised by interactional S&TS work on science and the state, as well as in feminist and cultural studies of science, concerns the direction of the influence of knowledge on power. Should power be seen as lodged in obdurate social structures which (as in work by Noble, Winner, and Haraway) constrain the production of potentially dissident knowledges; or is it fluid, immanent, and continually renegotiable, so that it can be captured or reformulated by inventive, upstart knowledge communities? Power, conceived in the former way, can be seen as continually reinscribing itself in the institutions, communities, practices, discourses, claims and products of science and technology, including not least our conceptions of human bodies and human nature. The problem of change, however, looms large if one adopts this stance too rigidly. If power is so entrenched and so hierarchical, replicates itself so freely, and reinscribes itself so effectively, then where does the impetus for change come from, and why are old orders sometimes suddenly overthrown?[12] On the other hand, refusing to acknowledge that some formations do retain power over long periods, and failing to ask how they achieve this stability, has embroiled S&TS scholars in charges of both moral relativism and prejudiced or uncritical subservience to paternalistic political orders. The co-production idiom, embracing as it does the constitutive as well as the interactional lines of thought, may offer at least a partial release from these dilemmas. It provides, following Latour and Foucault's later work, the possibility of seeing certain "hegemonic" forces not as given but as the (co-)products of contingent interactions and practices. These insights may, in turn, open up new opportunities for explanation, critique and social action.

Patterns of co-production

I have shown thus far that there is no dearth of work in science and technology studies from which to draw insights into the co-production of natural and social order. With greater and lesser self-consciousness, both the constitutive and the interactional traditions in the field have already made substantial inroads into social theory and political philosophy. The challenge is to piece together these theoretical contributions in a sufficiently programmatic form to open up a distinctive research arena for normatively minded students of science and technology, as well as to engage in a more ambitious discourse on power and culture with the traditional social science disciplines. Put differently, our aim is to make the idiom of co-production more tractable so as to encourage conversation with other approaches to political and social inquiry.

Theoretical synthesis, to be sure, seems inconsistent with the temper of a field that has tended to reject totalizing stories – whether positive or negative – concerning science and technology. The emphasis on the contingent, the locally and temporally situated, the tacit and the ambivalent in accounts of discovery and innovation stands in opposition to univocal grand narratives. S&TS research has repudiated equally the triumphalist themes of progress and emancipation associated with Enlightenment views of science, and the pessimistic images of technology as disciplinarian, despot or iron cage, ruthlessly imposing its instrumental rationality on human behavior, that have informed decades of European philosophical and sociological thought (Habermas 1975; Ellul 1964). In their place, S&TS has sought to create a picture that remains profoundly humanistic, stressing the roots of science and technology in human agency and will, but denying any singular logic or design. Accordingly, S&TS has generated a wealth of detail about accommodations made by particular practitioners to specific, messy, local challenges in encounters that smack more of *bricolage* than of an idealized scientific method. Skeptical of claimed patterns and *post-hoc* generalizations, such work offers at first sight inhospitable material from which to weave more general doctrines connecting natural and social order. Nonetheless, as this volume shows, the attempt is distinctly worth making.

Co-production's theoretical ambitions

Biological analogies are risky tools for the social sciences, as we know from numerous dubious or discarded research programs that built on biological models; examples include research on natural law, eugenics, race, and social Darwinism. Nonetheless, the problem faced by the social sciences today is not unlike the dilemma that Richard Lewontin describes for the biological sciences following the genetic revolution. If we recognize, as he and others have done, that exclusively genetic explanations of biological phenomena are impossibly reductionist, and that causes almost always entail reciprocal interactions between genes, organisms and the environment (Lewontin calls this the "triple helix" in contrast to DNA's double helix), then how can we meaningfully accommodate this level of complexity into our accounts of the world? As Lewontin (2000: 109) observes,

> It is easy to be a critic. All one needs to do is to think very hard about any complex aspect of the world and it quickly becomes apparent why this or that approach to its study is defective in some way. It is rather more difficult to suggest how we can, in practice, do better.

Can the co-productionist framework in science studies, like Lewontin's proposed program for evolutionary biology, avoid the trap of reductionism without falling into a mind-numbing holism?

We have already noted (see Chapter 1) that the idiom of co-production most readily aligns itself with the interpretive and post-structuralist turn in the social sciences (Jasanoff and Wynne 1998; Latour 1988b). Its aim is not to provide deterministic causal explanations of the ways in which science and technology influence society, or vice-versa; nor is it to provide a rigid methodological template for future S&TS research. Rather, it is to make available resources for thinking systematically about the processes of sense-making through which human beings come to grips with worlds in which science and technology have become permanent fixtures. Science and values, objectivity and subjectivity, and indeed intersubjectivity, can thereby be reintegrated into explanatory projects that conform more accurately to the lived experience of modern societies. The picture of human beings and their institutions as *knowing* agents fills some of the void left by statistically oriented social sciences that treat these entities as calcula-tive actors choosing rationally – which all too often means ahistorically and aculturally – among taken-for-granted preferences. Far from denying the reality or the power of science, co-production goes some distance toward explaining why the products of science and technology acquire such deep holds on people's normative instincts as well as their cognitive faculties.

We observed as well in Chapter 1 that work in the co-productionist idiom has tended to cluster around four recurrent themes. These are the *emergence and stabilization* of new technoscientific objects and framings, the staple concern of constitutive co-production; and, on the interactional side, the resolution of scientific and technical *controversies*; the processes by which the products of technoscience are made *intelligible and portable* across boundaries; and the adjust-ment of science's *cultural practices* in response to the contexts in which science is done. In each of these areas, work in the co-productionist idiom stresses, as we have seen, the constant interplay of the cognitive, the material, the social and the normative. Co-production, moreover, occurs along certain well docu-mented pathways. Four are particularly salient, as illustrated in the chapters that follow: making *identities*, making *institutions*, making *discourses* and making *representations*. It is useful to acknowledge and briefly describe these, because they help connect the science studies literature to work on similar topics in political and social theory.

Each of these instruments of co-production can serve varied functions in maintaining order. They can be *morally* or *metaphysically* sustaining, in that they divide the world of hybrids and cyborgs into less ambiguous categories that can easily be dealt with in law and custom. In spite of her ambivalent identity, for example, the cloned sheep Dolly remained for the duration of her short life firmly encamped in the company of domestic animals, as just another product of "ordinary" animal husbandry. Despite her unique ontology as a willed, exact genetic copy of another living creature, Dolly was not treated as something wild or unnatural that resists classification – as would, for now, a cloned Bill Gates or

Osama bin Laden. Scientific and technological products also do metaphysical work in preserving critical boundaries between self and other, structure and agency, state and citizen. The identities, institutions, languages and representations created by science and technology can be *politically* sustaining, by helping societies to accommodate new knowledges and technological capabilities without tearing apart (indeed, often by reaffirming) the legitimacy of existing social arrangements. Finally, they can be *symbolically* sustaining, providing surrogate markers for the continued validity of certain familiar dispensations when uncertainties threaten to overwhelm or disrupt them; examples include, in some liberal democracies, the presumed superiority of markets over state regulation, or the equally mythologized one-to-one correspondence between votes cast and voter intent (see Lynch 2001).

Ordering instruments

How, more specifically, does each of the four most common instruments of co-production operate at the nexus of natural and social order? How do they stabilize both what we know and how we know it?

Making identities

A staple category of post-structuralist social analysis, identity is particularly germane to co-productionist accounts because, whether human or non-human, individual or collective, it is one of the most potent resources with which people restore sense out of disorder. When the world one knows is in disarray, redefining identities is a way of putting things back into familiar places.[13] It is no surprise, then, that co-productionist writing in science and technology studies, concerned as it so often is with emergent and controversial phenomena, has consistently been absorbed with questions of identity. The formation and maintenance of identities plays an important role in several of the contributions to this book. The identity of the expert, in particular, that quintessential bridging figure of modernity, makes a prominent appearance in several of the chapters (Rabeharisoa and Callon, Lynch, Carson, Dear, Dennis). But collective identities are also contested or under negotiation in the working out of scientific and technological orders. What does it mean to be "European" (Waterton and Wynne), "African" (Thompson), "intelligent" (Carson) or a member of a research community, learned profession or disease group? And what roles do knowledge and its production play in shaping and sustaining these social roles or in giving them power and meaning?

Making institutions

Institutions play a crucially important role in co-productionist accounts of world-making, as they do in social analysis writ large. As stable repositories of knowledge and power, institutions offer ready-made instruments for putting things in their places at times of uncertainty and disorder. They may be regarded in this sense as society's *inscription devices* (see Latour 1987; Latour and Woolgar 1979) — vehicles through which the validity of new knowledge can be accredited, the safety of new technological systems acknowledged, and accepted rules of behavior written into the as-yet-unordered domains that have become accessible through knowledge-making. As Mary Douglas (1986) wrote in *How Institutions Think*, successful institutions classify, confer identity, act as repositories of memory and forgetting, and make life-and-death decisions for society.

Institutionalized ways of knowing things are continually reproduced in new contexts (Jasanoff 2001), either because they are socialized into actors and therefore unquestioningly reenacted, or because it would be too disruptive to reexamine them openly. For example, in market capitalism, the human subject is imagined as being able to form autonomous preferences, process information, make rational choices, and act freely upon the choices so made; the human subject's failure to behave as predicted is usually attributed to the market's failings (for example, barriers to information) and not to deficiencies in the underlying model of individual agency. As we have seen, such tacit models of human agency, and consequently of human nature, frequently underpin the technical discourses through which public institutions carry out their regulatory activities (Scott 1998; Irwin and Wynne 1994).

Institutions also serve as sites for the testing and reaffirmation of political culture. Through institutions such as legal systems and research laboratories, societies have access to tried-and-true repertoires of problem-solving, including preferred forms of expertise, processes of inquiry, methods of securing credibility, and mechanisms for airing and managing dissent. Solidified in the form of administrative routines, these repertoires offer constant fall-back positions from which responses to novel problems can be constructed. As all the chapters in this volume demonstrate to one or another degree, co-production could hardly be conceived in the absence of institutions, partaking of their resilience as well as their plasticity. When environmental knowledge changes, for example, new institutions emerge to provide the web of social and normative understandings within which new characterizations of nature — whether climate change, endangered elephants or agricultural science (Miller, Thompson, Storey) — can be recognized and given political effect. In other policy settings, institutions are required to interpret evidence, make law, standardize methods, disseminate knowledge or ratify new identities. Treating these functions as integral to the work of institutions offers an obvious point of contact between co-productionist work in science and technology studies and new institutionalist approaches in sociology and political theory.

Making discourses

Solving problems of order frequently takes the form of producing new languages or modifying old ones so as to find words for novel phenomena, give accounts of experiments, persuade skeptical audiences, link knowledges to practice or action, provide reassurances to various publics, and so forth. As many of the following essays illustrate, such strategies often involve the appropriation of existing discourses (legal, medical and ethical languages, for example) and their selective retailoring to suit new needs. In the process, scientific language often takes on board the tacit models of nature, society, culture or humanity that are current at any time within a given social order. As Rabeharisoa and Callon and Lynch most explicitly illustrate, but as is also suggested in several other chapters, social discourses such as law or the speech of patients may similarly incorporate and reinforce tacit understandings of science.

Discursive choices also form an important element in most institutional efforts to shore up new structures of scientific authority. Thus international environmental organizations, such as the European Environment Agency (Waterton and Wynne) or the Intergovernmental Panel on Climate Change (Miller), had to develop persuasive ways of speaking about the problems over which they exercised jurisdiction. Such efforts inevitably entail standardization, which may bring its own dilemmas of oversimplification and vulnerability to deconstruction in encounters between experts and skeptics (Carson, this volume; Jasanoff and Wynne 1998; Jasanoff 1992; 1986). While institutional discourses often tacitly merge normative and technical repertoires, as in many economic models, they may also enable reasoned action by defining the boundary between the promising ("natural" or "safe") and the fearsome ("unnatural" or "unsafe") aspects of nature and technology. Thompson's chapter on the substitution of a loosely managed, variably threatened African elephant for a globally threatened "endangered species" illustrates such a productive questioning and redefinition of boundaries.

Making representations

The nature of representation has been a core concern of S&TS since the earliest attempts to understand scientific knowledge in social terms. Much sensitive work has been done on the means, both human and material, by which scientific representations are produced and made intelligible in diverse communities of practice, but the connections between this work and that of political and social representation has not always been apparent. The contrast drawn earlier between Latour's analyses of representation and those of Anderson and Scott alerts us to the desirability of enlarging on the theme of representation in science studies, making its political implications more explicit. We may note in this context three aspects of representation that have begun to receive attention from scholars working in the co-productionist idiom, including those in this volume: historical, political and cultural influences on representational practices in science; models of human agency and behavior that inform representation, especially in the human and biological sciences; and the uptake of scientific representations by other social actors. The results of this broader engagement with the politics of representation are apparent throughout this volume, most particularly in Ezrahi's concluding chapter.

We are at last in a position to return to the questions posed early in this chapter as large challenges for the framework of co-production. Can this approach describe, explain, critique, and perhaps even predict phenomena in ways that make it a useful added resource in the project of social analysis? What, in sum, can co-productionist accounts add to our understanding of knowledge societies or of knowledge in society? Does co-production usefully integrate the insights of work in science and technology studies to provide something approaching a coherent research program, though one that can be pursued with a generous plurality of methods and objectives?

Most immediately apparent is the idiom's descriptive richness. It sweeps back into the analyst's field of vision connections between natural and social orders that disciplinary conventions often seek to obliterate, thereby doing injustice to the complexity as well as the strangeness of human experience. This ability to reframe the phenomena of the world in novel ways is what also gives co-productionist stories their explanatory power. Without being reductionist or monocausal, these accounts nevertheless attempt to answer certain kinds of questions that might otherwise remain baffling or, worse, not even acknowledged as important. How do new sociotechnical objects – such as climate change or endangered species, or for that matter Europe, Africa or democracy — swim into our ken, achieving cognitive as well as moral and political standing? How is knowledge taken up in societies, and how does it affect people's collective and individual identities, permitting some to be experts, others to be research subjects, and still others to be resisters or revolutionaries? By making visible such questions, and proposing answers that were not previously on the table, co-productionist analysis performs a neglected critical function. More conventionally, though no less importantly, it enables normative analysis by following power into places where current social theory seldom thinks to look for it: for example, in genes, climate models, research methods, cross-examinations, accounting systems or the composition and practices of expert bodies. Prediction is the hardest case, and one may well wonder why in our surprise-prone societies any social science ever purports to tell the future. But to the extent that co-production makes apparent deep cultural regularities, to the extent that it explains the contingency or durability of particular socio-technical formations, it also allows us to imagine the pathways by which change could conceivably occur. It illuminates, in this way, new possibilities for human development.

The essays in this collection should certainly lay to rest the charge that the field of science and technology studies is insufficiently normative and has little to contribute to macro-social analyses of culture and power. On the contrary, they demonstrate that some of the most enduring topics in politics and government lend themselves well to elucidation in a co-productionist mode. Among these are the emergence of new authority structures and forms of governance, the (selective) durability and self-replication of cultures, and the bases of expert conflict over knowledge in rational, democratic societies. The essays also establish a point that has become increasingly clear across the spectrum of S&TS research: that historical and contemporary voices in the field have a lot more in common than has been permitted to surface across institutionalized disciplinary boundaries. Regardless of the observer's standpoint in time, there is in these pieces a shared outlook on the nature of knowledge and its embeddeness in material and social forms. Perhaps as important, in one after another of these chapters, the distinction between "micro" and "macro" that has played so foundational a role in traditional social theory is shown to be, in significant part, an artifice of our own thought processes. In practical experience, the scales of analysis and action are frequently scrambled together. The national or global constitutional orders we recognize and live by are constantly remade in innumerable, localized engagements; without this perpetual reperformance they might as well cease to exist. Co-production, then, allows the bringing together of insights from anthropology and history, law and politics, cultural studies and social theory. It is an *integrative* as well as an interdisciplinary framework.

S&TS as a field has been criticized, finally, for making science too "social" — to the point, some say, of representing science as no different from any other exercise in the accumulation of authority. I have indicated already that this thin reading misrepresents the breadth and sophistication of the field's engagement with the social worlds in which science and technology function today as indispensable players. This book, at any rate, freely acknowledges the cultural uniqueness of science and technology, insisting only that their specialness arises from repeated, situated encounters between scientific, technical and other forms of life. More particularly, the volume invites readers to reflect on the plastic and infinitely varied adjustments through which science and technology infuse, and are infused by, other ways of knowing, perceiving, and making accommodations with the world. Unlike "laws of nature", the idiom of co-production does not seek to foreclose competing explanations by laying claim to one dominant and all-powerful truth. It offers instead a new way of exploring the waters of human history, where politics, knowledge and invention are continually in flux. On that voyage, we hope, this volume will serve as an informative companion.

Notes

1 Dolly, for instance, was incorporated for a time into the sequence of images that introduces CNN's news programs. These pictures are not only seen around the world wherever CNN has an audience, but constitute in the process a visual lexicon of instant recognizability whose elements require neither comment nor translation. They operate, in Ezrahi's terms as "outformations" (see his essay, this volume). They are part of the mass media's repertoire of reality that sometimes contravenes but sometimes also reinforces the realities produced by science.

2 To avoid any such implication, Bruno Latour and Steve Woolgar changed the subtitle of their seminal study of laboratory science from "The social construction of scientific facts" in the original 1979 edition to "The construction of scientific facts" in the 1986 edition (Latour and Woolgar 1979; see also 1986 edition).

3 An example of such black-boxing that has been widely discussed in the S&TS literature appeared in an article calling for science studies researchers explicitly to take sides with the "underdogs" in political controversies, since they could not possibly remain "neutral". See Scott *et al.* (1990). For a series of rejoinders taking apart the social black-boxes invoked by these authors, see Malcolm Ashmore and Evelleen

Richards (eds) (1996) "The Politics of SSK: Neutrality, Commitment and Beyond", *Social Studies of Science* 26(2): 219–468.

4   A parallel may be drawn here with Richard Lewontin's criticism of holistic theories in biology. Lewontin (2000: 110) observes,

> Everything is not effectively connected to everything. While gravitational pertur-bations do indeed spread out into the indefinite distance, one can stir a flower without troubling a star, because gravitation is a weak force that decreases as the square of the distance between objects.

Science studies has rightly questioned a realist view of the world that ascribes to science, writ large, something like Lewontin's gravitational force, with power to spread out into indefinite space. At the same time, the answer is not to substitute for the once unanalyzable category called "science" a term like "network", whose internal structure and function also resist sociological or normative analysis.

5   Scott evidently assumes that the children were in this manner expressing their resis-tance to their highly anonymous living circumstances. Having drawn precisely such pictures as a child in Calcutta, where houses with pitched roofs are virtually unknown, I wonder whether the experiment does not sooner illustrate a different and perhaps more insidious standardization of images of the "home" through children's books, films and other cultural materials produced in the West. Still, the basic point remains that none of the children "saw" the apartment blocks they lived in with suffi-cient clarity or sense of ownership to render them in their drawings.

6   Speaking of the lowest caste of outcasts during the Tokugawa period, Ruth Benedict says in her famous anthropological study, "They were Japan's untouchables, or, more exactly, their uncountables, for even the mileage of roads through their villages went uncounted as if the land and the inhabitants of the area did not exist at all" (Benedict 1989: 61). In Scott's terms, the outcasts were wholly illegible, and they remained so until the Meiji restoration of the nineteenth century. Their position contrasts strik-ingly with those of the other four castes – warriors, farmers, artisans and merchants – whose legibility the Shoguns ensured through a host of restrictions, from sumptuary laws to controls on vocation and movement.

7   I am indebted to Stefan Sperling for drawing my attention to this point. In the present period, a company like Amazon sorts and characterizes its readers no less effectively than hospitals do their patients; readers are thereby rendered legible. Moreover, such powerful marketing technologies, with their resulting consumer debts, may do as much to capture people and keep them in their place as official correc-tional institutions once used to do.

8   The point to stress here is that science was, for both Polanyi and Merton, *the* model polity. Both men were concerned to identify science with the liberal values that had been cruelly jettisoned by the mid-century's totalitarian regimes. Their views can be contrasted with Richard Rorty's statement that "the only sense in which science is exemplary is that it is a model of human solidarity" (Rorty 1989: 14–15).

9   Winner borrowed this example, which has become something of a byword in science and technology studies, from Robert Caro's (1974) biography of New York City's great and controversial planner Robert Moses. For an account that disputes Winner's reading of the example, see the article by Bernward Joerges (1999).

10 In his full account, Storey makes clear that the colonial regime did not wholly relin-quish its scientific advantage by giving the hybrid varieties to the small planters. To stabilize sugar production further, the government created a new "Central Board" to arbitrate disputes between factories and planters. The Central Board kept the millers from making unlawful deductions against the small planters' canes, but it also used chemical analysis to demonstrate the canes' inferior sucrose content, thus strength-ening the case for lower payments.

11 Ezrahi assumes the possibility of unmediated vision that allows citizens to see and judge for themselves the work of the state, as in America's space program of the 1960s. Recent "virtual wars" in places like Kuwait, Kosovo and Afghanistan have demonstrated the amount of work the state needs to do in order to make its displays perspicuous to citizens, from controlling its press releases to monitoring the media to selecting the pictures that will be available for distribution. At the same time, these globally televised wars underscore the validity of Ezrahi's basic point that technology has become an indispensable instrument for creating public displays of the state's legitimacy. In his essay in this volume, Ezrahi provocatively explores the contradictions between scientific and media representations of reality.

12 This problem is analogous to the issues that anthropologists have confronted in speaking about culture. If culture is taken as (relatively) unchanging, then how can one avoid falling into the trap of thinking that it is "stereotypically" reproduced? For an illuminating discussion, see Sahlins (1995).

13 For example, *in vitro* fertilization, combined with the possibility of using a surrogate mother for gestation, opens up the need to redefine the meaning of so basic a social identity as "mother". The discovery that the human genome is virtually identical in all human beings reopens the perennial controversy about the meaning of race. The recognition that the earth is an enclosed space with finite resources, a biosphere, calls for imagining the human subject as a global citizen.

3 Climate science and the making of a global political order

Clark A. Miller

The sum of research into the science and impacts of climate change makes it clear that nothing less than dramatic reductions in emissions of greenhouse gases will stop the inexorable warming of the planet. Nothing short of action which affects every individual on this planet will forestall global catastrophe.

(Mostafa Tolba, Executive Director, UN Environment Programme, 1991)

Taking a co-productionist idiom seriously is essential to understanding the processes of globalization transforming the postwar world order as we commence the twenty-first century. In recent years, public concern about a host of environmental, economic and security issues has given rise to a growing demand for global political cooperation.[1] Perhaps the most surprising and important is the transnational mobilization of public opposition to the US war in Iraq grounded on the failure of the Bush administration to secure multilateral backing for its aims. Not since the creation of the League of Nations immediately following World War I, and the United Nations after World War II, has the belief that humanity must act in global concert achieved a comparable level of public support. Responding to these concerns, policymakers have created a host of new global institutions, such as the World Trade Organization and the UN Framework Convention on Climate Change. None of these new institutions yet shares the comprehensive mandate of the UN. Nevertheless, their collective consequences for world governance in the next 100 years may ultimately rival changes made by 200 years of liberal individualism, and the spread of national expressions of political identity and the Enlightenment ideal of a rational politics geared to social needs.[2]

To date, the globalization of politics has not only failed to settle into a stable institutional framework, but has, in fact, exacerbated many of the uncertainties that haunt international relations. What is the proper division of authority between global and national political institutions? When is global intervention in national political choices legitimate? As global institutions acquire greater authority, do political actors other than nation-states – e.g. non-governmental organizations (NGOs), industry trade lobbies, local and regional governments, and individual citizens – acquire the right to participate in global policymaking? In what ways? Under what conditions and through what institutional arrangements are states willing to cede authority to experts and expert knowledge in global decisions? What normative principles will guide global procedural and distributive choices? Who will have the right to speak to those principles, and how will those rights be managed in practice? These questions, familiar from ongoing debates within a variety of new international organizations, demonstrate just how destabilizing the new global politics can be to an existing political order founded on the primacy of nation-states.[3]

Where does the power come from to call into question such entrenched political settlements? Part of the answer, I propose, is that existing normative and organizational frameworks for making public policy choices are now seen as inadequate for solving the kinds of problems humanity faces – problems that are conceived as explicitly global in scope. Faced with an array of challenges that seem to outstrip the knowledge and capacity of even the most capable states and multilateral institutions, people have begun to challenge and renegotiate the basic organization of global governance – founded on the sovereignty of nation-states, the exclusive legitimacy of national identity as a basis for political representation, and the exclusive rights of national governments to contract international legal agreements. Calls for a new, global politics draw an important part of their force from the work of transnational social actors – government officials, scientists, activists, business leaders and citizens alike – who have articulated persuasive accounts of the global nature of biological, geophysical, economic and/or social systems (cf. Takacs 1996; Jasanoff 2001; Miller and Edwards 2001). Hence, to understand where the impetus comes from to undermine existing, state-based political arrangements, we need to examine three issues: first, how and why people articulate their understandings of nature and society in explicitly global terms; second, how these global narratives become persuasive to diverse public and policy audiences; and third, how these audiences ultimately connect up global narratives to new moral and institutional frameworks for achieving social order.

I begin this chapter by inquiring into how and why people come to conceptualize the world in global terms. I then trace the process of globalization, so conceived, for the issue of climate change, using a detailed case study of the Intergovernmental Panel on Climate Change (IPCC). Subsequent sections explore two strategies of co-production the panel used to shore up its fledgling authority. First, I describe how the IPCC globalized the atmosphere by constructing a discourse that framed climate change as a risk to the global environment. This view differed from earlier discourses that had framed climate change as changes in the weather in specific locales. I then describe how, to further reinforce its authority, the IPCC articulated a new model of science and politics. In contrast to patterns of international governance founded on the power of states, the IPCC offered a model of global politics in which experts and expert knowledge, as politically neutral agents, were accorded significant power to define problems of global policy. The IPCC's efforts to shore up its contested authority in this manner have led it to draw on a variety of cultural norms and practices for warranting public knowledge, legitimating the use of power, and building trust. Most importantly, these included increasingly sophisticated institutional mechanisms and rhetorical strategies for drawing boundaries between — and in this way co-producing — distinct domains of science and politics in global forums. In the chapter's final section, I examine some of the implications of these observations for the politics of globalization.

The IPCC appears in this account as both an agent and a product of co-production. This is not a contradiction. The absence of an independent causal prime mover typifies co-productionist accounts, which ideally capture the messy reality of rapid intellectual and social change. A co-productionist idiom attunes the analyst to ways in which micro- and macro-categories, actors and dynamics connect up, directing careful attention to how, in their day-to-day routines and practices, institutions like the IPCC simultaneously reconfigure their ideas, their institutional forms, and the cognitive and social landscapes they inhabit.

What is globalization?

The sovereign state, which a decade ago appeared a permanent fixture on the global stage, today is frequently described if not as at death's door then at least as diminished in relation to suprastate and sub-state collectivities. The state is undergoing a "crisis of authority", we are told, stemming from its inability to address prominent issues on its agenda adequately in the eyes of its increasingly skeptical and skilled citizens (Rosenau 1992; Ezrahi 1990; 1984). Constructivist writers have reinterpreted the concept of sovereignty, arguing that it is properly understood not as the ability of autonomous states to exclude other states from their jurisdiction, but rather as a convergence of norms and practices in global society that change over time. Some have proclaimed "the end of sovereignty" (Camilleri 1996). Others that "sovereignty is being greened" (Litfin 1998). What seems clear is that many of the characteristics of sovereignty, at least as described by international relations theorists of past decades, will at least be subject to question in the new era. Most authors in the field today seem committed to the notion that there is something qualitatively different about world politics in the new millennium.

Less clear are questions such as how much change has occurred, precisely how and where discrete changes have taken place, and what drives processes of global change. Considerable attention has focused on the increasingly global reach of human networks and interconnections, built on new technologies of production, transportation and communication. Keohane and Nye (2001), for example, point to advances in technology that have increased the number and density of interactions among people in different parts of the globe, and to the emergence of new classes of policy problems, like terrorism and environmental change, that defy national solution. Working in a different intellectual tradition, Rosenau (1992) offers a similar account of dynamics of globalization:

Stated summarily, one of the five global dynamics involves the shift from an industrial to a post-industrial order and focuses on the dynamics of technology....A second is the emergence of issues, such as atmospheric pollution, terrorism, the drug trade, currency crises, and AIDS, that are the direct products of new technologies or the world's greater interdependence and are distinguished from traditional political issues by virtue of being transnational rather than national or local in scope....A third dynamic is the authority crises that stem from the reduced capacity of states and governments to provide satisfactory solutions to the major issues on their political agendas....partly because the compliance of their citizenries can no longer be taken for granted. Fourth, with the weakening of whole systems such as states, subsystems have acquired a correspondingly greater coherence and effectiveness....Finally, there is the feedback of the consequences of all of the foregoing for the skills and orientations of the world's adults who comprise the groups, states, and other collectivities that have had to cope with the new issues of interdependence and adjust to the new technologies of the post-industrial order.

(Rosenau 1992)

From a co-productionist perspective, however, globalization raises a different kind of question: why is it that, in the late 1980s and 1990s, people came to reconceptualize a number of prominent issues in explicitly global terms? Without inquiring into the changing categories in which people make sense of their world, discussions of long-term trends offer at best weak explanatory bite. Consider Rosenau's third and fourth dynamics, for example. Historically, it is difficult to argue that the capacity of states to implement effective policies and to compel citizen compliance is today at an all-time low. In the West, states today may have retreated somewhat from their peak powers in the 1950s and 1960s. Nevertheless, their ability to manage social conflict, mobilize force, and discipline citizens' beliefs and actions through such practices as the collection and standardization of information, surely remains at near-historic highs. If modernization programs succeeded at anything, it was in strengthening the capacity of states to know and manipulate their subjects (Scott 1998; Foucault 1979). If there is a crisis of authority in the West today, it is not because of absolute levels of state incapacity. At best, it is a crisis of expectations. Ironically, crisis conditions are arguably more prevalent in just those countries of the global South that have little or no presence at the forefront of globalization.

Other aspects of Rosenau's explanation seem similarly ahistorical. For each issue he lists as somehow more international today – e.g. AIDS, currency crises, terrorism, atmospheric pollution – one can point to earlier parallels that seemed equally world-spanning at the time: malaria, polio, recession in the 1930s, World Wars I and II, nuclear weapons, radioactive fallout, to name only a few. What, if anything, distinguishes the problems of this turn of the century so that people view them as beyond the capacity of even greatly expanded states, acting in consort? Moreover, if much of what underlies Rosenau's (and others') accounts

of globalization are continuous long-term trends in interdependence and technological change, how do such developments account for the specific timing of
globalization? Why have global discourses come to the fore just now? And, to
wander back into history again briefly, why did similar "one world" discourses
arise so prominently in the late 1940s, only to fade away again subsequently? If
interdependence has been building for many centuries, why has the late twentieth century been framed as a discrete disjunction in world affairs? If people
today seem to be simultaneously reworking the categories in which they understand the world and the institutions through which they address perceived
problems, can we identify and explain the processes by which this reworking is
taking place?

Aggregating the weather

Co-productionist accounts emphasize the power of ideas in shaping world order.
In this, they build on recent neo-institutional approaches to international environmental politics, which highlight the role of scientific knowledge of transboundary
environmental problems as a stimulus for the creation of new international institutions and regimes (e.g. Litfin 1998; Young 1998; Keohane and Levy 1996;
Hampson and Reppy 1996; Haas *et al.* 1993; Choucri 1993). They depart from
such studies, however, in inquiring into the sources of scientific ideas, as well as
their credibility and authority, in international settings (Jasanoff and Wynne
1998). Studies of environmental politics generally hold that ideas acquire political
authority because they mirror the realities of nature; correspondingly, expert
organizations acquire authority from their monopoly on objective knowledge
(Haas 1990; 1992). Considerable scholarship in the field of science and technology studies indicates, however, that this answer is inadequate. Scientific
accounts of nature exhibit persistent interpretive flexibility (Collins and Pinch
1982), and these interpretations can be taken up into competing frames of environmental and policy discourse (Miller 2000; Cronon 1992). Compelling
accounts of the power of ideas must therefore specify how ideas come to be
framed in particular ways, as well as how those particular framings acquire the
power to shape social and political order (see e.g. Jasanoff 1996b for an explicit
critique of Haas).

The historical evolution of climate change as a public policy issue exemplifies
the problem. In a speech to the Second World Climate Conference in November
1990 (see quote at the beginning of this chapter), Mostafa Tolba, then Executive
Director of the UN Environment Programme (UNEP), highlighted new scientific evidence for global warming and called for worldwide action to combat the
problem. Tolba imagined a new, worldwide political order of unprecedented
scope that could affect, as he put it, "every individual on the planet". The
following month, the UN General Assembly authorized the formation of a new
international institution – the Intergovernmental Negotiating Committee – to
develop an overall framework for global policy responses to climate change.
Eighteen months later, at the 1992 UN Conference on Environment and

Development in Rio de Janeiro, Brazil, the Committee completed the UN Framework Convention on Climate Change. The treaty, ultimately signed by over three quarters of the world's countries, established a suite of permanent global institutions to make global climate policy, and began the process of determining the norms and practices that would govern those institutions.

Tolba's views typify contemporary perspectives that link the global politics of climate to scientific understanding of the issue. They depart noticeably, however, from earlier framings of climate change. The claim that climatic changes will result from carbon dioxide buildup in the atmosphere has a long history. Nevertheless, prior to the late 1980s, scientists and other policymakers rarely connected this idea to a need to reorganize global politics. Why not? I will argue in the following two sections that they did not make these connections in part because, until recently, they represented and articulated their understandings of the atmosphere primarily in local and regional, not global, terms. Only when the Earth's climate was re-imagined as a *global* system, bringing views of the atmosphere into line with assumptions about the jurisdiction of international institutions, did claims about climate change begin to engage with debates about international politics.

For most of the twentieth century, the development of climatology as a field of scientific inquiry took place as part of the broader field of meteorology, and stemmed from the interests of meteorologists in understanding long-term weather patterns. From this perspective, climate and weather were not just intimately connected, they were essentially identical. The 1941 Yearbook of Agriculture, *Climate and Man*, published by the US Department of Agriculture in response to the events of the dust bowl years, presented the conventional mid-century view:

> The distinction between climate and weather is more or less artificial, since the climate of a place is merely a build-up of all the weather from day to day and the weather is merely a day-by-day break down of the climate. It seems to be a useful distinction, however, and there will probably continue to be meteorologists concentrating on the daily weather and climatologists concentrating on the long-term.
>
> (Hambidge 1941: 4)

This equating of weather and climate was reinforced by meteorological and climatological practices. Climatological knowledge derived from measurements of specific atmospheric variables (temperature, wind, humidity, etc.) made at specific locations over long periods of time. Historical records provided the data for deriving and verifying meteorological and climatological relationships and forecasting weather. Climatological conditions were computed for microclimates, local climates, and even regional climates by averaging data from one or more weather stations. Their day-to-day activities, then, as much as their philosophical predilections, connected meteorologists and climatologists with specific local and regional understandings of the relationships between human societies and long-term weather and climatic patterns. *Climate and Man* exemplifies these traditions, with the bulk of the volume (over 1,100 of 1,200 total pages) devoted to three related topics: (1) regional patterns of climate and agricultural settlement; (2) regional distributions of grain crops mapped onto climatic variations; and (3) specific climatic data for each state in the United States. As late as 1978, Robert White, Chief of the US National Weather Service and chair of the 1979 World Climate Conference, defined climate in almost the same terms as *Climate and Man*:

> The definition of "climate" and "weather" is a topic of endless discussion among meteorologists. For purposes of this paper, I consider climate to pertain to the statistics of weather parameters over time periods that are greater than those for which deterministic predictions of day-to-day weather are theoretically possible. As a practical matter, this means that the statistics of weather parameters over periods of two weeks and greater would qualify as climate.
>
> (White 1978: 109)

Put simply, climate remained merely another way of describing the weather, a statistical artifact constructed through mathematical averaging.

The ontological status of climate as an aggregation of local weather conditions over various spatial areas had important consequences for the politics of climate change, not least of which was the absence of any perceived need for international cooperation. The first formal, government assessment of anthropogenic climate change, published by the US National Academy of Sciences in 1966, wandered seamlessly across scales, making little distinction among various human activities that modified climate, such as urbanization, air pollution and smog, forest cover change, agriculture, supersonic transports, deliberate weather modification, and a host of other human activities, including carbon dioxide emissions. What linked these activities together in the report's discursive framework were their effects on "atmospheric properties and processes" that control long-term weather patterns:

> The subject of weather and climate modification is concerned with any artificially produced changes in the composition, behavior, or dynamics of the atmosphere. Such changes may or may not be predictable, their production may be deliberate or inadvertent, they may be transient or permanent, and they may be manifested on any scale from the microclimate of plants to the macrodynamics of the worldwide atmospheric circulation.

The report did acknowledge the potential seriousness of climate change, but framed the risks very carefully:

> [E]ven in the more extreme estimates of the possible climatic consequences of increased atmospheric CO_2, the calculated temperature changes have been of the order of a few degrees, generally less than five or ten. From glacial-geologic data, it is known with some certainty that North America

and Europe have, since the last maximum of the Wisconsin Glaciation, experienced climates that have averaged several degrees warmer than present. As mentioned earlier, *although some of the natural climatic changes have had locally catastrophic effects, they did not stop the steady advance of civilization.*

(NRC 1966: 88, emphasis added; for comparison, the IPCC today predicts a 1.5–4.5 degrees Celsius temperature rise for a doubling of carbon dioxide concentrations)

Far from linking changes in climate to a need for global policymaking, the report argued exactly the opposite. Carbon dioxide-induced climate changes, the report concluded, may very well have significant consequences for *local* communities, but they do not pose a *global* risk.

The climate system and global authority

Arguments such as those made by the National Academy in 1966, or Robert White in 1978, provide little support for the creation of an intergovernmental institution with the authority to make global climate policy. And yet that is exactly the step governmental leaders from around the world chose to take in November 1988, when they created the Intergovernmental Panel on Climate Change (IPCC). Prompted by a resolution of the UN General Assembly, the IPCC was created as a joint initiative of the UN Environment Programme and the World Meteorological Organization. Its brief was to "conduct a comprehensive review of the issue and make recommendations comprising 'elements for inclusion in a possible future international convention on climate'".[4] If, however, climate change was best understood in terms of long-term changes in local weather patterns (and those changes did not pose a global risk), why was an international convention on climate deemed necessary or desirable? One possible answer is that enough people around the world saw their local weather patterns at risk and came together to do something about it. In actuality, however, something very different happened: the *representation* of the Earth's climate in scientific and policy discourses changed dramatically between the mid-1960s and the late 1980s. What was this change, and how did it come about?

Two decades after its 1966 report, the Academy restated its sentiments that the risks of climate change were primarily local, not global, in its 1983 report, *Changing Climate*:

Viewed in terms of energy, global pollution, and worldwide environmental damage, the "CO_2 problem" appears intractable. Viewed as a problem of changes in local environmental factors – rainfall, river flow, sea level – the myriad of individual incremental problems take their place among the other stresses to which nations and individuals adapt. It is important to be flexible both in definition of the issue, which is really more climate change than CO_2, and in maintaining a variety of alternative options for response.

(NRC 1983)

As it had before, the Academy stressed in 1983 the local specificity of the natural and human systems involved, and sought to dissociate discussions of rising concentrations of carbon dioxide and other greenhouse gases from the need for global political action. This time, however, the Academy faced an uphill battle. By the early 1980s, there was an alternative to viewing climate as merely the aggregation of the weather. Based on computer models of the general circulation of the atmosphere, climate scientists increasingly represented the Earth's climate as an integrated, global system.[5] Conceptually, this system not only represented the atmosphere as a single entity, but also linked atmospheric dynamics and energetics to the world's oceans, vegetation, glaciers and ice caps. Moreover, it was this entire system that was now viewed as at risk from human emissions of greenhouse gases. The term climate had gone from signifying an aggregation of local weather patterns to signifying an ontologically unitary whole capable of being understood and managed on scales no smaller than the globe itself. Many scientists and other policymakers increasingly viewed climate change as posing risks to something that could reasonably be called the global environment. By pointing to the potential flexibility in framing climate change as either a global or a local problem, the authors of *Changing Climate* sought to reassert the credibility of prior, local interpretations of the risks of climate change against this global alternative. They thus hoped to counter what they viewed as an "intractable" framing of the issue. But the tide had turned. By 1988, a scant five years later, the IPCC's creation signified the ascendance of the view that climate change constituted a global environmental risk that could only be addressed through global political cooperation.

When formed in 1988, the IPCC derived its understanding of climate from the work of climate modelers. The IPCC produced its first assessment report in 1990 and its second in 1995. Building on earlier Academy reports on climate modeling and climate research from 1979 and 1982, as well as a subsequent report, *The Greenhouse Effect, Climatic Change, and Ecosystems*, published in 1986 by ICSU's Scientific Committee on Problems of the Environment (SCOPE), the IPCC reports adopted the climate system as their central metaphor and explicitly eschewed concerns with local weather and climates.

> Although the common definition of climate refers to the average of weather, the definition of the climate system must include the relevant portions of the broader geophysical system which increasingly interacts with the atmosphere as the time period considered increases. For the time-scales of decades to centuries associated with the change of climate due to the effect of enhanced greenhouse warming, the United Nations Framework Convention on Climate Change defines the climate system to be "the totality of the atmosphere, hydrosphere, biosphere, and geosphere and their interactions"
>
> (Houghton *et al.* 1996: 57)

The IPCC's second assessment report, *Climate Change 1995: The Science of Climate Change* (Houghton *et al.* 1996), opens with "The climate system: an overview", and proceeds to organize its entire account around the systemic view of climate and climate change. At its heart are three chapters devoted to the processes that govern the climate system, and climate model simulations of those processes. Three subsequent chapters examine environmental changes associated with changes in the global climate system: sea level rise, changes in terrestrial ecosystems, and changes in marine ecosystems. Other chapters examine radiative forcing of the climate system, observations available to validate climate models, and future work needed to narrow uncertainties in the assessment of human influence on the climate system.

The IPCC's internal organization and reporting strategy further reinforced this view of the atmosphere. Following a suggestion in the UN General Assembly resolution requesting its creation, the Panel divided into three Working Groups responsible for: (1) the science of climate change; (2) the impacts of climate change; and (3) possible response strategies. In the IPCC's 1990 assessment, Working Group I described the behavior of the climate system as a natural phenomenon being perturbed by human activities. Working Group II's report subsequently discussed the potential impacts of changing the state of the climate system. Working Group III's report concluded by describing the potential response strategies available to global society for inclusion in an international treaty. In all, policymakers were presented with a common (i.e. shared) global policy issue, and a set of possible responses for collective adoption.

In elaborating and reinforcing this global, systemic understanding of climate and climate change, the IPCC thus contributed to a vision of natural order that made clear the necessity for, and possibility of, a global politics of climate. By shifting the grounds of deliberation from changes in local and regional weather patterns to degradation of the global environment (that is, by globalizing the climate), the IPCC shifted consideration from what the US National Academy of Sciences report *Changing Climate* termed "local environmental factors...which take their place among the other stresses to which nations and individuals adapt" to what, only four years later, the World Commission on Environment and Development called "a common concern of humankind" (WCED 1987).

The globalization of science advice

In delineating the organization and work of the IPCC, I have thus far focused on the relationship of ideas about nature to ideas about the organization of politics. The creation of the IPCC in the late 1980s reflected the emergence of a global view of the Earth's climate and atmosphere. This view in turn helped underpin belief in the necessity of global political cooperation to prevent planet-wide environmental catastrophe. The IPCC helped strengthen both beliefs by further clarifying and extending the cognitive framework describing the global, systemic understanding of climate and climate change. Its efforts to depict climate change in global terms helped integrate that framework with conventional understandings of the jurisdiction and form of international organizations, thus reinforcing belief in the need for and possibility of global cooperation. By bringing concepts of natural order and political order into line with one another, the IPCC served to co-produce new arrangements of global nature and global civil society.

In this section, I turn to the normative, institutional and rhetorical resources with which the IPCC shored up its scientific claims. This is a second dimension of the Panel's role as an agent of co-production. Research in science studies has demonstrated that political institutions play a number of important roles in enhancing scientific credibility in public contexts. At a procedural level, legislative, executive and judicial bodies commonly participate in setting public standards for the conduct of policy-relevant scientific research, establishing criteria for scientific evidence in administrative and judicial proceedings, determining who counts as an expert in public forums, and demarcating boundaries between scientific and political authority (Jasanoff 1990; 1996a). At a more fundamental, ideological level, policy processes and political institutions also draw on deep-seated, cultural norms and practices for securing trust and credibility to repair scientific and social uncertainty (Brickman *et al.* 1985; Jasanoff 1986; Shapin 1994).

The IPCC, too, has deployed such resources, as we see if we track institutional changes in the panel's organization over the first several years of its existence. The initial authorizations of the IPCC by the UN General Assembly, UN Environment Programme, and World Meteorological Organization were deliberately vague on institutional specifics as a consequence of profound disagreements about how to organize the Panel. The UN Environment Programme, basking in the successful completion of the Montreal Protocol in late 1987, wanted to replicate the structure of the ozone negotiations in which a small group of internationally recognized experts participated directly in the negotiations alongside government representatives. The World Meteorological Organization, concerned that the structure of the ozone negotiations had allowed a small group of scientists to dominate the proceedings without satisfying the broader scientific community, wanted to strengthen the applicable peer-review requirements. Several governments, and particularly the United States, were concerned that the ozone negotiations had allowed experts to get too far ahead of political realities; they wanted to retain closer control over the production of scientific knowledge by appointing the Panel's members.

Differences between the US and German delegations to the initial meeting of the IPCC in November 1988, illustrate the confusion generated by these competing desires. The official purpose of the initial meeting was precisely to settle organizational issues. Invitations to the meeting went out from the World Meteorological Organization to their national contacts, the national meteorological services. The US government, interpreting the IPCC as a formal international institution dedicated to global policymaking for climate, sent a full national delegation of over twenty individuals from numerous agencies, headed by a delegation leader from the US State Department. Since the German meteorological office has no responsibility for either climate science or climate policy, however, it did nothing with the invitation until the week before the meeting. At that point the office forwarded the letter to the German climate research committee, which sent a single, academic researcher to the meeting. Once the meeting began, he quickly contacted the German embassy in Geneva, asking them to send a diplomatic representative as well.[6]

The organization that emerged from the initial meeting of the IPCC reflected a negotiated compromise among a variety of positions. The overarching plenary was established as a body of formal governmental representatives who would carry final authority over all actions taken by the Panel, including the publication of all reports. The plenary also established the IPCC Bureau, composed of a smaller number of government representatives chosen one from each of the six regional associations of the World Meteorological Organization. The IPCC established three working groups, with the six Bureau members acting as the chair and vice-chair of each. Working Group I was assigned the task of assessing the science of climate change; Working Group II was assigned the task of assessing the impacts of climate change; and Working Group III was assigned the task of developing response strategies. To accommodate the views of scientists present at the meeting, the rules for Working Group I provided for extensive peer review of the group's assessment, and allowed the group to recruit any scientist to work on the assessment, with the approval of the individual's national government. No comparable procedures were established for Working Groups II or III. Finally, the IPCC also established a secretariat, under the auspices of the World Meteorological Organization, and invited Bert Bolin, a prominent Swedish scientist, to chair the panel.

Here we see a variety of important efforts to draw upon political resources to shore up the authority of the IPCC. One involves the appeal to democratic norms and traditions of openness and participation in the Panel's organizational framework. Governments and experts from all sovereign states were invited to participate in the IPCC's activities, conforming to generally accepted practices of multilateral organizations within the UN system. IPCC reports prominently documented this widespread participation and drew on it rhetorically to support implicit and explicit claims regarding the fairness, impartiality and objectivity of the Panel's findings. In a paragraph similar to ones found in each of its reports, the Panel's *1992 Supplementary Report to the IPCC Scientific Assessment* notes:

> Generation of the background papers involved, either as lead authors or contributors, 118 scientists from 22 countries. A further 380 scientists from 63 countries and 18 UN or non-governmental organizations participated in the peer review of both the background material and the Supplement. The text of the Supplement was agreed in January 1992 at a plenary meeting of [Working Group I] held in Guangzhou, China, attended by 130 delegates from 47 countries. It can therefore be considered as an authoritative statement of the contemporary views of the international scientific community.
>
> (Houghton and Bolin 1992: xi)

The distinction between "delegates" at the Guangzhou plenary meeting and "scientists" in the production of the report refers to the formal approval of the final document by government representatives from forty-seven countries (even though many of these delegates were also scientists). Compared to the SCOPE assessment that preceded the IPCC, this reflects a substantial increase in the level of government oversight. Much as the US National Academy of Sciences legitimates many of its activities through formal relations with federal executive and legislative bodies, so, too, the IPCC has drawn legitimacy from the sanction of the government representatives who make up its plenary body.[7]

Differences arose in the first year of the Panel's operation, however, over how and why developing countries should participate in the IPCC, and what benefits the IPCC could expect to gain from developing country participation. In part, these differences reflected uncertainty about whether the activities of the IPCC were entirely scientific, clearly political, or somewhere in between – in other words, uncertainty about how to draw the boundaries of science and policy in international discussions of climate change.[8] To address the question of developing country participation, the IPCC established a Special Task Force in 1989 that reported in 1990, at about the time the IPCC's first report was published.

Some participants in the Task Force argued that the IPCC was a scientific organization. If so, developing country participation was only necessary insofar as scientists from these countries brought knowledge that was unavailable to other participants (e.g. of southern hemisphere climates and ecosystems). Developing country participants, by this reasoning, had to be disciplinary specialists. Other participants argued, by contrast, that the IPCC played an important policy role by helping to educate leaders about the dangers of climate change and possible policy responses. From this perspective, developing country participants could properly be generalists with the ability to digest the information presented in IPCC meetings and assessments, as well as with the political connections necessary to bring that information back to decisionmakers in their own countries. Still others saw the IPCC as necessary to confirm authoritatively that states needed to respond to climate change. From this perspective, the most appropriate developing country participants were well recognized experts who might or might not be connected to policymakers, but whose participation would lend credibility to the IPCC process back in their own countries.

Uncertainties also prevailed about how the IPCC should set criteria and develop policies for improving the effectiveness of developing country participation. For those who viewed the IPCC entirely in scientific terms, improving participation in the IPCC required the development of new research and training programs in developing countries. If the goal was to encourage social learning about climate change, however, then more broadly based information workshops seemed a better response. Finally, for those who viewed credibility as the most important reason for increasing developing country participation, the best short-term policy appeared to be to raise the status of those developing country representatives who already participated, and to add participants from other developing countries as quickly as possible.

Over time, the last indicated model of participation has received the greatest attention. The IPCC has increasingly funded the travel of developing country participants, but has used its limited resources primarily to fund individual representatives from each country to attend IPCC plenary meetings (Agrawala 1997). Donor countries have, for the most part, proved unwilling to extend large sums of money to developing countries to enable them to send multiple participants to the meetings of the IPCC working groups, or to begin to build credible climate science programs of their own. Developing countries, in turn, have opted to use their limited resources in other ways. Thus, while the number of non-OECD countries participating in the IPCC plenary rose to nearly a hundred by 1995 (Agrawala 1997), the number of individuals from developing countries listed as authors and contributors to the 1995 IPCC assessment remained much smaller and essentially constant over time (Kandlikar and Sagar 1997).

Many developing country participants, however, saw the need to participate in entirely different terms. In the 1990 report of the Special Task Force, for example, developing countries noted that many issues relevant to climate change are political. Poverty, development, equity, and access to technological and financial resources (including intellectual property rights) are fundamental, they argued, to any effort to respond effectively to climate change. At the Second World Climate Conference in November, 1990, Jean Ripert, the chair of the Task Force, noted:

> the struggle to master a very important aspect of the future of our planet cannot be dissociated from other efforts which the international community must make to favour a general process of development, to ensure an equitable rise in standards of living, and to equalize opportunities between peoples.
>
> (Ripert 1991)

If these were the objectives, developing country participation in the IPCC was woefully inadequate. Developing country leaders were certain that the IPCC could not act as an appropriate forum for formulating global responses to the problems of climate change, when framed in these broader political terms. This perception led them to reject the IPCC during UN debates over how to organize international climate negotiations. Between June and December 1990, the UN Environment Programme Governing Council and the UN General Assembly debated whether the IPCC should become the official institution for negotiating the Framework Convention. Although UNEP supported this choice, along with many industrialized countries, developing countries voted overwhelmingly to authorize the UN General Assembly to form another body for this purpose – the Intergovernmental Negotiating Committee.

To understand these events more fully, it is important to consider another resource that the IPCC has drawn upon over time to shore up its authority, namely the rhetorical and institutional separation, or bounding, of science and politics. Scientific judgments, we now know, inevitably involve tacit value assumptions and choices that can have important social and political consequences. At the same time, "boundary work" separating scientific and political domains of authority and action can be an important source of legitimacy in public policy contexts, although the boundaries drawn in any given instance inevitably involve negotiations among scientists, government officials, citizens and other policy actors. By appealing to widespread public understandings of science and politics as separate spheres of social activity, boundary work thus helps bring the forms and processes of public policymaking into line with prevailing Western expectations about the nature of democratic governance and rational inquiry (Gieryn 1996; Jasanoff 1990).

The confusion prevalent at the initial November 1988 meeting of the IPCC provided an ideal site for boundary work, and the separation of Working Group I (the science of climate change) from Working Groups II and III (the impacts of climate change and response strategies) demonstrates early efforts to distinguish between the scientific and political activities of the Panel. Not surprisingly, this separation took place not only in physical terms (separate working group meetings) but also in the rules and practices governing the production of the working group reports, as described earlier in this section. Over time, however, this separation proved inadequate in pragmatic terms as the IPCC grappled with the day-to-day problems of formulating and carrying out its work plans.

The problems of developing country participation offer one example of the IPCC's challenges in successfully presenting science and policy as bounded within the organization. When Mostafa Tolba, then UNEP Executive Director, began preparations for the climate negotiations to follow the publication of the IPCC's first report, he requested that the IPCC be delegated as the negotiating body for the Framework Convention. Tolba proposed to convene, under the Panel's auspices, technical working groups nominated by governments to establish parameters for various treaty components. These would then form the basis for subsequent negotiations by government representatives to the IPCC. Developing countries objected, however, arguing that many of the issues facing negotiators were political and not technical, and that the IPCC was an inappropriate body for undertaking such activities. Instead, as noted above, they supported, and obtained, the creation in early 1991 of a separate negotiating forum – the International Negotiating Committee – under the auspices of the UN General Assembly.

The institutional separation between the "political" domain of the International Negotiating Committee and the "scientific" domain of the IPCC had a number of important stabilizing effects for the climate regime as a whole. Developing countries, who had actively lobbied throughout the first two years of the IPCC for greater participation, eased their criticism of the organization with the apparent decrease in the Panel's ability to make political decisions. Subsequently, in late 1991, scientists, who had been highly critical of what they viewed as the political machinations and negotiations that had characterized Working Groups II and III, prevailed upon the IPCC to extend the rules of procedure and peer review initially established for Working Group I to the other two bodies as well. At the same time, the IPCC also established Technical Support Units for each of the three working groups, whose self-described purpose was to act as a buffer between the experts working on the IPCC reports and the special interests who would inevitably want to influence those reports. Finally, the IPCC set formal procedures for the production, review and acceptance of its reports, which established clear roles for both experts and government representatives. All of these activities went a long way toward bringing the Panel's institutional apparatus into line with the increasingly accepted view of the organization as a technical advisory body for the formulation of global policy. Some three years, and one complete report cycle after its creation, the IPCC had co-produced a global science and politics of climate change that would lead, in the subsequent five years to two major international treaties and the establishment of regular, ongoing global deliberations about the future of the Earth's climate.

Warning signs

One value of the co-productionist idiom is that it enables the observer to become attuned to the multiple ways that knowledge and order become coupled in the emergence of a new phenomenon like climate change. The IPCC, as we have seen, has actively engaged in two co-production processes. First, as a key component of its authority to speak on global policy issues, the IPCC worked to intertwine knowledge and power by explicitly representing the climate as a global-scale natural system. Second, the IPCC consolidated its own technical authority by articulating a narrative of global politics in which experts play a powerful role as politically neutral agents. Presented with a global science and politics of climate change, certified by an established technical authority, negotiators moved quickly to reach agreement on the UN Framework Convention on Climate Change. Even US president George Bush, who was initially skeptical of the issue, attended and signed the treaty in deference to public concern catalyzed by the IPCC report and the perceived need for global cooperation. The Framework Convention was signed in June 1992, two years after the publication of the IPCC's first assessment report. Article 2 of the Convention states: "The ultimate objective of this Convention and any related legal instruments...is to achieve...stabilization of greenhouse gas concentrations in the atmosphere at a level that would prevent dangerous anthropogenic interference with the climate system". Three years later, citing authoritative evidence in the Panel's second assessment, published in 1995, the Clinton administration accepted legally binding targets for greenhouse gas emissions, clearing the way for the negotiation of the 1997 Kyoto Protocol.

The co-production idiom is also useful, however, for the insights it provides into where coupled knowledge-orders remain unconsolidated, tentative and fragile. As the world seeks to bring into being new forms of global governance, such insights will be particularly valuable. The global science and politics put in place by the IPCC, for example, faces at least two major challenges. First, the global view elides major differences among human populations, treating everyone as a citizen of planet Earth. How such differences will be accommodated, especially between rich and poor, is a growing question mark. Skepticism toward the IPCC's "one world" vision of climate change persists in developing countries, and the place of these countries in the global order of the climate regime remains contentious. Critical voices in the global South have charged the IPCC and others who support worldwide action to reduce greenhouse gas emissions with a not-so-subtle form of neo-colonialism (Agarwal and Narain 1991). Developing country diplomats have insisted that rich, industrial states should take the first steps to reducing emissions, collectively refusing to adopt any emissions reductions targets themselves. In turn, this unwillingness on the part of developing countries to participate in a global regulatory framework has become a frequently wielded argument by opponents of climate policies, especially in the United States.

The failure of the IPCC to incorporate developing country voices and concerns about global politics into its "technical" framing of the problem, has also contributed significantly to concerns about IPCC science. Developing country researchers express doubt about the credibility of a picture of climate change that is founded on the work of laboratories and modeling centers in North America, Europe and Japan, and that ignores major features of the South's climate, such as the Indian monsoon (Kandlikar and Sagar 1997). Even when the IPCC has sought to accommodate critiques emanating from developing countries, its framing of the issue and its organizational norms and procedures have as frequently exacerbated controversy as reduced it. One major controversy occurred during the run-up to publication of the second assessment report, when calculations of the long-term economic costs of climate change turned out to have been based on assumptions that valued the lives of inhabitants of developing countries at only one tenth that of their counterparts in the West. More recently, during its third assessment report, completed in 2001, IPCC efforts to develop regional perspectives on climate change quickly ran into difficulties when the Panel could find few regional scientists who met its standards of expertise, and few regional studies that satisfied its stringent peer-review requirements. To build an understanding of climate change that speaks credibly to developing country audiences may well require the IPCC to renegotiate what counts as reliable knowledge and expertise within its assessments.

During the negotiation of the Kyoto Protocol, the climate regime also began to encounter significant resistance in the West. Particularly in the United States, conservative organizations and energy companies funded extensive media efforts to discredit IPCC science (Edwards and Schneider 2001). In early 1997, the US Senate voted 99–0 to oppose any treaty that appeared to disproportionately favor the economic interests of developing countries over those of the US by exempting them from global emissions reductions regulations. The Clinton administration never submitted the Kyoto Protocol for ratification, and when the George W. Bush administration took office in January 2001, it unilaterally declared the Kyoto Protocol dead, at least as far as the US was concerned.

Growing US opposition to the climate regime reflects several important features of the global science and politics co-produced by the IPCC. First, any vision of global government raises potential red flags for America's long-cherished traditions of sovereignty, political independence and individualism. When it declared the Kyoto Protocol dead, the Bush administration also declared the IPCC's conclusions to be "UN science", drawing on discursive repertoires in American political culture that paint the United Nations as an inept, highly political bureaucracy seeking to subjugate Americans to the capricious whims of a global state. The IPCC succeeded in quickly reasserting its technical authority, pointing out that well over half of its authors and peer reviewers were American scientists, and forcing the Bush administration to back down from its comments and at least formally accept the IPCC's scientific conclusions. In an ironic twist, however, the US government took advantage of the IPCC's effective boundary work by agreeing with the IPCC's science but nonetheless retaining its sovereign right to disagree over the political necessity of a global regulatory solution. In other words, the boundary drawing that the IPCC undertook allowed the very kind of unilateral exit that the United States made from the climate regime.

Similar challenges plague the IPCC regarding the boundary work it has done to differentiate its global view of climate change from more localized perspectives. Although people seem to respect the credibility of global climate science, and often point to global warming as a major policy concern, especially when in the throes of a hot summer or warm winter, their concerns remain locally grounded. Visions of global climate change have failed to generate much demand for costly policy responses. A great deal of uncertainty remains, for many, about just what climate change implies for their own individual lives and livelihoods, as well as about the capacity of global political institutions to map out and follow through on a strategy for achieving global sustainability. They fear global solutions that will impose unacceptable burdens and distribute them unfairly among the Earth's many inhabitants. The kind of incremental solutions proposed by the Clinton administration in 1993 (a 5 cent per gallon gasoline tax) and the Kyoto Protocol (a 7 per cent reduction in emissions from Western countries) fail to reassure people either that these are adequate to the task, or that the benefits they may bring from avoiding uncertain local risks will offset their very real costs.

The proper relations between the local and the global in a reconstituted global order remains a central dilemma faced by institutions of global environmental governance. Even if climate change is successfully projected as a global phenomenon, and even if a global perspective on the natural environment continues to permeate public discourse, just how human societies will rearrange themselves socially and politically to cope with the "demands of planet Earth" remains unsettled. Will we arrive at a world in which, as Karen Litfin puts it, sovereignty has been "greened" (Litfin 1998)? That is, will the nation-state, with potentially significant changes in its norms and practices, nonetheless remain the obligatory passage point of international governance? Or will, by contrast, some real or virtual institutional locus of global policymaking emerge in the twenty-first century, much as Washington DC replaced the fifty states of the United States as the locus of national policymaking in the late nineteenth and early twentieth centuries?

The evidence we have to date is ambiguous. Depictions of a new, global empire paint at best sketchy landscapes of its institutional and power relationships (Hardt and Negri 2000). Likewise, even the most forward-looking accounts of the need to reshape political order to redress global risks, such as the World Commission on Environment and Development's now canonical report *Our Common Future* (1987), are ambivalent about how to think about the new world order. The "our" of the report's title seems to presage the need for a single voice to speak for all humanity,[9] a sentiment reinforced by the report's opening line: "The Earth is one but the world is not". This simple phrase captures the challenge that global environmental discourses are said to pose to existing political institutions and arrangements. It is precisely the distinction between the global interconnectedness of environmental systems and the local dis-connectedness of social institutions for regulating and managing human behavior and natural environments, that the Commission singles out as the greatest cause for concern. Yet the report talks throughout not only of, but also to, nation-states. It seeks to imagine one new world, but it fails to escape existing political divisions.

Conclusion

In the case of climate change, the construction of a category of "global natural systems", at risk from human activities, has undermined important aspects of the postwar political order. No longer are sovereign nation-states viewed as an adequate organizational foundation for global governance. New global (as opposed to international) institutions must be created to cope with these new kinds of global environmental degradation. Precisely what form those institutions will take is not yet clear. The IPCC offers an increasingly influential model, although far from the only one, which several other regimes of emerging global governance have begun to emulate, including the Millennium Ecosystem Assessment of the Earth's ecological health and the InterAcademy Panel, an institution that aims to perform a scientific advisory role for global governing bodies comparable to that currently performed by the National Academy of Sciences for the US government. What is clear, however, is that the constitution of these new institutions will involve substantial changes to conventional political categories, such as sovereignty, the state, civic identity, and even science.

The history of the IPCC demonstrates that new constructions of natural and social order on global scales are highly interdependent. The nominally scientific construction of global environmental risks has helped underpin the legitimacy of claims about the need for new institutions of global political cooperation. Simultaneously, global political cooperation has proved equally necessary to underpinning the legitimacy and credibility of scientific claims about the existence of global environmental risks. Even as the IPCC has sought to portray climate change as a global phenomenon, the credibility of that view has depended on the IPCC's ability to construct itself as a legitimate institution of global cooperation. So long as the idea that the environment can be understood and managed on planetary scales was championed only by a handful of scientists from the United States and Europe, its credibility remained suspect in the eyes of elites and publics elsewhere. Only by re-presenting this idea through an institution that could credibly claim universal (i.e. global) representation could the idea secure the necessary authority to motivate global political change.

Much the same can be said for the IPCC's reconfiguration of the role of science and the state in global politics. For over a century, Western democracies have struggled to integrate expertise into the formulation and implementation of public policy. As comparative studies of scientific advisory processes have demonstrated, Western governments arrived at a broadly shared normative sentiment that science should inform policy but should be separate from politics. Over time, however, countries encapsulated this shared sensibility in very different institutional forms. Everything that one might normally expect to be universal to science – from evidentiary standards to norms of openness, transparency and public participation – is subject to different interpretation in the design and management of national expert advisory systems (see, especially, Jasanoff 1986; Brickman *et al.* 1985). Today, as supranational bodies like the IPCC seek ways of incorporating science advice in global policymaking, these same sets of value-laden questions face policymakers. Who will count as an expert? What will count as evidence? Who will be responsible for deciding such issues?

Science, in any event, will clearly retain considerable power to legitimize global policy institutions. Yet, as I have tried to illustrate in the case of the IPCC, the articulation of what counts as "good science" in global contexts will depend heavily on political institutions for support and legitimacy. This dynamic of co-production reinforces an observation made by Sheila Jasanoff. Securing the credibility of policy-relevant science in global contexts may well result not from seeking better science, in and of itself (which, as Jasanoff points out, "falsely presupposes the autonomy of scientific inquiry") but also and simultaneously from constructing more morally authoritative institutions of global governance (Jasanoff 1997).

Science and politics – as orderings of nature and society – are co-produced; solutions to the world's most critical problems of social order will require solutions to problems of knowledge, and vice-versa.

Notes

1 Note that the adjective "global" – pertaining to the globe in its entirety – differs from other adjectives, such as international or transnational – pertaining to relations among nation-states – that are often used interchangeably.
2 On the spread of nationalism, see Anderson (1983). On the rise of the instrumental state and its articulation in various Western democracies, see Ezrahi (1990) and Rueschemeyer and Skocpol (1995).
3 Demonstrations against the WTO in Seattle illustrate the increasing significance attached to global institutions and their potential to upset existing political settlements. Discussions of other case studies can be found in Chayes and Chayes (1995), who discuss the participation of countries in international legal regimes; Slaughter (1997), who discusses increases in networking among judges, legislators and other

political officials from around the world; and Miller (2001a), who discusses the challenges in constructing global expert advisory arrangements that can achieve credibility among multiple national audiences.

4   *WMO Bulletin* 38(2): 113.

5   The transition from a local to a global view of climate coincided with the development and spread of general circulation models as the principal tool for scientific inquiry into the nature of the climate. The history of this shift in the practices of climate scientists has been detailed by Paul Edwards, who describes climate models metaphorically as a "world in a box" (Edwards 2001). The construction of general circulation models began in the 1960s, and climate modeling gained credibility thereafter. The US National Climate Program, created in the early 1970s, specifically emphasized computer modeling as the central tool for climatological research. The 1979 World Climate Conference included discussions of climate models and statistical research alongside one another, particularly in its discussions of the impacts of climate change (WMO 1979). With the publication of two Academy reports in 1979 and 1982, these models began to displace statistical aggregation as the central focus of climatology in policy discourses (NRC 1982; 1979). The 1979 and 1982 Academy reports (also known as the Charney and Smagorinsky reports) are the first reports in which carbon dioxide is treated independently of other human activities that affect the weather on local scales. Another indicator of how climate models shifted the discourse of climatologists is the "First Annual Conference on Statistical Climatology" held in 1979. Prior to the late 1970s, there was no reason to refer to *statistical* climatology, as there was no other form of climatology to distinguish it from.

6   I conducted interviews with several individuals who attended this meeting.

7   Overall, the IPCC's organization was a hybrid mix of elements borrowed from the practices of scientific advisory committees and international diplomacy. For a more theoretical discussion of hybrid institutions like the IPCC, see Miller 2001b.

8   Similar boundary drawing occurs all the time within nation-states in accordance with well established procedural understandings in legal, administrative and advisory settings. See Jasanoff 1990.

9   Cf. Anderson (1983) for a similar account of the emergence of possessive language as an indicator of new forms of identity in the case of nationalism.

4 Co-producing CITES and the African elephant

Charis Thompson

In her introduction to this volume in Chapter 1, Sheila Jasanoff analyzed a number of aspects of "co-production" typical of contemporary uncertain multi-sited scientific and technological practice, including developments around representation, identity, discourse and institutions. In this chapter I describe a transition in the status of the African elephant, from a universal species of charismatic megafauna endangered enough to need protection from all off-take, to a regionally differentiated species needing absolute protection in many areas but susceptible to regulated sustainable off-take in some locations. For this transition to occur, CITES (The Convention on International Trade in Endangered Species of Fauna and Flora), the international treaty which legislates international trade in endangered species, also had to change. In its early years it had emerged as a convention whose famous "appendices" listed and thus protected endangered flora and fauna under the banner of unified scientific species making up an imaginary universal commons. This effectively banished those who disagreed with decisions to include certain species or sub-species on the various appendices to trading outside the convention. The decision regarding the African elephant that I describe here was part of CITES' subsequent transition to an instrument capable of contextualizing sub-populations of endangered species by using its appendix listings conditionally, depending on local and regional conservation criteria. This effectively internalized differing opinions on the viability of trade in particular species to the convention, and thus meant that varying levels of protection and trade could be regulated within the terms of the convention. This co-production of an evolving African elephant and an evolving treaty reflected intense efforts by African conservationists and other stakeholders not just to intensify, but also to indigenize biodiversity conservation and its associated tourist economies in line with African regional and local perceptions about development, land use, wildlife, and local people. The more indigenized African elephant became a means of negotiating these African priorities, and the evolution in CITES allowed the differing philosophies and circumstances of those owning and managing the land and wildlife in question to be incorporated in the treaty itself. Interestingly, this indigenization of the African elephant allowed it to make demands on the global conservation community that the earlier more universal elephant did not. This transition has wide-ranging implications for the future of biodiversity conservation, and was achieved precisely through the "parallel processing" shifts in representation, identity, discourse and institutions of which the introduction speaks.

I examine the shift in question through a decision taken at the Tenth Conference of the Parties (COP) to CITES in June 1997 to down-list from Appendix I to Appendix II some Southern African populations of the African elephant, and the reprisal of this decision at the 2000 COP. The situation entering the tenth COP represented a re-emergence of a difference in opinion that pre-dated the listing of elephants on CITES Appendix I, and centered around the claim by many wildlife management experts in Southern African states that the ban on sustainable off-take and trade in ivory was unnecessary, if not outright bad for biodiversity conservation in their region, where many elephant populations were seen as being too plentiful for the land in question. East, Central and Western African range states (states where significant wild African elephant populations are found), however, still by and large viewed their elephant populations as both critically endangered and highly vulnerable to illegal and dangerous poaching activity. How could some elephant populations be down-listed without threatening all African elephants by exposing them to the brutalities and lawlessness of poaching and an unregulated ivory trade? How could the sensibilities of sustainable development that Southern range states were advocating be reconciled with the more preservationist needs of other range states? And, relatedly, how could the debate take on the appropriate African tenor, so that the more preservationist states' demands were not simply equated with a wealthy Western animal-rights position that sought to protect universal species at the expense of local people, and that had increasingly come under attack from member states? One East African delegate explained the extent to which the principles of sustainable utilization associated with African and other developing countries had become de rigueur as background to the tenth COP:

> The philosophy of sustainable development was given great prominence at the meeting. Every proposal appeared to go through the scrutiny of whether or not it contravened the basic principles of sustainable utilization of natural resources.
>
> (Kenya Wildlife Service 1997)

The tenth COP had to negotiate these regional differences in perceived elephant abundance, as well as broker the conflicting conservation philosophies through indigenization. Novel proposals for scientific monitoring and enforcement were the means through which the relevant changes in representations, identities, discourses and institutions were coordinated with one another.

CITES

CITES, or the Convention on International Trade in Endangered Species of Fauna and Flora, is a global treaty that regulates trade in species that are considered threatened or endangered. The treaty was needed to plug the perceived holes in GATT and NAFTA as regards trade in wildlife products. As neither GATT nor NAFTA differentiate between sources of wildlife product, they are impotent to regulate a sustainable trade in endangered wildlife, and CITES took on this trade regulation role. The estimated value of the annual worldwide wildlife trade in 1994 was US$10 billion, with $2–3 billion being a conservative estimate of the illegal portion of that trade (Hemley 1994). The treaty, sometimes called the Washington Convention, was signed in Washington DC, on 3 March 1973, and entered into force in July 1975. It is thus roughly contemporaneous with the domestic US Endangered Species Act, and reflects much the same political and scientific understanding of species endangerment. There were twenty-one initial signatory nations, and by the 1997 meeting, 139 states were parties to CITES. CITES party nations meet approximately every two years at the Conference of the Parties to amend appendices.

The convention has three appendices on which threatened and endangered species are listed. If a species is listed on Appendix I, no commercial trade in the species or specimens derived from the species is permitted. A species on Appendix II can be traded in a regulated manner by stakeholders who obtain permits which are dependent on conservation considerations such as sustainability. Appendix III listings mandate international cooperation from member states in restricting the trade of locally endangered species. The three appendices together form the instrument of the convention. All signatory states are required in theory to accept all listings, unless a given state has taken out a reservation on a particular species. States can take out reservations on individual species when a species is first listed, or when a state first joins the convention. A state with reservations is treated as a non-party as regards these species. The criteria for listing, down-listing and removing species from the CITES appendices are only loosely codified. Member states request listing changes, and, with information from the Animal and Plant Committees and other technical sources, the Standing Committee drafts resolutions for debate at COPs. Any state can nominate members for the technical committees. Listing changes must be approved by a two-thirds majority of voting parties.

The convention names "peoples and states" as the relevant political units for control over wildlife, maintaining that they are "the best protectors of their own wild fauna and flora". In accordance with the Charter of the United Nations and the principles of international law, sovereign integrity is paramount despite the transnational nature of the convention. Nation-states are the default bearers of political legitimacy, and states and peoples are treated as the kinds of entities that can "own" natural resources.[1] Under the convention's terms, each party must accede independently, and must provide its own management and scientific authority to carry out the convention's obligations, such as the preparation of annual wildlife trade reports, and the enforcement of import and export regulations. The convention is supposed to co-exist with domestic wildlife laws, and is typically implemented by enacting domestic provisions for carrying out CITES obligations.[2] States must also set their own penalties for contravention of trade terms. The convention depends upon each nation fulfilling its rights and responsibilities, regardless of technical and political capacity. While this lends the convention the strengths associated with flexible interpretation and implementation, it also means that there is a wide disparity in compliance with the convention.[3] For example, it is typical for only slightly over 50 per cent of nations to produce their annual report for the CITES secretariat. Enforcement, being the responsibility of the individual signatory countries, is considered highly variable. As Norbert Mumba, head of the Zambian delegation in 1992 expressed it:

> Departments of Customs in all the States in the subregion are extremely important if trade is to be monitored effectively. Today I can tell you Mr. Chairman, that most of the customs officers don't even know the difference between an elephant tusk and a banana.

In addition, wildlife laundering through non-signatory countries is common, so that the nation-based structure enables those who so desire to undercut the convention's supranational goal of regulating international trade in endangered species.

Despite being organized around sovereignty, the convention is notable for the roles it specifies for international organizations (IOs) and for non-governmental organizations (NGOs). Environmental problems derive much of their political intransigence, urgency and theoretical interest from the fact that global and local constituencies – not just nation-states – have compelling claims to the natural resources or states of nature in question (cf. Jasanoff and Martello forthcoming). The CITES convention recognizes "international cooperation" as essential "against overexploitation through international trade", and has explicit provision for the non-voting presence of international organizations at the COPs. UNEP (the United Nations Environment Programme) funds the treaty secretariat, and the convention is financed by voluntary contributions calculated according to the UN scale, so that, for example, the US is responsible for 25 per cent of the costs. CITES also recognizes the non-voting presence of NGOs at COPs. NGOs function as watchdogs, represent stakeholders and evolving conservation philosophies, fund delegates to travel to CITES meetings, and collaborate with other technical bodies in the collection of scientific data (cf. Mann 1991). In addition, the working of CITES is dependent upon the activities of a few major transnational but Western-based wildlife NGOs: WWF (World Wildlife Fund) funds, and jointly oversees TRAFFIC (Trade Record Analysis of Flora and Fauna in Commerce), with IUCN (the International Union for the Conservation of Nature and Natural Resources). TRAFFIC, with WTMU (the Wildlife Trade Monitoring Unit), collects worldwide data on CITES species, and these data are housed at the WCMC (World Conservation Monitoring Unit) in Cambridge, England.[4]

When CITES was drafted in 1973, the protection of fauna and flora was justified in terms very similar to the bipartisan Endangered Species Act, namely, that "wild fauna and flora in their many beautiful and varied forms are an irreplaceable part of the natural systems of the earth", and that wildlife has a plurality of values, including "aesthetic, scientific, cultural, recreational, and economic". The impetus behind the treaty in the 1970s was principally to curb international trade in a few highly visible and highly endangered species, such as the spotted cats, chimpanzees, and crocodiles. The language contained in the major wildlife conservation legislation of the 1970s was pluralistic in value but catholic in appeal, speaking of a shared human heritage whose multiple benefits could be reaped by and for any or all. By the mid-to-late 1980s, however, there was pressure to use CITES as a different kind of instrument, reflecting the general move in conservation practice and philosophy away from individual universal species protection and toward localized biodiversity conservation (Tackacs 1996: 41–99). Among other things, moving conservation science and policies from the fate of species to the fate of ecosystems raised legal and social issues such as land tenure, wildlife use rights and land use to primary relevance, and greatly increased the potential number of stakeholders. This change had the result of "politicizing" CITES.[5]

The ivory wars and counting elephants

Scientific consensus is elusive at the best of times, and, befitting the size of the beast and the personalities involved, territorial claims are unusually large and hotly contested among elephant biologists. Add to that the public kudos of saving the elephant, and you have the makings of an almighty battle.[6]

Saving elephants is a large-scale endeavor, with obvious social, political and economic consequences. Many African elephant range state economies are heavily dependent on the foreign exchange earned from their wildlife tourism. It is thus a significant state interest to mitigate factors that are thought to affect tourist revenues. For example, the so-called "big five" (elephants, rhinos, buffalo, cheetahs and lions) are considered critical for tourist satisfaction in savannah habitats, and rapid declines in wildlife, especially inside wildlife parks, threaten tourist satisfaction.[7] While there might be state as well as other scientific, conservation and moral arguments for ensuring the healthy long-term survival of all these species and more, optimally managing elephant populations is not as simple as making sure that enclosed parks are well stocked with the species in question (Thompson 2001). An adult African elephant can eat 170kg of vegetation a day, and except where kept in forcibly, elephants move in and out of wildlife parks, seasonally following rainfall gradients, and daily moving away from water sources which are often at the center of parks, and then back again in the evenings. Left to their own devices, elephants move over large areas somewhat constrained by, but without particular regard for, human land tenure systems and land use patterns. Their "trespassing" can be very destructive of crops, property and human life.

One of the most fundamental components of even beginning to manage wildlife populations involves counting the number of animals present in a given ecosystem, over time, so that trends of growth and decline of populations can be established, and threats and healthy population levels can be gauged. Even though elephants are large and easy to differentiate one from the other, and inter-observer reliability is not as big a problem as for many species, counting elephants has always been highly contested.[8] The initial decision to list the African elephant on CITES Appendix I, which was taken at the seventh COP in Lausanne, Switzerland, in 1989, followed over a decade of fierce debate as to how many elephants there were in Africa, and whether or not their numbers were declining to unsustainable levels. The so-called "ivory wars" are sometimes dated to Iain Douglas-Hamilton's pan-African survey of African elephant numbers, which was carried out under the auspices of IUCN in 1977.[9] Douglas-Hamilton, an ex-patriate living in East Africa, and at that time head of IUCN's African Elephant Specialist Group, sent questionnaires asking about elephant numbers to wardens, conservationists and scientists throughout Africa. He received responses ranging from counts of particular populations, through estimates and extrapolations of various kinds, to outright guesses. Using this heterogeneous data, he argued that elephant numbers were precarious across vast areas of Africa, and that dramatic measures were needed to curb poaching and habitat destruction. The translation of the claims of the *Pan African Survey* into the million-dollar Elephant Action Plan supported by WWF was partly a reflection of the mediagenic Douglas-Hamiltons and their association with anthropomorphism toward, and thus attribution of individuality to, elephants. Nonetheless, the survey itself was part of a developing East African perception that there was an elephant survival problem.

Douglas-Hamilton's results were rapidly challenged by conservationists from South Africa, who had a very different view of the conservation status of the African elephant. Most vocal among the dissenters from Southern Africa was Ian Parker (also an ex-patriate), who was perhaps the foremost exponent of the Southern African position of sustainable consumptive utilization of elephants as a way to manage them and pay for their conservation. Parker compiled his own two-volume report, countering Douglas-Hamilton's conclusions with his own Malthusian models of sustainable off-take based on the highly managed game reserve populations that predominate in Southern Africa (Parker and Amin 1983). Parker argued that many elephant populations, far from being on the brink of extinction, needed culling to prevent overpopulation and consequent mass die-offs. At the first All-Africa meeting of the Elephant Specialist Group in Wankie National Park in 1981, Parker leveled a "bad science" attack at Douglas-Hamilton, claiming that over 90 per cent of Africa's elephant populations could either sustainably support off-take at current levels, or were of unknown status. Because Douglas-Hamilton's survey results were so easy to show up as bad science, the fact that Parker and Douglas-Hamilton were using distinctively different models of elephant well-being that reflected their regional identities and conservation philosophies remained somewhat submerged. The submerged positions were to resurface later.

In the meantime, the triumph of the "bad science" attack ironically left Parker's own position vulnerable to being overturned by more complete evidence and accurate counts of the elephant populations of Africa. The constituencies which continued to coalesce around alarm at elephant population declines (crudely, East Africans concerned about poaching and wildlife-human conflict, and Western animal-lover NGOs concerned about the protection of elephant rights) took on the task of filling this gap in scientific evidence. A multiple NGO study of the ivory trade by the Ivory Trade Research Group, and the African Elephant and Rhino Specialist Group, was undertaken, in part with funds from the US-based Claiborne-Ortenburg Foundation. In addition, the CITES secretariat secured funds from the Kowloon and Hong Kong Ivory Manufacturers Association to commission work on the impact of the ivory trade. Contrary to the expectations of many Southern Africans, their report also came out against the sustainability of Africa's ivory trade. These studies collected elephant population graphs from aerial counts across much of Africa, recorded rapid increases in the price of ivory and a steep drop in poached tusk weights, generated computer model predictions of elephant population crashes, and noted spent cartridges and overgrown elephant trails in forests. After a decade of data collection and arguments on either side of the question of how many elephants there were and how many there needed to be, the sixth COP to CITES held in Ottawa in August 1987 adopted the African Elephant and Rhino Specialist Group's collated findings that unless poaching was stopped Africa's elephant populations would dwindle below viability. Nothing was done about the ivory trade until the seventh COP, but the momentum was set. In the months between the sixth and seventh COPs, the media played an important role in galvanizing public opinion, beginning in 1988 by naming elephant poaching the "elephant holocaust" and portraying the vanity of ivory consumers.[10]

Loxodonta africana, the African elephant, was first listed in 1976 on CITES Appendix II. Resolutions to control the ivory trade were passed at subsequent COPs, including the introduction at the fifth COP of management quotas, but none of these measures sufficed to control the illegal ivory trade and poaching. The species was voted onto Appendix I of CITES at the seventh COP in a vote that passed 76–11, with eight Southern African range states opposed. The new listing was made more palatable by an amendment that specified terms for the transfer of elephants from Appendix I to II at a future date, should expert opinion or the status of elephants change. This amendment, the so-called "Somali agreement", specified that for a population of elephants to be downlisted, it must meet two criteria: it must demonstrate ability to withstand off-take, and controls against ivory smuggling in importing and exporting countries must be demonstrably reliable. The Appendix I listing represented widespread public opinion in support of the ban on trade in elephants and elephant trophies, combined with the fact that the more accurate scientific evidence appeared to have spoken authoritatively against the sustainable utilization view. Zimbabwe, Zambia, Botswana, Malawi and South Africa, convinced by local knowledge of their own successful elephant management practices, took reservations against the Appendix I listing. Namibia joined them in 1990, when it joined CITES. The 1989 listing decision, then, was achieved more through a combination of media attention and a piling up of scientific evidence of threats to East African elephants, than through achieving a common framing of the different ways of counting (head counting, and valuing) elephants. As the vote came in, the conservation NGOs fought to take credit for the consensus on banning the ivory trade, announcing the decision on television simultaneously in the US (WWF, with backing from the New York Zoological Society) and in Switzerland (WWF), but not in Africa. The major involvement of NGOs included not just the well known conservation NGOs, but also animal rights groups such as the International Foundation for Animal Welfare, the Environmental Investigation Agency, the Humane Society of the United States, Friends of Animals, and the Animal Welfare Institute. Animal rights groups such as these were to become explicitly linked to colonialist views by the 1997 decision, but their backing of the original listing decision, combined with the Western staging of media announcements of the ivory ban, suggests that a coalition between animal rights and East African anti-poaching and desires to curb wildlife–human conflict was more helpful than not in 1989.

In the years following the 1989 decision, the Southern African countries did not trade outside of the convention, partly because of the drop in export markets and the contraband status of ivory, and partly out of a desire to preserve the convention's efficacy as an instrument of conservation. Ivory confiscated from poachers or derived from problem-animal control or management culls began to accumulate in range states, its very existence serving as a constant reminder of the high cost of CITES to local and national development and to conservation in lost legitimate ivory revenue. The temptation to realize the value of growing ivory stockpiles was ever-present. The position that sustainable utilization of certain elephant populations was viable kept resurfacing, and managed gradually to become the position associated with the growing demand in conservation for social justice for developing countries. Southern African states minus South Africa initially formed SACIM (Southern African Centre for Ivory Marketing), which was subsequently symbolically renamed SACWM (Southern African Convention on Wildlife Management). The argument gained ground that if environmentalists and others in the West were so keen to see elephants saved, they should help pay for them to be saved, including compensating those actually living with the elephants for their care of the elephants and for elephant-inflicted losses. Short of meeting this obligation, conservationists and animal lovers in the West had no moral authority to prevent Africans from making elephants pay their own way in a sustainable trade. This North/South equity logic gradually became irresistible, and represented a shift from a universal endangered elephant to a global one whose preservation made different geopolitical demands on different people in different places.

The Southern African claim that there were in fact plenty of elephants kept re-emerging after the 1989 decision, even though it was invisible in the elephant's official CITES status. Elephant counts became more thorough and more systematic, and the IUCN began to codify the rawness, heterogeneity and uncertainty that had been the downfall of Douglas-Hamilton's data at Wankie. By the mid-1990s, elephant count data was represented in a manner that indicated which of nine survey categories had been the source of the count, and used a scale of 1–3 to gauge the reliability of the count.[11] With these more organized data, Southern African countries began pursuing the idea of splitting Africa's elephants into different populations, and amending CITES to reflect the fact that some populations could withstand off-take while others could not. There were a number of risks involved in this strategy, however, including that of undercutting the convention's unit of conservation, namely the species as a whole. Treating the species as composed of distinct groups had to be part of a combined trade strategy for the entire species: it was necessary to show that African elephants would fare best as a species if managed in distinct – and opposing – ways depending on the population in question.

The idea of keeping the populations apart in the name of the well-being of the whole species gave rise to a number of immediate practical problems. For example, it required that customs officials and others enforcing CITES trade restrictions be able to tell whether ivory came from one of the populations that would do better if culled, or from one of the populations for which an absolute ivory ban was appropriate. Various methods were attempted to distinguish ivory source populations. A reliable and easily implemented method for distinguishing among all populations proved elusive, however. Measuring isotopes of heavy metals like strontium in the ivory appeared to distinguish among Southern African elephant populations, but not among East African populations. It was suggested that this was because the Southern African populations are relatively geographically isolated one from another, as reflected in their management, whereas East African elephants roam over larger areas (including human-inhabited areas) and are less reproductively isolated from each other. Just like the earlier elephant counts, the scientific attempts to trace ivory to source populations of African elephant worked within, but not between, two different kinds of elephant populations in East and Southern Africa. In any case, it was felt that signatory countries could not realistically be relied upon to have the necessary monitoring capacity.

Down-listing of *Loxodonta africana*, Harare, June 1997[12]

The 1989 consensus forged between science and popular opinion, and between elephant endangerment and elephant rights, could no longer hold at bay the demands from a newer coalition between ideas about North/South equity and calls for sustainable utilization of some elephant populations for African development. The 1997 COP vote looked poised to become a show-down between the preservationism associated with the Appendix I listing of 1989, and the sustainable use philosophy associated with a possible Appendix II listing and the countries that had taken reservations on the 1989 listing. While there were some dissenters, the ban was largely considered to have been successful in halting poaching. For example, Jean Mbeng, the Director of Wildlife and Hunting for Gabon, said in June 1994, "it is clear that the ban on trade in ivory has caused the decline in poaching". The perception of success began to be read more as a measure implemented to stabilize the poaching situation that had already done its work. The Panel of the Experts Report has been pleased with the sustainability of Southern elephant herds since 1992. Their report added fuel to the view that CITES appendices were too rigid and so were no longer functioning as a tool in conservation. If species get stuck on Appendix I regardless of their conservation status, the appendices risk becoming means of enforcing one conservation philosophy over others (one associated with developed countries) rather than being instruments responsive to changes in endangerment. As David Western, Kenyan delegate to CITES, expressed it in his record of the events of 1997:

> The rift grew into a crisis of confidence in CITES itself. According to many southern hemisphere countries, CITES has become a preservation instrument dominated by the western conservation lobby with no prospects of down-listing species and encouraging trade even when the species in question has recovered and no longer faces extinction. The southern African countries among others have threatened to abandon CITES unless the convention permits legitimate sustainable trade which pumps money back into conservation and local communities.
>
> (Western 1997b)

In 1992, the SACIM countries and South Africa had drawn up formal proposals to have their elephant populations down-listed. Kenneth Kaunda's government fell in Zambia, however, and the new government withdrew both its reservation and its support from SACIM, putting a chink in the united Southern African position. Again in 1994, South Africa, this time with Sudan, submitted proposals to transfer their elephant populations off Appendix I. Other African states refused to join them at this point because several African countries recorded an upsurge in poaching immediately preceding these COPs, which was attributed to anticipation of the lifting of the ivory ban. Increased poaching stoked fears that it was premature to lift the ban. By the ninth COP, however, the CITES secretariat urged the thirty-seven African elephant range states to seek consensus on proposals before the tenth COP was convened. There was general consensus that Southern Africa would not have accepted postponing the decision until the next COP. As John Waithaka (1997) expressed it, continued antagonism with Western animal rights NGOs had stretched the tolerance of Southern African countries to the limit:

> The presence of a multitude of pressure groups opposed to the down listing of elephants appeared to have pushed the proponent countries to state categorically that they were ready to trade outside CITES.

Namibia, Zimbabwe and Botswana, supported by Malawi, submitted proposals for transfer of their elephant populations to Appendix II, with annotations restricting trade to live animals, hunting trophies and stockpiled ivory. Importantly, their proposals were not for a down-listing of all populations of *L. africana*, and they were only for export to a single market. Japan was approved in these proposals as the sole market for import of ivory from the populations of elephant in question, and it was proposed that it function only as an internal market. In a significant gesture of support for international conservationist networks, all three countries proposed to direct the revenues to elephant conservation and to community management programs like Zimbabwe's CAMPFIRE. At the lead up to the 1997 COP, support for these down-listings was very high. The major conservation NGOs, including international ones such as WWF, IUCN and TRAFFIC, and African ones such as the African Wildlife Fund, and Wildlife Conservation Society, had all circulated position papers in favor of the down-listings at this point, further isolating the animal rights NGOs, who continued to push for a total ban on the ivory trade. The CITES Secretariat, with a Japanese chairman of the Standing Committee, Nobutoshi Akao, had also come out in favor of the down-listings.

The preservationist side was by this time no longer the default position, and was represented chiefly by observers and delegates from animal rights groups and countries where these perspectives predominated. To make matters worse for their bid to keep all African elephants on Appendix I, delegates from developing countries complained of nuisance calls and other harassing tactics by members of the NGOs opposed to the down-listing. Needless to say, this played further into the North/South resentment, and the animal rights position was referred to as "colonialism" both during the build-up to the COP and at the meeting itself.

Saving the convention from becoming ossified, and the vote from being a showdown between preservationism and utilitarianism, seemed to require getting some sort of third position onto the COP agenda. A meeting to try to establish a pan-African position had taken place in Dakar, Senegal, in November 1996. Two days before the CITES meeting, the thirty-seven African range state delegations met again, at Darwendale, Zimbabwe. This meeting started with thirteen Francophone states, most Southern region states, and Eritrea, Sudan and Ethiopia from the Eastern region supporting the down-listing proposals. After once almost ending without agreeing on conditions that might modify the down-listing decision, the meeting was reopened. Eventually consensus was reached on conditions that would have to be met if the ivory ban was to be lifted. These included independent verification and monitoring procedures, and the establishment of databases to observe the effect of lifting the ban, and a provision for immediate re-listing on Appendix I if the opening of the market was abused. It also included a period of twenty-one months to put all this into effect, effectively prohibiting the resumption of trade before the next COP. If the African states could get these conditions onto the COP agenda, and approved before the listing decision itself, a vote in favor of the down-listing proposals would mean something very different from either the Appendix I or Appendix II choice that the decision had seemed to involve.

Kenya had seized the international limelight in the period around the 1989 ivory ban by staging dramatic and widely televised public burnings of huge pyres of stockpiled ivory. It had since continued to play a leading role in the ivory wars, and had also been influential in giving local and regional arguments for the ivory ban that were not simply mouthpieces for Western positions. The Kenyans were thus well placed strategically to broker an acceptable consensus. They added an additional provision during the CITES meeting which used the North/South equity momentum, and which also provided a solution to the question of the fate of highly contentious ivory stockpiles. They proposed an amendment that would have developed countries buy out and then dispose of ivory stockpiles, thereby directly tying the problem of stockpiles to the idea that North/South equity should be a consideration in the protection of the elephants as "global commons".

In the middle of the final CITES debate on the elephant listing proposals, a halt to discussion was called by the Secretariat because the current seemed to be running strongly in favor of down-listing and sustainable utilization. It was suggested that delegates proceed immediately to a vote, and this motion was approved. With frantic diplomatic activity, the vote on the resolution was halted, pending a vote on the African conditions agreed in Darwendale. The African states also called for a secret ballot to decide this, claiming years of Western intimidation in the open votes to date (so much for transparency!). The conditions were passed by over 75 per cent of delegates. In addition, Kenya's amendment for the disposal of ivory stockpiles was passed by over 90 per cent. The down-listing vote then passed comfortably.

As one delegate said after the decision: "Because of the non-confrontational approach and continual stress on conditionalities, we were able to (forge) dialogue and eventually a consensus". The official US delegate to CITES had arrived at the meeting opposed to down-listing, reflecting the powerful hold of the animal rights groups on US popular opinion. At the conclusion to the meeting he declared in an interview on National Public Radio that he had found the compromise decision – down-listing with conditionalities based on North/South equity, science as a tool or method, and provisions for more rapid and conservation status-sensitive movement between appendices – "uplifting".

By the eleventh COP in 2000, TRAFFIC's Bad Ivory Database System had been transformed into the Elephant Trade Information System (ETIS), a global monitoring instrument designed to compile data on all ivory and elephant product seizures since 1989. ETIS' goals were reported prior to the eleventh COP as being threefold. The intention was to learn about the common patterns of illegal trade so as to alert those involved in monitoring the trade; to eventually build up the monitoring, law enforcement, and reporting capacity of each country involved in the trade to acceptably reliable levels; and to be able to use the comprehensive database to phase in legal trade between particular source and trading countries. While great strides were reported in the development and funding of ETIS over the period between COPs, the second goal in particular was felt to be in need of extensive improvement from an independent body.

Despite its limitations, as of the time of writing, the competing scientific and regional frames of reference are being more or less successfully subsumed into the scientific data collection efforts of ETIS. The transition marked by the assertion of regional differentiation was articulated with the help of these technical and institutional instruments that helped forge the new space of this global regime to protect the indigenized elephant, in place of the earlier international regime preserving the universal elephant.

Co-production in CITES and African elephant monitoring

The above account of African elephant conservation under CITES is an account of the co-production of representations, identities, scientific and other discourses, and institutions, to affect important elephant conservation change, and contain dissent.[13] Successive scientific instruments, materializing successive changes in the identities at stake, the representations with power, the institutions of relevance, and the discourse and practices of making the changing phenomenon objective, are illustrative. The trail from early non-standardized counts of the 1970s (how many African elephants are there, and are they endangered?) leading to more standardized counts with error estimates in the 1980s and 1990s (evidence that many populations are in serious decline or face serious threats), and then to the very recent comprehensive monitoring database (means to differentiate between populations so as to promote regionally specific and socially just conservation) – form one facet of the transition, and mark the increasing technical and institutional capture by the changing convention of the debates around trade in African elephants.

The trajectory of the convention itself drew on and in turn contributed to broad tendencies in environmental treaties and conservation during this period, including the increased centrality of social justice, and increased importance both of global and local or regional identities to environmental action. The Declaration of the United Nations Conference on the Human Environment, adopted at Stockholm in June 1972, is usually credited, along with the Club of Rome reports of the 1970s, with putting the environment and development together on the international political agenda (e.g. Escobar 1995: 192–199; Norgaard 1994: 11–13). The International Union for the Conservation of Nature and Natural Resources (IUCN) made sustainable development measured by intergenerational equity its conservation framework when it published *World Conservation Strategy: Living Resource Conservation for Sustainable Development*. And when the United Nations World Commission on Environment and Development, chaired by Gro Harlem Bruntland, issued *Our Common Future* in 1987, sustainability had acquired a geographic as well as temporal dimension of equity, implying that environmental stewardship should be spread equitably across the globe as well as passed down equitably from generation to generation. The version of the debate over sustainable use versus preservationism that permeated the 1997 CITES meeting was also influenced by the precedent set by the 1987

Montreal Protocol to limit the worldwide production of CFCs, and some African conservationists involved in the African elephant listing decisions mentioned the Montreal Protocol's role in establishing a precedent for North/South equity.[14] The regionally differentiated but global regime that was part of the transition effected by voting to down-list certain Southern African elephant populations with conditions was presaged by Principle 7 of the Rio Declaration, drafted in 1992.[15]

The explicit assertion of novel identities was also very important to the transition in question. During the ivory wars of the late 1980s, the predominant identity groupings were not made particularly explicit. The most significant difference was between East and Southern Africa, and this mapped onto two different legacies from older colonial relations in the two regions. Southern African conservationists tended to invoke a single colonial enemy, pitting colonial settlers (and presumably their various first-world backers) against "indigenous" Africans, with most conservation activities seen as an extension of colonialism. M. P. Simbotwe, a Southern African Resource Management consultant, expressed the Southern African position as follows:

> The question African people ask is: for whom are we conserving wildlife? While there is an urgent need to conserve it, history reveals an almost total indifference and ignorance among colonial settlers toward indigenous perceptions of wildlife conservation.

East African conservationists likewise tended to invoke the similarities between land-grabbing conservation and colonialism. But they also blamed helter-skelter post-independence efforts at modernization, which resulted in habitat loss and land degradation. Compare the Southern African statement just quoted to Moringe S. Ole Parkipuny's and Dhyani Berger's East African portrayal of these two distinct anti-conservation forces:

> Maasailand has been reduced to primarily semiarid land on two separate fronts. First, commercial agriculture and spontaneous encroachment by peasants have advanced, under the flag of national interests and common rights to resources. Second, exclusive wildlife protection areas created for the purpose of wildlife conservation, and maintained for tourists from abroad, have claimed a large share of land.[16]

The Kenyan position, which was the best represented on the CITES technical committees of the East African range states at the time, was aligned with Western sentiments in its support for, and lead in, establishing the ivory ban, and on the value of continent-wide assessments of elephant endangerment. As the home to a portion of the species that was highly vulnerable to poaching and to wildlife-human conflict, Kenya stood to gain from the strongest species protection plan that could be passed. Kenyan conservationists who were important actors in the ivory wars tended either to be strong advocates of Western-style thinking about park protection and animal rights, or to be proponents of a distinctively East African version of community-based conservation. Many of the prominent researchers of the African elephant, such as Cynthia Moss and Iain Douglas-Hamilton, worked in Kenyan wildlife parks, and became (in)famous for the practice of individually naming elephants, which then became obvious candidates for protection in the Western media-heightened imagination. The community-based conservationists pointed out that in East Africa, land-use and wildlife-human conflicts are high, in part because of rapidly changing land-tenure patterns to do with modernization pressures. Aligning with the West on elephant protection could be a strategy to protect open range lands for elephants and resist state pressure to settle nomadic pastoralists and fence off elephant migration routes.[17] Most East Africans were also aligned with Southern Africans on the principles behind sustainable utilization, however, and disliked the colonial undertones to strict preservationism for elephants in areas of the world where humans didn't even enjoy basic rights. East Africans emphasized, as a way of connecting their sympathy for the ivory ban with their postcolonial African identity, the critical role of local people's custodianship of wildlife outside parks in any conservation solution.

The Western animal rights NGOs of the period tended to be extremely unreflective about the colonial overtones of their positions. One group used the slogan "Either you're for killing elephants or you're not". Susan Lieberman, a representative of the Humane Society of the United States, exemplified this with her statement on behalf of animal rights groups in 1989:

> I represent twelve animal welfare groups with a combined membership of at least two million Americans. The American people overwhelmingly support the maximum protection for the elephants. They want to bequeath a world where elephants remain free in Africa.

The main conservation NGOs (as opposed to animal rights and animal welfare NGOs) changed from supporting the ban in 1989, to supporting the down-listing to Appendix II in 1997, roughly tracking the shift from species conservation to biodiversity conservation documented above, and responding to the need to address social justice issues in the latter conception of conservation. The ivory trade organizations initially opposed the ban, and the Japanese and Hong Kong trade associations expressed anger in 1989 that they had not been told by the CITES Secretariat or by their Southern African trading partners that the elephant was endangered. The head of the Hong Kong Ivory Trade Association is reputed to have dropped a live shrimp into a cauldron of boiling water at the pre-CITES meeting in 1989 and said "here's what we Chinese think of animals". After the ban was passed, however, the ivory trade associations re-crafted themselves in co-productionist institution and capacity building manner, either as wildlife management bodies (as in the case of SACIM/SACWM) or as lobbying and capacity-building organizations for the future possibility of opening up a restricted ivory trade. This allowed the ivory trade organizations to provide the possibility, if not yet the reality, of fulfilling down-listing with conditionalities when the 1997 COP arrived.

The 1997 decision required a pan-African consensus and corresponding identity in a way that the 1989 vote had not. As argued above, North/South equity was an obvious conduit for this, as was evident in the pronouncements of conservationists throughout the range states. There, differences between East African and Southern African representations of North/South equity and conservation remained, but the narrative was more readily available for both. For example, a young East African environmental consultant lamented the lack of Western underwriting for the maintenance of the wildlife heritage, and said that the appropriate African response to colonial donor relations ought to be "Asante ya punda ni mateke;" ("thanks of a donkey with kicking", or, "looking a gift horse in the mouth"). A Taita (a southern Kenyan tribe) conservationist with the Kenya Wildlife Service contrasted two tribal responses to Western wildlife conservation. In so doing, she illustrated the potential power of local alliances with the international community, in this case the possible alliance between nomadic pastoralists and the global community against national modernization goals:

> The Maasai have a weapon; they can connect with the international community because if they don't like what the Wzungu (Whites) do they just kill the elephants. A Taita man lets his land be taken, and then asks if the trespasser will please get off his toes, so that he can better move out of the way for the newcomer.

Tawona Tavengwa, of Zimbabwe's CAMPFIRE, put the contrast between North and South more bleakly (as is typical of the Southern African view): "To all rural Africans, elephants look the same. It is the Western animal protectionists who need to have their eyes examined" (these two examples from Lewis and Carter 1993). Gilson Kaweche, the Zambian deputy director of National Parks and Wildlife Service, made the same point in especially poignant form:

> Too often non-Africans insist on imposing their views....Such people walk into my office while still jet-lagged to ask questions and request papers dealing with management recommendations submitted to previous directors.

The differentiated and conditional down-listing that came out of the 1997 COP and the institutional and technical capacity that has followed, were possible because the differences between East and Southern African positions were made internal to a greater African identity as the indigenous home of the endangered wildlife in question. This African consensus took cues from, and in turn reinforced the North/South global identities that Western conservation NGOs were increasingly accepting. What resulted was a global conservation regime for the elephant that recognized that the costs of supporting the elephant's survival fell disproportionately on those housing the elephant, and that this cost ought to be shared equitably. Both the African range states and many Western NGOs (although not the animal rights groups) were part of, and called for, this shift from a universal species living "free in Africa" to a species located on the ground in Africa. This indigenization of the elephant turned Africans into the primary stakeholders and main spokespeople for the African elephant. The earlier split between East African and Southern African elephant management patterns and colonial relations did not go away, but it no longer separated the regions. Instead, the indigenization of the African elephant, and the acceptance of differentiated global responsibilities toward the species thought of like this, allowed for the expression of different conservation circumstances in different parts of Africa. Befitting its original heterogeneous position, East Africa was able to broker the decision so that it wasn't simply a question of the opposed philosophies of sustainable use versus preservationism, but reflected the different circumstances for these different elephant populations.

In sum, the case study discussed in this chapter illustrates the way in which institutions, representations, discourses and identities change together in this kind of co-productionist multi-sited, global environmental issue. The analysis allows us to see that change is possible, yet that it takes action on a wide range of fronts that must somehow be coordinated enough to change the dominant paradigms of conservation. It also allows one to see that change does not mean that the legacies of older representations, identities, discourses and institutions disappear, but rather that they realign and reemerge. And finally, it allows us to see how important bureaucratic and technical and institutional capacity is in temporarily stabilizing one frame or another for work to be done. The kind of transition marked by the shift from a frustrating and frustrated universal species protection to the more differentiated global responsibility for an indigenized species, represents an important turning point for biodiversity conservation. With careful attention to these processes, broad gains in both conservation and social justice should be possible.

Acknowledgements

My knowledge and understanding of this case would not have been possible without the generosity of David Western, a key player in the African ivory wars, with whom I worked for a number of years in the mid-to-late 1990s, and who continued to enlighten me with his insight through the decision of the 2000 COP. The primatologist Shirley Strum provided deep insight and warm hospitality, both of which were more than helpful. I am also extremely grateful to John Waithaka for taking me to see elephant science and politics "on the ground" and for sharing with me his great expertise on the African elephant, and to the employees of Kenya Wildlife Service, African Conservation Centre, New York Zoological, the San Diego Zoo, and the Liz Claibourne/Art Ortenburg Foundation and others who talked to me about these matters.

Notes

1 The principles of the Rio Declaration on Environment and Development, in a kind of "ontogeny recapitulates philogeny" logic, serve as a good summary of trends in global environmental treaties (see below). On the primacy of sovereign rights and responsibilities, see Principle 2:

> States have, in accordance with the Charter of the United Nations and the principles of international law, the sovereign right to exploit their own resources pursuant to their own environmental and developmental policies, and the responsibility to ensure that activities within their jurisdiction or control do not cause damage to the environment of other States or of areas beyond the limits of national jurisdiction.

2 E.g. in the US, the ESA, boosted by the Lacey Act, with the US Fish and Wildlife Service as the scientific and management authorities.
3 For details on the history of CITES and case-studies (including the African elephant) by important Southern African and Australian conservationists and zoologists, and CITES secretariat members, see Hutton and Dickson (2000).
4 See Ramachandra Guha (1998) for an example of an early and influential critique of one strand of Western environmentalism. Referring to Daniel Janzen's call for a worldwide network of protected areas under the jurisdiction of biologists, he says

> This frankly imperialist manifesto highlights the multiple dangers of the preoccupation with wilderness preservation....As I have suggested, it seriously compounds the neglect by the American movement of far more pressing environmental problems within the Third World. But perhaps more importantly, and in a more insidious fashion, it also provides an impetus to the imperialist yearning of Western biologists and their financial sponsors, organisations such as the WWF and the IUCN. The wholesale transfer of a movement culturally rooted in American conservation history can only result in the social uprooting of human populations in other parts of the globe.
>
> (Guha 1998: 272)

5 The CITES sourcebook uses this formulation, and it is a commonly expressed view about CITES. This should not be taken as saying that the species CITES was initially envisaged as protecting were free from political contestation; it seems clear that they were not. What people mean by the claim that CITES became politicized in this change is that political disputes became internal to the convention, instead of being thought of as external to the convention.
6 For a gripping account from one of the major participants in the ivory wars, see Western 1997a: 220–254. The quote is from p. 231. See e.g. Joyce Poole (1996) for an account of the ivory wars from an East African elephant researcher, rather than a conservationist. The connections between the Western animal rights perspective and the elephant researcher perspective are clear in this memoir of one of the actors.
7 Tourist satisfaction is probably highly malleable. In conversations with park rangers and wardens in Kenyan wildlife parks (1994–1997), I was told that a very small amount of tourist education can rapidly alter tourist perceptions. For example, Western tourists seeing nomadic pastoralists inside a wildlife park tend to respond that seeing people in the park decreases their sense of being in nature and spoils their experience of the animals. If as little as five minutes is dedicated to explaining that the people and animals need each other to reproduce a flourishing landscape, however, then the approval rating after seeing pastoralists in parks goes up dramatically. Similarly, if a park is described as "deforested", tourists feel that they are seeing

nature in decline; if the same dusty vistas are described as the drought part of natural weather cycles, the dust becomes much more palatable.

8 Cf. Alexander De Waal (1989), who wrote that

> (p)re-famine estimates of animal numbers in Dafur varied by factors of two-and-a-half....Market statistics can be misleading, as the principal markets (those for which figures are available) represent a varying proportion of animals and crops sold, and prices in these markets are varyingly representative of prices in rural markets. Even rainfall figures can mislead. During the 1980s, as the drought worsened, many rainfall monitors in north Darfur ceased recording, as they were no longer receiving payment for this task....*Statistical data have the quality of becoming "harder" the further one is from the process of their collection and analysis.* It is best to limit their use, and be skeptical.
>
> (5, my emphasis)

9 E.g. Western 1997a :193. Iain Douglas-Hamilton is married to the granddaughter of Jean de Brunhoff, author of the *Babar* books. The world of wildlife conservation in Africa is characterized by larger-than-life actors, especially male ex-patriates, who tend to become "charismatic megafauna" just as much as the animals on whose behalf they work.

10 Describing the role in the 1988 ivory wars of the combination of NGOs, public opinion and the media that accompanied these scientific studies, David Western has written:

> Within a few months, the media blitz launched by conservation groups and lobbyists changed the imagery and did for the elephant what it had done earlier for the Vietnam war: it brought the carnage and trauma into American and European living rooms. The film clips of elephant carcasses with hacked-off faces were gruesome enough, but these paled beside scenes of entire herds crumpling like discarded sacks as tiny orphaned babies raced around their fallen mothers trumpeting in abject fear. Worse still, the victims as often as not included game guards lying face down, riddled with AK-47 bullets sprayed by poachers scouring the continent for ivory.
>
> (Western 1997a: 239)

11 IUCN world elephant data (Western 1997a: 239).

12 My understanding of the Kenyan perspective on these events is based in large part on the notes of D. Western; Western 1997b; Waithaka 1997; Kenya Wildlife Service 1997.

13 In addition to my own fieldwork notes and interviews, sources from which I have drawn in portraying the divisions and similarities among different African community-based perspectives include: Lewis and Carter 1993; Overseas Development Administration 1994; Kiss 1990; Western *et al.* 1994.

14 The Montreal Protocol laid out a differentiated timetable for CFC phase-out, requiring faster compliance from developed than from developing countries, and placing the financial burden for alternative technology development on the West. The West had to phase out more quickly to make up for its much greater per capita influence on the ozone layer to that point, and it had to take financial responsibility for the change in technologies to make up for the financial gain it had received, often at the expense of developing countries, from CFC-producing technologies to this point.

15 Principle 7 of the Rio Declaration states:

> In view of the different contributions to global environmental degradation, States have common but differentiated responsibilities. The developed countries

acknowledge the responsibility that they bear in the international pursuit of sustainable development in view of the pressures their societies place on the global environment and of the technologies and financial resources they command.

16 Parkipuny and Berger (1993: 115).
17 Nomadic pastoralism, as practiced by the Maasai in southern Kenya, for example, is considered to be one of the kinds of human land use compatible with keeping range open for elephants. Nomadic pastoralism is considered by some to be counter to Kenyan modernization, however. Excessive fencing of land can be counterproductive to elephant conservation because it restricts their range, and thus leads to deforestation and rapid land degradation.

5 Knowledge and political order in the European Environment Agency

Claire Waterton and Brian Wynne

Introduction

The discourses of science and politics have perhaps always been confused by the interpenetration of hybrid ideas of both natural and human orders. Indeed, since well before the establishment of a field of science and policy which explores such potent theoretically laden issues, anthropologists had noted the fundamental correspondences between notions of human and natural order in non-modern societies (Horton 1971; Douglas 1966; 1975). In considering the subtle relations between natural knowledge and social-political orders, the political and cultural flux of late-modern Europe may be an especially interesting site for observation and analysis. From early beginnings in a purely economic arrangement, a Common Market, more explicit ideals of a politically and culturally unified Europe began to find expression among Western European leaders. Successive versions of a European Treaty gradually strengthened the momentum towards ideas of a political union. At the same time, original expectations and ambitions of a European superstate along modernist lines have been complicated by a combination of forces which could be called both "traditional" and "postmodern" – a stubborn refusal to relinquish local identifications (witnessed in pockets all over Europe), as well as a more pervasive cosmopolitan sense of global relativity. Whatever their particular shape however, it is clear that knowledge and, in particular, the projection of emergent idioms of natural knowledge, have been central factors in the struggle to define and stabilize competing visions of institutional and political order such as we see in post-Cold War Europe.

In this chapter we examine a contemporary European institution whose purpose is to produce natural knowledge about the environment in Europe.[1] Through an analysis of ways in which the European Environment Agency (EEA) negotiates what kinds of natural knowledge are appropriate for use and dissemination as official EU "environmental information", we can see instances where quite clearly what we are looking at is the simultaneous emergence of science and a (super)state. There is a strong sense in which this "co-production" of knowledge and state is both a hugely influential and powerful process, yet at the same time an undertaking that is full of contingencies, uncertainties and unknown consequences. As other authors in this volume do, we look both at the undeniable force and power of the processes and networks within which the EEA is implicated (science itself, the institutions and culture of the European Union, processes of standardization and the stabilization of scientific knowledge into policy-useful "information"), as well as more subtle shifts and indeterminate tensions detectable within those processes and networks. The making of an appropriate vocabulary and identity for itself in the heady and pressured world of European environmental policymaking has been one of the most difficult tasks this new agency has had to undertake. This "identity question" is manifested in defining practically stable and shared expectations and assumptions about the EEA; in setting out proper boundaries of agency in policy-advocacy and influence; and delineating, in member state affairs, who has sovereignty to define legitimate knowledge agents and processes.

As in several chapters in this book, the institution we have analyzed is an institution-in-the-making. Therefore, in the following pages, we try to convey the sense that making environmental knowledge (and stabilizing it as "environmental information") within the EEA is, in effect, a contribution to the making and constant re-ordering of Europe as an institutional and political entity which we may otherwise read about in the daily newspapers. There is a sense in which, in carrying out its responsibilities, the EEA is engaged in crafting new institutional forms in a position where it is right at the edge of institutional creativity, at the very brink of ongoing changes and adjustments in Europe. Yet it would be wrong to convey the EEA as being at the helm of change in the sense that those acting within it have autonomy and power. What we can see, rather, is the constant wrestling with and exchange of identities and influences from one scale to another, so that it almost seems as if the shaping of knowledge (and power) lies outside any particular human actor's will or agency – hence the feeling of individuals within this institution itself that the EEA is "in the eye of the hurricane" – in the midst of conflicting forces greater than itself. Examining this institution, we witness knowledge in the making, and history in the making, yet with no particular actor at any supposed wheel. The metaphor of co-production allows us to describe this emerging nature/society state-of-play in all its complexity, mutuality and multiple dimensions.

The European Environment Agency

The European Environment Agency (EEA) is one of a new suite of European agencies formally independent of the European Commission yet designed to fulfil the objectives of European Treaty commitments. Conceived in the mid–late 1980s – at a time when so much importance was beginning to be attached to environment, but also to "information" as a means of political agency – and when European political unification goals were probably waxing most confident and powerful, this agency's main constitutional responsibility was to provide "objective, reliable and comparable" information about all aspects of Europe's environment, in order to inform the Commission, the EU member states, the European Parliament, other policy actors and the wider public. A key ambiguity here which was later to be more openly contested, as we discuss later, was whether the European citizenry was to be informed and involved in various more direct ways, or only through the formal agency of the EEA-informed member-state central governments and the European Commission.

The foundation of the EEA rested upon the fact that scientific information concerning the environment in Europe was uneven and inconsistent. As such, disparate information sources did not create a basis for imagining a larger unit within which member-state comparisons carried meaning; and many of the sources of information themselves were deemed unreliable. Hence clauses in the EEA's founding regulation define the Agency's task as follows: to ensure "the consistency of information on the state of the environment"; provide "uniform assessment criteria for environmental data to be applied in all member states"; and "help ensure that environmental data at European level are comparable and, if necessary, to encourage by appropriate means improved harmonization of methods of measurement" (CEC 1990). In a nutshell, the task was to provide "objective, reliable and comparable" information, of European significance, for European policy. It was clear that environmental knowledge in Europe fell a long way short of such an ideal, and the articulation of an imagined epistemic order of this kind can be seen as the expression of a normative model, of how environmental knowledge and information *should* be shaped and developed. But this epistemic model in turn involved a corresponding tacit model of the agents of such knowledge production, quality control, formation for policy, and its use – in other words of an institutional policy order and its forms of agency. What was therefore being constructed or envisaged in the articulation of this model of European environmental information? And how did it relate to pre-existing institutional arrangements for the production and use of environmental information for policy?

To begin to answer this question, the EEA's mandate needs to be viewed in a somewhat larger political context – one that takes into account ongoing presumptions in the drive to create a unified Europe. Agencies like the EEA were based on the conviction that more Community institutions and activities were necessary to achieve Community Treaty goals.[2] But they were also established, in part, to balance out the excessive unaccountable power of the European Commission in the promotion of a unified Europe. These agencies were intended to be independent, impartial, immune to member-state politics and particularity, and impermeable also to the Commission's tendencies to act in politically insulated ways with regard to member states. But, as Kreher notes, such agencies were "not provided with the power to replace existing procedures or institutional settings within the nation states". In the operational sense they were all conceived as being "complementary to existing regimes or procedures" (Kreher 1997: 228). Of the new agencies the EEA was perhaps the most significant, as environment was already not just a strongly waxing public concern within Europe, but a focal point of political conflict between some member-state governments and critical environmental groups. It was also the arena in which public information and access to state-held information was the most pregnant with political conflict.

Although the EEA was not granted direct regulatory power (for example, in regard to inspection and policy enforcement), its official remit was both ambiguous and also vast. Since its practical inception in December 1993, it has been struggling to define a workable, satisfying and legitimate identity for itself, both in relation to what we might call the environmental agenda in Europe, and in relation to other bodies and institutions it has to work with. But while it was expected that the EEA would provide information so as to be relevant to and effective for EU environmental policy, it was nevertheless also expected that this new institution would avoid trespassing into areas of policy prescription or advocacy. This policymaking terrain was jealously protected by the formal policy institution, the Directorate-General for Environment, DGXI of the Commission.[3] In setting up the EEA in this way, the European Commission had assumed that it would be possible for the Agency to provide information without directly influencing policy. This basic assumption has been the root cause of many clashes between the EEA and DGXI of the Commission, as we shall describe.[4]

As we have suggested, the relationship between DGXI and the EEA was set up formally to be close, with DGXI being the most prominent policy-user in a world of increasing user-sovereignty over knowledge. However, whereas the EEA had been given a relatively clear run (albeit with intense pressure from different interests) on the production of appropriate information, DGXI has, in the last two decades, seen its policy territory and influence shrink. This has partly resulted from the apparent success of sectoral integration of environmental policy goals in the EU; but it has also been in large measure due to an aggressive nationalism, led by the Conservative British government until 1997, which saw environment as the main platform rationalizing a sinister plot to build a European superstate that would suffocate liberal free-market enterprise. Thus in the virulently anti-European repatriation of policy power from the Commission in the late 1980s and early 1990s, environment was the most heavily raided policy sector,[5] and DGXI the most emasculated of all the Commission services. A resulting hostility to environmental policy, unless it is very carefully tailored to the needs or capacities of big business, has continued to shape DGXI's approach, to the disillusionment of many environmental specialists throughout Europe.

As part of this trend towards ecomodernization and redefinition of environmental policy in terms of corporate industrial and commercial capacity, and corresponding with cross-sectoral environmental policy integration, "the environment" has also come to be seen as a legitimate part of the remit of other more powerful DGs within the Commission – agriculture, transport, energy and trade, for example. So, at the very time when DGXI's policy terrain has been reduced and its ambitions and powers sharply curbed, it has had to establish a working relationship with a new, independent EEA – an agency explicitly inspired by enthusiastic popular environmental advocates in the European

Parliament, the thorn in the flesh of many Commissioners. DGXI's evident anxiety to avoid being drawn into a position of undue prominence and radicalism, combined with its suspicion towards the EEA's possible over-enthusiasm and appetite for policy influence, has coloured its approach to this key institutional relationship. Thus it soon became unclear after the establishment of the EEA as to whether it and DGXI were, in fact, partners, or whether DGXI was the prime client of the EEA, or whether they were, on the other hand, competitors. These different models of the relationship involve different corresponding images of both the larger institutional order of Europe and the epistemic order of environmental knowledge to be established for Europe.

From its inception, the EEA worked hard to differentiate itself from DGXI. Much of this effort revolved around the EEA's belief that DGXI was attempting to enforce a rigidly conservative definition of environmental information, in at least three respects:

1   Basic data: first, DGXI wished to restrict the EEA to providing basic data on the *state* of environmental media such as water, air, nature conservation, etc., at the cost of attending to upstream factors which produce environmental problems, or to analytical work which might help elucidate priorities;
2   No policy role: DGXI attempted to keep the EEA away from any possible policy-influencing role;
3   No public axis: third, DGXI attempted to force the EEA to provide information only for the formal policy bodies of the Commission, especially DGXI, and member-state central governments. It was implacably opposed to the idea that the EEA should actively generate information for the public, and civil society actors, as well as for official central policy bodies. Likewise, it rejected the idea that knowledge sources such as NGOs, local authorities, or even university scientists, outside the editorial control and sanction of central governments should be treated by the EEA as legitimate interlocutors for an "independent Agency". In common with most member-state government officials, DGXI saw the public and society as properly informed by their official government bodies, and thus in no need of other autonomous information networks.

The DGXI-EEA relationship is crucial to understanding how natural knowledge idioms began to be carved out and produced as "environmental information" within the EEA. Both institutions have defined themselves in relation to the other, in ways that shaped their knowledge-making practices and sculpted their interface with wider cultural transformations taking place in the production of knowledge more generally. We now turn to our observations of the EEA and of its emerging practices in the forging of new information about the environment in Europe. We identify two contrary modes of knowledge-making simultaneously in play. The first is allied to a sense of Europe as an emerging centralized superstate, with all the requirements of standardization and harmonization across cultures which that political vision implies.

The second mode of knowledge-making involves a much more exploratory and effervescent view of what might be possible or desirable in the as-yet-still-nascent European state. In this second mode, old confidences (in formal scientific knowledge, in the possibility of harmonization, in the idea of the European superstate) are broken down and the uncertainties and contingencies of the process of making knowledge into hard and fast information are brought more clearly into view. This is Europe as civil society which is part real and already extant, part imagined community, in the throes of self-definition and establishment.[6] It is this imagined community which the EEA (certain key senior staff and close supporters) has intuitively sensed is vital to the public legitimacy not only of the EEA itself, but of those institutions of formal EU policy with which it has often locked horns.[7] These two visions are not mutually exclusive, as we discuss later.

Objective information and the development of an EEA "mission"

In giving practical interpretation to its information mission, the EEA had at least two guiding principles. First, there was its founding regulation, which gave it ideas about what kind of institution it *could* possibly be. Because of the constitutional novelty of the very concept of an "agency" in the European Union, and because of the lack of precedent and norms, Council Regulation 1210/90 became a important "boundary object" (Starr and Greismer 1989: 387–420) – an anchoring device which became the focus of intense interpretative work by the new agency staff as well as by others – DGXI officials, environmental NGOs, MEPs, academics, member-state governments, and so on. As we have indicated above, DGXI's interpretation of the EEA regulation conformed more to a politically conservative and positivistic notion of information provision, with no imagined corresponding influence over policy or policy networks. Interpretations of the founding regulation by the European Parliament, by NGOs and by actors within the EEA itself, in contrast, encompassed a far more ambitious vision of the role of information in society. In effect, both these competing visions were consistent with the founding regulation – hence the conflicts that inevitably ensued.

Second, the EEA had ideas about what kind of institution it did *not* want to be. A prominent fear was that "it could become completely controlled by its clients and partners" (European Environment Agency 1996). As an information and not a policy-advising nor policy-*initiating* body (the latter being a constitutional role of the Commission Directorates), the EEA neither wanted to become like DGXI, nor did it want to be controlled by DGXI or any other of its working partners. On the contrary, it had a much clearer sense of two connected developments:

1   its own territory, in which a more traditional European regulatory role combining inspection and enforcement across the EU had been rejected in favour of a less interventionist *information* role, connected with the broader deregulatory liberal economic aspects of economic globalization; and

2   the growing role of public information in the new post-1980s policy culture in which information explicitly overspilled its traditional boundaries, empowering citizens' groups to demand greater accountability and more effective policy progress once visible gaps between policy targets and practical results were shown.

Given the expectation to cooperate with existing Commission structures including DGXI, the EEA had to work on many fronts, and in politically astute ways, to carve out its independence. Not long after its inception, it gave an important symbolic rebuff to attempts to circumscribe its activities by transforming the unwieldy terms of the founding regulation into a neat and transmissible "mission statement". This mission statement cleverly incorporated a normative version of "objective information" in direct contra-distinction to that supposed by the Commission – creating an altogether new vocabulary by which to define the sort of information it expected to provide.

We have suggested elsewhere that the term "objective" for the Commission is associated with what Sharon Traweek calls a "culture of no culture" belonging to knowledge (Waterton and Wynne 1996; Wynne and Waterton 1998). As the EEA became well aware, objectivity is assumed by the Commission to have no culture, to be in effect "neutral". In this sense, claims to objectivity (in environmental information, for example) can therefore be used as a brilliant rhetorical device in the unstable, semi-formed state of Europe – a means of legitimating and enabling supranational diplomacy and negotiation in the face of conflicting interpretations of conditions in the (diverse and culture-laden) member states. As Porter has explored in a variety of contexts, the more insecure institutional bodies feel themselves to be, the more they tend to indulge in the discourse of objectivity and decontextualized quantification (Porter 1995). Objectivity is a term that is understood, in the political context, as being consistent with, almost a building block for, the idea of European harmony and unity, a term that carries such strong associations with the possibility of a unified view that it is taken as a surrogate for unity itself. If objective information about the environment can be gathered, then practices impinging on the environment are capable of being harmonized, so goes the conventional wisdom.

"Objective" for the EEA, however, soon began to develop a different meaning from "objective" for DGXI and the Commission. For the EEA, the concept came to mean independence from the Commission and from the member states, and correspondingly, an implicit rejection not only of the Commission's understanding of objectivity but also of the corresponding idea of policy and the policy order. It was as if the EEA, in its attempt to distance itself from DGXI, had recognized just how *en*cultured the Commission's culture-free understanding of objectivity was in practice. As a free-standing institution in its own right, the EEA constructed a version of objectivity that was manifestly a negative imprint of that understood by the Commission. This interpretation appeared in various guises, using new vocabulary, but most assertively and publicly in the EEA's "mission statement":

Through the provision of timely, targeted, relevant and reliable information
to policy making agents and the public, the EEA aims to help achieve significant and measurable improvement in Europe's environment.

What the EEA did here was to appropriate a new vocabulary (timely,
targeted, etc.), thereby asserting an institutional interpretation of the founding
regulation that was consistent with the spirit of the regulation, but which also
clearly extended and enlarged the implicit understanding of the EEA's role
within the Commission. The idea was that the EEA should produce information
that is:

- "timely" (i.e. that which "must coincide with the political agendas and
  related deadlines of key clients");
- "targeted" (i.e. that "the products of the EEA should be aimed at the unmet
  needs of key clients");
- "relevant" (in the sense that it will have to be relevant to policymakers);
- "reliable" (defined as acknowledging that "uncertainty and data gaps will
  always be with us" but that information should be "good enough to be relied
  upon by policy makers who want action");
- "significant" (in that it helps others to make a "real difference");
- "measurable" (in that the EEA must be able to show improvements in the
  environment).[8]

All these qualities, we argue, are qualities which indicate that the model of
information that the EEA is working with is a thoroughly encultured and
explicitly "pro-environment" normative model. Note that many of the adjectives used to describe the kind of information that the EEA would produce do
not include the kind of universalistic, neutral image generally associated with
"scientific" knowledge. Rather, an explicitly normative and even political
vocabulary has been incorporated. By using vocabularies of adequacy and
relevance at the same time as talking about "objective information", the EEA
was creating an independent identity for itself in relation to pre-existing structures, institutions and beliefs. An example of the tensions this generated was
the pressure it created on DGXI to explicitly state its political agenda for the
environment in sufficiently precise terms for the EEA, in turn, to use this to
define its environmental information work programme. To make such assertive
and positive commitments in the face of increasingly economically and envi-
ronmentally insecure commitments from member-state central governments
was challenging for DGXI. The EEA, in other words, had begun a process of
imagining not just how they would go about defining the kind of (objective)
information they should procure and disseminate, but simultaneously of imagining a new and alternative information-policy order. This imagined vision was
in direct opposition to the culture-neutral model of "objective information"
described in the founding regulation of the EEA – and familiar to the DGs of
the European Commission.

The mission statement was soon prominently displayed in EEA public documents, as well as on the back of EEA staff-members' personal cards, giving the statement mobility in such a way that it became both linked to EEA staff, yet also had a more public distribution and display. To anyone familiar with the official remit of the EEA, the mission statement was a clear indication that the EEA was determined to stand its ground as a free-standing institution – within the European political context, but by no means under the wing of the Commission.

But how did the EEA put its mission into play, accepting the need to work in genuine partnership with DGXI, yet determined to play an autonomous role within European environmental politics?

New policy and political orders?

As we have suggested, the approach of DGXI and the European Commission towards the EEA, projected an implicit model of the policy order which was both normative and descriptive, and which comprehensively shaped its imagination of what might be proper environmental knowledge or information within the EEA's remit. It is worth identifying the main features of this model, since it retains a powerful influence upon the EEA's practices, despite the new agency's attempts to adopt new modes of knowledge-generation and use as indicated above.

In DGXI's and the Commission's terms, legitimate policy agency is constituted only with official, representative political institutions and appointed administrative bodies, incorporating a highly formalized structure of political legitimacy which takes little account of the less tidy realities of *de facto* democratic deficits, public alienation from formal policy institutions and processes, and the rich and vibrant, if unofficial and oblique, tapestries of representative public life conducted through myriad agents of civil society.

Consistent with this norm, only central state government agencies have been allowed to control information flows from member states to the EEA. Although this central control has inevitably been extensively breached, and healthily so, it has nevertheless been strongly assumed and articulated as a righteous principle. European policy is therefore taken to be constituted by centralized member-state governments exercising univocal stances on issues and operating according to official procedures. In this model there is little or no room for unofficial information and extra-institutional agency – hence no need for relations of knowledge-generation, quality-control or uses with any other bodies but official central state organs and their designated scientific agents. Thus, in this scheme, proper information for environmental policy should pass from official scientific sources through officially controlled channels, in comparable units and formats according to standardized, universal protocols of measurement, aggregation, analysis and normalization, to the EEA, which is to render them reliable objective and comparable, to then pass it on to European policy officials. Legitimate executive agency within the EU is via the secretive Council of Ministers of member-state central governments, with a more marginal role for the more populist, transparent and unpredictable European Parliament.

Risk assessment and GMOs

An example of the information dimensions associated with the risk assessment of genetically modified organisms (GMOs) in agricultural crops illustrates the implicit normative force of these so-called "neutral", "objective" procedures. In the case of GMOs, European regulation of deliberate experimental and commercial-scale environmental releases takes place under a 1990 Directive (EEC 1990), the so-called "DRD", "Deliberate Release Directive", which has undergone several amendments, culminating more recently in a major revision (Levidow and Carr 2002). This framework involves a case-by-case and step-wise escalation of risk assessment before final full-scale release may be licensed. Proceeding to the next larger scale (and cost) of testing only occurs if the preceding step shows no evidence of harm. Thus gradual escalation may go from laboratory bench to enclosed greenhouse, to confined garden plot, to limited and confined field trial, to larger-scale but still confined field trial, and finally to full-scale commercial release. Before the most recent amendment added such issues as possible effects on biodiversity, and non-target organisms, the regulation was criticized for requiring only a limited set of risk tests before commercial release was allowed; but even with these additions it is still subject to criticism. Debate is still unresolved about whether monitoring for unexpected and possibly longer-term environmental effects should accompany commercial planting, and about what liability arrangements should cover such unanticipated effects. Irrespective of that, however, this EU-wide framework of GMO risk assessment and regulation is called "precautionary", invoking the implicit claim that scientific risk assessment can and does comprehend all relevant uncertainties. Yet not only does this ignore equivalent questions about scientific ignorance and intrinsically unpredictable effects – in the case of GMOs it also overlooks a further problem for the prevailing idea of European union.

GMO regulation and risk assessment is based on the constitutional principles of the European single market: in order to accommodate free trade, a satisfactory risk assessment and licence for release given in one member state has to be accepted as valid by all other member states. This principle was challenged by some member states (France, Austria, Denmark) partly on the grounds that existing EU risk assessment rules are unacceptably narrow and reductionist, for example ignoring agricultural interactions surrounding GM crops, cumulative and indirect impacts, and (before the latest revision) wider effects such as on "biodiversity".

Some such as Wynne (1992) more generally, and von Schomberg (1996) in the GMOs case, have argued that when scientific risk assessment is not just uncertain but indeterminate, it logically requires public deliberation about the social needs, purposes and claimed benefits of the activities whose risks are being assessed. Thus regulation would need more than scientific determination, and would also have to include something like the so-called fourth-hurdle deliberations proposed by European parliamentarians but rejected for the original self-proclaimed "precautionary" 1990 Directive. As von Schomberg has noted for GMOs, and Wynne and Lawrence (1989) have described for European toxic wastes policies, such forms of public deliberation could only conceivably be conducted at member-state level, which could lead to divergent practical interpretations of risk assessment and the precautionary principle between member states. This kind of member-state divergence over the implicit cultural underpinnings of regulatory science did lead in the toxic wastes case to compromises with the assumed principle of standardized EU-wide risk assessment criteria that had been built into the 1986 Directive on Transboundary Movement of Hazardous Wastes. In the GMOs case, the same neglect of scientific indeterminacy and cultural and political differences (brought about by assuming that what was thought to be deterministically objective risk science could dictate standardized policy closure) would mean inadvertent but direct confrontation between the *symbolic* commitment to precautionary regulation, and the *practically* more fundamental principle of unitary political order in Europe as reflected in the European Single Market. This is still the constitutional principle under which much European environmental policy has to be justified in order to gain acquiescence from member states. It is difficult not to conclude that the enthusiastic adoption of single market commitments in the 1980s wholly overlooked the cultural standardization demanded by such market unification, including the normative standardization of a supposedly "objective" intellectual order of environmental risk assessment.

GMOs have not yet been a part of the EEA's formal work programme, although a chapter broadly reflecting Wynne's and von Schomberg's interpretive line on uncertainty and precaution was published (despite Commission opposition) in the high-profile EEA Report, *Europe's Environment at the Turn of the Century* (European Environment Agency 1999). The main points of this for the present analysis are that, despite its recognized environmental importance across Europe, this GM issue was not part of the EEA work-plan, and only made its way into the 1999 EEA report because of the huge public controversy about the environmental uncertainties over GM crops and foods in Europe, and the perceived inability of the regulatory system to recognize and address these uncertainties properly. Because the GM issue was relatively novel, its environmental impacts could not be subject to the standard "downstream" measurement of state-of-the-environment parameters which the Commission defined as the prime role of the EEA, and the report instead made observations about pressures and stresses (test-releases and applications, the gaps in the system of regulation, and scientific questions which had not been included in regulation) which could give rise to environmental changes. This more upstream focus was the preferred idiom of the EEA, against Commission disapproval because it more directly identified and implied possible policy initiatives and needs. It also happened to be at this more upstream level that a non-universalistic, non-standardized and non-unified Europe became more visible.

The more formal and positivistic stance of the Commission with respect to scientific determinism and universality (notwithstanding the recent major revision) could be argued to have been a key factor in the widespread opposition throughout Europe towards the official policy (until June 1999) of promoting the commercial licensing and use of GM crops through the prevailing "precautionary" regulatory system. Several unilateral member-state decisions which contravened the 1990 EU Directive under forceful and diverse public pressures led eventually to an EU moratorium on further licensing, and the utter confusion of official EU policy on GMOs. This was further complicated in November 1999 by the reported divergence of the designated EU official to the World Trade Organization talks in Seattle from the agreed inter-ministerial line on the global trade in GM products, and especially the EU's wish to oppose imports of US GM crops and foods on grounds reflecting public concerns about the extremely reductionist risk criteria of the US and the WTO.

Here, then, we can see an emergent EEA concept of both the epistemic grounds of more upstream regulation and policy agency, and the corresponding less centralized (ideal?) political order. This markedly contrasts and conflicts with the unquestioningly modernist, positivistic and deterministic epistemic assumptions, and correspondingly centralized, standardized institutional and political order, articulated by the Commission. One can see in the tensions here that the EEA was operating in a wholly contingent, fragile, in-effect experimental and exploratory way, in trying to reconcile these conflicting visions, commitments and pressures. As the EEA continues to open up interpretive spaces which allow it to put into question the very way that environmental information and policy interact, it recurrently encounters some of the most entrenched values holding together the European Union.

Comparability of data

A major part of the EEA's task as defined by its founding regulation is to ensure the comparability of environmental information across different member states and knowledge cultures. But the very concept of comparability across Europe invokes a necessary universal standard of environmental quality and value against which state-to-state comparison of environmental performance in relevant sectors can occur. Because of the emphasis given to the comparability of data, and the relative lack of emphasis traditionally given to looking at pressures or specific impacts on the environment, environmental data "of European significance" has sometimes come to exclude important sources of environmental pollutants such as, for example, environmental radioactivity, which are not necessarily Europe-wide. One major source of such radioactivity, of global as well as European significance, is the UK's nuclear reprocessing plant at Sellafield on the Irish Sea coast. However, in terms of European comparability, Sellafield's environmental significance is anomalous, since, apart from the Cap de la Hague plant in France, it has no comparable counterparts, and European comparative environmental data cannot therefore be provided.

It may be that the neglect of environmental radioactivity until 1998, when the EEA scientific committee noted this lacuna and recommended it be repaired, reflects the implicit formalistic model of policy and of policy-useful environmental information. The major policy preoccupation of DGXI has been to use the EEA to make up for its lamentable dependency with respect to information on member states' environmental performance, and to exert pressure on badly performing member states to invest in the basic infrastructure of environmental monitoring, by producing clear evidence of backsliding. This formalistic model of the policy order also partly explains DGXI's resistance to anything but a focus on "state of the environment" monitoring, where unambiguous evidence of, say, worsening bathing beach quality, urban air quality or drinking water quality can be translated fairly simply into political pressure from the Commission to relevant member states. More ambitious attention to upstream social driving forces and pressures, such as intensity of motor-car use, strategic energy planning, or waste-generation coefficients per unit of economic activity – measures and information whose need is implicit in formal EU commitments to precautionary, integrated and preventive policies – are inherently more difficult to render "objective and comparable", and are inherently more politically sensitive. Thus DGXI has not pursued information or analyses of these upstream forces and commitments, and it has tried to stop EEA from addressing them in its official work-programme.

Imagining new policy orders – chemical risk assessment

The previous example has shown the kind of cultural pressures bearing on the EEA to standardize and to achieve comparability, which serve in turn to reinforce the Commission's implicit vision of an appropriate European policy order. But on the other hand, and consistent with more strategic and constructivist interpretations of its information responsibilities, the EEA has begun to open up the black boxes of the scientific knowledge which are its raw materials for generating useful information. In the sphere of chemical risk assessment, for example, it has done this in ways which actually challenged conventional assumptions that scientific risk assessment could provide a definitive framing of environmental policies. In addition, and consistent with the cultivation of a more open idea of "policy", "policy actors", "information actors" and "information uses", the EEA has explicitly addressed the issue of ignorance (beyond any acknowledged uncertainty) by reporting on the quality and completeness of environmental information which is in play.

In the field of chemicals, this was manifested by EEA's focus on the yawning holes in data about the environmental and health effects of the many thousands of human-made chemicals circulating in the environment. This focus highlighted the fundamental inadequacies of even the best scientific risk assessments to comprehend, let alone quantify, the effects of such chemicals, especially once chemical interactions in the environment are taken into account. Based on examination of the *quality* of environmental data (including how complete data sets are), the EEA justified its emphasis in focusing policy attention more seriously upon exposure (and therefore emissions reduction at source) rather than on the false assumption that there was adequate knowledge to perform risk-screening and control further downstream, after emissions had taken place.

In this example, what the EEA did, in effect, was to acknowledge the existence of ignorance *within* knowledge, and the artificiality of scientific risk knowledge which is framed as if chemicals have effects in the environment that are completely isolated. Then it used that acknowledgement of ignorance to open up a further interpretive space within which to explore the meaning of "precaution" relevant to the case. This produced a more stringent and ambitious expression of the officially endorsed precautionary basis of policy than the formal policy institutions conventionally accepted. Through the legitimate responsibility of reporting on environmental information quality, therefore, the EEA escaped from the straitjacket of keeping scientific ignorance of environmental processes out of the category of "policy-useful information" which the Agency is asked to generate.

In doing this, the EEA has imagined an alternative policy order — and not just in the sense that this process would, if established, radically intensify precautionary pressure on industries. The acknowledgement of ignorance and the extension of the precautionary mode in policymaking also implies a fundamental revision of policy responsibility between science, formal policy institutions and civil society. For once the essential indeterminacy of scientific risk assessment has been acknowledged, then the usual boundary between expert knowledge and public responsibility is dissolved. It becomes necessary for public debate to focus on questions of value and utility rather than risk alone: if it is not possible to predict the risks of this or that chemical, then the question arises: do we *need* it and the social purposes it is serving; and do we want the uncontrollable uncertainties which its use brings? So by acknowledging ignorance underlying science and by re-interpreting the meaning of precaution in specific cases, a radically different kind of policy order is implied and projected by the EEA. In this new model, civil society is called on to play a much larger role in articulating public values, supplementing the formal representative (and administrative) institutions of parliamentary democracy.

"In the eye of the hurricane"

We have seen in earlier sections how the EEA has defined itself explicitly in contradistinction to the Commission, its intimate neighbour, and how a different model of "objective information" and its relationship to policy has emerged partly as a result of the EEA's current need to establish itself as an independent actor within that relationship. For the EEA this has meant observing and facilitating emerging changes in the social distribution of knowledge, as well as re-thinking what counts as appropriate knowledge in a changing European policy context. We want to stress that the forces that are acting upon such knowledge networks are not attributable to rationalizable interests or deliberate design

– rather they are integral parts of wider cultural, social and epistemic shifts whose origins are complex and not necessarily confined to the European arena. The more distributed nature of knowledge-agency that such shifts imply should perhaps be portrayed as what the EEA is working in the midst of, rather than what the EEA is producing in mastermind-like fashion. It is from within this context of flux that the Agency sometimes self-consciously encourages new versions of European policy culture to be tried out – versions that involve shifts in "natural" as well as social orders of knowledge and information. We focus in the following section on how Agency staff are handling such shifts, looking in particular at the implications they feel in letting go of traditional assumptions of knowledge orders based upon universal science and expert rationality.

Early in its career, the EEA developed a strategic vision of environmental information in a context where information overload was already a dominant concern. Under an indiscriminate flood of information, the EEA surmised that what people appear to crave is an adequate supply of information whose provenance and trustworthiness can be evaluated – whether correctly or not is beside the point. Thus people can express the apparently self-contradictory anxieties of being information-overloaded, yet at the very same time information-starved. In the words of EEA staff, information needs to be invested with *meaning*, which needs to be inspired by its ultimate purposes, *environmental improvement*. The EEA saw not only that overly centralized, decontextualized and officially sanctioned information was worse than useless for public credibility and effectiveness (which increasingly emphasized broad social partnership and widely shared responsibility). It also recognized the opposite danger: that information, no matter how copious or accessible, without a strategic framework of meaning was also useless, paralysing and potentially disempowering; its meaning in relation to broad normative goals – like quality control, precaution, integration, or distance-to-target indicators – also had to be articulated with it. This strategic vision of information, however, risked transgressing the ambiguous and (to DGXI) highly sensitive boundary with policy advice, as one of our interviewees in the EEA was well aware. We report below part of an exchange with one of us which shows how entwined the EEA's reflexes with regard to DGXI are with the desire to create a radically different information and policy order:

EEA ANALYST: When we produced the '95 report on "The State of the Environment", right, we [the EEA] were in a position to analyse and to make some "distance to target" analysis. And here (*showing the graph*) we have the political target, for example, in waste generation. Right? This is the target we set in our programme. So, based on the information we have been able to collect, based on some analytic criteria, and so on, we have been able to really make this "distance to target" analysis. And [thereby], to deliver a clear message that, given the actual policy in place, [and] given the actual development in the economic [sphere] and so on, we are *not* in a position to meet the target. So, this is providing information. But then, DGXI is saying, "What are you doing? What are you doing? This is information which is *confidential* information from our side. So, if you want to give us this information, good! But it is for *us* [DGXI] to then make the political statement!".

What they are saying is that, once this analysis is done, our role, in their understanding, is before publishing the report, to go to them, to show the draft, to show the result of the analysis, and for…them to say, "Oh! This is not very good for us!", for example, "Er, we would not like you to publish this information.".

INTERVIEWER: So, how do you resolve this? Do you just…stand firm? I mean, what's been the result of this problem?

EEA ANALYST: The result of this problem is to say, "We are doing our job.".

INTERVIEWER: OK.

EEA ANALYST: And then we put that in our report. And this information is in the public domain. We are fulfilling the obligations of the Directive: access to information.[9]

Evident uncertainties underlying what appears to be a defiant stance taken by the EEA here are compounded by the sense that, in many respects, the EEA is constantly relating its work and strategy to an (over-)exposure to the tremendous variability of knowledge, knowledge sources, and knowledge forms about environmental issues in Europe. In the situation of flux described above, the Agency is experiencing challenges not only about what kinds of actors produce, and should produce, environmental knowledge (scientists? citizens? "stakeholders"?) but about what forms of knowledge are appropriate. An epistemic complexity, in other words, has inevitably accompanied the re-ordering of social networks involved in the production of knowledge. In the new configurations that are being played out case by case, sector by sector, within the EEA, such new social/natural networks mean an attempted re-establishment of bonds of trust that had largely been taken for granted within the Commission. As Gibbons, Nowotny and others have argued, the roles of traditional academic scientists are no longer taken for granted as the sole providers of "natural" knowledge. One of our interviewees attested to this at the same time as expressing an ambivalence as to how to proceed in a situation where it is no longer clear who should provide knowledge and what such knowledge should be:

I think all of us would like to do the scientific good stuff. It's…we would all like to do that, but reality is not quite like that…I wouldn't want the scientific world to disappear. I mean that's what we need. And that's, for instance, why we want to have this connection to the European Vegetation Survey [a group of plant community scientists], because it's where the scientific foundation is. We just can't work with it like that, but we want to hold on to that.…We want to hold on to what others are doing, but…*we* need to do something in between.

The EEA is in the midst of a tremendous cultural shift in knowledge production and information provision. This shift is complex. It is less like the replacement of one form of rationality by another and more like an ongoing struggle surrounding the emergent construction of new, but very tenuous forms of knowledge and order. These new orders are shaped both by an emergent vision of explicitly recognized, multivalent interpretive possibilities *and* powerful existing forces and constraints based on assumptions of a univalent "voice" of nature. An institution formed as recently as 1993 might reasonably be expected to be innovative and bold with respect to the way in which it defines credible knowledge or "information", and how that fits into a contemporary sense of what "Europe" might be. Yet the entire shift appears beset with ambiguities. The EEA is in the process of defining not only its charge, but in a fully co-productionist move, its own identity, in a Europe which is undergoing considerable expansion and change in itself, as this last excerpt from our interviews reveals:

EEA ANALYST: I would say that we are in the eye of the hurricane. Because integration is really a hurricane....And if we are not able to stay in the eye, then we will be completely, ourselves, disconnected from what we have to achieve....Because our mission is really to support the policy process....But that means that if we are not able to provide the public debate with a common understanding of the issues then we are not going to respond to the demands. And in order to design this information, in such a way that it really provides this common understanding, this common language, it is quite a challenge, of course....And we have to involve partners in all the different sectors. If we are doing that, then we will be, in the end, providing a kind of parallel way of analysing things. So, it could sound pompous. Because that means, "OK, so you are the one providing the truth!" I mean, it's not that! The agency is unique. At the European level. It is unique. Which other institution can do it? There is no other institution in charge of doing that. So we have to take advantage of this unique role and unique position....We have to send good signals to the public; we have to send good signals to the socio-economic partners; the different industries; the different people working in the different activities, and so on; and we have to send the right signals to the NGOs....So that's why I think we are, we have to stay, in the eye of the hurricane.

In effect this EEA analyst is recognizing that to *serve* the policy order, with appropriate knowledge, is also inevitably to help *form* that policy order, or to reinforce its potential formation.

Conclusions

As various authors have noted (Etzkowitz and Leyesdorff 2000; Gibbons *et al.* 1994; Nowotny *et al.* 2001), the conventional models of how scientific knowledge is produced and translated into rational policy uses have been superseded by more multicentric and hybrid models, involving not only more pluralistic policy actors, but also broader notions of "knowledge-users" as also being "knowledge-authors", and of "extended peer-communities" including non-scientific user or stakeholder groups. This intellectual shift from positivist linearity appears to correspond to a profound cultural transformation affecting – and affected by – the foundations of political and institutional order. The forces acting upon institutional (re)construction and intellectual articulation run deeper than rationalizeable "interests" and deliberate choices or commitments; and traditional forms of human solidarity and trust appear to be in flux as much as do "natural" forms of knowledge. To what extent new articulations of European environmental knowledge show an implicit awareness of the corresponding need to build new patterns of solidarity and trust, and not just to reflect old ones, has become an interesting question.

What we have described does not illustrate a gradual slide away from positivism reflected in the EEA. We have seen, rather, a much messier picture in which two very different versions of natural/social orders co-exist uneasily within this new institution. Both versions are simultaneously operating within the agency, and both are tied into correspondingly different notions of society and the European polity. We suggest that these two models – of knowledge, knowledge-authors and users, and of the policy order to which they correspond – are in tension precisely because questions concerning the institutional identity of the EEA and the surrounding political order of "Europe" are also more open now than they have been for some time.

The first version is characterized, in epistemic political and institutional spheres, by positivism, universalism, formal legalistic assumptions of authority, and projected confidence in defeating uncertainty and ignorance. In short this version belongs to a highly resistant and durable modernist paradigm, in which deterministic ideas of a linear progression from expanding objective knowledge to rational policy and progress prevail. It ties in with, and relies upon, a modernistic conception of science as culture-neutral, universalistic and objective – a clear lens on the world as it is. Whilst this deterministic model of intellectual order reinforces, and is reinforced by, a centralist model of policy order and of Europe, the alternative intellectual order, which recognizes the indeterminacy of knowledge, inspires a correspondingly more open imagined policy community, and view of European identity.

In this second model of objective knowledge and information, much of politics and human political energy is conducted in diverse independent forms outside the official channels of political institutions, and outside the idioms of explicit, deliberate choice. Independent information framing occurs along with autonomous forms of knowledge-generation, and value-generation – perhaps elaborating official forms and channels, perhaps bypassing or replacing them. Correspondingly, unofficial autonomous forms of legitimate information-transfer, validation and use also occur, which validate (or contradict) those emergent social networks beyond the powers of identification of formal institutional politics and collective life.

Culturally and politically, it is essential for the EEA to keep the first model in play. This first model is tied into many of the most fundamental and long-standing assumptions and practices which collectively constitute what is now known as the European Union (EU). In this model information works *for* the idea of European unity. It is an instrument that illustrates that unity, coherence, and a detached, objective and Platonic overview of the whole of Europe. This model of information makes possible the idea of a harmonized Europe, a Europe with only minor internal political and cultural barriers, which may be overcome through the effort of human cooperation and technical integration.

The second model on the other hand, is allied less to ideas and concepts of unity than to pragmatism, indeterminacy and the acknowledgement of complexity. Through the use of the second model, players have an implicit sense of the cultural and technical plurality and variability of information sources, of information forms, of information uses, and thus of information qualities. They may also be aware of the different yet legitimate social relations that information may reflect and uphold. This model of information makes possible a vision of a complex and heterogeneous map of Europe in which there are different cultures, heterogeneous practices and variable ways of knowing — and relating — within Europe. It implies a different sense of social order.

Both models of information draw on implicit models of the role of science in constructing knowledge and information. Scientific knowledge is not discarded in the second model. Scientific input is an integral part of both models, but in the second it evokes entirely new and alternative understandings of its explanatory power: it is judged as just one contribution among many others that the Agency takes on board in the making of environmental information. Of course this is true also of the first, formal model; but in this more formal model other input may be concealed and deleted from public acknowledgement.

It is not possible, and not right, to pretend to identify more than the skeletal outline features of the more multicentric, fluid, decentralized and diverse "civil society"-based model of a European policy order. By definition it is more attenuated, tentative, pluralist and overtly open-ended, changing the conventional boundaries of the instrumental deterministic presumptions of science. A further important aspect of this more indeterminate civic culture is the correspondence between the self-conscious exploration of new models of human subjectivity, which it shows as a response to the environmental-sustainability problematic, the cultural forms of civil society "sub-politics", and the rejection of the modernist-centralist institutional order assumed and imposed by the formal institutions of policy. It is not that these institutions, whether of the nation-state or of the incipient European "superstate", deny altogether the place of civil society actors. DGXI, for example, has for a long time accommodated environmental NGOs in its consultative mechanisms, and even funded them. However, not only have these mechanisms been severely cut back in recent years, but the implicit model of the proper role of the agents of civil society remains one in which the formal institutions are taken for granted as representing a legitimate democratic voice, which the NGOs and others may amend but not fundamentally diverge from. A deeply deterministic, monolithic rationality still lies at the heart of this political culture, and this is evident from the kind of information culture which it projects, and which in turn projects it.

Consistent with the "discursive turn" in social science, knowledge actors are always, in producing and projecting knowledge or information, also projecting an imagined information-subject, a social/political agent who can, and hopefully will, *use* that information. The EEA demonstrates this kind of projective and performative element through the ways in which it has attempted to articulate and establish a new information culture. It has attempted to identify the kinds of agent, and agency, in civil society, outside of the formal institutions of policy, which could energize, pressurize, supplement and legitimate official policy commitments, which are in practice compromised by conflicting political commitments at powerful levels of the European economic and political arena.

What might once have been commonplace descriptions or indicators of environmental quality or purity have become insecure within the EEA. This has happened partly in response to the Agency's institutional surrounds, but also in response to a wider imagined order, which is in the process of being "performed". It is the fundamentally emergent nature of the EEA's practices that make it an institution at once bold, yet vulnerable. The EEA, like other European knowledge-articulating agents, is in the very process of describing the natural and human world, attempting to bring a particular vision of the world into being. Staff at the Agency have described themselves as being "in the eye of a hurricane": in the swirling mass of a still unconceptualized Europe, there are very few stable rules determining what environmental knowledge should be. But this is not our main point – the crucial aspect lies precisely in the open-endedness of the social/institutional order of Europe at this point in history, which is both enabling, and potentially paralysing. The EEA will go on making moves that show both its courage and its vulnerability. A stable order has to be there for knowledge to be meaningful and usable. At the same time, articulating such knowledge is a necessary means for establishing such an order.

Notes

1   This analysis is based upon a combination of empirical fieldwork in and around the EEA. One author, BW, was a full member of the EEA Management Board and Scientific Advisory Committee from its initiation in 1993 until 2000, when his term was completed. During that time he attended many meetings of both committees and many further seminars, informal discussions and other meetings connected with EEA business and EU environmental policy, including with the European Parliament's Environment Committee which he represented as an EEA board member. For each of the seven years involved in this, he spent approximately twenty-five days on such work at the EEA. In effect this constituted ethnographic fieldwork allowing very close-quarters observation of and involvement in the formal and informal processes of EEA work. Fieldwork notes were kept and issues discussed with various EEA and DGXI staff, including the then director of EEA, Domingo Jimenez-Beltran, the then chair of the Scientific Committeee, Philipe Bordeaux, and the then chair of the Management Board, Derek Osborne. In addition to this extensive ethnographic field-work, CW also conducted more formal interviews for the present study with several

relevant senior EEA staff, as part of the UK ESRC-funded research grant to CSEC, on "Science, Culture and Environment", 2nd phase 1995–1998. After 2000, BW continued to be involved in EEA work but as an outside academic colleague working mainly on editing and drafting for the EEA book on the precautionary principle, *Late Lessons from Early Warnings* edited by Poul Harremous, David Gee, Sofia Vas, Andrew Stirling and Brian Wynne (Copenhagen: EEA, 2001; London: Earthscan, 2002); but he was no longer involved as an insider with formal roles in the EEA. Therefore the account on which this analysis is based finishes in 1999–2000. Although the detailed issues and context have naturally developed since this period, for example over the expansion of the EEA formal constitution, work-plan and working networks with the forthcoming accession of new states to the EU, regular but less intense later observation causes us to have confidence in the continuing salience of the analytical perspective given.

2   Other new European agencies include the European Training Foundation, the Office of Veterinary and Plant Health Inspection and Control, the European Monitoring Centre for Drugs and Drug Addiction, the European Agency for the Evaluation of Medical Products, the Agency for Health and Safety at Work, the European Monetary Institute, and the Office for Harmonization in the Internal Markets (Trade Marks and Design).

3   DGXI (now DG Environment) is one of a range of specific policy-sectoral DGs which make up the Commission. It is responsible for the environment, and nuclear safety (Consumer Protection was split away in 1996). Each DG's main tasks are the identification of policy needs in its sector; the preparation of policy proposals and draft formal Directives, Regulations and Communications; the coordination of member state implementation of those European policies; and the ongoing assessment and where necessary "enforcement" of member-state implementation. The Commission is able to propose new policy to the Council of [relevant sector member-state] Ministers, the ultimate EU executive body.

4   This is one example of the many instances in our area of work (science and policy-making) where basic science studies insights might be said to apply directly to practical policy situations. The simple point made by Latour that "[I]t is impossible to dominate nature and to dominate society separately" (1999: 287) would explain precisely why the Commission made a basic mistake in assuming that DGXI and the EEA could harmoniously co-exist. Each inevitably stepped into the other's designated territories.

5   This corresponded with the general trend towards reassertion of national member-state scepticism and autonomy with respect to the Commission, and over areas of policymaking like environment, which were felt to have been excessively taken over by central authorities of the so-called "superstate". The most aggressive leader of this reaction was the UK Thatcher government, but it was taken up more broadly across the EU member states. As described later, EU environmental policies over such issues as GM crops were forthrightly subjected to autonomous – and divergent – national stances, but so too were less contentious issues such as air and water pollution standards, and nature conservation. In an increasingly neo-liberal pro-business and competitive global economic climate, DGXI was forced onto the back foot and a more insecure position, which may have fuelled the conflicts with the new, creatively energetic and ambitious EEA.

6   In referring to different modes of knowledge production we can see many connections and parallels with the work of Gibbons *et al.* (1994). We borrow the term "imagined community" from Benedict Anderson's work (Anderson [1983], 1991).

7   This understanding of the problems of public engagement and support facing EU institutions, especially those with scientific policy missions, in relation to civic involvement, was expressed in the EU White Paper on Governance of July 2001. A chapter

of this was devoted to "Science and European citizens", referring to new dialogue processes and greater involvement of civil society in expert areas of policy.

8 The interpretation of these keywords has been taken from an EEA presentation outlining the EEA's mission to an outside audience.

9 This excerpt and those following are derived from interviews with three senior representatives of the European Environment Agency, conducted by Claire Waterton at the European Environment Agency, 3 October 1997.

6 Plants, power and development

Founding the Imperial Department of Agriculture for the West Indies, 1880–1914

William K. Storey

Where does the idea of "development" come from? The word itself has been used in several ways for centuries, but the specific use of the word, to mean the economic and social uplift of a disadvantaged country, has its origins in the "New Imperialism" of the late nineteenth century. Ever since then, development policy, even in its scientific and technological aspects, has been heavily freighted with imperialist ideology. In the British Empire, ideologically driven scientific and technological development was first instituted in the West Indies. Discussions about the founding of the Imperial Department of Agriculture for the West Indies were highly important for the elaboration of development policies, and indeed for the very idea of development. In particular, the Imperial Department, and the institution of its development policies, was closely linked to Social Darwinism and colonial paternalism. These ideologies provided a rationale for those who wished to disseminate scientific agriculture throughout the colonies. By the turn of the century, the new Imperial Department of Agriculture for the West Indies was serving as a model for the creation of state research institutions and development policies in many other colonies. The Imperial Department embodied imperial rule and helped sustain patterns of scientific power and interdependence between Britain and the colonies.

Today many believe that "third-world development" will be achieved, in part, through neutral "transfers" of science and technology. The history of the Imperial Department of Agriculture related in this chapter tells a different story, more consistent with the theme of co-production. As Jasanoff points out in Chapter 1 of this volume, the formation of new institutions is often a moment to observe co-production at work. I show in this chapter how the local needs of the British West Indies became translated into imperial institutions through a blend of discourse and practice. We will first consider how the local needs of the West Indies were rooted in the "sugar crisis" of the late nineteenth century, a crisis that was simultaneously natural and political. We will then examine the ways in which the British government addressed the crisis while creating new, closer imperial ties to the colonies. In doing so, Britain institutionalized a new discourse of intervention, called development, as well as the practices associated with it. Development entailed a new way of thinking about the Empire's social responsibilities, quite different from the laissez-faire approach that preceded it, at the same time as it made British knowledge more easily available to island farmers. The result was a new Imperial Department of Agriculture for the West Indies, whose practices became so thoroughly normalized and naturalized that modern-day scholars and development workers have lost any awareness of how it originated in an ideologically freighted move away from earlier colonial policy.

Sugar cane ecology and plantation society

To understand development in the British West Indies, we must first understand the political and social aspects of the sugar cane, the plant that dominated the islands' economies. Since the days of the Crusades, increasing demand for sweeteners in Europe spurred farmers in suitable locations to cultivate canes. In turn, the plant's botanical characteristics influenced the creation of particular methods of production. Sugar cane is a large, perennial grass, of which there are five species. Three of these cannot survive without cultivation, making them completely dependent on people, while the remaining two can grow wild. The most important species is *Saccharum officinarum*, which originated in New Guinea and was widely known as the "noble cane", a name that demonstrates how political and social qualities may be attributed to a plant. During the eighteenth and nineteenth centuries, a noble cane with the noble name of "Bourbon" was the most popular cane on European colonial plantations because of its large size, high sucrose content, and relative ease of harvesting.

Europeans created sugar colonies as part of one of history's most repugnant episodes in cross-cultural encounter. To produce a commodity used to sweeten foods and beverages, Europeans spread cane cultivation gradually from the Mediterranean, to the islands off the West African coast, and then to the Caribbean and Brazil. In doing so, they reduced indigenous populations by means of war, disease and enslavement. Then the colonists brought slaves from Africa to make up the resulting shortfall in labor, initiating one of the most horrific forced migrations in world history. Over time, European cane cultivation spread further throughout the Americas to islands in the Indian and Pacific Oceans and to other parts of the world.

Large European sugar cane farms, called plantations, were among the first large-scale capitalist agricultural enterprises. They were cruel places where managers exercised quasi-legal jurisdiction over workers. As Philip Curtin argues in *The Rise and Fall of the Plantation Complex*, the most notable features of the sugar cane Plantation Complex were the widespread use of forced labor; the existence of populations that did not increase naturally; the integration of trade into long-distance networks; and the acknowledgement of the authority of remote European rulers. Wherever the Plantation Complex took hold, it transformed ecological systems and interrupted historical continuities in the distribution of land, labor and capital.[1]

Knowledge of sugar cane botany has always influenced the processes of sugar production. Sugar cane grows best in wet, warm tropical conditions, and yields the most sucrose when a warm, wet season is followed by a cooler, drier season. These climatic requirements restrict it to tropical and subtropical regions, which ideally do not experience frosts. Sugar cane botany also makes special demands on field laborers. Cane-cutting is difficult and unpleasant; it requires strength, skill and agility. Cane also has peculiar processing requirements that stem directly from its botanical properties. Soon after cutting, the cane's sucrose content diminishes, reducing the value of the crop. Producers must process canes into sugar as soon as possible, preferably within twenty-four hours. Sugar factories must be near the fields, and the factories must process canes when they contain the most sucrose. This aspect of sugar cane botany dictates a sporadically intensive labor regime. During the harvest period, which can last several months, factories typically operate around the clock. To ensure the factory always has enough cane, field laborers must work long hours to harvest as much as possible. After the harvest in most cane-producing regions, laborers replant the fields of the oldest ratoons, which is also heavy, skilled labor. But afterwards, there are only light tasks to perform such as weeding, and it is not economical for a large-scale factory-farm to employ the full contingent of workers used during the harvest. This production schedule poses a problem for sugar producers: how to ensure a ready supply of labor during each year's harvest, when it is to the laborers' advantage to find steady, year-round employment, rather than six months of back-breaking work followed by six months of comparative idleness.[2]

Sugar cane botany explains, in part, the plant's historical connection with colonialism and coerced labor; it also helps to illustrate the broader point that new technologies often require new political and social arrangements. In the British West Indies, the labor requirements of capitalist agriculture and the botanical requirements of the sugar cane plant were served by high degrees of social stratification and control. Planters subjected laborers to numerous legal disabilities and strict controls. Social boundaries between Europeans and non-Europeans were often rigid, although small communities of poor whites, free Africans, and free mixed-race "Coloureds" or "Creoles" made niches for themselves in between these sharp boundaries.[3]

In the middle of the nineteenth century, the Plantation Complex entered a period of crisis. The emancipation of the slaves caused turmoil in the 1830s, and after the repeal of the Corn Laws in 1846, Britain's free-trade policies forced the islands to compete with protected foreign sugar producers. During these years, some of the colonies, especially British Guiana and Trinidad, imported indentured laborers from India. But these workers, while important, could not stem the tide against the latest threat to the Plantation Complex: the sugar beet industry of Europe, which was supported by state subsidies and scientific research. By the 1880s and 1890s, sugar planters in the British West Indies were clamoring for more protection and better plants than the ones they had. The Imperial Department of Agriculture was formed in response to this crisis, but its institutional history lay in earlier British engagements with colonial botany.

Science, politics, and responses to crisis

In the 1890s, it seemed to island planters that in London there were ideological obstacles to creating government-supported scientific research institutions. On the surface, Great Britain still adhered to strict laissez-faire policies. And yet, as Richard Drayton reminds us in *Nature's Government*, Britain supported scientific institutions that had the potential to make powerful, constructive interventions in colonial economies. Even as Britain embraced free labor and free trade, the professionalization of the state bureaucracy allowed for London to centralize its authority through administrative and technical means. The Royal Botanic Gardens at Kew coordinated a network of colonial research gardens, resources for plants and knowledge that had the potential to prop up dependent colonial economies. Kew, the product of older imperialist interventions, was in effect a natural resource for distressed planters in the British West Indies.[4]

Kew's connections with domestic and imperial power are traced well by Drayton. He reminds us that Kew is the site of a royal palace, on whose grounds kings and queens patronized horticulture. During the eighteenth century, the Hanoverians, especially George III, were keen to impress their usefulness upon the public. Royal help placed the monarchy squarely behind the progressive landlords who might otherwise have challenged the king. And thanks to Sir Joseph Banks, the powerful landlord who had sailed on Cook's first voyage, Kew also patronized botanical exploration overseas. Under Banks's oversight, "economic botany" was centralized at Kew. His nineteenth-century successors, Sir William Hooker, Sir Joseph Hooker, and Sir William Thiselton-Dyer, all professionalized botany at Kew. The key step was taken in the 1830s, when the botanists successfully transferred the gardens from the crown to the government, which itself was becoming more professional and bureaucratic. As Drayton writes, at Kew, "The professionals of Science and Imperialism found common advantage in the idea that knowledge might guide the best management of nature."[5]

As the Empire grew during the late nineteenth century, Kew coordinated the research of colonial botanic gardens increasingly closely. At the same time, gardens in the colonies were paid for out of local funds, and were accountable to local landowners, who often had significant lay knowledge of agriculture and botany. This was especially true in two sugar colonies: Barbados, in the British West Indies, and Mauritius, the Indian Ocean colony that routinely produced as much sugar as all the islands of the British West Indies. In Mauritius, the Franco-Mauritian sugar planters had a long tradition of agronomical research and political engagement. They exerted a considerable influence over the colonial state and its government botanists. During the sugar crisis, when it seemed that the government was not doing enough to support research, the Franco-Mauritians founded their own private Station Agronomique in 1892.[6] In Barbados, local planters did make efforts to improve their factories and their fields, although they were not as vocal, independent or successful as the Franco-Mauritians. In 1812, Barbadian planters established an Agricultural Society.

They were not able to improve factory methods, which stagnated in comparison to the rest of the Plantation Complex.[7] It was in cane selection, though, that Barbados planters had notable success. Planters, together with their workers, made some of the most important breakthroughs in the science of selecting and propagating new varieties. The cane is usually propagated by planting cuttings, and for centuries, Europeans had believed that the cane was sterile and could not produce seed. During the 1850s, a Barbadian field hand named Iranaeus Harper discovered the first seedlings while weeding. His discovery was followed up by James Parris and four other Barbadian planters, who are known to have experimented with cane seedlings.[8] After several years of experimentation, the new canes produced mediocre results. Kew refused even to recognize the possibility of cane seeds.[9] Gradually the planters ceased their experiments.

When sugar prices plummeted during the 1880s, Barbadian planters, local officials, and Kew's scientists combined their efforts to improve the cane plant. In 1883, the governor and the plantation owners initiated discussions about acquiring new canes.[10] One prominent planter and the governor wrote separately to Kew asking for suggestions.[11] Kew's director, William Thiselton-Dyer, recommended that the Barbadians establish contact with his protégé Daniel Morris, who was then serving as director of the state botanical gardens in Jamaica. Morris had just acquired a shipment of thirty-five new noble cane varieties from Mauritius, which Kew and the Colonial Office hoped to disseminate throughout the British West Indies.[12] In 1884, Morris shipped eighteen of his canes to Barbados, initiating small-scale experiments with varieties. Unbeknownst to Morris, his new canes harbored diseases that would hasten the downfall of the widely planted Bourbon variety throughout the West Indies. Islanders did not recognize the proliferation of new diseases until the 1890s.[13] Even so, the diseases could not have bolstered Morris's credentials as a scientific expert. Local efforts to propagate canes began, too, and in 1884, members of the planters' Agricultural Society joined the Island Professor of Chemistry, John B. Harrison, in planting out plots of canes on four estates so that they could make comparisons with Bourbon.

On the advice of Morris and Thiselton-Dyer, colonial governments in the Caribbean began to create a network of small experimental gardens.[14] In 1886, the Barbados experiments moved to the government's new station, established, as a cost-saving measure, on land at Dodds Reformatory. This move undermined the credibility of the research program among the plantation owners. First of all, the land at Dodds was not suited to agriculture, although the boys' reformatory provided plenty of cheap labor. Furthermore, the governor named Harrison and John R. Bovell to manage the experiments, a choice that did not exactly inspire the planters' confidence. Harrison was a chemist who knew very little about the practical side of planting. Bovell owned a small sugar plantation and supervised the reformatory, but he had no training in botany or chemistry.

Experiments, as we know from prior work in the history and sociology of science, succeed, in part, by persuading relevant witnesses that they have worked.[15] Initially the results achieved by Harrison and Bovell did not impress plantation owners. They conducted trials on the new sugar cane varieties, but their first priority was to study soil chemistry and manures.[16] An article in the planters' *Agricultural Gazette* complained that the Agricultural Society had been excluded from the work, stating that

> the Society knows little, and can vouch for little, that goes on at the Station, and this is a great pity, as the testimony of a few (say two) practical planters, of which one should be the president of the Agricultural Society, would certainly not weaken the reports, and may cause them to be more generally believed in.[17]

The re-discovery of sugar cane seedlings at Dodds buoyed the station's local credibility very briefly. Bovell and Harrison presented their seedlings at the Agricultural Society's Exhibition, where Harrison reported that large numbers of planters examined them and remarked on their differences from the original noble varieties. James Parris, the Barbadian planter who had grown seedling canes during the 1850s, even assisted in verifying the results at Dodds – here was an expert with the best credentials that an amateur local scientist might have.[18] Bovell opened Dodds to visitors, some of whom came from other parts of the West Indies to verify the discovery.[19] The West India Committee pressed the Colonial Office to grant more funds to the experiments on seedlings, judging their potential to help the entire region.[20] Members of the Barbados Agricultural Society pressed the governor unsuccessfully for money to expand Dodds and to build a second research station.[21]

As time passed, the Barbadian scientists, in contrast to their counterparts in Mauritius, could not interest the local elite permanently in seedling canes. This may have been partly the fault of the government, which kept budgets at a minimum, and partly the fault of Bovell and Harrison. Their written techniques for publicity were noticeably weak; they buried their exciting discovery in the *Report on the Reformatory and Industrial School for 1888*, which was devoted primarily to the activities of a hundred juvenile delinquents, and in the back pages of the *Report of the Results Obtained on the Experimental Fields at Dodds Reformatory, 1888*, which contained mostly statistical reports of fertilizer experiments. At least this method of publicity did not incur much government expense.[22]

Weak publicity hurt. The Barbadian planters also began to lose interest because the seedlings appeared to be useless. In Bovell and Harrison's words, they were "exceedingly delicate in their nature and very susceptible to injury by the sun and wind."[23] By 1890 a drought was killing them.[24] In early 1892, a local newspaper report upbraided the Barbadian planters for their "indifference" to the new cane varieties at the most recent agricultural exhibition, yet who could blame them?[25]

Bovell and Harrison's abilities were now also being questioned at Kew. In September 1888, Harrison wrote to Morris, now Kew's assistant director, to relate the discovery of cane seedlings. Harrison stated modestly that "if we can establish the fact of the cane occasionally and under certain favourable conditions producing fertile seed, it will open an important field of investigation." Morris placed a red check mark next to Harrison's remarks, indicating his support.[26] Then he proceeded to publish the results as quickly as possible in the *Kew Bulletin*, which circulated around the world.[27] Harrison objected to the rapid, unexpected publication of his results. He entered into a long-running controversy with Morris that spilled over into the British and West Indian newspapers. Morris dismissed Harrison's illustrations of cane seeds as amateurish. Harrison retorted bitterly that Morris was trying to take credit for the discovery of the cane's fertility.[28] Nevertheless, however skeptical Morris may have been about the professionalism of science in Barbados, he made sure that Kew still supported overall research there. As planter support for research waned after the seedling discoveries, Morris arranged for Thiselton-Dyer, Kew's director, to write in support of Bovell's experiments to the Colonial Office.[29]

Turmoil in the appointments to the Dodds station also sapped the credibility of early sugar cane research in Barbados. In 1890, Harrison resigned his position to occupy a more senior scientific post in British Guiana. The government named J. P. d'Albuquerque, a chemist with credentials from London and Berlin, to replace Harrison as Island Professor of Chemistry. Initially d'Albuquerque did not participate in the work at Dodds, which, among other things, led the planters to complain openly in the newspapers that the work at Dodds was slipping. Although Bovell was one of their own, they expressed concern that he did not possess any recognized scientific training. In the wake of Harrison's departure, they desired more control over Dodds's Board of Management in order to increase the reliability of the station's work.[30] After several years of support for Dodds, even the local planters' press turned against it. The *Agricultural Gazette* called the station "a mere apology, serving only to show what could be accomplished if only a proper station was provided." The same writer argued that Bovell's trials of sucrose contents in the factory were also inadequate. D'Albuquerque began to participate more in the work of the station, but his efforts did not seem to match Harrison's. Bovell remarked testily that many of the local planters lacked even a rudimentary understanding of agronomy, but in the end the planters got their way.[31]

Sugar estate owners sought to unite tacit knowledge of local agriculture with metropolitan scientific methods. The Barbadian planters had succeeded initially in combining Harrison's British scientific training with Bovell's practical local knowledge. The collapse of this arrangement left the Barbadian planters in a predicament: Bovell was managing the Dodds station, even though he did not hold any externally recognized scientific qualifications. The resulting crisis in confidence among the large-scale sugar growers of the island, along with the perilous state of the island economy, provided a rationale for creating a new kind of state scientific institution.[32] Justifying this move required a new discourse of intervention built on the notion of development.

Instituting development

During the 1880s and 1890s, Barbadian planters began to realize the potential of scientific research to support the old Plantation Complex. Laissez-faire science policy, like laissez-faire economics, was failing to sustain the British West Indies, a clutch of diverse colonies that had prospered most in the days of slavery and mercantilism. It happened that colonial agricultural research was centralized at Kew Gardens, an institution that also had its origins in the days of mercantilism, and whose directors retained a taste for authority and interventionism. As Drayton has demonstrated, along with other historians of the British Empire, while the nineteenth century was the heyday of laissez-faire, during these years authoritarianism remained a strong element of colonial administration. The Secretary of State for the Colonies, the cabinet member who headed the Colonial Office, had to give public support to laissez-faire policies. Most importantly, the Colonial Office expected each colony to raise enough taxes to support itself. The Treasury and the taxpayers disliked giving financial support to the colonies, except in cases of natural disaster.

In the midst of the sugar crisis, Barbadian planters began to hope for some assistance from Britain. The ideological balance in the Colonial Office and in the government at large was beginning to tilt away from strict liberalism in favor of economic interventionism in support of imperialism. During the 1870s and 1880s, several high-ranking officials in the Colonial Office began to support this shift in policy. These officials were at the forefront of a new movement in British politics: Constructive Imperialism, which would come to dominate colonial policy between 1895 and 1903, when Joseph Chamberlain served as Secretary of State for the Colonies. Chamberlain supported capitalism, but together with other imperialist ideologues such as Alfred Milner, Field-Marshal Roberts, and Halford Mackinder, he rejected classical liberalism's anti-imperialism and libertarianism. Chamberlain and his supporters believed in Social Darwinism, but respected the growing power of the working class enough so that they sought to unite capital and labor against socialism. The Constructive Imperialists, also known as Social Imperialists, advocated "national efficiency," which was simultaneously more nationalist, imperialist, and protectionist.[33]

Joseph Chamberlain was the best known and most influential Constructive Imperialist. He began his career as a manufacturer of screws and only later became a politician. He was known to be hostile to the members of the landed classes who still controlled British finance and government. When Chamberlain entered politics as a radical Liberal, he received strong support from fellow industrialists. Unlike them, he believed in the importance of securing colonial markets for British manufactured goods. In 1886, Gladstone, the Liberal Prime Minister, decided to support Irish Home Rule, which prompted Chamberlain to switch his allegiance to the Conservatives.[34]

The Conservatives supported the expansion and consolidation of the Empire. Benjamin Disraeli had supported imperial expansion during his premiership of 1874–1880, and his successor as Tory leader, Lord Salisbury, also did so during his three premierships (1885–1886, 1886–1892 and 1895–1902). It was long thought that the old Conservative leadership supported expansion mainly for strategic reasons, even as they remained wedded to laissez-faire economic policies and sought to stabilize the interests of British investors in colonial production. Starting with the work of historians Antony Atmore and Shula Marks, published some thirty years ago, historians have increasingly seen that Conservative policy in the colonies did favor businesses, particularly those that sought to maximize settler access to indigenous labor.[35] Economics and imperial grand strategy went together. Chamberlain, a manufacturer, was strongly in favor of business as well as imperial expansion. When he became Secretary of State for the Colonies in 1895, he and his fellow industrialists were concerned about declining prices, trade unionism, and foreign protectionism. Many industrialists believed that expanded colonial markets might help to sustain the domestic *status quo*, if only the government would help the colonies to build infrastructure and to conduct research. Chamberlain began to formulate a nationalist, neo-mercantilist vision for Great Britain.[36] On 22 August 1895, Chamberlain explained aspects of Constructive Imperialism to the House of Commons:

> I consider many of our Colonies as being in the condition of undeveloped estates, and estates which never can be developed without Imperial assistance. [Cheers] It appears to me to be absurd to apply to savage countries the same rules which we apply to civilized portions of the United Kingdom. Cases have already come to my knowledge of colonies which have been British colonies, perhaps, for more than 100 years, in which up to the present time British rule has done absolutely nothing; and if we left them today we should leave them in the same condition as we found them. How can we expect, therefore, either with advantage to them or to ourselves that trade with such places can be developed. I shall be prepared to consider very carefully myself, and then, if I am satisfied, to confidently submit to the House, any case which may occur in which, by the judicious investment of British money, those estates which belong to the British Crown may be developed for the benefit of their population and for the benefit of the greater population which is outside. [Cheers][37]

Chamberlain seems to have been among the first high-level officials of the British government to use the word "development" in this modern sense. The word and the concept had been in use for some time, of course, but this seems to be the first time that a British official used the word to describe a policy for an entire colony.[38] When Chamberlain referred to the colonies as "undeveloped estates," he made a significant elision in meaning between private properties and political regions, an elision that reflected a deep-seated paternalism, and that would have significant ideological consequences.

Chamberlain was not just introducing a new vocabulary. Development, attached to Social Imperialism, would inform British colonial policymaking for much of the twentieth century. Colonies were not just supposed to develop *from* some latent condition; they were supposed to develop *into* more prosperous markets for British goods. State subsidies could be justified on the grounds that the economies of "savage countries" adhered to different "rules" than "civilized portions of the United Kingdom." Some years later, in 1914, Alfred Milner, the former Governor-General of South Africa, wrote that in British East Africa, West Africa and the West Indies, "the years 1896–1903 were years of progress, and mark the transition from the old system of laissez-faire stagnation to the new policy of activity and development."[39]

Chamberlain was re-defining prior notions of development so that he could talk about colonial economies and societies in new ways. To make his case persuasively and overcome his laissez-faire opponents at the Treasury, he had to support his new discourse with evidence. It was widely known that in the 1890s the plantation economies of the British West Indies were hurt by the metropolitan state's imposition of free labor and free trade, although it is hard to gauge exactly how much these policies hurt the British West Indies. And yet there was no evidence to support Chamberlain's assertion that the colonies "never can be developed without Imperial assistance." To remedy this, he persuaded the Cabinet to fund a Royal Commission to enquire into the state of Britain's West Indian colonies. The commission was chaired by General Sir Henry Norman, a former governor of Jamaica. Between 31 December 1896 and 28 May 1897, Norman and his three colleagues examined 380 witnesses in each of Britain's West Indian colonies, as well as in London and New York.

In their final report, the Commissioners recommended the policies of economic development that Chamberlain supported. The colonies needed substantial assistance from the British Treasury. In Barbados, the sugar industry could still be propped up by centralizing factories, which would be supported by government guarantees to loans of £120,000. The commission also recommended direct grants totalling £90,000, a large amount of money in those days, to aid some of the other colonies, partly for debt relief, and partly to support construction projects. With the exception of Barbados, Antigua and St Kitts, the West Indian colonies were encouraged to settle peasant proprietors on the land and to diversify agriculture. The report also stated that sugar prices would rise if the British government entered into negotiations with the Europeans to get them to reduce the subsidies they paid to beet farmers. The chair, General Norman, went so far as to advocate slapping a tariff on foreign sugar entering the British market, but his colleagues did not support this position. Still, the commission listened to the complaints of islanders about the laissez-faire policies of the previous seven decades, and in the end the commission supported unprecedented state intervention in colonial economies.[40]

It was not enough for the Commissioners simply to present these conclusions to the Colonial Office and the Treasury. They had to sell their plan. They did so by inventing an official discourse of obligation to the colonies that bears an uncanny resemblance to commercial marketing techniques. First, salesmen demonstrate and describe the product, next they create a sense of social obligation to buy the product, and finally they reveal the price.[41] This was, broadly speaking, the structure of the Norman Commission's report. The Commissioners began with a detailed description of West Indian problems and discussed the possible solutions. Before they summarized their findings and recommended specific expenditures, they inserted a section entitled "Obligations of the mother country."

The Commissioners began their discourse of obligation by showing how the "race" of slaves found themselves in the Caribbean under "artificial" conditions:

> The black population of these Colonies was originally placed in them by force as slaves; the race was kept up and increased under artificial conditions maintained by the authority of the British Government.

The state created this unnatural situation by placing the "race" of African slaves in the West Indies; therefore the state was responsible for their advancement:

> What the people were at the time of emancipation, and their very presence in the Colonies at all, were owing to British action…we could not, by the single act of freeing them, divest ourselves of responsibility for their future, which must necessarily be the outcome of the past and of the present. For generations the great mass of the population must remain dependent upon British influence for good government, and generally for the maintenance of the progress that they have made hitherto. We cannot abandon them, and if economic conditions become such that private enterprise and the profits of trade and cultivation cease to attract white men to the Colonies, or to keep them there, this may render it more difficult for the British Government to discharge its obligations, but will not in any way diminish the force of them. We have placed the labouring population where it is, and created for it the conditions, moral and material, under which it exists, and we cannot divest ourselves of responsibility for its future.[42]

"Charity creates a multitude of sins," wrote Oscar Wilde in *The Soul of Man under Socialism*, and while Wilde was aiming his comments at socialists, his insight might also be applied to his Social Darwinist contemporaries. The Norman Commission proposed a number of innovative solutions to the economic problems of the West Indies. The Commissioners encouraged the British government to negotiate for the abolition of European subsidies on beet sugar, although the Commissioners disagreed over the possible imposition of retaliatory duties. The Commissioners did agree that peasants ought to be encouraged to grow alternative crops, and they also proposed government grants to some colonies for debt relief, road building and steamship lines. The commission also proposed to create a government department of agriculture to support research on sugar cane, based on the recommendation of Daniel Morris of Kew, who filed a special report on West Indian agriculture that the commission appended to its own report.

In his appendix to the commission's report, Morris sketched an outline of the proposed scientific department of agriculture. It would be headquartered in a central experiment station in Barbados, where the director, "a competent Imperial officer," would "develope the agricultural resources of the Windward and Leeward Islands and Barbados," while supervising the research of the old botanic gardens located in the larger colonies of British Guiana, Jamaica and Trinidad. According to Morris, "Careful experiments will also be necessary to obtain by selection the richest and most suitable canes, to determine for each soil the best manures to be applied, while the most recent appliances are introduced to economise labour to the utmost extent." Morris also proposed that the Imperial Department become involved in agricultural education and extension services, through schools, publications and shows.[43]

Instituting federation

The Imperial Department of Agriculture was to be the first state institution to transcend the boundaries of all of Britain's West Indian colonies, each of which had a separate administration reporting directly to London. As such, the Imperial Department could be seen as part of a particular trend in imperial politics. During the second half of the nineteenth century, the idea of an imperial federation received support from a handful of activists and intellectuals, among whom was Joseph Chamberlain. The idea of federating all the colonies never got very far, but movements to federate smaller colonies into larger colonies proved successful. In the heyday of the British Empire, three major federations were created: Canada in 1867, Australia in 1901 and South Africa in 1910. In South Africa, Chamberlain had connived with Cecil Rhodes in the overthrow of the Boer republics, first by supporting the Jameson Raid in 1895, and next, in 1899, by helping to start the Boer War.[44]

At the same time as war was becoming the instrument of federation in South Africa, science was becoming the instrument of federation in the West Indies. Chamberlain's attempts at federation in the West Indies suggest that he understood what Yaron Ezrahi argues is one of the hallmarks of modern statecraft: the use of seemingly "pure" science as a way of "depersonalizing" or "depoliticizing" the exercise of political power and in "rationalizing government actions as actions taken…supposedly for the sake of the people."[45]

At first Chamberlain resisted the recommendations to extend grants to the West Indian colonies, for reasons that may have had more to do with political deal-making than anything else. But the Cabinet decided to support the commission's recommendations, most of which became official policy.[46] Accordingly, Parliament approved the funds to create what was to be called the Imperial Department of Agriculture for the West Indies. Chamberlain secured the appointment of Daniel Morris to lead the Imperial Department, arguing before Parliament that Morris held strong metropolitan scientific credentials and that he had also had practical experience in the West Indies.[47]

Morris activated the Imperial Department quickly, demonstrating a flair for organization. The Imperial Department began small: in 1899 Morris only had one traveling superintendent and two clerks on his staff, but he added an entomologist and a mycologist in 1900. Subsequently he added more professional staff members, and he also coordinated the work of researchers who were already in place in all the West Indian colonial botanic gardens.

As we have seen, before the creation of the Imperial Department, significant sugar cane breeding experiments had taken place in Barbados, and to a lesser extent in Trinidad and British Guiana. Experimental plots in diverse locations could only help the Imperial Department's research program, which was, however, hindered by long-simmering disputes between the directors of the old botanic gardens in both colonies, especially with Harrison, who was now in charge of sugar cane research in British Guiana.[48] Perhaps as a result of these disagreements, Morris centralized the most important sugar cane breeding and agronomical experiments in Barbados under Bovell, d'Albuquerque, and himself.

Morris worked hard to establish the credibility of sugar cane research and the Imperial Department among the West Indian elites. Most of the scientists whom Morris recruited held metropolitan credentials, much sought after in the Caribbean. Morris also used his impressive reports and his ties with Kew to maintain good relations with members of the British parliament, who voted most of the Imperial Department's funds. Almost every year, he convened in a different colony a conference attended by scientists, planters, teachers, religious leaders and state officials. In his address to the first conference, he emphasized sugar cane breeding above other aspects of research. At one point in his speech he even brandished a new seedling cane called B.147 to illustrate its superiority to the old, widely planted Bourbon cane.[49] At all subsequent conferences, sugar cane breeders had opportunities to publicize their results alongside the research of pathologists and agronomists. Over the course of ten years, Morris convened seven conferences, five in Barbados, one in Jamaica and one in Trinidad, to which he invited planter representatives from all British West Indian colonies. The transcripts, printed in the Imperial Department's *West Indian Bulletin*, circulated throughout the West Indies and also throughout most of the world's cane-growing regions. This was significant. Morris was bringing together planters from around the West Indies, highlighting the ways in which island planters shared the same concerns. His Imperial Department was the only federal institution in the West Indies; while he could not bring together the islands completely, he did at least unite island planters in standard ways of describing and discussing scientific research.

Standardizing discourse was not a matter of Morris enforcing his scientific and political will on the planters. Imperial Department publications reveal that Morris actually shared the planter elite's conservative political outlook. In his address to the first West Indian agricultural conference, Morris employed Social Darwinist rhetoric to describe the islands' economic situation. "In commercial, as in natural life," he stated, "the perpetual struggle for existence necessitates continual adjustment to new and fresh conditions. When this adjustment is wanting or imperfect, the industry, or being, is pushed aside and disappears." Morris proposed that with his help, the West Indian planters would overcome their economic problems, especially the "labour difficulty," so that the colonies might "realize the destiny designed for them by nature, and they will become happy and prosperous communities."[50] In this speech, presented at the time when the Imperial Department was first establishing its credibility with the West

Indian elite, natural metaphors were invoked to show that political decisions were justifiable on allegedly biological grounds.

Morris felt strongly about preserving the existing social order in the West Indies. When the British government reduced troop strengths in the West Indies in 1905, Morris was alarmed. The withdrawal, he advised Thiselton-Dyer,

> is not wise, as we are always liable to a disturbance among the blacks, who are easily carried away by the excitement and lose control of themselves. It is proposed to increase the police force, but as most of the men are black themselves, too much reliance can't be placed upon them.[51]

He also expected his staff members to share his social opinions and his strategic sense. He complained to Thiselton-Dyer about one new appointee from Kew whose "tendencies are distinctly to associate with the lower rather than the higher class of white people in these colonies. This means a lot as regards his future usefulness."[52] Morris's political outlook was not unusual for a turn-of-the-century European in the colonies. It probably helped him to establish rapport with both the planters and the colonial administrators whose power was closely intertwined with the power of the Imperial Department.

It is significant that the Imperial Department was founded on the notion that established economic and social relations were natural. It is also significant that imperialist ideology was becoming part of the Imperial Department's research and extension programs. During Morris's tenure as Imperial Commissioner of Agriculture for the West Indies, 1899–1911, the Imperial Department established two different tracks for research and extension. Both tracks encouraged the production of cash crops. One track supported the owners of sugar cane plantations, who were mostly white. The other track encouraged the descendants of the African slaves and the Indian indentures to buy small plots of land and to cultivate exportable agricultural commodities, like bananas and citrus.

The commission could not imagine that the West Indies might develop any non-agricultural industries, so the Commissioners encouraged emigration, a drastic and unpopular solution, or peasant cultivation. By encouraging peasant cultivation, the Imperial Department was following the recommendations of the Norman Commission. The Commissioners said that one good way to deal with the decline of the sugar industry was "to enable the mass of the population to support themselves in other ways than as laborers on estates." Some Africans and Indians had already tried peasant cultivation in the West Indies, and even though the sugar estates preferred them to work in the cane fields, the commission believed these peasants to be a success:

> The cultivation of the sugar-cane has been almost entirely carried on in the past on large estates, but both the negro and the coolie like to own small patches of land by which they may make their livelihood, and take a pride in their position as land-holders, though in some cases they also labour at times on the larger estates, and are generally glad to have the opportunity of

earning money occasionally by working on such estates, and on the construction and maintenance of roads and other public works. The existence of a class of small proprietors among the population is a source of both economic and political strength.[53]

As much as the commission hoped to settle laborers on the land, the Commissioners believed that there were some obstacles in the way of such progress, namely in the attitude of the laborers:

> The labouring population in the West Indies is mainly of negro blood, but there is also, in some of the Colonies, a strong body of East Indian immigrants, and the descendants of such immigrants. The negro is an efficient labourer, especially when he receives good wages. He is disinclined to continuous labour, extending over a long period of time, and he is often unwilling to work if the wages offered are low, though there may be no prospect of his getting higher wages from any other employer. He is fond of display, open-handed, careless as to the future, ordinarily good humoured, but exciteable and difficult to manage, especially in large numbers, when his temper is aroused.
>
> The East Indian immigrant, ordinarily known as the coolie, is not so strong a workman, but he is a steadier and more reliable labourer. He is economical in his habits, is fond of saving money, and will turn his hand to anything by which he can improve his position.[54]

It fell to Morris and the Imperial Department to blend the best traits of the "coolie" with the best traits of the "negro."

While Morris was serving as Commissioner, the Imperial Department's *West Indian Bulletin* was filled with articles about how agricultural instructors were encouraging peasant cultivation. Until we know more about the peasants and their relations with the Imperial Department, it is premature to measure the success of Morris's program. Nevertheless, in 1911, on the occasion of his retirement, Morris did offer some opinions on the subject. In a speech to the Royal Colonial Institute that was published in both *United Empire* and the *West Indian Bulletin*, Morris noted the extension of cacao, cotton, fruit, rice, rubber and tobacco cultivation throughout several different West Indian colonies. The Imperial Department had also led training sessions in agricultural instruction for every West Indian elementary school teacher, while the Imperial Department itself opened schools in Dominica, Jamaica, St Lucia and St Vincent.[55]

Morris argued that he had achieved the Norman Commission's objective of using agricultural science to liberate West Indians from the vicissitudes of the sugar market, but it is difficult to accept these claims. It may have been better to grow fruit than to cut cane, but Morris's Social Darwinist beliefs caused him to hold what was still a rather limited vision of progress for West Indians.

The evidence from the Norman Commission's report and the official publications of the Imperial Department suggest that the science of the Imperial

Department reflected deeper divisions within colonial state policies. During this period, British domestic politics moved decisively toward democratization, while colonial governance remained authoritarian. The science of the Imperial Department of Agriculture was inspired by both liberal and authoritarian political practices, producing racial and economic stratification as in places like South Africa, where Chamberlain's federationist notions extended rights to "white" settlers while stripping them away from "blacks."

The bifurcated research and extension program of the Imperial Department embodied Chamberlain's Social Imperialist vision for the Empire. Diversification to other cash crops was the best way to help colonial blacks, while improvements to the sugar cane would be the best way to help colonial whites. The program would also enhance Britain's economic self-sufficiency. Under Morris's leadership, between 1899 and 1911 the Imperial Department centralized and expanded experiments on sugar cane breeding in Barbados. Morris continued to employ Bovell and, to a lesser extent, d'Albuquerque as cane breeders, but Morris also hired young, metropolitan scientists for the work. Morris's first hire to help in breeding was L. Lewton-Brain, a Cambridge graduate who conducted basic research on the botany of the sugar cane. In his 1904 article, "The hybridization of the sugar cane," he presented the first detailed analysis of the flowers of the fifty-one cane varieties available to breeders in Barbados.[56]

Yet even this new information was not enough to stabilize the cane-breeding program. The widely divergent ecosystems of the West Indian islands made it necessary to enroll the support of the planters and the colonial botanic gardens in other colonies, so that the breeders could test their new varieties. While research on the cane now involved metropolitan botanists, it still depended upon local planters for their expertise. Planters were not easily satisfied. In the second conference, held in 1902, a planter from Trinidad and a planter from Barbados attacked the cane selection trials for being too small and for being not as rigorous as the trials going on in Hawaii and Louisiana.[57]

Despite these criticisms, Morris was making the sugar cane breeding program more rigorous. One of the key figures to emerge in Morris's breeding program was young Frank Stockdale, a recent Cambridge B.A. with a first in the natural sciences tripos. Stockdale had the added qualification of coming from a family of East Anglian farmers. He had plenty of practical agricultural experience, in addition to being a talented scientist. He was appointed by Morris to be "Mycologist and Lecturer in Agricultural Science" in 1905, but soon he found himself working with the Barbadian breeders.[58]

In 1906, Stockdale and Morris published a "state of the art" report on sugar cane breeding in Barbados. Breeding work had begun in the 1880s, twenty years before European scientists rediscovered Mendel's research on variation and heredity. By the time of Stockdale and Morris's experiments, sugar cane research still depended upon empirical principles of selection. Stockdale, Morris and Bovell selected canes by looking for variations in vegetative vigor and sucrose content. Then they took their selections and crossed them in the hope that some of the progeny might prove to be useful. Sugar cane was a relatively easy plant to cross in this way, and early, non-specialist breeders like Bovell, Morris and Stockdale could produce thousands of new varieties every year. The problem was that the sheer number of new varieties made it difficult to select the best canes.[59]

These early breeding experiments could not predict results with any great accuracy, but Barbados breeders did develop new techniques to enhance their selections. Many of these techniques spread to other breeding programs around the world, as I described in *Science and Power in Colonial Mauritius*.[60] Still, Morris and Stockdale recognized that even the latest empirical methods were awkward and impractical, and they wrote that they were looking forward to a day when Mendel's laws of heredity, just recently rediscovered, might allow sugar cane breeders to develop ways to conduct their research in a more systematic and predictable fashion.[61]

Scientists still knew very little about the genetics of the sugar cane plant. In fact, judging from hindsight, it is impressive that the Barbados breeders had any success at all. The breeders had no inkling of the difference between genotype and phenotype, which means that they could not tell the difference between true genetic traits and other observable traits. They also did not know that the gene pool of the noble canes was fairly limited, which meant that inter-varietal hybrid crosses had less potential than inter-specific crosses with some of the wild species of cane. Still, Barbados did produce several canes that helped to bolster the West Indian sugar industry. As J. H. Galloway shows in his article, "Botany in the service of empire," the Imperial Department produced several good seedling canes, most notably a cross of two noble varieties called B.H. 10/12 that came to be planted extensively throughout the world's sugar-growing regions.[62]

The legacy of the Imperial Department

As important as B.H. 10/12 became, the Imperial Department of Agriculture had a more lasting legacy. By the time of Morris's retirement in 1911, he believed that many other colonies had used the Imperial Department of Agriculture for the West Indies as a model when forming their own scientific departments of agriculture. The largest was the new Imperial Department of Agriculture in India, but there were also smaller departments of agriculture formed in the colonies of British East Africa, the Federated Malay States, the Gold Coast, and Southern Nigeria.[63] In Mauritius during the decade of the 1900s, the Franco-Mauritian sugar planters, who had long been involved in independent agronomical research, were demanding their own department of agriculture.[64] By the 1920s, nearly every significant British colony had a scientific department of agriculture. In addition, as historian J. H. Galloway has demonstrated, the Imperial Department also served as a model for state agricultural institutions in Caribbean colonies that belonged to the United States, Denmark and France.[65]

The idea of a scientific department of agriculture was replicated throughout the British Empire, although as Geoffrey Masefield points out in his history of the colonial agricultural service, the organizational structure of these institutions did not become stable until the 1920s. As in the West Indies, the original officers appointed had to conduct research across the disciplines, simply because there were so few of them on the ground. But eventually, as more agricultural officers came to work in the departments, research came to be divided among established disciplines such as entomology, plant genetics and veterinary services.[66]

One aspect of Chamberlain's program did not survive: in the West Indies, the federated Imperial Department was split up into individual colonial departments. When Morris retired in 1911, the larger colonies of British Guiana, Jamaica and Trinidad had already established their own departments of agriculture, along with some of the smaller colonies, and Barbados was about to follow suit.[67] But the colonies did agree to continue to cooperate in some aspects of agricultural research. Sugar cane breeding continued to be centralized in Barbados, while all the colonies supported the agricultural college in Trinidad. There, the Imperial College of Tropical Agriculture, founded in 1921, became the central training institution for many of the agricultural officers in Britain's tropical colonies.[68]

Morris ensured his legacy by placing many of his West Indian subordinates in key colonial positions. Harrison, despite initial skepticism, went on to serve as director in British Guiana, Bovell served as director in Barbados, and Francis Watts, who had also served in the Imperial Department, took over Morris's position as Imperial Commissioner. Several other former employees moved on to careers in Fiji, India and Malaya.[69] Frank Stockdale became one of the most important civil servants to work on colonial development. He directed the departments of agriculture in Mauritius (1913–1916) and Ceylon (1916–1929), then between 1929 and 1940 he served as the agricultural advisor to the Colonial Office, where he helped to found the Colonial Agricultural Service. Later Stockdale held two more influential positions: Comptroller for Development and Welfare in the West Indies, and Vice-Chairman of the Colonial Development Corporation.[70]

The same is true of another Morris protégé, Harold Tempany, a chemist who began his career under Morris in the West Indies. Tempany directed the departments of agriculture in Mauritius (1917–1929) and Malaya (1929–1936), then served as assistant agricultural advisor to the Colonial Office (1936–1940) and as agricultural advisor to the Colonial Office (1940–1946), serving simultaneously as governor of the Imperial College of Tropical Agriculture, located in Trinidad.[71] Tempany, like Stockdale, may have carried on Morris's legacy in the field of colonial development, but he also has not yet been the subject of any biographical study. Further research is needed before we can come to a full assessment of the influence of Morris's ideology on later efforts at colonial development. The influence of Morris's protégés makes some connection likely.

Morris's Imperial Department grew out of the ecological and economic crises that the British West Indies faced during the late nineteenth century. The Norman Commission's report on the West Indies blended together several ideas:

Chamberlain's nationalist notions of federation, protectionism and development; imperialist notions of racism and Social Darwinism; and a belief that science could be used as an instrument to remedy a problem that originated in a complex mix of biology, economics and politics. The Commission recommended that Parliament create an Imperial Department of Agriculture to address all these problems.

Following the Commission's recommendations, Morris harnessed agricultural research and extension services to a paternalistic effort to raise the cultivation standards of peasants on the economic and geographic margins of the British West Indies. He hoped to integrate them more closely into the export economy, promoting alternative crops like bananas and citrus as a way of shoring up social stability. The *West Indian Bulletin* was filled with reports from Imperial Department officials, itinerant agricultural instructors and missionary teachers writing about the best ways to accomplish these goals. Morris's knack for self-promotion and networking almost certainly spread these ideas of agricultural extension to other tropical colonies.

On the occasion of his retirement in 1911, Morris quoted from the words of Charles Lucas, a senior civil servant who worked in the Colonial Office from 1877 to 1911:

> Not long ago Sir Charles Lucas, who is so intimately acquainted with colonial matters, happily remarked that, while the eighteenth century saw the greatness of the West Indies, the nineteenth their distress, the twentieth century, he hoped, would witness their regeneration. The latter in part is becoming true, for Lord Crewe, the late Secretary of State, was in a position to announce, in February last, "that not one West Indian Colony was now in receipt of grants-in-aid."[72]

In Morris's view, imperial support for the Imperial Department had been entirely justifiable, and any laissez-faire fears were unwarranted. After all, a small expenditure on research and extension had produced budgetary surpluses, removing the need for aid. Bovell even calculated "that more profit was derived from the introduction of new seedling canes on one estate in Demerara than would cover the whole cost of the experiments at Barbados over a period of twenty-six years."[73]

One wonders about the real cost of the Imperial Department's activities. Morris believed that the eighteenth century had been the best of times for the sugar industry, even though he must have known that these were times of terrible oppression. He hoped that the Imperial Department might "regenerate" the former greatness of the West Indies, an interesting choice of metaphor to represent a reactionary political agenda as natural. Morris strove to achieve this objective by using and creating natural artifacts, sugar canes and other plants, to further an agenda that was ideological. Politics did not simply influence science, and science did not simply influence politics. Science and politics provided a rationale for each other, a rationale that was replicated far beyond the "distressed" colonies of the British West Indies. In Barbados and Kew, in Bridgetown and London, politicians, planters and scientists produced new plants and new ideologies together, resulting in a strongly interventionist policy of paternalistic scientific development. Today, as we again contemplate better development policies based on science in an atmosphere of more intensive globalization, it is worth considering whether or not our new ideas of development reflect a similar co-production of ideas of nature with ideologies of imperialism.

Notes

1 P. D. Curtin, *The Rise and Fall of the Plantation Complex: Essays in Atlantic History*, Cambridge: Cambridge University Press, 1990, pp. 11–13.

2 W. K. Storey, *Science and Power in Colonial Mauritius*, Rochester: University of Rochester Press, 1997, pp. 4–10.

3 Curtin, *Plantation Complex*, p. 83. H. M. Beckles, *A History of Barbados: From Amerindian Settlement to Nation-State*, Cambridge: Cambridge University Press, 1990, pp. 41–42, 69.

4 R. Drayton, *Nature's Government: Science, Imperial Britain, and the "Improvement" of the World*, New Haven: Yale University Press, 2000.

5 Drayton, *Nature's Government*, p. xvii.

6 Storey, *Science and Power in Colonial Mauritius*, pp. 97–108.

7 Beckles, *Barbados*, pp. 129, 148–149. R. Drayton, "Sugar Cane Breeding in Barbados: Knowledge and Power in a Colonial Context," A.B. Honors Thesis, Harvard University, 1986. J. H. Galloway, "Botany in the Service of Empire: The Barbados Cane-Breeding Program and the Revival of the Caribbean Sugar Industry, 1880s–1930s," *Annals of the Association of American Geographers* 86, no. 4, 1996, pp. 682–706.

8 G. K. Parris, "James W. Parris: Discoverer of Sugarcane Seedlings," *The Garden Journal* 4, no. 5, 1954, pp. 144–146.

9 Fryer to Oliver, 23 June 1871, Archives of the Royal Botanic Gardens, Kew, Miscellaneous Reports 15.6, *Barbados. Sugar Cane Cultivation, Department of Agriculture, &c. 1871–1918*.

10 Robinson to Derby, 29 October 1883, 5–6; "The Agricultural Society," *Barbados Agricultural Gazette*, November 1887, 46. Both these sources are found in the Archives of the Royal Botanic Gardens, Kew, Miscellaneous Reports 15.6, *Barbados. Sugar Cane Experiments. 1883–1900*.

11 Carrington to Dyer, 11 May 1883, 1–2; 22 November 1883, 14–15; Robinson to Dyer 28 October 1883, 3; all in Kew, Miscellaneous Reports 15.6, *Barbados. Sugar Cane Experiments. 1883–1900*.

12 Wingfield to Dyer, 19 November 1883, 7–11, Kew, Miscellaneous Reports 15.6, *Barbados. Sugar Cane Experiments. 1883–1900*.

13 *Report of the Results Obtained upon the Experimental Fields at Dodds Reformatory*, Kew, Miscellaneous Reports 15.6, *Barbados. Sugar Cane Experiments. 1883–1900*.

14 Drayton, *Nature's Government*, pp. 251–253.

15 S. Shapin and S. Schaffer, *Leviathan and the Air-Pump: Hobbes, Boyle, and the Experimental Life*, Princeton: Princeton University Press, 1985.

16 *Report of…Dodds Reformatory*, 1886–1887, Kew, Miscellaneous Reports 15.6, *Barbados. Sugar Cane Experiments. 1883–1900*.

17 "The Agricultural Society and the Dodds Experiments," *Barbados Agricultural Gazette*, November 1887, 46, Kew, Miscellaneous Reports 15.6, *Barbados. Sugar Cane Experiments. 1883–1900*.

18 Harrison to Morris, 7 January 1889, 47, in Kew, Miscellaneous Reports 15.6, *Barbados. Sugar Cane Cultivation, Department of Agriculture, &c. 1871–1918*.

19 *Report of…Dodds Reformatory*, 1889, in Kew, Miscellaneous Reports 15.6, *Barbados. Sugar Cane Experiments. 1883–1900*. Demerara *Argosy*, 13 April 1889, 48, in Kew,

Miscellaneous Reports 15.6, *Barbados. Sugar Cane Cultivation, Department of Agriculture, &c. 1871–1918*.

20 West India Committee, Circ. 41, 8 July 1889, 56, in Kew, Miscellaneous Reports 15.6, *Barbados. Sugar Cane Cultivation, Department of Agriculture, &c. 1871–1918*.

21 *Barbados Agricultural Gazette*, June 1891, 131–132, in Kew, Miscellaneous Reports 15.6, *Barbados. Sugar Cane Experiments. 1883–1900*.

22 These reports are enclosed in Kew, Miscellaneous Reports 15.6, *Barbados. Sugar Cane Experiments. 1883–1900*.

23 *Report of...Dodds Reformatory*, 1888, 36, in Kew, Miscellaneous Reports 15.6, *Barbados. Sugar Cane Experiments. 1883–1900*.

24 *Report of...Dodds Reformatory*, 1890, Kew, Miscellaneous Reports 15.6, *Barbados. Sugar Cane Experiments. 1883–1900*.

25 "Dodds and the Exhibition, 1889," Barbados *Agricultural Gazette*, February 1890, 79–80, Kew, Miscellaneous Reports 15.6, *Barbados. Sugar Cane Experiments. 1883–1900*.

26 Harrison to Morris, 17 September 1888, 43–4, Kew, Miscellaneous Reports 15.6, *Barbados. Sugar Cane Cultivation, Department of Agriculture, &c. 1871–1918*.

27 *Kew Bulletin*, December 1888, 295.

28 "Sugar Cane Seed, from a Correspondent," Manchester *Examiner and Times*, 29 July 1890; Manchester *Courier*, 5 August 1890; Morris, "Letter to the Editor," *European Mail*, 20 August 1890; Harrison, "Letter to the Editor," Manchester *Examiner and Times*, 22 August 1890; Harrison to Morris, 28 August 1890, 72; all in Kew, Miscellaneous Reports 15.6, *Barbados. Sugar Cane Cultivation, Department of Agriculture, &c. 1871–1918*.

29 Dyer to Secretary of State, 27 June 1893, Kew, Miscellaneous Reports 15.6, *Barbados. Sugar Cane Experiments. 1883–1900*.

30 *Agricultural Gazette*, 12 February 1892, 104–105, in Kew, Miscellaneous Reports 15.6, *Barbados. Sugar Cane Experiments. 1883–1900*.

31 *Report on the Reformatory and Industrial School for 1892*, 3, in Kew, Miscellaneous Reports 15.6, *Barbados. Sugar Cane Experiments. 1883–1900*.

32 *Agricultural Gazette*, September 1892, 166, Kew, Miscellaneous Reports 15.6, *Barbados. Sugar Cane Experiments. 1883–1900*.

33 M. Havinden and D. Meredith, *Colonialism and Development: Britain and Its Tropical Colonies, 1850–1960*, London: Routledge, 1993, pp. 45–52. H. A. Will, "Colonial Policy and Economic Development in the British West Indies, 1895–1903," *Economic History Review* 2nd series, vol. 23, no. 1, April 1970, pp. 129–130. B. Semmel, *Imperialism and Social Reform: English Social-Imperial Thought, 1895–1914*, Cambridge MA: Harvard University Press, 1960.

34 P. J. Cain and A. G. Hopkins, *British Imperialism, vol. 1: Innovation and Expansion*, London: Longman, 1993, p. 213.

35 S. Marks and A. Atmore, "The Imperial Factor in South Africa in the Nineteenth Century: A Reassessment," *Journal of Imperial and Commonwealth History* 3, no. 1, 1974, pp. 105–139. N. Etherington, "Labour Supply and the Genesis of South African Confederation in the 1870s", *Journal of African History* 20, no. 2, 1979, pp. 235–253. R. L. Cope, "C. W. de Kiewiet, the Imperial Factor, and South African 'Native' Policy," *Journal of Southern African Studies* 15, no. 3, 1989, pp. 486–505.

36 S. Constantine, *The Making of British Colonial Development Policy, 1914–1940*, London: Frank Cass, 1984, pp. 10–11.

37 *Hansard Parliamentary Debates*, 4th series, vol. 36, 1895, cols. 641–2.

38 The *Oxford English Dictionary* says "development" was not used to refer to a region or a people until the British Parliament discussed South Africa in 1902, but Chamberlain seems to have been using the word to mean precisely this in 1895.

39 As quoted by Constantine, *The Making of British Colonial Development Policy*, p. 11.

40 *Report of the West India Royal Commission*, vol. 1, C.8655, 1897, pp. 64–70.

41 C. Clark and T. Pinch, *The Hard Sell: The Language and Lessons of Street-Wise Marketing*, London: HarperCollins, 1995, pp. 97–111, 250–253.
42 *Report of the West India Royal Commission*, vol. 1, C.8655, 1897, p. 64.
43 D. Morris, "Subsidiary Report on the Agricultural Resources and Requirements of British Guiana and the West India Islands," in *Report of the West India Royal Commission*, vol. 1, C.8655, 1897, pp. 82, 145.
44 D. Judd, *Empire: The British Imperial Experience from 1765 to the Present*, New York: HarperCollins, 1996, pp. 161–165, 214–216.
45 Y. Ezrahi, *The Descent of Icarus: Science and the Transformation of Contemporary Democracy*, Cambridge MA: Harvard University Press, 1990, p. 13.
46 Will, "Colonial Policy and Economic Development", pp. 136–138.
47 *West Indian Bulletin* 1, no. 1, 1899, pp. 4–5.
48 Morris to Dyer, 24 Dec. 1898, 18–19; 21 Jan. 1899, 20–21; 31 Jan. 1899, 57–62; 19 Jan. 1900; 30 March 1901, 102–103; 25 May 1901, 106–107; 6 Dec. 1901, 112–113; 16 Jan. 1902, 114–115; 28 Feb. 1902, 124–128; 1 Dec. 1902, 147; 3 Dec. 1907, 235; all in Kew, Miscellaneous Reports 15.6, *West Indies. Commissioner of Agriculture Letters, 1898–1914*.
49 *West Indian Bulletin* 1, no. 1, 1899, pp. 13–14.
50 *West Indian Bulletin* 1, no. 1, 1899, pp. 16, 19. See also Drayton, "Cane Breeding," p. 104.
51 Morris to Dyer, 20 December 1905, 209–210, in Kew, Miscellaneous Reports 15.6, *West Indies. Commissioner of Agriculture Letters, 1898–1914*.
52 Morris to Dyer, 19 January 1900, 57–62, in Kew, Miscellaneous Reports 15.6, *West Indies. Commissioner of Agriculture Letters, 1898–1914*.
53 *Report of the West India Royal Commission*, vol. 1, C.8655, 1897, p. 17.
54 *Report of the West India Royal Commission*, vol. 1, C.8655, 1897, p. 17.
55 *West Indian Bulletin* 11, 1911, pp. 233, 238–240, 368–370.
56 L. Lewton-Brain, "Hybridization of the Sugar-Cane," *West Indian Bulletin* 4, 1904, pp. 63–73.
57 Remarks of G. T. Fenwick and W. D. Shepherd, *West Indian Bulletin* 3, 1902, pp. 36–8.
58 C. Jeffries, "Sir Frank Arthur Stockdale," *Dictionary of National Biography*, 1941–1950, pp. 840–841.
59 D. Morris and F. Stockdale, "Improvement of the Sugar Cane by Selection and Hybridization," *West Indian Bulletin* 7, 1906, pp. 345–50. G. C. Stevenson, *Genetics and Breeding of Sugar Cane*, London: Longman, 1965, p. 2.
60 Storey, *Science and Power in Colonial Mauritius*, pp. 98–103.
61 Morris and Stockdale, "Improvement of the Sugar Cane," pp. 353–355.
62 Galloway, "Botany in the Service of the Empire," pp. 695–699.
63 *West Indian Bulletin* 11, 1911, p. 242.
64 Storey, *Science and Power in Colonial Mauritius*, p. 104.
65 Galloway, "Botany in the Service of Empire," pp. 692–695.
66 G. B. Masefield, *A History of the Colonial Agricultural Service*, Oxford: Clarendon Press, 1972, pp. 31–39, 53–59.
67 *West Indian Bulletin* 11, 1911, p. 242.
68 Masefield, *Colonial Agricultural Service*, pp. 38–44.
69 *West Indian Bulletin* 11, 1911, p. 242.
70 Jeffries, "Stockdale," pp. 840–841. Stockdale's career is also discussed in Storey, *Science and Power in Colonial Mauritius*, and also in D. J. Morgan, *The Official History of Colonial Development, Vol. 1: The Origins of British Aid Policy, 1924–1945*, London: Macmillan, 1980.
71 *Tropical Agriculture* 32, no. 4, October 1955, pp. 337–338. Tempany's career is also discussed in Storey, *Science and Power in Colonial Mauritius*.
72 *West Indian Bulletin* 11, 1911, p. 233.
73 *West Indian Bulletin* 11, 1911, p. 236.

7 Mapping systems and moral order

Constituting property in genome laboratories

Stephen Hilgartner

Introduction

Genome research is simultaneously creating important new forms of property and exponentially growing quantities of data in the public domain. In this context of rapid scientific change and extensive commercial activity, the appropriation of genes, genomes and DNA fragments has inspired ongoing controversy. Most discussion of genomic property has focused on legal rule-making concerning patents, treating property issues as a matter of law and policy rather than science. In general, these discussions have assumed that the Patent and Trademark Office, the legal brief, and the court decision – not the laboratory – are the critical sites of property construction. Making knowledge and making property rights are treated as two distinct moves, separated temporally and institutionally. Knowledge is made in the laboratory; property is secured in the worlds of law and commerce.

This chapter argues that understanding the creation of scientific property requires looking not only at the law but also at the laboratory in order to appreciate how appropriation mechanisms are institutionalized in specific systems for conducting scientific work. Legal knowledge and practices do not exist in a universe that is somehow separate from scientific knowledge and practices (Jasanoff 1995; Cambrosio and Keating 1995). To restrict the study of the creation of high-technology property to the legal decisions that "follow" it, while neglecting the laboratory, is to cripple analysis; for property – and practices that shape the boundaries of ownership – are deeply embedded in laboratories and the routines of scientific life, and they shape a laboratory's internal operations and relations with the outside world. In particular, I argue that institutionalizing new forms of scientific work involves the co-production of technical and social orders capable of simultaneously making knowledge and governing appropriation. An analysis of an effort to build a system for genome mapping at the end of the 1980s provides an empirical example. Data are drawn from a study of genome mapping and sequencing using participant observation and interviewing in genome laboratories and other relevant sites.

Appropriation in science

Before proceeding, the terms *property* and *appropriation practices* call for clarification. In everyday discourse, people talk of property as if it consisted of concrete entities, such as houses, money or shares of stock. Legal scholars, however, construe property not simply as things that are owned but as bundles of rights with respect to those entities, whose limits must be specified and sometimes tested. Property entails certain limited rights (such as to sell a house – but not to transform it into an establishment for retailing illegal drugs), and it also imposes certain burdens (such as to shovel the front walk – or to pay damages when someone slips). Possessing property thus embeds people in a fabric of rights and obligations; this fabric, not the entities themselves, constitutes the functional meaning of property. The term *appropriation practices* designates practices that constitute such rights and obligations.

Although the notion of a bundle of rights represents a significant refinement of everyday understandings of property, understanding how property operates in social life entails considering forms of "property" that may not be explicitly recognized by the legal system. In many instances, the relevant property in scientific exchange includes not only formally recognized intellectual property (such as patents, copyrights and trade secrets), but also what one might call "informal" types of scientific property – such as the rights and obligations of the parties in a "collaboration" or of the authors of a scientific paper. These features of the "moral economy" of science (Kohler 1994) are consequential in the research process and beyond in the wider world of law and policy. Thus, rather than resting analysis on a concept of property limited in scope to a narrow world of legal discourse, it is useful to consider property to be profoundly embedded in wider discourses, practices and systems of exchange that partially order collective definitions of owners, ownable entities, and property rights.[1]

The role of laboratories in creating property has been obscured not only by commonsense understandings of law and science as wholly separate activities, but also by a simplistic conception of scientific exchange. Much discussion of scientific exchange envisions the process as highly individualistic and discrete. Mertonian sociology of science, which remains influential among scientists and specialists in science policy, typically describes scientific exchange as a transaction between the individual scientist and the scientific community. Production and exchange are conceived of as two distinct steps; a scientist first produces a "finding" (conceived of as a well defined, neatly bounded research result) and subsequently publishes it or shares it with colleagues (thus transforming it into community property in exchange for credit). Other researchers proceed to incorporate those findings into the next cycle of research, producing new results that, in turn, are published or otherwise entered into exchange (Hagstrom 1966; McCain 1991).

Critics of this oversimplified picture of scientific exchange describe a much more collective and continuous process. Analyses grounded in actor network theory have emphasized the fluidity of scientific work and the emergent forms it produces (e.g. Callon 1994; Latour 1987). In this much more dynamic vision, the identities of individuals, laboratories and other actors are continuously subject to redefinition. Appropriation takes place in many linked sites and involves subtle yet consequential changes in everyday practices and in "practical cosmologies" (Cambrosio and Keating 1995). Laboratories are conceptualized not as producers of "research results," but as producers of a heterogeneous stream of entities – including a wide range of inscriptions, processes, materials, skills, techniques and other resources. These diverse entities – which for convenience can be grouped under the rubric of "data" – do not begin their existence as well defined objects, neatly packaged and clearly bounded; instead, they are embedded in complex assemblages that evolve continuously as scientific work proceeds (Hilgartner and Brandt-Rauf 1994a).

The continuous and emergent properties of these evolving streams of data and materials – which are collectively produced both within and among laboratories – raise interesting questions for analysts of scientific property. What kinds of practices regulate the flow of various forms of data? How are discrete entities separated from these assemblages and packaged as property? How – especially in research enterprises that involve many scientists and span the boundaries of laboratories – are transactions surrounding data and materials managed, and how are these transactions implicated in granting scientists authorship (Biagioli 1998; see also Foucault 1977) or property rights in data?

To explore these questions, this paper examines the property relations embodied in one mapping strategy – the "reference library" strategy – developed and partially implemented at the outset of the genome project during the late 1980s and the early 1990s. The reference library strategy was developed in the Genome Analysis Laboratory, directed by Hans Lehrach, at the Imperial Cancer Research Fund (ICRF), a private charity, in London. This strategy represented an ambitious means of organizing trans-laboratory cooperation that sheds light on the role of laboratory practices in constructing scientific property and illustrates how deeply property relations are built into institutions for conducting scientific work. Although the first maps of the human genome were produced in other laboratories using different strategies, at the time, it was unclear which mapping strategies would prove successful, and the reference library strategy was often described as "unique", "original", "promising" and, above all, "clever" – even by its critics.[2] More importantly for our purposes, the reference library strategy provides an especially clear example of an effort to constitute a new social and technical order in genome research.

Genome mapping in the early 1990s

Before considering the reference library strategy, it is necessary to examine the state of play in genome mapping when Lehrach first devised it. At the close of the 1980s, as the Human Genome Project was formally initiated, genome researchers faced not only impressive technical obstacles but also the task of creating systems for managing collective work on a new scale (Hilgartner 1995).

The challenge of mapping and sequencing the human genome, along with the genomes of other targeted organisms, was beyond the capabilities of any existing laboratory, and was expected to require extensive cooperation, ongoing exchanges of data and materials, and the construction of new, larger laboratories. Cooperation is problematic in molecular biology, as Karin Knorr-Cetina (1999) documents, because its culture features highly individuated epistemic subjects. Molecular biology research traditionally takes place in small, "bench work" shops, each run by an "autonomous" lab head who personifies the lab, speaks for, and directs, its "own" "independent" research. The new context of genome mapping raised many questions about how control over research, and ownership of research products, should be distributed to project participants – both among and within laboratories. Because the existing exchange practices of molecular genetics were deemed inadequate, genome scientists experimented with a variety of what they called mapping "strategies" – schemes for institutionalizing ways of mapping on a larger scale through a combination of technical and social innovations.

In the early years of the genome project, most human genome research was aimed at producing basic, low-resolution maps of the genome rather than delineating its complete nucleic acid sequence. Mapping research tended to focus on one of two major lines of work: global mapping and gene hunting. A number of centers for genome research sought to produce global maps of the human genome (or, more frequently, of particular chromosomes). These laboratories pursued a number of strategies and produced several different kinds of map, each of which represented the spatial relations among different kinds of landmarks (Hilgartner 1995). Many mapping labs, for example, were busy constructing so-called "contig maps", created by shattering the human genome into many small pieces and then reassembling the fragments into a contiguous array. Accomplishing this for even a single chromosome required years of effort and cost millions of dollars.

In contrast to global mapping, with its goal of producing a broad overview of the genome, gene hunting involved finding the precise location of small "objects" within it, namely, genes – most often those implicated in human disease. Human disease gene hunting was (and remains) an extremely competitive area of research. In the late 1980s and early 1990s, only a relatively small number of genes – such as those implicated in cystic fibrosis, Huntington's disease, neurofibromatosis, and the muscular dystrophies – provided gene hunters with attractive "targets", and fiercely competitive races often developed among groups of researchers seeking the same gene. Since only one team could win each race, gene hunting was a zero-sum game in which prestige and potentially valuable patents were up for grabs (Hilgartner and Brandt-Rauf 1994b). Moreover, gene hunters could expect to spend years searching for a gene. Global genome mapping was also quite competitive, because large grants were required to fund major mapping laboratories, and only those deemed productive were likely to survive.

Despite the different goals of gene hunting and genome mapping, both lines of research involved creating maps, and each could contribute useful data to the other.[3] Although gene hunters built high-resolution maps of the regions where they believed a gene of interest was located, while genome mappers created low-resolution maps of much larger regions, the two types of maps could share landmarks, so data originally developed for one purpose could be incorporated into the other. Moreover, many – indeed most – global genome mappers of the early 1990s had a dual identity as active gene hunters. As a result, scientists were often reluctant to share important resources, such as DNA samples used to construct maps. In this context, the question of how to motivate cooperation and harness competition became a salient one for funding agencies, for their science advisors, and for researchers developing mapping technology (Hilgartner 1998). The reference library strategy was designed to address these problems.

The reference library strategy

The reference library strategy was an effort to create an institution capable of sustaining a new kind of more collective and collaborative genome research. Although it was only incompletely implemented, it represents an important strategic vision for engaging hundreds of geographically dispersed laboratories in a collaborative network. This chapter provides an ethnographically informed reading of that strategic vision, focusing on its technological and moral logic, rather than giving a detailed history of the effort to implement it. The strategy was ambitious, because trans-laboratory cooperation on a large scale represented a significant departure from the usual pattern in the individuated and competitive world of molecular genetics. To make such cooperation into an efficient way to build maps, the reference library approach aimed at nothing less than to constitute a new social order. The word *constitute* here is meant to evoke not only the notions of composing or establishing, but also (see Jasanoff 2003) the idea of a political constitution: for the reference library approach sought to create a social order in which a set of actors – endowed with specific powers, rights and obligations – would interact in an ongoing, rule-governed way. This social order (simultaneously and irreducibly also a technological order) was designed to draw together a collectively produced stream of data, while at the same time separating it into "public" and "private" parts and apportioning property rights among participants. To constitute this new way of ordering mapping, Hans Lehrach and his colleagues envisioned creating a network of laboratories bound together by reliance on shared biomaterials, shared technology, shared data, and mutually-beneficial exchange relations. Let us take a closer look at the "constitution" of the reference library strategy and the materials, concepts and procedures in which it was inscribed.

Orderly libraries

Lehrach's work on what evolved into the reference library strategy began with a focus on how to create orderly "libraries" of DNA samples, as well as the tools, such as computerized databases and robots, for managing and manipulating them. In the parlance of molecular biology, a "library" is a large collection of DNA samples derived from a particular DNA source, such as the human genome. Libraries were (and remain) important tools in molecular biology, and Lehrach sought to make them more useful by creating systems for organizing them and using them to build maps. To create a library of human DNA, scientists break the genome into many small fragments, each of which is spliced into an individual bacteria or yeast cell using recombinant DNA technology. The cells containing the human DNA fragments are called "clones", and these clones can be grown in the laboratory, allowing scientists to replicate the human DNA. Clones can also be stored in a freezer or mailed to other scientists. Clones thus provide a convenient way to preserve, copy and distribute DNA samples.

Even so, creating and using libraries requires considerable work, especially given the numbers of clones involved. For example, a library designed to "cover" the human genome – that is, to include clones containing fragments of DNA from the entire human genome with no significant gaps – might consist of tens of thousands of individual clones. Each of these clones must be carefully stored and protected from contamination, so working with libraries is time consuming. In addition, when a library of clones is first created it is completely uncatalogued: no detailed data are available about the individual DNA samples that make it up. Information on the individual samples only emerges as they are studied. Lehrach's initial work on what ultimately developed into the reference library strategy began with an effort to construct systems for ordering these libraries, for example, by creating robotics for manipulating clones, by storing each clone in a separately numbered location, and by building a database about the clones.

Orderly maps

Using these libraries, robots and computer systems, Lehrach's group also developed a novel method for genome mapping – hybridization with high-density filters. This technique was designed to produce large amounts of data about the clones in a library and use those data to build contig maps. The method relied on a "spotting robot", designed in the Lehrach laboratory, to array thousands of DNA samples in a grid of tiny dots on a single "filter" – a flat sheet of DNA-binding material somewhat larger than an ordinary piece of paper. Each of these tiny spots was addressable, because each clone was assigned a number and a computer recorded its position on the filter; its coordinates in the grid were thus linked to the original sample. Initially, the spotting robot could array 9,216 samples on a single filter. (This density allowed a library covering the entire human genome to fit on a handful of filters. Later this density, already considered impressive in the early 1990s, was doubled.) These filters could then be analyzed using a standard technique called hybridization. In this technique, radioactively labeled DNA samples, known as "probes", are poured over the filter, and the probes bind (or "hybridize") to any samples on the filter containing DNA matching the probe. After washing off excess radioactive material, the filter can be used to expose X-ray film, producing a pattern of black dots, known as an "autoradiogram", indicating which samples contain the probe. In this manner, a list of "positive" clones – that is, those matching the probe – can be rapidly produced: the high-density filters permitted testing a probe against thousands of clones in a single experiment.

Lehrach deployed high-density hybridization in two kinds of experiments. The first involved experiments designed to identify samples that contained particular probes. In the competitive world of human genetics, an "interesting clone" could be an important resource; if the probe was believed to lie near a gene that was the object of a gene hunt, the sample could be extremely valuable to a gene hunter. The second was designed to produce a contig map of DNA samples known to overlap. Identical filters could be repeatedly tested with probes designed to reveal shared DNA sequences; the large amounts of data that accumulated, ultimately, could be analyzed to produce a contig map. Lehrach demonstrated that this approach could work, at least with the relatively simple genomes of microorganisms, by creating a contig map of the yeast *S. pombe* (Maier *et al.* 1992).

An orderly network of laboratories

A critic of the individualistic orientation of molecular genetics, Lehrach believed that a research enterprise that drew many scientists into competitive, zero-sum races wasted resources and led to duplication of effort. As Lehrach and his colleagues at the ICRF worked to develop the technique of high-density hybridization – a task that involved creating libraries, robots, software, and so on – they also began thinking about how these tools might be used in trans-laboratory collaboration for genome mapping. For example, if many laboratories all used the same set of libraries as a shared point of "reference", these labs would be tied together by virtue of working with the same biomaterials. Such ideas grew into the reference library strategy, an ambitious attempt to use the tools constructed by Lehrach's group to constitute – in both a material and sociopolitical sense – a new institution for mapping genomes based on orderly exchanges among a network of laboratories.

The constitution of the reference library strategy pertained to two main categories of social actors – the central laboratory and the "participating laboratories". The central laboratory, which Lehrach and his colleagues set up at the ICRF, was charged with coordinating the network, creating and storing biomaterials that it needed, and maintaining a central database. (For clarity, I will use the term "Reference Library Laboratory", or RLL, to designate the central laboratory; in practice the referent of the term "reference library system" was ambiguous, sometimes designating the system as a whole and sometimes the central laboratory.) The strategy framed the "participating laboratories" as "users" of the system and also, as we will see, contributors to it.[4] The typical participating laboratory was expected to be an ordinary human molecular genetics lab, not a large center of genome research. As such, it was expected to be likely to be hunting genes and racing to find map landmarks near the genes it was seeking.[5]

The design of the reference library strategy integrated the material elements of the systems, such as biomaterials, tools and techniques, with a set of rules of exchange between the RLL and the participating laboratories. These rules were intended to specify the terms of trans-laboratory cooperation, apportioning property rights in biomaterials and research results, and governing the main kinds of transactions.

One type of transaction involved the use of reference library filters. The RLL used its spotting robots to create many identical copies of high-density filters covering its libraries. These filters were distributed to laboratories who wanted to participate in the network. In the typical transaction, once a participating laboratory received filters, it would do a hybridization using a probe of its choice. The participating laboratory would then report back to the RLL its hybridization results, providing the RLL with the coordinates of the positive signals, with a copy of the autoradiogram, and with some information on the probe. The RLL would then identify samples that were "hits" – that is, those positive for the probe – and send those samples to the laboratory.

For the participating laboratory, this type of transaction offered a very efficient way to identify useful samples in a genomic region of interest (such as near the putative location of a coveted gene). In the early 1990s, the ability to test a probe against 10,000 or 20,000 clones in a single experiment was impressive, and this capacity provided an incentive for laboratories to participate. For the RLL, transactions of this form were attractive in part because they could assist participating laboratories in their research. But beyond this "service" function, the RLL benefited directly from the exchange: it incorporated the data from the hybridizations into its database, where data about which probes "hit" which clones accumulated. Such data could raise the value of the clones in the reference library, perhaps by providing information about their biological significance or about their chromosomal location, which helped to "anchor" small contigs on the genome. In this way, the reference library strategy aimed to link the work of many laboratories into a central database while simultaneously contributing to the particular research projects underway at each laboratory.

A second type of transaction involved requests for clones known to be positive for particular probes. Outside laboratories could examine the reference library database and obtain individual clones of interest from the RLL. The laboratories could then incorporate these clones into their research projects. Transactions of this type allowed a gene hunter, for example, to obtain clones that might be important in a gene hunt. However, a significant competitive advantage was unlikely to be obtained through this route, given that the RLL database was public and other laboratories hunting for the same gene would probably obtain the same clones.

Orderly property

The constitution of the RLL was designed not only to enable sharing and making data public, but also keeping data private. The rules of exchange made it possible for data and biomaterials from the reference library to be incorporated into work of participating laboratories, and, at the same time, for data produced in the participating laboratories to be fed back into the RLL's database. But the system also constructed boundaries to keep these data separate. For example, the RLL kept the libraries themselves – in a sense, its core resource – "private"; they were distributed, if at all, only to the closest collaborators. Filters were distributed, but without access to the original clones, it was impossible to recreate the libraries. The filters thus served as a means of providing limited access to the libraries, which could be used by the participating laboratories without being transferred to them.

The rules of exchange also compelled participating laboratories to send experimental results back to the RLL, but this compulsion rested not only on moral suasion but also on the intrinsic characteristics of the material and data that the RLL released to the participants. Once a laboratory elected to participate, was sent filters, and conducted hybridization experiments, it could obtain useful information *only* by sending the experimental results back to the RLL. The autoradiograms alone were useless: the positive signals they displayed were meaningless dots until their coordinates had been entered into the RLL database, which linked those filter positions to the underlying clones. To benefit from the exchange, the participating laboratories therefore had to send their hybridization results to the RLL, and doing so automatically provided the RLL with information that enhanced the value of its libraries and its genome maps. In this way, the technological structure of the system helped to reinforce the rules governing the transactions.

The rules also explicitly defined the boundaries of collectively produced results. Thus the RLL stressed that "the distribution of filters and clones from the Reference Library does NOT establish a collaboration (e.g. co-authorship)".[6] Through this emphatic statement, the RLL clearly signaled that it had no interest in intruding into the autonomous world of the individual laboratory. The participating laboratories were asked merely to send reprints of publications arising from the use of RLL materials and to acknowledge the origin of RLL clones – both normal courtesies in the prevailing exchange practices of molecular biology. In a symmetrical way, this statement denied the laboratories any ownership right, such as co-authorship, over the RLL's libraries, databases and maps.

The rules of exchange also allowed the participating laboratories to draw on reference library resources while preserving a zone of "private" data of their own. The typical gene hunting laboratory not only considered it very important to obtain relevant clones quickly, but also wanted these clones to remain unavailable to its competitors. This was especially true in the case of "unique" probes that the laboratory had developed itself, and which were unavailable to competitors. In contrast to well known "public" probes, which were widely available (often from public repositories of biomaterials), these "unique", "private" probes might produce a competitive edge over other labs. Accordingly, the RLL built protections for the participating labs into its system: it offered participating laboratories the option of keeping the clones identified by certain probes "confidential" for a period of six months (expandable to a year – and even beyond in some instances). These clones would be available to the laboratory that had performed the hybridization, but not to others (including other participating laboratories). The existence of confidential data would be registered in the database and made public, but neither the information about the probe nor the clones it "hit" would be made public until confidentiality expired.

Social and technical order

As the above discussion suggests, the reference library strategy was much more than a system for analyzing DNA; it was also the blueprint for an institution for conducting genome mapping work in a new, more collaborative way. Lehrach and his colleagues sought not only to create orderly libraries and maps, but also to use the technological successes of his library construction and robotics projects to form a network of researchers linked by shared materials, create orderly systems of exchange among them, and institutionalize rules for ownership of research products emerging from the network. Put otherwise, the reference library strategy was simultaneously a technological project and an effort to engineer social change in genome science. Successfully making genome mapping into a more collaborative venture entailed constituting a technical and social order capable of underwriting this new kind of work.

The RLL only achieved this goal only partially. Hundreds of laboratories did participate in the network, but their commitment was quite limited; most of them appear to have been interested mainly in using the RLL to obtain a few interesting clones, and their involvement did not persist for a sustained period of time. Moreover, critics attacked the system with both technological and sociopolitical arguments. On the technological side, hybridization was said to have an unfavorable signal-to-noise ratio that made the system less "robust" than approaches, such as STS-content mapping (Stemerding and Hilgartner 1998), that were gaining prominence in the United States. Similarly, the "cleverness" of the reference library strategy, which even critics saw as ingenious, was said to be appropriate for experiments that only had to work once, but unworkable for the repetitious work of genome mapping.

Other criticisms carried explicit moral messages, such as objections to the centralization inherent to the strategy (e.g. "I don't want to rely on one place to do this. I don't think it's the way it should be done"[7]). Some raised questions about the moral integrity of the system: How do we know that the databases will be secure? What if information gets leaked? Could the central laboratory suddenly change the rules? To many researchers in human genetics, a mapping strategy that required this degree of dependence on, and trust in, another laboratory seemed naive.[8] People worried that the databases might not be secure, that information might not remain confidential, that clones might be secretly distributed to favored colleagues in violation of the rules. Many genome scientists and geneticists decided not to participate in the emerging reference library system, even as several hundred laboratories chose to participate in its work.[9]

Ultimately, the RLL never produced a map of the human genome, and the first physical maps of the human genome were published by French and American groups that employed completely different strategies.[10] The institutional changes that Lehrach sought to implement did not materialize, and the reference library strategy — an example of a "failure" of co-production — remains of interest owing mainly to its significance as a road not taken.

Conclusion

Laboratories do not only produce facts and machines, they also produce property and owners. The reference library strategy was an ambitious blueprint for constituting a new technological and moral order for mapping genomes, and it illustrates clearly how deeply property relations are embedded in the fabric of scientific life. This chapter suggests that analysts who examine the law but neglect the laboratory may miss crucial dimensions of the processes that constitute scientific property. Appropriation is not a *post-hoc* "add on" to scientific success. On the contrary, appropriation practices are built deeply into the technical and social order of laboratories, and they constitute an inseparable part of their technological structure, moral order, strategic logic, and everyday operation.

Notes

The author acknowledges the support of the U.S. National Science Foundation, Grant No. 0083414.

1 Boyle's (1996) insightful analysis of the role of the "romantic author" in shaping legal decisions about intellectual property provides an excellent illustration of how such wider discourses can be used in cultural explanations of property law. However, Boyle does not address laboratory practices or "science in the making", and generally treats inventions and creations as stable entities that are fitted into property regimes *after* they come into existence.
2 These statements appear repeatedly in my fieldnotes and interview transcripts collected for an ethnographic study of the genome mapping and sequencing community. See also Jordan (1993: 58).
3 On philosophical issues involved in cartography and the use of map making as an analogy for science, see Kitcher (2001), esp. ch. 5.
4 See e.g. *Reference Library News Update*, May 1991.
5 On the crucial importance of speed in genomics, see Fortun (1998).
6 *Reference Library News Update*, May 1991, p. 8.
7 Interview, fieldnotes at 04100.37.
8 See Hilgartner (in press) for a discussion of distrust among molecular geneticists of large centers of genome research.
9 See *Reference Library News Update*, October 1992, pp. 2–3.
10 The first physical maps of the human genome were produced at Genethon in France and at the Whitehead Institute in the United States. For an ethnographic account of Genethon's "victory", among other topics, see Rabinow (1999).

8 Patients and scientists in French muscular dystrophy research

Vololona Rabeharisoa and Michel Callon

Introduction

Lay people are becoming more and more involved in scientific and technical debates and activities they are concerned with. Their intervention poses questions on the way scientific and technical issues are raised and decided upon, and on the nature of knowledge that is mobilized through this process. These debates relate to the shaping of a new regime of relations between science and society, that the notion of co-production aims at capturing.

Co-production translates an intertwined transformation of the relations between science and society. The first transformation manifests into the expanding list of actors who participate in scientific and technical debates and activities. In particular, the publicization of scientific controversies calls for an extended dialogue with all concerned groups, be they experts or lay people (Bailey *et al.* 1999; Barthe 2000; Brown 1992; Callon *et al.* 2001; Collins and Evans 2002; Kerr *et al.* 1998; Rip, forthcoming; Wynne 1996). In some cases, this dialogue ends up in actions that these concerned groups design and perform altogether. From this perspective, co-production refers to the emergence of collective action and the shaping of new identities. The second transformation relates to the shaping of objects of shared interest that could not have emerged without this collective action. This is a crucial point for certain concerned groups that try to bring into the public sphere problems that were formerly either unknown or ignored. From this perspective, co-production refers to knowledge and collective mobilization being conjointly produced.

In this chapter, we present a model of co-production that stands as an original example of the two perspectives mentioned above. This model has been developed by the French Muscular Dystrophy Association (Association Française contre les Myopathies or AFM). It combines: (i) the mobilization of research communities around neuromuscular diseases (MD) that were orphan hitherto; and (ii) the active participation of patients and their families in the orientation of biological and clinical research and the production of knowledge on these diseases. The originality of the AFM is its capacity to invent tools and procedures for organizing research and collective mobilization around MD.

The AFM contributes to a general evolution of patients' associations. Apart from financial back-up to research teams and laboratories (Rangnekar 2002), traditional pressure exerted on public decisionmakers (Dresser 2001), and patients' participation in clinical tests, some associations are indeed starting to have an impact on the orientation, management and evaluation of research programmes concerning their diseases. This development raises the question of whether the intervention of patients' associations in research policy promotes the emergence of original ways of constructing knowledge and mobilizing research communities that transform relations between patients and specialists. To this question there is obviously no general answer. The associations supporting research related to certain categories of disease reveal a wide diversity of configurations (Rabeharisoa and Callon 2002). Yet the emergence of original configurations seems plausible, at least for some of them. For example, offensive strategies implemented by AIDS associations in the field of therapeutics, attest to increased intervention by patients in areas formerly reserved for experts (Epstein 1995; Barbot 2002). But in France, long before AIDS and in a very different way, neuromuscular diseases benefited – as they still do – from active participation in research by the AFM.

The AFM was created in 1958. It includes patients suffering from MD and their parents. Today, the AFM has 4,500 members,[1] 400 employees, and an annual budget of 90 million euros, 80 per cent of which is provided by the Telethon©.[2] In contrast to chronic disease patients' groups that blossomed in the 1950s in France, the AFM soon realized that there existed neither robust knowledge on MD, nor organized action against these pathologies. In order to overcome this disinterest, and the ignorance that it induced, the AFM decided very early on to include supporting research on its agenda, alongside traditional endeavours such as helping families and fighting for social recognition.

Since the launching of the Telethon© in 1987, the AFM has allocated over 200 million euros to all kinds of research. These efforts culminated in 1991, with the launching of Genethon laboratory. Genethon provided the first physical maps of the human genome in 1993, and thus gained an international reputation. But it is above all a unique research structure (Kaufmann, forthcoming), entirely imagined, set up, monitored and financed by a patients' association, at least in France. Even before that, when resources were limited, the existing muscular dystrophy associations devoted approximately 40 per cent of their annual budgets to research (Barral *et al.* 1991). Furthermore, unlike some associations which became entirely dependent on doctors and researchers, the patients and their families have successfully maintained control over the association since its inception in 1958 and, more specifically, over the orientation of research (Rabeharisoa and Callon 1999). That is why the AFM seemed an appropriate context for reflecting upon co-production, and studying the way it is organized.

This study is part of a long-term research project which is now completed. Our research objective was to characterize the actions that the AFM undertook between 1981 and 1995[3] for developing research on MD and securing social recognition for MD patients. We also paid increased attention to the articulation between research and social investments, for this helped to understand the emergence of MD into the public sphere. In this chapter we focus on the support given by the AFM to research. We organized our inquiry around three main questions:

(i)   the content of the AFM's research policy during the period under study (if such policy ever existed);
(ii) the tools implemented by the AFM for the orientation, the steering, and the evaluation of its support to research (the forms of expertise it relied upon; the role of its scientific council);
(iii) the nature and scope of the relations it established between patients and specialists (the structure of these relations, and their effects on the very definition of MD and MD patients' identity).

We proceeded with a wide range of investigations. The first step was a detailed and exhaustive analysis of the minutes of meetings held by the scientific council (SC) and the board of administrators (BA) of the association, between 1981 and 1995. These archives, of remarkable quality (they include, notably, numerous and extensive literal transcriptions of several brainstorming sessions), enabled us to study the association's research policy in the making. Then we went through the archives of two of the association's patient groups: the spinal muscular atrophy group and the myasthenia group. We participated in meetings held by these groups. This enabled us to get a view of patients and their families' contributions to the understanding of their diseases. We also traced the history of working groups gathering patients and specialists on specific themes such as orthopaedics. Finally, this material was completed by interviews with about forty patients and their parents, researchers, clinicians, employees and administrators of the association.

These investigations confirmed the validity of our initial hypothesis. Through the years, the AFM has progressively developed forms of production of knowledge and mobilization of research communities which help to redefine the modalities of relations between patients and specialists. The purpose of this chapter is to present some of the mechanisms through which the AFM comes to formalize an original model of co-production that we call 'mutual learning'.

We shall emphasize two specific dimensions of this model. In the first section, we show that the association inscribes, in its very functioning, a long-lasting collaboration between patients and specialists. Patients and their parents play an active role in the production of knowledge about diseases. They conceive and implement "proto-instruments" which enable them to become both subjects and objects of research and investigation, identifying problems and going, in certain cases, as far as the creation of know-how and even of formal knowledge. This enables them to engage in collective experiments with specialists, the remarkable effect of which is the mixing of lived experiences and laboratory results in the characterization of MD. In the second section we provide some indications of the way this doing of research relates to an original model of mobilization of research communities. We highlight the importance of what we suggest calling "intermediary discourse" that the AFM invents to formulate its own strategic orientations as regards research. We also describe the procedures that the AFM calls upon for mobilizing expertise and controlling specialists, yet securing their cooperation. To conclude, we suggest that this model could illustrate the appearance of a new form of collective action – that of the reflexive organization.

The emergence of MD as an object for research

Throughout the association's history, patients and their families have been deeply involved in the definition and implementation of research policy aimed at improving knowledge and control over the various forms of MD. In this section we show that this involvement is far more than a matter of financial support or strategic decisions. It consists of the active participation of patients and their families in the formulation of knowledge and know-how. Patients neither limit themselves to being specialists' auxiliaries, nor do they reject laboratory research. They mobilize a vast array of tools and devices in order to create a dialogue with specialists, through which patients' experiences and experiments on the bench are mutually enriched. We first describe the role of patients in the primitive accumulation of knowledge that makes this dialogue possible. We then show how patients and specialists become partners in the writing of the natural history of MD, through collaborative mechanisms that the AFM has progressively implemented. This mutual learning, embedded in the very functioning of the association, transforms both patients' identites and the status of their diseases.

The role of patients in the primitive accumulation of knowledge

> So I took the phone directory and I called a few GPs. We needed a good one, one we could rely on, who was available and attentive, who'd go a long way with us. "My son's got muscular dystrophy, Duchenne's disease, I'm looking for a family doctor". A kind of call for tenders. Three of them came round. The first one was reluctant and fled. The second one was sure of himself and tried to capture the market: "Yes, yes, I know the Aran Duchenne disease, no problem". Areng? Haran? Hareng!…Next please.
>
> (Barataud 1992: 19–20)

Numerous accounts describe the vicious circle of abdication and ignorance: when a disease is unknown the professionals turn away from it because it highlights their powerlessness. This disinterest, in turn, maintains the state of ignorance because it paralyses all efforts at carrying out research on these diseases. In such situations, the only knowledge on the pathology is that developed by the patients and shared with their families. This was how, very early on, faced with the abstention of the medical profession, the AFM promoted a series of actions to gather information on the disease, in other words, to undertake what could rightly be called a primitive accumulation of knowledge. By noting their observations and circulating, comparing and evaluating them, patients and their families transformed their familiarity with the disease into a body of knowledge which could serve as the basis for the systematic production of expertise.

One of the association's first contributions was to make an inventory of patients. This required systematic and repeated inquiries, especially in hospitals, as well as the organization of press campaigns. One of the consequences was that groups of patients were able to organize the collection of DNA. It was, however, particularly in a third type of contribution that the originality of the association's involvement was manifested. By mobilizing proto-instruments, the patients and their families put themselves in a position to create quasi-formal, transportable, accumulable and debatable knowledge.

For example, at a very early stage Madame de Kepper, who founded the AFM in 1958, started filming her children, who suffered from myopathy. Her stated intention was to monitor the evolution of the disease, drawing comparisons between her different children suffering from the same disease, and providing documents to the few doctors interested in it (de Kepper 1988). One of these films made in the early 1960s bespeaks this intention:

> The film shows the hesitant way in which Edouard and Philippe walked, their exhaustion after dancing with the little girls, and their increasing difficulty in climbing the stairs. Fifteen months later the contrast is striking. The commentary underscores the inexorable development of the disease and the slow decline to death: "Remember the frolics, the dancing, the stairs. This is what myopathy can do to your children"....Time passes. One day, a day like any other, the child wants to play with a car on the window-sill but can't grasp it: "How can I get my car?" The film also shows the progression of the disease, making the degeneration of the muscular functions visible and analyzable.
>
> (Notes taken during the projection of the film made by the
> de Kepper couple, during our visit on 15 October 1996)

Films made by the association or its members, photographs taken and shown by parents, accounts written by patients or their parents in the form of books for the general public, testimonies that were requested and spontaneous letters, were all ways of formalizing and publicizing knowledge which had hitherto remained confined to the intimacy of private life.

From this point of view, photos are a very effective tool for producing knowledge on the intermediary form of type II SMA (spinal muscular atrophy) in children. Defined in a residual way as being neither fatal in the short term nor non-evolutive in the long term, its degree of gravity can be qualified only by comparison, with each parent trying to situate their child's development in relation to that of other children suffering from the same disease. Photos play a significant part in this comparative evaluation because they act as tools for visualization[4] which make it possible to compare children's abilities to act. The patients and their parents are never without their photo albums, which they exchange and comment on at every opportunity, often trying to interpret the other parents' silent reactions from the look in their eyes. These discussions and evaluations are comparable with those of researchers around the inscriptions produced by their laboratory instruments. What is important is the qualification of the child's state and trajectory. This effort is based on the different procedures of visualization, i.e. the proto-instruments (camera, VCR, drawings and sketches) used to produce, discuss, spread and share information.

Apart from films, photo albums and accounts, patients also use more classical methods such as surveys. These consist of long questionnaires (generally about ten pages with over fifty highly detailed questions) which are sent out regularly. Their formulation and the processing of the answers serve to review the disease, including its development, symptoms, treatment and the effects of the treatment. They play an important part in building up and sharing patients' knowledge and know-how. Thus, during a meeting called to prepare a questionnaire on SMA, the parents (G) responsible for the group pointed out that:

> The body temperature of a child with SMA is 36°C or 36.5°C, and not 37°C. Some parents have noticed that after ventilation the temperature rises. G asked Professor X about this but she was unable to answer. "But do we have to include this as a separate item?". Finally, a proposal is made to add a question on the usual body temperature. "It will enable us to submit the problem to the medical profession".
>
> (notes taken during the group meeting, 9 January 1997)

This discussion shows that parents have progressively accumulated knowledge on their children's disease, which professionals do not necessarily have. It also shows that this knowledge, which is enriched by being shared, is also a source of questions that patients put to doctors. These means not only constitute vectors for the diffusion of information on the disease (Carricaburu 1993), they also help to ensure that objects of investigation, which without this primitive accumulation would probably not have emerged, are taken into account.

Moreover, patients' competencies are not limited purely to practical matters and to the compilation and certification of data resulting from elementary observations. Patients and their representatives frequently go as far as detailed statistical treatment, as in the case of a questionnaire on facio-scapulo-humeral myopathy (FSH), subsequently published in academic journals. This proximity to academic science is not exceptional. Because of the rareness of these diseases – one of the consequences of which is their weak presence in both the teaching[5] and practice of medicine – patients and their association acquire knowledge that is likely to enhance the efficiency of medical services. That is why they put so much effort into gathering all existing publications on a subject, and into writing syntheses which they then circulate among specialists to inform and teach them. Thus patients and their association are the origin of numerous documents on the effects of drugs, and readily discuss such issues with specialists, as equals. The case of the SMA group is, from this point of view, an excellent example. The leaders of the group, all volunteers – patients or their family members – scan the international literature, translate articles considered to be important, and write syntheses. These they update every six months, give to specialists to read through during meetings which sometimes last a whole day, and then disseminate among families with whom they organize work sessions to answer questions.

The active participation of MD patients and their families in the primitive accumulation of knowledge undoubtebly results from historical contingencies. Confronted to the absence of research programmes on MD, they had no choice but to launch investigations, and they could only rely upon their own experiences (Brown 1992). The originality of this action stems from patients and families' capacity to mobilize proto-instruments for collecting, formalizing, circulating and discussing these experiences, among themselves and with specialists. For the first time, the latter are provided with elements they can reflect upon. One could say that the AFM has helped to make MD debatable, and therefore objectifiable. From this point of view, the AFM clearly departs from patients' associations that seek to emancipate themselves from academic knowledge, in order to affirm the subjective character of their lived experiences (Rabeharisoa 2003). On the contrary, MD patients and families become real objects and subjects of research, by establishing a dialogue with specialists, rooted in what they know about themselves. We now turn to the impact of this method of research on the way MD has come to be qualified.

Mutual learning and collective experiments

Once the process has been launched, the disease recognized and the objects of investigation identified, one might expect that the patients would, in a traditional manner, delegate the exploration of their diseases to experts who are now aware of the diseases and have basic information on them. This is not, however, the case. The AFM, supported by numerous specialists, constantly multiplies the number of meetings, discussions and forms of cooperation between patients, scientists and clinicians: discussion forums (every two years the association organizes a conference on MD, open to all concerned); personal interaction between members of patient groups and professionals; periodic visits by patients to laboratories; participation by families in epidemiological surveys; the constitution of patients' DNA banks; the creation of work groups for addressing patients' specific problems, at the initiative of certain mixed commissions of the scientific council; and, last, the creation of the Myology Institute, which groups together, on the same site, research, teaching and consultations. Each of these devices might be described as a 'hybrid forum' (Callon and Rip 1992), that is a place where groups of diverse origins mix. They interact, discuss and negotiate, seeking answers to questions on the research to undertake, the evaluation of results obtained, and the programmes to support. The main characteristic of these forums is that they organize collective experiments: experts are in constant dialogue with lay people, and actions are decided together after joint analysis of the results obtained. Each of these forums has its own specific characteristics, but taken as a whole they establish a rich network of diversified relations between specialists and patients, caught together in the production of the history of the disease.

The work groups, spurred by the clinical commission of the AFM scientific council, clearly illustrate this common will and interest of researchers and patients to co-author the history of MD. These groups emerge as soon as the AFM becomes involved in a certain area of research. One of the first groups to be formed was the one in charge of orthopaedic matters. Surveys carried out among patients were then used to make an inventory of prostheses. Conferences followed, where cases were discussed and good practice progressively defined. As information spread on the right way to handle patients, their lives were prolonged. However, because these diseases are evolutive, this simple fact led to a series of unexpected observations:

> Patients with Duchenne's disease died because they were not ventilated. Now that they're ventilated, they live longer but at the same time heart problems that we never suspected have cropped up.
>
> (a clinician)

As a result, a new direction for research emerged for the "heart group", i.e. the study of relations between those heart-attacks that were related to neuromuscular diseases and those that were not. A specialist recommended that a theme be defined in relation to molecular biology research, concerning muscular expressivity which varies depending on individuals and families of a single genetic alteration. Similar processes have taken place for breathing, sleep, anaesthetics, and evaluation of the quality of life. The groups which were formed around these subjects all recognize the patients' own abilities to draw up a list of critical problems related to their disease, and all give them the chance to express these problems. They also all transform these problems into clinical and scientific research questions, and then go back to the patients to assess the results and launch other projects.

This investigative work, embedded in the very functioning of the AFM, endows patients or their direct representatives with a long-lasting identity, as both the objects and the subjects of research. Objects because the mere fact that they survive – whereas they were dying – provides research with new questions. Subjects because they become directly involved in the production of this knowledge, as the collective experimentation progresses and in relation to the results obtained and the trials experienced in the process. Diseases themselves are produced as entities made of intimate links between experiments on the bench and patients' lived experiences. This method of research translates into an original model of mobilization of research communities. In the next section we characterize this model, and the procedures that the AFM has invented for giving it shape.

Towards a new model for mobilizing research communities

The originality of the model conceived over the years by the AFM appears clearly when it is compared to the two reference models usually taken to support and orient applied scientific research: the public action model and the market model (Dasgupta and David 1994).

In the public action model the government delegates to specialists the tasks of defining and developing research themes in keeping with the main guidelines defined by policymakers. This delegation is inevitable because only scientists have the information required for deciding on relevant research programmes, and evaluating the quality of the results obtained. In this model the government is confronted with two difficulties: choosing "good" scientists on whom it can rely for selecting research subjects and evaluating the results; and ensuring that those scientists strive to act in accordance with the guidelines set. To overcome these difficulties, it sets up incentives enabling it to identify competent researchers and to ensure their loyalty. Irrespective of the nature of these incentives, they are based on a high level of autonomy of the scientific community.

The market model is totally different from the public action model. Research programmes are chosen by industrial decisionmakers in relation to the state of the demand, its solvability, and the nature and intensity of competition. In this model the researchers are, to a large extent, instrumentalized. Their activities are closely supervised, monitored and controlled. The evaluation of their efforts and results is mainly external, that is to say entrusted to non-specialists who are particularly attentive to economic criteria.

Apart from their differences, both models assume that it is possible to define research programmes *ex-ante*. In other words, they assume that one can deduce – whether this deduction is made by researchers (public action model) or decisionmakers (market model) – the scientific objectives to achieve, based solely on the identification of non-scientific objectives. The limits of this type of assumption are highlighted by the particular case of MD. The AFM administrators, in their efforts to develop research on effective therapies, soon realized that (i) researchers were unable to plan and to clearly define programmes that met their expectations; (ii) as patients or parents of patients, they were not in a better position to design such programmes. This type of situation disqualifies both the public action and the market model, as well as any combination of the two, since between research demand and supply there is a huge gap that cannot be bridged.[6] Moreover, the precise content of demand and supply is constructed simultaneously through the translations and interactions which make its formulation and compatibility possible. To know exactly what it wanted and to formulate it in scientifically relevant terms, the association had to multiply consultations and discussions, particularly with the researchers it planned to support. On the other hand, to understand what the patients were expecting from them, the researchers had no alternative but to immerse themselves in the world of the patients and their representatives. Without this constant interaction, strategic choices would have been impossible and debate precluded, for at no time would it have been possible to link political guidelines to scientific options.

In the first part of this article we have drawn on a few examples to demonstrate the existence and originality of this interaction. They suffice for formulating the model conceived by the AFM – a model which cannot be compared to those of public action and the market, since both imply a clear separation between decisionmakers and specialists. But the association has taken political and organizational innovation even further by ensuring that, in this interaction and cooperation, roles and responsibilities are not confused: the power of decision must remain in the patients' hands. This constant preoccupation has led the association to conceive of a series of devices to promote collaboration between patients and experts, while maintaining control by the former over the latter.

Two examples can be used to give an idea of the nature of these devices: the first is the progressive invention of what we propose to call an intermediary discourse, midway between scientific content and strategic considerations; the second is the setting up of procedures and structures which make cooperation and control compatible.

The invention of an intermediary discourse

The most outstanding of these innovations is the progressive elaboration, by the association, of an intermediary discourse. This is a discourse which is neither purely technical nor purely strategic, which enables patients to go into the content of research without getting lost in it, that is to say, without losing sight of the goals. With this discourse, the fine adjustment between an intention and actions to accomplish it is made plausible, as the following dialogue during a recent board meeting indicates:

AN ADMINISTRATOR: With regard to contracting party X, I have two questions: Is any progress being made in the programme? At what stage are the 5'?? Has progress been made on the neuromuscular part? Have samples been taken?

THE SCIENTIST BEING QUESTIONED (WHO WAS INVITED TO THE MEETING): I'm answering on the aspects concerning promoters. X launched a programme aimed at sequencing a large number of promoters. The promoting part is next to the promoting sequences. They can be reached. The programme aims at sequencing the adjacent parts, that is to say, the 5' of the cDNA. It's worked well, it's original, it was done by a researcher, Z, who used to work for the Genethon in the Y team and who did the work taken over by X. 28,000 5' sequences have been done, of which 20,000 are original. But they haven't sequenced the promoter regions yet. They'll be doing 5' until the end of the year. But they won't be doing promoting sequences.

ANOTHER SCIENTIST: I'm answering the second question. The AFM provided
    X with the neuromuscular material. It seems they focused only on the
    skeletal muscles.
ANOTHER ADMINISTRATOR: We must limit our relations with X. When are
    they going to sequence the promoter regions?
THE FIRST SCIENTIST: They're doing 5' only. The contract is only till the end
    of the year. They sold a project they couldn't do in such a short space of
    time. They bluff their way through things.
(notes taken during the board meeting, 3 October 1996)

This extract is interesting because it shows that the decisionmakers (here, the
administrators), as non-specialists, are capable of asking technical questions.
These questions are not to obtain information on the results themselves (one of
the administrators admitted after the discussion that he did not really know what
these 5' sequences were); they are asked because their answers will enable the
decisionmakers to know whether or not the actions for achieving the objectives
have been undertaken.

Apart from improvised dialogue such as the one we have highlighted
above, the AFM has progressively formalized this intermediary discourse
through what we suggest calling strategic tables. These strategic tables are to
be found in the AFM's political statements, in the synthesis it produces on the
state of the art on MD, in working documents that circulate within the association. These strategic tables list the actions to be undertaken in relation to the
targets set, the order in which they must be carried out, and possible changes
of direction to foresee, depending on the nature of the results obtained. This
schedule is often in the form of tables with numerous arrows and options.
The table used most often within the AFM and by researchers, shows how the
association starts off with patients' problems and then, after a series of successive research operations, comes back to them one day with effective
treatment. In the above dialogue, the table as such is not drawn up, but it is
easy to imagine: one witnesses a programme taking shape, aimed at systematically exploring certain entities of which the relative positions and the links
between them are described.

This intermediary discourse in the form of tables is strongly supported by the
logic of a type of research which identifies and maps entities and their modes of
action. In fact biology, at least in the fields concerned here, is very close to a
science of action, but an action that is highly diversified and sophisticated, and
that brings into play a host of varied entities which discover one another and
their functions as the investigations progress. As the research advances, the
details of the overall scenario become more and more clear. This reveals, by
contrast, the remaining grey areas. The genome map, to which the AFM is so
attached, must not be taken metaphorically (Kerr *et al.* 1997). All of the association's actions and all its energy is aimed precisely at drawing strategic maps of
the diseases, of the sequences of elements (proteins and others) linking genes to
muscles, in order to identify paths to take and obstacles to overcome. This is

what the AFM's committee is constantly striving to do, as the following short extract from a long speech by the president, on future treatments, shows:

> The problem of dystrophy clearly illustrates the difficulty of going from a gene to the physiological function. It is not enough to have the protein in order to understand its function. One also has to consider other elements such as glycoproteins or all the signals going from the outside of the cell to the inside.
>
> (SC, plenary session, 9–10 January 1993)

The emergence of this intermediary discourse – which, in particular, enables lay persons to understand and to describe genes and bodies in action – is greatly facilitated by the constant interaction between the members of the AFM and the numerous specialists cooperating with them. A scientist who judges another scientist during debates organized by the association, will talk of content (even if only to give their opinion on the relevance of choices and the quality of results) without, however, veering towards technical questions, for the aim is often to propose avenues for research so that they can be approved. The researchers who work with the AFM are thus directly involved in the formulation of this intermediary discourse. For example, during the sixth Conference on Neuromuscular Diseases organized by the AFM in 1996, most of the scientists made systematic comparisons between their own hypotheses and experimental protocols and those of colleagues working on similar subjects. The constraint of public justification imposed by the association on the researchers it finances, plays an important part in this type of event. It demands that experts jettison popularized discourse (which conveys information on science without giving its addressees the opportunity to act on it), in favor of a discourse which proposes conceivable choices and (potential) results associated with them, in the form of schedules of commitments to make.

To summarize, one could say that this intermediary discourse presents itself as a guide for action whose final objective is known – to come back to the patient with medical treatments – but whose path is tortuous and unexpected. Elements that shape this guide (projects, protocols, results of research) are not intended for public understanding of science, but for signalling the directions in which the teams supported by the association are actually moving. By discussing and revising this guide regularly with all concerned, the AFM is able to develop a strategic thinking. This does not prevent risky decisions, but it allows patients and families to formulate a judgement on these risks, depending on the objective they set up, as we will see later on with the launching of Genethon and gene therapy programmes. The capacity of this intermediary discourse to guarantee patients' ability to enter into strategic relations with specialists, is enhanced by consultancy and decisionmaking procedures implemented by the AFM for defining and monitoring a research policy for its patients. That is what we shall now consider.

The adjustment of research orientation and expertise procedures to the association's objective

During the period 1981–1998, the AFM engaged simultaneously in two logics for supporting research: a logic of exploration, and one of exploitation. Each of these logics has been linked, through trial and error, to specific forms of organization and procedure. The ways in which experts are consulted have been modified and made more complex. This evolution proves that, despite the pressure of certain SC researchers to maintain and amplify an exploration logic more in keeping with their own professional interests, the AFM board and its committee have consistently refused to relinquish any of their strategic power. The launching of Genethon in 1991, and soon after, the AFM's engagement in therapeutic research, are clear cut illustrations of this strategic power. It manifests the capacity of the association to call upon expertise procedures adjusted to the problems encountered and the projects forseen.

The separation of power between specialists and patients is inscribed in the structure of the AFM itself. Since its inception in 1958, the board of administrators has been composed either of patients' parents or of adult patients; it has no representatives, as such, from the scientific or medical professions. The reasons why professionals were originally excluded from the board of administrators are not clear. Apparently it was not a deliberate choice aimed at asserting the monopoly of parents and patients, but the consequence of an observation: at the time, there were no researchers or doctors who were involved enough for their presence to be considered essential. Furthermore, patients and their parents did not fully trust the specialists, whose competence seemed limited. Partly because the professionals were reserved, and partly because parents were not convinced that professionals were able to play a determining role, formal power was, from the outset, placed in the hands of patients and their families.[8] That was where it was to stay (Barral *et al.* 1991; Rabeharisoa and Callon 1999).

The constant assertion of the association's only *raison d'être* – the eradication of these diseases – prolongs this structural separation of power, accentuated by the perpetual use of war or military metaphors. Words such as war, struggle, battle, resistance, enemy, opponent, are omnipresent in the association's language. They form the framework for a common identity and give substance to a dynamic that has lasted for years.

From our point of view, the use of this type of language has two significant effects: first, it makes the need for a single command (that of the association) obvious; second, it suggests that the road to achieving the set goal is tortuous and that success depends on the maintenance of a sound position and the ability to take advantage of the situation and of circumstances. The AFM board and its committee, without ever neglecting their responsibility, are thus capable of opportunism and even Machiavellism. We witness a power struggle in the way they supervise researchers and practitioners, without reducing them to pure instruments of a policy imposed from the outside, which would undermine their capacity for making proposals.

A fine example of this strategic opportunism is provided by the evolution of procedures implemented by the association for defining its research and therapeutic development policy. Faced with the atomization of the medical field – which was, moreover, very restricted – the AFM initially set up a scientific council representing the different specialisms likely to be concerned. It also used calls for tenders as a tool for exploring, mobilizing, guiding and coordinating the relevant scientific communities.[9] The structure was fleshed out as the years went by, and reached maturity with the 1991 reform which defined the council's full form and ambition. The council now consists of a board of twelve directors, and of three theme-related commissions (biological, clinical and genetic), each with about ten members and a president. In its very form the scientific council, with the call for tenders as a working tool, is the locus of open exploration. It is what enabled the association, very early on, to place molecular biology alongside traditional clinical themes and, reciprocally, to maintain these themes – enhanced by progress made in other fields – when genetics officially came onto the scene. This plurality, maintained throughout the period under study, constitutes what we have called the thorough basis of the AFM's research policy, motivated by the obsession to do everything in its power and not to miss the slightest lead which could help to relieve or heal patients. The progressive creation of commissions and the putting out of general calls for tenders on neuromuscular diseases were intended to absorb the diversification of these themes, and to enable the association to constitute a scientific community around its patients.

In regular contact with researchers, through its council and calls for tenders, the association formed an opinion on the most promising avenues for moving towards treatment. This exploratory strategy, maintained throughout the period under study, also served as a basis for carefully and progressively launching major mobilization programmes – particularly those of human genome sequencing (Genethon) and gene therapy.

The decision to create Genethon for locating and identifying the genes responsible for MD, in particular, was a turning point in the history of the association. But this break with the past concerned the nature of the procedures implemented for defining and managing the AFM's research policy, rather than the policy itself. Engagement in the Genethon adventure was by no means improvised. The fruit of long preparation, it seemed to be a perpetuation of the policy of exploration and information gathering followed by the AFM in the 1980s. But this strategic continuity concealed a profound discontinuity in decision making mechanisms. For the association, regardless of the uncertainties, investment in this type of programme was a necessary choice since its only *raison d'être* was to try everything – even if it seemed risky and adventurous – to get the better of the disease. This difficult decision provided an opportunity for the AFM's administrators to become aware of the limits of the scientific council and the calls for tenders that it managed. When the time came to invest in the heavy equipment which was to automatically locate and identify the genes responsible for MD, the AFM committee found itself confronted with dissent among its community of experts. Moreover, this created a rift within the scientific council itself. Debates were stormy, for while some considered that the risk was too great, that the programme was premature and that it was better to focus on basic research; others thought it advisable to give it a try. Confronted with this divergent discourse and these clearly contradictory interests and projects, the administrators had only themselves to turn to. It was at this point that the board of administrators set up a new, informal procedure for consulting experts and for programming research, which was better suited to focusing efforts on mobilization programmes.

The Genethon is, to be sure, a research project, but it is more than that. It has technological, economic and organizational dimensions, and requires international cooperation. To assess these issues, define the main features of the programme, and launch and manage it, the AFM consulted people both within the scientific council and, above all, outside it. It thus obtained a wide range of advice and viewpoints. Faced with this change in procedure, the SC felt left out and there were rumblings of discontent. The AFM had little choice, however, for the circle of the scientific council was too limited and its members were unable to agree on important issues. It was therefore natural that, confronted with choices of which the nature and scope were changing, the association should transform the modalities of consultation with experts, without undermining the pre-eminence of the board.

This partial but profound reconfiguration of procedures became increasingly clear with the entry of the association into the era of therapeutics, announced by the AFM's president in 1993 during the scientific council plenary session. The decision was taken, despite the reluctance of several members of the council, to undertake a set of actions which would lead it to establish cooperation with several firms, to develop animal models, and to support the creation of gene therapy centres and specialized rooms for patients. The AFM also undertook research higher upstream, devoted mainly to the development of vectors for introducing genes into diseased cells. On all these projects, which have to be coherent in relation to one another and which require constant coordination with outside partners or competitors, the association is surrounded by numerous experts capable of advising it on specific aspects of the programme (legal, financial, industrial, etc.) and its various components.

The AFM considers that these actions must henceforth be judged on the strength of the overall strategy underlying them, and not on their scientific dimension alone. This will result in increasingly systematic and varied consultation with outside experts (scientists, but also firms, lawyers, financiers, etc.), and in the appointment of specialists commissioned to participate in the design and management of these programmes. The scientific council in its existing form can be of limited use only. Designed for exploratory actions, it is not equipped to run mobilization programmes, that is to say, to manage an operational logic, for evaluation and decisionmaking procedures have changed profoundly. Moreover, this operational logic which is emerging alongside the more traditional one of exploration, pervades the projects presented more classically in the framework of calls for tenders, as this extract from the Gene Therapy Commission shows:

In the field of gene therapy, projects submitted to the AFM are examined by a specialized scientific commission composed of members of the AFM SC and outside experts chosen for their competence and their involvement in the field of gene therapy. Another characteristic of the functioning of this commission is that each of its members has to assess all the applications for funds or research support. These evaluations are then synthesized and discussed, file by file, during a commission meeting.

(Gene Therapy Commission, 31 March 1994)

The formalization of this new organization, after being debated at length within the association, has now reached its conclusion. New structures have been set up, composed of a strategic council with a small number of experts with diverse competencies, and of a scientific council. The council is in charge of the commissions, which will also undergo change, and covers all fields of intervention of the association in clinical and biological research.

To summarize, one could say that the most original characteristic of the association is probably this steadfast will to inscribe, in its advisory and decisionmaking procedures, the radical alterity between its prerogatives and those of the experts.[10] The idea is thus always to be able to consult specialists, but in forms which depend on the nature of the orientations decided by its own policymakers.

Conclusion: mutual learning and reflexive organization

In recent years, several patients' associations have played a highly active role in the mobilization of clinical and biological research. Numerous studies would be required to define the full diversity of the modalities of this engagement. The aim of our research on the AFM is to assess the extent to which and the way in which the intervention of patients or their direct representatives transforms traditional models, and impacts not only on the patients themselves but also on their relations with practitioners and scientists, and indirectly on scientists' activities.

As suggested in this chapter, over the years the AFM has set up an original model of production of knowledge and research mobilization that we call "mutual learning". Patients and their families play a crucial role in the primitive accumulation of knowledge and know-how on their diseases. The fact that they are grouped together into an association is, from this point of view, decisive. Not only do they act as a driving force in the recording of information on patient populations; they also, by means of proto-instruments, put themselves in a position to produce formalized knowledge and practical know-how, collectively and in close collaboration with specialists. The setting up of tripartite structures (patients, clinicians, biologists) for work and discussion, enables them to build on learning and to circulate and evaluate results. Patients thus become both subjects and objects of research.

This enterprise does not eliminate the division of labour established between the different protagonists in this collective adventure. The knowledge produced by laboratories and doctors is specific and irreplaceable, but it is nurtured and deployed by the actions of organized patients, and irrigated by the flow of knowledge and questions they formulate. It would be wrong to say that this form of investigation and experimentation leads to different knowledge (in relation to what?), or that it has effects on the content of knowledge. It is enough to recognize that the production, dissemination and implementation of knowledge and know-how on MD requires this form of organization, and would probably be impossible without it.

The establishment of mutual learning does not, for all that, do away with the asymmetry between the board and its committee, on the one hand, and the experts – whether they are grouped into a single scientific council or spread between several internal or external bodies – on the other. During the period under study, strategic initiatives and the ability to take risks remained in the hands of the association. This body maintained its pre-eminence, but without reducing researchers to instruments of a policy defined elsewhere. We have highlighted the important role played by two elements in the establishment of this bounded autonomy. The first is the progressive constitution of an intermediary discourse which allowed the discussion and evaluation of choices made by the researchers. The second, more traditional element, is the setting up of decision-making bodies and procedures which adjust the modalities of consultation with experts in relation to the nature of the actions to develop and support.

Active participation by patients in the production of knowledge and know-how concerning them, and strategic supervision, by the association, of researchers and practitioners, are the two complementary characteristics of the model designed and tested by the AFM. Throughout this chapter, we have emphasized the importance of procedures that the AFM has invented and mobilized to give shape to this model. If we recall that co-production implies a collective action and mobilization, then the work for organizing it imposes itself as a prominent issue. But there is more in the case of the AFM. Throughout its history, the association has put a lot of effort into designing and discussing procedures, whereas few debates have occurred on the very content of its policy. From this respect, the AFM stands as a particular organization that we tentatively qualified as a "reflective organization". We would like to complete this chapter with a final comment on this point.

Since the early 1980s the AFM has clearly stated and stuck to its main policy guidelines, reflected in specific structures and procedures. Moreover, the existence of the Telethon© has imposed a demand for transparency and for public justification of the actions undertaken. In these conditions, it would be easy to believe that the association's strategic choices were debated within it, since they were so visible, explicitly expressed and claimed. Yet the archives attest to the fact that at no time was an alternative project articulated and discussed. Throughout the past two decades AFM policy has had the strength of an obvious fact. The minutes of board and committee meetings show that decisions and commitments made were the outcome of discussions and explanations that reveal very wide consensus on the content.

It would be wrong to think that this unanimity was entirely imputable to the charisma or authority of the president. On the contrary, it is primarily due to the nature of the decisions to be taken. Consider, as an example, the case of gene therapy, in which the association invested heavily in the early 1990s. It was a risky decision, huge sums of money were spent and the probabilities of failure were considerable. Whereas outside the AFM pessimistic predictions were heard from all sides, no voice within the association was raised against this gamble – which had, moreover, been prepared at length. In this case critique could be based only on very subjective hypotheses or judgments. The decision may have been risky, but it was taken in a context of profound ignorance. For further information on the realism and content of the programmes, there was no alternative but to implement them, to start experiments in order to obtain the first results. Information permitting calculated, argued and convincing decisions was the consequence of these decisions and not their condition. In such situations, where risk and ignorance progressively disappear as the programmes are launched and start to bear fruit, strategic debate on alternatives is futile, for it soon turns into a dialogue of the deaf and an ideological confrontation. To illuminate decisions the only option is to take them; that is the price to pay for obtaining information. What counts are all the procedures used to monitor the experiments, so that intermediary results can be evaluated and discussed, in a contradictory manner. This explains why the association devotes so much time and so many resources to sustained reflection on procedures, structures and organization charts, which it constantly amends. The debates, discussions and conflicts are continuous, but they focus on procedures and not on policies. We could say that a reflexive organization is one which constantly questions the procedures and tools enabling it both to learn, i.e. to accumulate competence and knowledge produced collectively, and to evaluate this competence and knowledge so as to decide on future actions to undertake. This reflexiveness through which the action is put into perspective, ends up being confused with the action itself (Knorr-Cetina 1996). We would suggest that reflexiveness is at the core of organizations that are capable of mobilizing resources for redefining their own identity, by entering into sustained dialogue with their environment, and inventing and implementing new forms of co-production.

Acknowledgements

We wish to thank the AFM for its support and openness, and for its help in consulting its archives. We also wish to thank Catherine Barral, Nicolas Dodier, Florence Paterson, Janine Bardot, Duana Fullwiley, Alain Kauffman, Paul Rabinow and Bénédicte Rousseau, as well as the anonymous referees, for their comments and suggestions.

Notes

1 They represent about 10 per cent of the 40,000 families concerned with the hundred MDs identified so far by the WHO.
2 A TV fund-raising event inspired by North American telethons.
3 Paterson and Barral (1994) have studied the history of the AFM from 1958 to 1981. Their work has provided extremely valuable insights into the early dynamics of the association. It was in 1981 that the AFM begun to inscribe support for research into its very structure. Its scientific council (SC) was set up in this year.
4 As we know, visualization and inscription are essential in the production and certification of scientific facts (Latour 1995).
5 According to a researcher-clinician, medical students receive no more than two hours of training in neuromuscular diseases.
6 For the complete demonstration of this point, see Rabeharisoa and Callon 1999.
7 I.e. five prime.
8 The authors: "Why were there no doctors on the first board of administrators, apart from the parents of patients who happen to be doctors?". Mrs De Kepper: "We didn't want them". She then added after a moment of hesitation: "We probably thought they were too ignorant. And then, it just turned out that way!" (interview with Mr and Mrs De Kepper, 15 October 1996).
9 The list of research themes publicized with the general call for tenders in 1988 illustrates this mechanism:

   (i)   the heart and muscular diseases: clinical and biological aspects;

   (ii) mitochondrions and muscular diseases: clinical and biological aspects;

   (iii) molecular genetics and Duchenne's disease, Becker's disease, and other neuromuscular diseases;

   (iv) genetic map of neuromuscular diseases with genes that have not been located;

   (v) nerve–muscle interactions and muscle regeneration;

   (vi) biochemistry of proteins (surface antigens, membrane proteins, rare proteins, receptors, growth factors);

   (vii) pharmacology: experimental models and human applications.

   (SC, 24 May 1988)

10 We must stress this separation that the AFM is able to maintain between the advice that experts lavish on it and the decisions that it takes for its patients, by way of the original procedures it sets up. This in no way resembles the situation described by Carricaburu (1993) in respect of the French Haemophiliacs' Association. There, the system of co-option of doctor-advisors, the auxiliary medical role assumed by the patients, and the friendship between doctors and their patients, end up making any critical thinking as regards new and uncertain situations impossible (in that case, possible contamination by the AIDS virus).

9 Circumscribing expertise

Membership categories in courtroom testimony

Michael Lynch

Abstract concepts like "science" and "expert" are subject to varied academic and ordinary usage. When considered as names for worldly things, the words "science" and "expert" denote, respectively, a modern social institution and an agent (person or professional body) accredited with specialized knowledge. However, especially when used as adjectives, "scientific" and "expert" convey evaluations: they are used to claim or confer special status for activities, agents and agencies, statements, and evidences. The words "expert" and "science"/"scientific" are indexical expressions (Bar Hillel 1954; Garfinkel and Sacks 1970). When used under different circumstances, such expressions hold highly variable meanings and pragmatic implications. Moreover, "science", "scientific", "scientist" and "expert" are *membership categories* (Sacks 1972): in many formal and informal situations they are used tendentiously to claim or confer authority and credibility. In circumstances in which potential incumbents of such categories confront others who are in a position to accept, contest or deny membership, it becomes apparent that *calling* someone an "expert" or *accepting* a statement as "scientific" involves concrete (and sometime contestable) courses of action and interaction. The use of these words, and the performance of relevant actions to contextualize their use, is not simply a cognitive process of extending conceptual categories to cover new cases.

Formal definitions and rules of use (whether provided by dictionaries or legal statutes and precedents) can only take us a certain distance when we aim to appreciate the social significance of "science" and "expert". For all their pleasures and advantages, scholarly analyses, and even reflective inventories of "ordinary" usage, are likely to miss the surprising moves generated in lively occasions of interaction. Armchair analysis – even when oriented to the "ordinary" – limits the imagination in some ways while it licenses it in others. Consequently, an examination of "actual" occasions of action and interactions (or their tape-recorded and transcribed proxies) can be useful, not – or not only – as a means of access to real worldly social activities, but as an "aid to a sluggish imagination" (Garfinkel 1967: 38). A distinctive empirical, though not empiricist, orientation – akin to the phenomenological herald calling us "to the things themselves" – is implied in a painstaking examination of just how actions related to the great themes of epistemology are performed on singular occasions. In previous work (Lynch 1993), I have dubbed these themes "epistopics" – recurrent topics of epistemological reflection and debate, respecified ethnographically in terms of practices performed in singular organizational circumstances. Peter Dear (2001) makes a similar recommendation – with more of a methodological accent – with his neologism "epistemography", signalling an historiographic or ethnographic orientation to the themes of epistemology: observation, knowledge, truth, experience, interpretation, and so on. Along these lines, the present chapter examines some uses of the categories "expert" and "scientist" in testimony during the appeal case (*R. v. Deen*). The study examines the local articulation and circumscription of vocabularies that, when viewed as "concepts", have fundamental significance for law and social science.

In this examination of excerpts from the *Deen* transcript, we shall pay close attention to the local work of articulating and circumscribing categorical terms and fields of "expertise". Although deploying relevant linguistic concepts, specified in terms of a legal background of definitions and precedents, such local interactional work is *pre-conceptual*, in the sense that it is more nuanced, less stable, and less fixed to textual reference points. To say that such work is pre-conceptual does not imply that it is based in cognitive "preconceptions" about science and expertise that are unconscious, confused, and in need of clarification by a more rigorous legal or social science definition.[1] Instead, it means that such usage exhibits an intelligibility that is not readily contained in the conceptual glossaries of law or social science. And yet, at the same time, such usage informs us, and the courts, about what we are talking about when we use the words "expert" and "science" as social concepts or legal categories.[2]

In terms of the co-productionist idiom, the instances described in this paper involve *the co-production of expert and non-expert domains of knowledge*. Following Latour's (1987) original coinage, "co-production" usually is referenced to distinctions between nature and society, or natural facts and political machinations. Accordingly, when the scientific and technological innovations are examined "in action" – before uncertainties and controversies about them become resolved – there is no clear separation between "technical" or "natural" factors and "social" or "political" factors. Indeed, talk of any "factors" is premature until the dust settles. The idiom also has affinity with Foucault's (1980) conception of power/knowledge: the idea that disciplinary orders not only "reflect" the ideas of historical control freaks and serve to repress the powers of the body and spirit, but that they provide conditions for the production of "scientific" (centrally administered) knowledge of, and about, human subjects; including knowledge viewed as liberating. Co-production can be applied usefully to other distinctions, such as the law-science distinction. As Jasanoff (1995) demonstrates, science not only supplies cadres of experts who assist the law in its effort to resolve and regulate technical matters; law becomes deeply intertwined with the production of science, technology and medicine. Not only does law interact with (or, as some would have it, interfere with) activities in scientific, technological and medical fields; it frames innovation, influences experimental protocols, and even provides problems and incentives for innovative research. In this paper, the co-production idiom is shifted to yet another practical-conceptual field: the co-production of stable categories (expert, science) and instances of those categories (a particular expert witness, a specific field credited with, or denied, status as a science).

Many expert witnesses are identified as, and identify with, the legal-epistemic category of "science": they claim or disclaim expertise in particular fields of science; and together with their interlocutors they articulate how they stand *with* science and *as* experts. For those who like to think in structuralist terms, the axes of co-production are comprised, first, by the legal/epistemic (and even ritual) categories of "expert" witness and "scientist", and, second, by the moves, claims and disclaimers that play on (and off of) those categories, their immediate relevancies, and their longer-term implications. Neither axis is sufficient on its own; instead, the legal/epistemic categories (expert, scientist) and interactional production of testimony come together in the production of a *case*. The case is a site of co-production that interweaves legal categories, and their normative implications, with the indexical expressions and interactional manoeuvres of participants in a courtroom hearing.

Situated vocabularies and legal boundary work

As C. Wright Mills (1940) pointed out in the case of the social-psychological (and legal) concept of "motive", the banal observation that "motive", "motives" and "motivation" are commonplace *words* has far-reaching theoretical implications for professional disciplines that endow those words with conceptual significance. Anticipating the linguistic turn in philosophy, Mills advocated a shift in sociological perspective from a treatment of "motives" as a technical term referring to substantive "springs of action" to be elucidated through empirical research and incorporated into causal social-psychological models, to an empirical examination of situationally-specific uses of "vocabularies of motive" to assign blame, offer excuses, or publicly justify or discredit actions.[3]

Studies of communicative actions that followed through with the shift in perspective that Mills advocated never became a dominant perspective in the social sciences (Mills himself did not follow through in his later work), but they did provide a persistent counterpoint to the predominant structural and technical trends in sociology. In the late twentieth century, studies inspired by pragmatist, phenomenological, and ordinary language philosophies provided alternatives to the combination of functionalist theory and survey methodology that dominated sociology in mid-century. Harold Garfinkel (1967) developed an entire research programme – ethnomethodology – that investigated ordinary, pragmatic and constitutive uses of expressions associated with sociology, epistemology and formal law. An entire roster of fundamental concepts – method, meaning, evidence, action, structure, reasons, rationality, reality, fact, etc. – became open to respecification (Garfinkel 1991). Instead of defining these terms and treating them as key theoretical and methodological concepts for a social science, ethnomethodologists examined how they were deployed in ordinary conversations and organizationally situated activities such as jury deliberations, courtroom hearings, classrooms, meetings, and so forth. After such research got underway, it became common to draw a contrast between studies that deployed key terms as stable, more or less well-defined, theoretical concepts and method- ological variables, and studies that described situated, *ad hoc* and "negotiated" uses of those terms. In polemical contests that surfaced from time to time, proponents of structural theories and quantitative methods sometimes expressed exasperation with the way an emphasis on situated actions and vocabularies seemed to divest sociology of its stable conceptual and methodological tools, while "interactionist" or "interpretive" sociologists sometimes seemed to disdain the very idea of formal social structures as well as the "objective reality" that structural terms supposedly stood for.[4]

To return to the terms introduced earlier – "expert" and "science"/"scien- tific" – we can begin to appreciate opposing perspectives when we contrast a referential use of these terms as standing for real-worldly statuses and institutions with a contingent, flexible and interactional use of such words in situated discourse. Contrary to earlier efforts to demarcate science from non-science or to define science as a distinct and autonomous institution, it has become common- place in social studies of science to disavow any possibility of giving "science" a stable definition that distinguishes "it" from non-science. Instead, it is more common to follow Tom Gieryn's (1999) advice to study the science/non-science distinction as a conceptual resource that is used flexibly, and is resolved contin- gently, in historical and contemporary situations of "boundary work". Understood in terms of the co-productionist idiom, boundary work does not simply trace or re-trace a "line" that is already inscribed at the boundary between science and non-science; it is more like a "line in the sand" that contentiously, provocatively, and sometimes successfully, divides science from its "other".

The theme of "boundary work" provides a compromise, of sorts, between an orientation to the objective, social-structural, existence of science and a radical relativist denial of any such (institutional) *thing* that goes by that name. Gieryn's cartographic metaphor invites us to imagine that there are relatively settled terri- tories or "states" in which science is an established and uncontested (if not exclusive) public identity. These states are bordered by frontiers, battlefronts and demilitarized zones in which efforts to claim the territory in the name of science are fiercely contested. The territorial arrangements, contested margins and lines of demarcation are institutional (or socially constructed) realities that frame and inflect what we call "sciences" and "scientific" matters. The sociologist's task, for Gieryn, is to survey the territories and write chronicles of the boundary disputes. Such chronicles can establish how currently established conceptual and institu- tional territories owed their formation and current stability to a history of colonial ventures, uneasy truces, revolutions and schisms, as well as an array of covert and *ad hoc* arrangements.

Legal proceedings – especially in an adversary setting – can seem ready-made occasions for examining boundary work;[5] indeed, notable cases can be viewed as spectacles of boundary work which provide vivid public tutorials on the flexible and contentious way in which parties negotiate the boundaries between science and non-science, and expert and non-expert knowledge (Jasanoff 1990; 1995; 1998). It can be argued that the very idea of boundary work is internal to legal traditions in which borderline cases are resolved in terms of settled bodies of concepts and statutory definitions. The categories of "expert", "science" and "scientist" are contested in adversary trials, appeals and admissibility hearings, especially when one or both parties to the hearing call expert witnesses. Studies of landmark cases, for example of the US Supreme Court decisions in *Daubert v. Merrell Dow Pharmaceuticals, Inc.*[6] and *Kumho Tire v. Carmichael*,[7] elucidate the conceptual ambiguities and competing interests involved in court efforts to define and apply the categories of "expert" and "science" (Jasanoff 1995; Edmond 2002). At the same time, these studies (together with the *Daubert* court's, and later courts', accounts of the decision) make clear that landmark decisions and rules of evidence provide trial judges with considerable latitude in their "gatekeeping" role. More generally, in any given case in which experts (particularly, experts who purport to represent a science) are vetted and interrogated – whether in an admissibility hearing held in a US state or federal court that recognizes *Daubert*, or a hearing, trial or appeal held under different standards in the US or another country – the categories of "expert" and "science" can be subjected to a considerable degree of free play that is not predicated upon statutory definitions, legal precedents, judicial guidelines and rules.

Membership categories

Membership categories are embedded in ordinary as well as technical language-use. They are expressed through words, but they do more than assign names to objects. "Science", for example, is not *just* a name for an institutional entity. A distinctive form of insight can be gained by examining just how this word is used and what hinges upon its use. This shift in perspective is not necessarily incommensurable with viewing science as an institution; indeed, it is a way to get purchase on the kind of institution it is. "Science" (along with related terms like "scientist", "scientific", "scientific knowledge", "expert" and "expertise") is an instance of what Harvey Sacks (1979) once called a "members' category". It is a distinctive kind of "actor's" category. Not only is it a category used by persons in a society to classify things, people and activities; it is an expression that *incumbents* of the category use in reference to *themselves* and their activities. In many contexts, "science" is more than a label; it is a term of praise and a mark of privilege. Persons whom others call "scientists" are likely to be happy to use the same term self-referentially;[8] more likely, for example, to identify with that term than with the vernacular expression "boffin".[9] Indeed, a "scientist" can often express a strong investment in the "correct" use of the category (for example, objecting to appropriations of the term "scientist" by unqualified persons and groups).

Not all membership categories are also *members'* categories. A members' category like "mother", when used in association with the category "family", is available to incumbents as well as others (including administrative agencies) who classify the incumbent. In contrast, the terms "schizophrenic", "child abuser", "terrorist", "alcoholic" and "moron" can be used to classify a person in a way that they are likely to resist. Bureaucratic agencies (sometimes staffed by former members or members "in remission") sometimes struggle to get members to accept membership in vernacular, moral, and/or administrative categories typically controlled by non-members. Except, perhaps, when maternity is disputed or disclaimed, no such struggle is necessary when a "mother" is required to register herself as such.[10] Other terms tend to be favoured by members of a category, but not by outsiders and administrative authorities.[11] There are many nuances, systematic changes and instabilities associated with the interplay of insider and outsider control of vernacular categories. For example, vernacular expressions used by non-members to insult others can be used by (presumed) members in a playful way, and even as a term of endearment. History and politics are often explicitly at stake when presumed members and non-members employ, avow, disavow or revalue categories like "gay" and "queer". Currently, we tend to be acutely aware of the non-equivalent pragmatic and political connotations of the words "woman", "lady" and "female".[12]

Close studies of interactional and pragmatic uses of membership categories show that the effective use of such categories is much more than a matter of employing a label, sign or symbol to assign a social, occupational, moral or legal status to an incumbent. Erving Goffman (1959) observed with regard to symbols of status that titles and terms of address like "Doctor", "General" or "Your Majesty" are controlled and supported by networks of rights and obligations, corroborative supports and credentials, and administrative tests. For some of the more tightly controlled membership categories it is possible, but not very easy, for an impostor to "pass" without being noticed. In the case of the family of terms associated with science (and the related, but not identical, term "expert"), the assignment of persons, activities and facts to that category has well known strategic advantages, and thus efforts are made to control such assignment.[13]

Law courts proceed case-by-case, but they relate the details of each case to events outside the courtroom, and they use relatively stable procedures and principles of interpretation. The courts are thus responsible for determining the significance of events and placing them in history.[14] With regard to questions about science and expertise, the courts make reference to rules of evidence and bodies of law, while bringing them to bear upon the unique circumstances of a case at hand. Courts also express and rely upon conventional understandings of what counts as expert, scientific and legal knowledge. These are performative as well as interpretative relations, because a given court's way of handing a singular case goes on record and can have lasting consequences. Subsequently, judges, lawyers, journalists and scholars, when pursuing an appeal, searching for precedents or conducting historical research, are able to consult the record. The literary residues of courtroom orality take on a life of their own, and feed back into case-by-case judgments. Cases in which science and expertise are prominent provide an especially apt setting for examining the situated articulation of written definitions, rules of evidence and precedents for assigning persons and activities to the categories of "expert" and "science".

"Scientist" and "expert" as legal membership categories

The categories of "science", "scientist", "expert" and "scientific expert" are perspicuous in criminal cases involving DNA profiling. Courts establish local relations between "science" and "the state" whenever they designate witnesses as "experts" and relevant areas of activity as "scientific". Moreover, as we shall see, expert testimony articulates limits, and otherwise situates itself within court-specific understandings of "science" and "expertise". Disputes that arise in particular cases indicate that "scientific expertise" is not simply a matter of reproducing a witness's relation to established epistemic categories; it involves an element of casuistry that lends creative flexibility, and occasional instability, to the relevant categorical relations.

In the Anglo-American courts, science is a type of expertise and scientists are one type of expert witness.[15] Expert witnesses need not be scientists, but an identity as a scientist in a recognized discipline virtually qualifies a witness as an expert on relevant matters. (What exactly is "recognized" and "relevant" in a particular case can, of course, be contested.) One of the jobs the courts perform is to classify particular activities as "scientific" and to recognize particular witnesses as "scientific experts". The courts distinguish "scientific" and "expert" knowledge from the trier of fact's presumptive capacity to make "common sense" judgments about the elements of a particular case. So, for example, in a traffic court it is assumed that the presiding judge need not have studied Einstein's theory of relativity in order to resolve a discrepancy between a police officer's and a motorist's accounts of the speed of the motorist's car at a particular place and time.[16]

"Expert" is a special category of witness, and "scientist" is a special category of "expert". Both formal and informal privileges are associated with the testimony of these types of witness. Among the formal privileges is the right to give "hearsay" testimony on behalf of members in a relevant profession or field of expertise. Informal privilege arises from lay participants' deference to the specialized education, training and experience of a recognized expert, all of which can make it difficult for the non-specialist to understand, let alone to contest, the basis for the expert's judgments. When expert testimony is uncontested jurors may accept it as indisputable fact, and when it is contested jurors may become confused by contradictory expert claims. Like other marks of special privilege and status, "expertise" is subject to administrative controls and checks against misuse. In a trial court, the authorization of expertise is internal to the trial, but like the evidence presented in a trial, such authorization calls into play public credentials, records, tests and standards of judgment which are presumed to be intelligible to non-specialists and which refer beyond the immediate circumstances of the trial to relatively stable identities and organizational matters in a world at large.

In the courts, and in the criminal justice system more generally, scientific and expert identities are embodied in administrative documents. The adversary dialogues in the court can discount, destabilize, and pursue the implications of such identities. For example, the curriculum vitae of Professor Houseman, the MIT scientist who was an expert for the defence in *Florida v. Andrews*, provided a record of a large number of publications and other conventional indicators of high academic standing. However, the document was not simply submitted for the record, it became the subject of a ritual production in the courtroom. In the following instance, a prosecutor is requesting that the court recognize "Professor Houseman" as a witness for the prosecution:

Q: Professor Houseman, I will show you what's been marked for identifi-
         cation purposes as State's exhibit A and ask you to look at it and tell
         me if you recognize it. Tell me what it is, sir?
A: Yes, sir, I will. This document is what is called my curriculum vitae.
         This represents the activities, professionally, that I have been engaged
         in since receiving my degree. And it indicates the list of publications in
         the field of genetics that I have published under my name.[17]

In this instance, the CV is discursively framed as an "exhibit". Moreover, the designation of it as "exhibit A" identifies it as a *first* exhibit in a series. The attorney's instruction "will you look at it and tell me if you recognize it" places the exhibit in a series of other evidence exhibits which is likely to include things like photographs, memos and physical objects (e.g. an item of bloody clothing, a murder weapon, etc.). The CV is thus placed in a series of things with which it otherwise might seem to have little in common. Note that the witness is specifi- cally instructed to "tell" the court, not only "if" he recognizes the exhibit, but also to state aloud "what it is". The witness then gives a name for the exhibit – specifically designating it as a "document" with a conventional name, "curriculum vitae" – and he specifies what it "represents". The attorney had referred to the witness as "Professor", so that Professor Houseman's reference to "my degree" can be heard as a reference to a Ph.D. The witness further specifies the relevance of *professional* activities, a list of *publications*, and the field of *genetics*. This simple ritualistic exchange thus identifies the witness with a public, docu- mented constellation, or network, of categorical references: "Professor Houseman" assigns an academic rank (and a recognizably high one) to the witness; the "degree" associates the rank with an educational credential, the "professional activities" and the "publications" are headers for a list of academic and research activities, and "the field of genetics" identifies the relevant domain of those activities. Moreover, the ritual exchange establishes that the witness himself explicitly *testifies* to his incumbency in the relevant set of categories, and to the authenticity of the CV as a document.

All of this should seem obvious – indeed, I take it that the exchange was *produced* to be obvious. Something else also should seem obvious: the categorical references used in the exchange are "ordinary". Genetics may be a specialized field, but the word "genetics" is commonplace (far more commonplace than technical terms used by geneticists like "oligonucleotide" or even "amino acid"). Few of us would be able to comprehend the titles (let alone the contents) of Professor Houseman's publications, but we should be expected to recognize that he has a long list of them. What is not so ordinary is the way "curriculum vitae" is linked to a series of exhibits in a trial, or the way "Professor Houseman" is asked to "look at" and "recognize" his CV as a court-specific object. Moreover, Professor Houseman's identity is distinctively shaped through a juxtaposition of references that make some, but not others, of his attributes relevant. The ritual dialogue *makes* relevant that he is a professor with publications in the field of genetics, but nothing is said about his marital status, where he grew up, or what he does for recreation, though such matters could be made relevant. For the present, his identity and relevant activities are framed in a locally (and institutionally) distinct way, and yet the terms that establish his identity and relevant activities refer to categories which are conventional, public, and otherwise trans-situational.

Note, however, that the adversary setting provides an opportunity to recontextualize what, in this case, might seem to be a self-evident record of impressive expertise. For the court, the key issue is the *relevance* of those credentials to the case at hand. For example, during the summary phase of *Florida v. Andrews*, the defence attorney referred to Professor Houseman's "impressive" credentials, but then proposed that Houseman had a vested interest in the promotion of DNA profiling techniques.

> I would suggest by that that while Doctor Houseman's credentials are impressive, to say the least, that he is not a totally dispassionate, totally disinterested member of the scientific community and may well have a career interest in having this test determined to be reliable by coincidence, since he also draws his paycheck by virtue of doing five to ten of these a week. And if the test were not found to be reliable, he might well suffer some career damage from that.[18]

This argument did not carry the day, and Andrews was convicted, but it illustrates how disputants attempt to invert or undermine conventional administrative indicators. It is also relevant that the attorney makes use of the Mertonian (Merton 1973) normative category of "disinterestedness", treating it as an absolute standard for assessing Professor Houseman's credibility as a scientific witness. In another case (*New Jersey v. Williams*) a defence attorney similarly associated the impressive knowledge and weighty CV of a prosecution witness with a vested interest (in this case the witness is Henry Erlich of Cetus Corporation, a co-inventor of PCR): "if a juror cannot quite understand allele drop-out or mixed samples, the issue should not be admitted because Dr. Erlich wears a five hundred dollar suit and has a CV four pounds in weight".[19] The attorney draws the analogy between an expensive suit (not a lawsuit in this instance) and a weighty CV to express scepticism about their relation to credible knowledge. Not incidentally, the analogy encourages class resentment by associating a knowledge gap (Collins 1988) with a socio-economic gap between Erlich and the jurors. Again, this argument apparently did not persuade the jury. Unless such challenges are made, and made successfully, the conventional indicators can stand proxy for the "expert" and "scientific" identities they denote. However, such challenges can alert us to aspects of the local production of expertise which do not follow from the formal credentials of a witness.

Circumscribing expertise in testimony

A more elaborated "CV ritual" is presented in an exchange of questions and answers at the beginning of the direct testimony of an expert witness (Peter Donnelly) in the appeal of the trial court's guilty verdict in *R. v. Deen* (1993).[20] *Deen* was a rape case involving multiple victims and suspects in the Manchester area. In 1989, a semen sample (referred to as a "swab") was recovered during the examination of one of the victims. Andrew Philip Deen later was arrested and the police took a sample of his blood. DNA analysis of the swab and blood samples was conducted using the multi-locus probe (MLP) technique invented by Alec Jeffreys of the University of Leicester, and marketed under the name "DNA fingerprinting" by Cellmark Diagnostics. This was the first DNA profiling technique to be used in criminal justice work. Professor Peter Donnelly, a statistician and proponent of Bayesian analysis, testified for the defence and raised a number of challenges to the DNA analysis used by the prosecution. The following sequence ensued shortly after Professor Donnelly was sworn in during the appeal. He is questioned in direct examination by Deen's barrister, Michael Mansfield, QC:

Q: Professor Donnelly, first of all in terms of qualifications, you are a Bachelor of Science with a First Class Honours Degree from the University of Queensland?

A: Yes.

Q: A Doctor of Philosophy, from the University of Oxford?

A: Yes.

Q: Since 1988, you have held the Chair of Mathematical Statistics in Operational Research at Queen Mary and Westfield College in the University of London?

A: Yes.

Q: You are a Chartered Statistician in the Royal Statistical Society?

A: Yes.

Q: Have you been elected as a member of the International Statistical Institute?

A: Yes.

Q: And there are other memberships, but I shall not go through them, relating to statistics. Clearly you have been engaged over the years in research, is that right?

A: Yes.

Q: And one of the particular and major areas of your research has concerned the application of probability and statistics to genetics?

A: That is correct.

Q: And you have published a large number of papers – in the region of thirty – in scientific journals; half of those have been concerned with that issue?

A: That is correct.

Q: Since the middle of 1990, has your group, and the members of your research group, been concerned with the statistical aspects of DNA profiling?

A: That is correct.

Q: Are you in receipt of two research grants from the Science and Engineering Research Council which specifically relate to the area again of population genetics?

A: That is correct.

Q: And as it is very current – in fact today – you are the joint organizer of the Royal Society Discussion Meeting on mathematical and statistical aspects of DNA and protein sequence analysis?

A: I am.

Q: That is where you should have been today, is that right?

A: Yes.

This dialogue – up until the last two questions about the Royal Society meeting – can be read as a form of "transcription" from one textual register to another. Instead of simply designating the CV as a textual exhibit, barrister and witness perform a duet: the barrister orally recites a series of CV items, and the witness confirms each of them with an unelaborated "Yes". or "That is correct". Donnelly's tokens of agreement are not incidental, as they declare that he acknowledges, and thus takes responsibility for the accuracy of, each of the items recited. The sequence is transcribed by the court reporter as part of the official record of the case, so that the text of the CV is re-written in the form of the above dialogue. The reading of the CV is more than a matter of transferring information from one textual register to another, as it elaborates upon a selected sequence of items and specifically marks their relevance for other court partici-pants (most significantly, a panel of appeal court judges). The sequence is interesting, when considered as a progressive *assembly* of the witness' relevant identity. The recitation starts with educational credentials conventionally placed at the beginning of an academic CV: credentials that have generic significance for a wide variety of institutional readings of the document. It continues with a statement about the witness's current position, and then specifies his membership in apparently exclusive and honorific statistical societies. From the point at which the questioner says "And there are other memberships, but I shall not go through them",[21] the recitation becomes progressively more focused on immediately rele-vant aspects of Donnelly's expertise. One can imagine a kind of homing-in operation, starting with "broader" academic credentials and fields, and then moving gradually to narrower fields of application: statistics; probability and statistics in genetics; statistical aspects of DNA profiling; and population genetics.[22] The questioner not only mentions Donnelly's involvement in these fields, he designates impersonal items of record (presumably recorded on the CV). Each one of these items designates Donnelly's membership, research record, and public recognition in particular fields. The zooming-in operation proceeds through a selected recitation of listed CV items: professional associations, publications and grants. There is also a temporal aspect of this operation, which is evident in the final reference to the Royal Society meeting Donnelly had organized for "today" on "mathematical and statistical aspects of DNA and protein sequence analysis". This mention effectively identifies Donnelly with a prestigious, highly pertinent and up-to-date event, and also makes evident that he has interrupted his academic schedule in order to appear in the court.

The ritual presentation of the CV displays for the court an array of general social categories. The CV is evidence in its own right. It is also a document of institutionally specific identities that are relevant to the case at hand. In this case, the CV ritual lends special authority to what a particular "expert" will be allowed to testify. The remainder of this paper goes into less ritualistic[23] aspects of testimony that display and circumscribe "expert" identities.

As noted earlier, Goffman (1959) points out that legal and professional standards and tests are designed to control membership in restricted social categories. Some membership categories can be impersonated with impunity, whereas others are more strictly controlled. This is a complicated matter, and not just a question of the rank, status or desirability conventionally assigned to the category. It is illegal in some circumstances for a sighted person to pretend to be blind, for an ineligible vehicle to park in a "handicapped" space, or for a wealthy person to claim the "rights" of the impoverished (for example, to be eligible for earned income tax credit under US tax law). "Expert witness" is a privileged category. Whether or not the controls over incumbency in that category are rigorous, or rigorous enough, is a matter of some dispute (Huber 1991). In North American and British courts, tests are necessarily limited to what an expert witness can quickly and conveniently show to a non-expert audience (non-expert in the particular field of expertise).[24] In many cases, witnesses are accepted as experts in fields of science on the basis of educational credentials, professional certificates and other documentation of "experience" in the relevant fields. Employment in a university or research lab and a record of publications in refereed journals are often treated as sufficient evidence of scientific expertise. In the US, UK, Canada and other nations, individual witnesses (including expert witnesses) can be subject to a *Voir Dire* examination of relevant credentials. In US state and federal law, fields of expertise are themselves subjected to tests in admissibility hearings under the *Frye* "general acceptance" standard, or the list of factors specified in the *Daubert* decision. These tests have been the subject of widespread discussion and debate, which I will not go into here (see Jasanoff 1995).

Aside from formal credentials and criteria for deciding whether a person is an "expert" or a type of evidence is based on "science", the expertise of a person and the scientific standing of their field also may be tested during the trial phase of a hearing, especially during cross-examination. Such discursively situated tests are endogenous to the courts, but they also make use of documents that originate from other institutions. Moreover, the courts rely upon conventional judgments about expertise and science that they presume are shared by a broad public.

An examination of testimony can illuminate how expert authority and credibility are circumscribed and subject to distinctive forms of undermining in the courts. It is important to keep in mind that interrogation is a *dialogical production* that is supervened by a non-participating (or, in the case of a judge and the adversary attorney, occasionally participating) audience. An organizational feature of testimony, which has been called *conditional relevance* (Schegloff 1968), distinguishes utterances in dialogue from monological statements, propositions or pronouncements. Conditional relevance means that the sense and relevance of an utterance depends upon its placement in an unfolding dialogue composed of utterances produced by at least two parties.[25] No single party controls the dialogue, and the records, reports and narratives that arise from the dialogue do not reflect the hand (or mouth) of a single author, although some have more control than others. For example, an interrogator asks questions and often demands that the witness limit replies to simple "yes" or "no" answers. The interrogator may try to get the witness to confirm a series of statements (minimally formatted as questions, or quietly accepted by the court, and even transcribed, as though they were questions). Lines of related questions build up, step-by-step into monological arguments or narratives, but the production and logical implications of such lines are contingent upon the witness's compliance to the terms of each question, as well as the audience's possible (not always demonstrated) understanding of their sense and relevance.[26]

Particular sequences of interrogation demonstrate that the court's acceptance of a witness as an expert in a particular field is not the end of the story. Both interrogators and witnesses do a great deal of work to circumscribe just how the witness is or is not "qualified" and "experienced". For example, in the *Deen* case, Professor Donnelly is asked the following question during direct examination:

Q: Is there research indicating that when you take known samples from the same individual, you may not get the same [DNA] profile?
A: I am not well placed to comment on research. I have heard forensic scientists, including Professor Jeffreys, give evidence of this.

(Donnelly goes on to say that "people with expertise in the field" sometimes agree and sometimes do not agree about the possibility of getting different DNA profiles when analysing known samples from the same individual. His references to such "experts" makes clear that he is not one of them. By disclaiming expertise about forensic lab procedures, he circumscribes his own expertise on statistical matters. Such circumscription of expertise is picked up at the beginning of Donnelly's cross-examination by Mr Shorrock for the Crown.)

Q: Professor Donnelly, first of all I would like to explore with you the different role that you play as a statistician from the genetic scientist or forensic scientist in these cases. Do you understand?

A: Yes.

Q: You are not a microbiologist, are you?

A: No.

Q: You are not a forensic scientist?

A: No.

Q: You are not a genetic scientist?

A: No. I suggest I have expertise in population genetics, or certainly I do research in that field, so it depends a bit on what you mean by genetic scientist. There is a whole range there from people who do experiments with DNA – I certainly don't have expertise in that area – to people who ask questions about genes and gene frequency and evolution, and that in fact is a major area of my research.

Q: Scientists in all fields, forensic scientists, microbiologists, microchemists, use statistics as a tool, do they not?

A: In many fields, yes.

Q: So they have a working knowledge of statistics as part of their trade and training?

A: To a varying degree, yes.

Q: That clearly is the case in this art of interpreting the DNA profiles. It is necessary to have a working knowledge of statistics?

A: Ideally, yes. I am in some difficulty because some of the things that have been said and some aspects of the models that have been used suggest that the people using them do not have what I would regard as satisfactory knowledge.

Q: Someone like Professor Alan (*sic*) Jeffreys, he is not a statistician?

A: No.

Q: But he uses statistical models to explain and evaluate his science?

A: Yes, and in some cases he gets it right and in some cases he gets it wrong.

Q: We will come back to that in a moment. So far as the forensic scientist is concerned, he is the person who prepares the blot, does the methodology that their Lordships have been told about. You have no experience at all of that?

A: No.

Q: Presumably you are not able to say whether a band is independent or not?

A: Independent of what?

Q: The bands in a particular profile are independent or not?

A: With respect, that is exactly a statistical issue. That is something that can only be assessed by looking at data.

Q: Is it? You see, this is where you and I, I suspect, begin to part company. Is it not, apart from being a statistical matter, a matter for the experience of the reporting officer and the scientist, using his collective experience and day-to-day knowledge and doing these things week in and week out?

A: The only way one can assess whether bands are independent is to look in the population and see whether possession of bands are independent within members of the population. Now, if the person you are speaking about has done that, then they are entitled to say they are independent. But that is not something one would gain knowledge about from looking at particular DNA profiles.

Donnelly's disclaimers of expertise appear to authorize his credibility in the field of "statistics", but the cross-examination brings out some interesting ambiguities on this point. Shorrock begins with a series of questions of similar design, each of which invites Donnelly to disclaim expertise in a named field (microbiology, forensic science, genetics). Interestingly, each of these questions is a negative version of the opening lines of the direct examination we discussed earlier. Where Mansfield earlier had asked Donnelly to confirm his membership in a series of relevant categories, Shorrock now asks him to confirm that he is *not* a member of another series of relevant categories. Both series of questions work progressively to situate Donnelly's expertise within an ecology of categories. The lines of question differentially exhibit, circumscribe and articulate the relevance of his testimony to the case at hand. These lines of interrogation are preliminary, not only because they occur at the start of the witness's direct and cross-examination, but also because they set up the relevance and significance of the "expert" testimony that will follow. The evident differences between Mansfield's and Shorrock's lines of question make perspicuous how such placement in an ecology of relevant, and broadly familiar, "expert" categories is contingent upon the local, and adversary, dialogue that constitutes the trial.

After Donnelly speaks up for his expertise in a sub-field of genetics (population genetics), Shorrock then begins another line of interrogation suggesting that scientists in a series of fields (including forensic scientists) develop a "working knowledge" of statistics. He mentions "the art" of interpreting DNA profiles, and he emphasizes the role of practical experience. In this instance, Shorrock suggests that knowledge invested in personal experience (related to the theme of tacit knowledge) should be held in higher esteem than formal knowledge.[27] Donnelly gives qualified answers to the effect that forensic scientists (and even academic scientists, such as Sir Alec Jeffreys, who was knighted for the invention of the DNA profile technique used in the case) sometimes get the statistics right and sometimes do not. Things get troublesome for Shorrock when he mentions a substantive judgment about the independence of bands, which he suggests requires "working knowledge". Donnelly counters by reclaiming the basis of such judgment for his own statistical expertise. Shorrock contests this by trying to elicit acknowledgement that such judgments are a matter of practical "experience" and not just statistical analysis.

From this exchange, we can begin to appreciate how the circumscription of "expert" categories can bring into play diverse associations and implications. Shorrock's initial questions seem designed to partition the relevant specialties that bear on the case at hand, so that Donnelly's expertise is restricted to only one type. Donnelly effectively resists such partitioning, first by associating his "statistical" expertise with an area of "genetics" and then by reclaiming for his own expertise what Shorrock presents as an example of a different kind of expertise involving practical judgment and laboratory experience. In addition to circumscribing Donnelly's expertise in terms of a set of named disciplines and sub-fields, and establishing its relevance (or lack of relevance) to substantive problems at hand, Shorrock's questions introduce a distinction between practical "experience" (and associated "working knowledge") and statistical calculation. He implies that Donnelly's "expertise" is extrinsic to the practice of forensics, and perhaps irrelevant to the experienced practitioner's knowledge. This is a common theme in testimony (and also interviews with forensic practitioners), and it sometimes provides a basis for technicians selectively to invert epistemic hierarchies within a laboratory. Practitioners who "get their hands dirty" sometimes distinguish their own know-how from the "academic" or formal knowledge assigned to more credentialled scientists.[28]

Like any organizationally situated interaction, this interrogation occurs in a particular context, but knowledge of *the relevant* context is not just a necessary background for understanding the dialogue. This is because numerous interwoven contexts are made relevant in and through what the parties say. The naming and circumscription of fields of claimed and disclaimed expertise simultaneously produce "expert" testimony and establish possible "contexts" for understanding what sort of expertise is being claimed or disclaimed. Moreover, particular utterances refer to what was said during previous testimony, and they specify longer-term histories and set up inferences about actions that "reasonably" follow from prior actions.

To situate categories like "science" and "expert" in particular occasions of action does not require a sceptical analytical attitude toward the existence of science or the fact that an expert has specialized knowledge; instead, it requires an orientation that is uncommitted to the referential adequacy (or inadequacy) of particular academic and ordinary uses of the terms in question. To return to the theme of "boundary work" mentioned earlier, we can begin to appreciate that the witness and interrogating lawyers – as well as the panel of appeal judges and other members of their audience – are not simply partitioning conceptual landscapes into binary regions of science and non-science or expert and non-expert knowledge.

When we compare the opening sequences of the direct and cross-examinations, we can begin to appreciate that circumscribing an expert witness within specific "fields" of expertise is not a matter of placing the witness within a shared matrix of disciplinary boxes. While Donnelly and his interlocutors locate his expertise within the category "statistician", and not in the category "forensic scientist", Donnelly claims (and this claim is not directly challenged) to be expert in the area of "population genetics". What he is entitled to say about particular forensic judgments becomes more contentious. Shorrock suggests that adequate judgment about the results of a laboratory preparation properly rests with the experienced practitioner who does the hands-on practice. Donnelly contests this by asserting that a judgment about the independence of bands on an autoradiograph is "exactly a statistical issue". In Donnelly's view, the practitioner sees one preparation after another, without necessarily taking stock of aggregate patterns and probabilities in an entire population. The expression in Shorrock's question "whether a band is independent or not" may be a source of ambiguity: Shorrock may be referring to a visual judgment about the quality of the bands on a given autoradiograph – Are they distinguishable (independent) of other possible bands above and below them? – whereas Donnelly may be referring to the Hardy-Weinberg equilibrium assumption of the "independent" probabilities assigned to different genetic loci that are labelled (and show up as "bands") in a given autoradiograph.

The contentious interchange also implicates the social distribution of knowledge in a way that is not bounded by the categories "statistics" and "forensic science". Shorrock suggests that "statistics" is used in several fields, and that many forensic scientists have an adequate "working knowledge" of statistics. He also mentions Jeffreys – a scientist whose credentials as an expert might seem to be beyond dispute – and yet Donnelly does not fully credit Jeffreys' use of statistics. Shorrock and Donnelly differ in their assessments of the extent to which "statistics" is relevant to forensic practice, and of how much statistical knowledge is necessary for making adequate forensic judgments.

Conclusion

The excerpts from *R. v. Deen* discussed in this paper, along with briefer excerpts from two US trials, document the *local interactional production* of areas of expertise and of associated domains expert knowledge. Familiar disciplinary categories and academic credentials, and the authority granted to experts in courts of law, feature prominently in the excerpts. By paying close attention to the interactional uses of those categories to claim, discount or circumscribe "expert" testimony, we can begin to appreciate that the co-production of legal authority/scientific knowledge is a relentless and rather subtle undertaking. It is not simply a matter of slamming together two global sectors of a public sphere, of inscribing, erasing or transgressing epistemic boundaries, or of projecting disciplinary order into a lifeworld. There can be no question but that the excerpts from specific cases, and the cases themselves, are embedded in historically developing legal institutions, but a specification of formal structures, rules and decision criteria is insufficient to handle the local contingencies arising within an adversary dialogue.

The particular variant of co-production exhibited in this chapter has to do with the interactional production of expert and non-expert knowledge and identity. A close reading of the excerpts presented above showed that academic or "scientific" credentials were translated into case-specific evidence in a court of law. A witness' membership in academic fields and status within those fields, as documented on a CV, was read aloud in a dialogue that displayed, circumscribed and (in the cross-examination) contested the relevance of the record to the evidence at hand. The CV was co-produced in, and for, the case, as *legal* as well as academic evidence. The local articulation of relevant fields of expertise, and the placement of the candidate witness in those fields, was an interactional production of the "law set" (Edmond 2002), consisting of the witness, the examining attorneys, and the audience (a panel of appeal court judges in this instance). The witness produced evidence of his educational credentials, and of his activities within a recognized field of academic expertise, but his interlocutors held him answerable to adversary understandings of just how his expertise related to the case. Claims and disclaimers of authoritative knowledge spilled over the apparent boundaries between the membership categories "statistician" and "forensic scientist", and the audience was then faced with having to resolve discrepant accounts of the witness' expertise and its bearing on the evidence.

By considering "expert" and "scientist" as membership categories that are deployed in moment-to-moment, institutionally embedded, discursive interaction, we can become apprised of the way parties position themselves and one another with respect to those categories and their conventional associations. The categories are not boxes with stable boundaries between inside and outside. Instead, the discursive movement of self-identification, qualification and disavowal, and other-attribution and challenge, simultaneously resolve the configuration of the category and place the candidate member within it. Both the category ("expert", "scientist", "statistician", etc.) and the terms of its membership are co-produced in dialogues presented to the court.

Notes

1   Durkheim's first rule of method states that "*One must systematically discard all preconceptions*" (Durkheim 1982 [1895]: 72, italics in original). He invoked Descartes and Bacon in support of this agenda. He speaks of "emancipation" from political and religious belief, and recommends "cold, dry analysis...repugnant to certain minds". He even likens the sociologist's orientation to that of a vivisectionist, who offends popular moral sense while pursuing objective truth.
2   See Garfinkel (2002: 181) on perspicuous settings.
3   See also Winch (1958), Peters (1958), and Lynch (1995).
4   For a debate about the concept of motives in social research, see Bruce and Wallis (1983; 1985); and Sharrock and Watson (1984; 1986). This and related debates did not simply pit "qualitative" sociologists against "quantitative" sociologists. The radical challenge that Winch (1958), and in a different way ethnomethodology, raised for the use of words as explanatory or structural "concepts" implicated a whole range of "qualitative" studies in sociology and social anthropology that deploy semiotic schemes and nominal typologies.
5   Disputes in the US courts over the status of "creation science" and evolutionary "theory" provided a perspicuous site for investigating boundary work concerning the science–religion distinction (see Gieryn *et al.* 1985; Nelkin 1982). The creationist controversy provides a difficult case for scholars who disavow demarcationism, because philosophers and social scientists are likely to be appalled by the substance and implications of creationist arguments, and thus tempted to join efforts to place "creation science" beyond the pale of science. See, for example, Quinn (1984) and Ruse (1986).
6   *Daubert v. Merrell Dow Pharmaceuticals, Inc.,* 113 S.Ct. 2786 (1993).
7   *Kumho Tire v. Carmichael,* 119 S.Ct. 137 (1999).

8 As conversation analysts point out, the *correct* use of a membership category (in this case "scientist") is not settled by whether or not the person so designated *is* a scientist. Whether or not calling somebody, or calling oneself, a "scientist" is relevant and appropriate depends upon the salience of that identity on some occasion. It would be odd, except perhaps under the most unusual of circumstances, to say that "the scientist changed her baby's diapers", or that "the scientist made an illegal left turn at the intersection".

9 This is not always the case, however. In conversations, terms that normally convey "high" status can be used sarcastically and cuttingly.

10 A term like "mother" can of course be used incorrectly, sarcastically and insultingly, even when the person so designated is in fact a mother.

11 Sacks (1979) gives the example of "hotrodder" in one of his best known lectures.

12 See Jayyusi (1984), Coulter (1982; 1996), Suchman (1994), Watson (1978), and Hester and Eglin (1997) for extensive discussions of membership categories and categorical politics

13 As Goffman (1959) also observes, informal use of such terms opens up a range of ironic and sarcastic uses. For example, neighbours and family members can have fun at the expense of an officious person by calling him "the General", when it is clear to all concerned that the person is not an army officer. More subtle uses have been explored by conversation analysts.

14 See Garfinkel (1967) on jurors, Sudnow (1965) on "normal crimes", and Lynch and Bogen (1996) on master narratives.

15 The US Federal Rules of Evidence state (Rule 702):

> If scientific, technical, or other specialized knowledge will assist the trier of fact to understand the evidence or to determine a fact in issue, a witness qualified as an expert by knowledge, skill, experience, training, or education, may testify thereto in the form of an opinion or otherwise.

16 See Pollner (1987) for a study of "mundane reason" in a traffic court. Also see Goodwin (1994) and Jasanoff (1998) for cases in which the distinction between what anyone can see and what an expert can show becomes problematic. An accused person might very well be able to employ a physicist to question the adequacy of a police radar reading; or an accused perjurer who insists that receiving oral sex does not amount to having "sexual relations" might consider enlisting the services of an anthropological linguist to explore the semantic nuances of "sex" in Ozark-region male discourse.

17 *Florida v. Andrews*, 533 So.2d 841 (Fla. App. 5 Dist. 1988), review denied 542 So.2d 1332 (Fla. 1989) transcript, 20 October 1987.

18 *Florida v. Andrews, ibid.*, transcript, p. 66.

19 *New Jersey v. Richard Williams*, 599 A.2d 960, N.J. Super.L. (May 1991), transcript.

20 *Regina v. Andrew Philip Deen*, no. 90/1523/X3, Royal Courts of Justice, The Strand, London, December 1993, transcript.

21 This particular use of an "etcetera clause" (Garfinkel 1967) signals that the written exhibit "contains" unspecified orders of detail that surpass the recited and transcribed *record* of the case. Even if the CV document is inspected no further, it has been marked as readable evidence with a surplus of potentially relevant details. We sometimes imagine that formal documents are reduced versions of the "realities" they stand for, but in this instance, the written document is treated as being a reality in itself, the evidentiary value of which has been glossed in the present scene.

22 "Population genetics" is more general than statistical aspects of DNA profiling, but when considered in the context of DNA profiling, it is a particular area of statistical application.

23 By "ritualistic", I mean an interactional routine in the court that tends to recur, often at the start of a phase or sequence. A CV "ritual" involves many variable elements – it is not a strict recitation, but it adheres relatively closely to the conventional format of a CV document. Later phases of a direct examination also rely upon notes, but they involve more frequent departures from a detailed pre-scripted agenda.

24 The US and UK courts differ in their procedures and guidelines for admitting expert testimony. Although these differences are relevant in many respects, the specific features of testimony described in this paper can be found in both systems.

25 See Schegloff (1984).

26 See McHoul (1987) for a discussion and examples of how witnesses can resist an interrogator's control. Lynch and Bogen (1996) describe how Oliver North – with much help from his friends – disrupted, resisted and redirected his examination by the majority counsels for the House and Senate, and used the interrogation opportunistically to make speeches and give counter-narratives, while also denying that he was doing so.

27 See Lawrence (1985) and Anderson (1992) for studies of the polemical use of themes akin to tacit knowledge in medical disputes.

28 Shapin's (1989) account of "invisible technicians" discusses the division of epistemic authority between natural philosophers and various early-modern precursors of today's technician. See Kathleen Jordan (1995: 135–140) for examples of complaints about notable scientists who "do not get their hands dirty". Also see Park Doing's (2002) account of the tensions between technicians and scientists in a physics laboratory. A related issue came up in two Appeal Court rulings in 1996 and 1997 on the case *R. v. Adams*, Court of Appeal (Criminal Division) (*The Times* [London] 9 May 1996). Donnelly was also an expert witness for the defence in *Adams*. In that case, the "boundary work" was not between forensic scientists' practical "experience" and statistical analysis, but between jurors' "common sense" weighing of all of the evidence in the case and statistical analysis of all, or some, of the evidence. See Gieryn (1999) on boundary work, and Lynch and McNally (2003) on the *Adams* case.

10 The science of merit and the merit of science

Mental order and social order in early twentieth-century France and America[1]

John Carson

On 16 February 2001, Richard C. Atkinson, president of the University of California, announced that he was proposing to abolish the SAT/ACT requirement for applicants seeking admission to any school in the university system. Atkinson justified his decision, the culmination of decades of controversy surrounding college aptitude tests and their role in American society, on the grounds that such tests were "not compatible with the American view on how merit should be defined and opportunities distributed" (Schemo 2001). Atkinson's proposal marked a decisive shift in the understanding of the role of aptitude/intelligence tests in the American educational system. From their development at the turn of the century up to the 1960s, mental tests were promoted precisely as a means of defining merit scientifically and thereby ensuring that all who took them would be treated equally. To their advocates, testing was an invaluable agent of reform, able to move the distribution of opportunities away from the privileges of birth or money or power. It could produce, they believed, a system that preserved equality by providing objectivity and accountability while still allowing for the extraordinary heterogeneity of the locally administered system of US primary and secondary education (Lemann 1999). Instruments such as the SAT, in their eyes, promised to help negotiate an issue of fundamental importance to American democracy in the twentieth century: how to distribute coveted and limited social goods such as educational opportunities in ways that would appear fair and equal even to those least successful in garnering rewards from the system. As Atkinson suggested, increasing public skepticism about the ability of intelligence tests to fulfill this function – to make the decisionmaking processes seem legitimate and fair by being based solely on merit – placed the tests in a precarious position *vis-à-vis* their continued utility for questions of college admissions.

This problem of how to satisfy demands for both equality and merit within a democratic political culture, and specifically the recourse to scientific objects and instruments and methods of quantification/classification to manage the tension between them, forms the subject of this essay. Adopting a co-productionist perspective, I will emphasize that "the ways in which we know and represent the world (both nature and society) are inseparable from the ways in which we choose to live in it", as Sheila Jasanoff states in Chapter 1. I suggest that technologies of merit such as intelligence tests are best understood not as invented apart from and then applied to the social realm, but rather as developed in tandem with other elements of the social order, together producing the reality in which all must operate (Jasanoff 1987; 1990; 1999). To sustain this position, I examine the emergence and response to intelligence and its tests in the early twentieth century, first in their birthplace, France, and then in the United States. By so doing, I explore how two distinct political cultures recast their approaches to equality and merit according to the possibilities that the ability to measure intelligence provided. It is a story at once about the fashioning of a scientific instrument to fit the needs of democratic political culture, and the fashioning of political cultures to fit the findings of an instrument.

The modern intelligence test provoked little interest in France upon its formulation by French psychologists Alfred Binet and Théodore Simon in the period 1905–1911. Conceived of, at best, as a supplement to other ways of analyzing human psychology, administrators and public officials deemed it of slight relevance to a system of merit already thought to be well served by public education. Thus French culture experienced few of the paroxysms of worry over intelligence and its measurement that would be engendered in the United States. Deemed useful in certain limited contexts, intelligence assessment generated little enthusiasm within a society that had already institutionalized a means to resolve, or at least channel, frictions between the claims of meritocracy and democracy through a highly standardized, universal system of education. The ability of that system to both produce and justify social hierarchy – through its training of the political/technocratic elite – while still representing such a social hierarchy as potentially open to all, was critical to the French approach to linking equality and merit. Intelligence, whatever its ontological status in French psychology, had little role to play in justifying such determinations, and, as a consequence, its purview remained highly circumscribed.

France's indifference to intelligence and intelligence tests contrasted markedly with the situation in the United States, where psychologists and administrators embraced both object and instrument and promoted them as a means of making a range of social decisions seem objective and fair. The most important early success of the American mental testers occurred soon after the Binet test arrived in America. During World War I, the exigencies of coping with mass mobilization made the US Army receptive to the initiative of a number of American psychologists to establish the nation's first large-scale intelligence testing program, for the purpose of classifying and sorting new recruits (Carson 1993). In the aftermath of the war, the results of that testing, particularly the widely reported finding that the average American soldier had the mental age of a thirteen-year-old, provoked an intense debate over the implications of intelligence for democracy. Waged in a number of journals, articles pitted leading mental testers such as Lewis M. Terman and Guy M. Whipple and their allies against a range of critics, including the educator William C. Bagley and such prominent public intellectuals as Walter Lippmann and John Dewey.

At its most basic, the controversy swirled around the figure of thirteen years: did it imply that a significant proportion of the American population was of limited intelligence and would remain so, or did it reveal flaws in the testing process that belied the psychologists' more exuberant claims about the knowledge they were producing? More broadly, issues of the nature of merit, equality and democratic citizenship were pushed to the fore. Could a democracy, some wondered, provide the same kinds of citizenship to all of its adult members if there were significant individual differences in the ability to be, or even choose, a good leader? The proponents of intelligence testing, by and large, argued that what was fundamental to a democracy was equality of opportunity, which meant only that each person should be afforded educational opportunities commensurate with their abilities. The critics of mental testing, on the other hand, considered the hierarchies of merit that testing could create inimical to a democracy, and stressed instead an equality founded on uniform treatment of all. For both sides, questions of democratic citizenship were intimately linked to understandings of human nature, and buried within the debate was an argument as well over who, if anyone, had the right to decide what individuals were, in fact, capable of accomplishing (Callon forthcoming; Rabeharisoa and Callon this volume).[2]

The contrast between the very different trajectories of intelligence and its tests in the United States and France reveals how culturally specific were the objectivities by which concepts such as "equality" and "merit" were made socially real in each nation. Drawing on a tradition of the celebration of individual rights derived from Britain, Americans since the eighteenth century had consistently turned to notions of nature and natural rights as one means of grounding and justifying political claims. Within American civic discourse, nature was framed as standing outside of society and as a counterweight to it, a source of rights independent of the vagaries of particular governments or social arrangements, and also a source of difference that could undercut claims to such rights (Rodgers 1987). Intelligence and its tests, in this context, could be seen as a seemingly natural means of determining what equality could and should mean, what differences were and were not real, independent of state or partisan influence. In France, on the other hand, republican discourse since the eighteenth century, while celebrating the need to replace tradition with reason and imbued as well with the presumption that nature was the ultimate source of rights, provided a far greater role for society as a whole (Nord 1995). Rousseau's notion of the "general will" and a commitment to sovereignty lying not in individuals but in the nation, formed the core of French republican doctrine, and in practice it was not so much nature as the good of society that served as the justification for various attempts at reform or revolution. Within this political culture, where citizenship was conceived of as communal and corporate as well as individual, the state served as the primary vehicle to ensure equality for all citizens. It accomplished this primarily through the establishment of national institutions, theoretically competitively open to every citizen, whose purpose was to bring the cream of the nation to its service. The objectivities provided by intelligence and its tests, in such a context, were not only superfluous, but might even have been the source of rival claims to elite privilege on the basis of criteria unmediated by the collective influence of the nation.

The Binet-Simon scale in France: a solution without a problem

Ironically, in view of its eventual uptake, the story of the modern intelligence test begins in France. When Alfred Binet commenced work in 1904 on the first version of his measuring scale, published in 1905, the direct impetus was his appointment to a ministerial commission on children lagging in school (Binet and Simon 1905b; Binet and Simon 1916). The scale began, as Binet and his colleague Théodore Simon explained at the Fifth International Congress of Psychology in Rome (1905), as a new means of diagnosing idiocy, imbecility and feeblemindedness (*débilité*), and distinguishing these subnormal types of intelligence from normal minds lacking sufficient training (Binet and Simon 1905a: 508). Their initial goal was to replace the "arbitrary" classificatory methods of doctors and educators with a procedure for defining degrees of intellectual deficit that was more objective, precise, and above all scientific. "It is a hackneyed remark", Binet declared, "that the definitions, thus far proposed, for the different states of subnormal intelligence, lack precision" (Binet and Simon 1916: 10). The thrust of Binet's work in the 1905 scale was to remedy this lack of precision by creating a series of tasks that would differentiate unambiguously between the normal mind and the three pathological classifications of intelligence enumerated above.

In subsequent years, Binet and Simon's conception of the possible applications of the scale and the social roles it could fulfill altered, and as it did, the instrument itself evolved correspondingly (Reuchlin 1968: 390). Almost immediately, French physicians proved hostile to a diagnostic technique that apparently challenged their authority, a reaction that pushed Binet to reorient his intelligence work away from medical diagnosis and "toward practical and social questions", as he declared publicly in 1908 (Binet 1908: v). By the scale's 1911 revision, Binet and Simon had substantially transformed the notion of intelligence embedded within it. In place of the meaning common in French psychology before their efforts – intelligence as the composite name for a diversity of faculties of interest for diagnosing intellectual pathologies – they had substituted the notion of intelligence as a singular, quantifiable entity applicable to the entire population (Gould 1996: 150–152; Tuddenham 1963: 490; Wolf 1969: 235–236).[3] The scale equated normal intelligence functionally with the ability to make judgments, comparisons and decisions in line with broadly accepted cultural norms, and statistically with the mean performance of its sample population on the items in the test. In the process, Binet and Simon extended the potential social applications of the scale well beyond simple classification of the feebleminded, instead envisioning it as a way of objectively ranking entire populations and allocating resources to meet a variety of needs:

the practical applications of this study [of intelligence] are evident in recruitment for classes of the abnormal, in the formation of classes for the supernormal, in the determination of the degree of responsibility of certain feeble mindeds [*débiles*], etc., without even taking account of the great interest that a parent or a schoolmaster could find in knowing if a child is intelligent or not, if his scholastic performance [*succès*] is related to his idleness or intellectual incapacity, and towards what kind of career it is fitting to direct him.

(Binet 1911: x)

As the range of these applications suggests, by 1911 Binet and Simon had conceptualized the metric scale primarily as a mechanism for assisting institutions in the management of individuals. Having removed much of the clinical feel of the 1905 version, they had rendered Binet-Simon intelligence instead as something quantifiable and unidimensional, a social technology advertised as providing impartial mediation between the rationalizing imperatives of various social institutions and the levels of ability of the citizenry. Binet and Simon's representation of intelligence as universally distributed and of fundamental significance in assessing human potential allowed them to argue that use of the scale could bring objectivity and accountability to a range of administrative practices and social decisions. Its employment, they suggested, could shift the basis for action from subjective choice to scientific determination (Wise 1988).

The potential ramifications of such a social technology, if truly enlisted to perform all of the tasks that Binet and Simon envisioned for it, might have been far reaching and profound. However, the actual uses to which the metric scale was put in France turned out to be rather modest. Binet's sudden death in 1911 at the age of fifty-four deprived the scale of its most important champion, and Binet's Sorbonne laboratory, symbolic home of his activities, was entrusted not to Binet's disciple Simon, but to a younger rival, Henri Piéron (Piéron 1939; 1965). While most French psychologists acknowledged that the Binet-Simon scale was a measuring instrument of some practical value, few found it of more than limited relevance to their own research programs. The orientation of French psychological investigation in the early twentieth century was overwhelmingly toward clinical studies of individual pathology or laboratory experimentation on basic psychological functions, not toward the practical applications of psychological science to social problems (Brooks 1993; Carroy and Plas 1996; Danziger 1985; Reuchlin 1978).

Even those psychologists, such as Piéron and his wife Marguerite, who did produce studies of intelligence and its development during the 1910s and 1920s, employed a focus significantly different from Binet's. In one form or another, they sought to investigate the complexities of intelligence and to understand it as a multi-faceted phenomenon, whether ultimately singular or compound in composition. For them, it was not Binet's metric scales of intelligence that served as a model, but his 1903 study of his daughters, *L'Etude expérimentale de l'intelligence* (Binet 1903). As Henri Piéron noted in 1927, "[t]hough we always employ the same word, intelligence, for the aptitude to solve problems, it is still necessary to understand that under this term the mental action may be quite different, depending on the nature of the problems to be solved" (Piéron 1929: 178–179). In other words, intelligence was not one thing but many, a sentiment echoed by Benjamin Bourdon in 1926 when he argued that proficiency in one area, even to the level of genius, did not insure ability in any other domain (Bourdon 1926).

Such a stance did not mean that the connection of intelligence with the practical needs of the individual and the state disappeared completely in France. The Piérons, along with the physiologist Henri Laugier and psychologist Jean-Marie Lahy, devoted significant time and energy to the development of the field of occupational testing (*orientation professionnelle*), and the Binet-Simon scale was an important component in their repertoire of investigative tools. In addition, the psychiatrist Georges Heuyer used the intelligence scale extensively in his studies of abnormal children – in particular juvenile delinquents who were required to have psychological examinations before appearance in court – but again the Binet-Simon test was only one of a number of ways in which these individuals were assessed (Schneider 1989; 1992). As historian William Schneider has observed, recourse to a single, global measurement of intelligence as a primary means of social decisionmaking did not even become a serious public issue in France until the mid-1930s, when the Popular Front suggested a nationwide survey to determine the percentage of retarded and abnormal children requiring special educational services. Postponed with the defeat of the leftists in the late 1930s, the proposal was resuscitated with the advent of the Vichy government in 1940 – spurred on by its own interest in the health of the nation and the family – but only finally reached conclusion under the Fourth Republic in 1954, with the report "The intellectual level of school-age children". And even at this point, the role for global intelligence remained limited: a means of categorizing certain intellectual deficits that were deemed of particular relevance to French educators and state administrators.

In the end, what is most apparent about this story of the emergence of intelligence and its tests in France is how circumscribed the claims for them came to be. When French psychologists or psychiatrists needed to investigate the nature of an individual's intellect, as we have seen, they used not one assessment technique but a whole battery of them, in which Binet-Simon intelligence might be, at most, a single element. What is more, rarely did important voices in French culture suggest that intelligence measures might stand in for, or even substantially contribute to, culturally sanctioned methods of judging individual merit, outside the diagnosis of particular pathological conditions. As important as the issue of merit was in Third Republic France, it was addressed primarily through a different type of examination, the *concours*, whose purpose was not to identify individual potential (or deficit), but to choose at each level a cadre of high achievers for advanced training to meet the needs of state and society.

Since at least Napoleon III's Second Empire, republicans had routinely included demands for rule by the most able in their plans for the reconstruction of the French polity along more democratic lines.[4] Instead of intelligence, however, at the heart of the French republican vision of merit lay the system of education, with its institutional commitment to equality and excellence through competition and selection. One of the central institutions of Third Republic culture, and both manufacturer and employer of many of the Republic's most ardent proponents, the educational system had already developed by the early nineteenth century a highly elaborated system for winnowing the "best" from the school-age population and directing them to special institutions of higher learning (Clark 1973; Mayeur 1981; Smith 1982; Weisz 1983). A series of competitive examinations (the *concours*) and ever more elite schools, culminating in the Ecole Normale Supérieure or Ecole Polytechnique and the *agrégation*, served to select and make available to the French state *la crème de la crème*, a group of extremely well trained young people whose very success in negotiating the system defined them as the most talented in the nation (Clark 1973; Smith 1982; Shinn 1980).

Although the percentage of primary-age children enrolled in the French educational system continued to increase throughout the nineteenth century, this expansion had little effect on the system's pyramidal structure or its ability to generate sufficient numbers of "superior" products to meet the needs of state and society. Rather, consumed with their battle with the Catholic church over control of education (and convinced that public instruction was the bulwark of the republic), leading republicans of the left and right – all products of the lycées and grandes écoles – viewed the educational system as the guarantor of the triumph of talent over tradition. Thus few in positions of authority perceived any real need for new mechanisms of selection and classification within most arenas of French life, and they routinely rejected as superfluous additional methods for selection, even one purporting to measure something as fundamental as intelligence.[5] For them, merit and equality had to be seen as byproducts of a system potentially open to all, and not lodged in a faculty presumably present from birth.

In the United States, on the other hand, intelligence was quickly seized upon and promoted by psychologists as a major constituent of merit. The systems of social sorting that had worked tolerably well during the antebellum period proved largely unable to cope with the powerful transformations reshaping late nineteenth-century American society and culture. Large-scale urbanization and industrialization, rapid shifts between prosperity and depression, unprecedented labor unrest, massive immigration from eastern and southern Europe, and the emancipation of millions of formerly enslaved African Americans changed the nature of community life. A multitude of new languages and cultural practices were introduced into urban areas increasingly segregated by race/ethnicity and class, and new practices of control and exclusion were fashioned.[6] At the same time, worries about cultural degeneration and the deleterious influence of the abnormal, and particularly the subnormal, spread widely in the United States, anxieties both fueled by and fueling interest in eugenics (Cravens 1978; Degler 1991; Kevles 1986). Faced with the emergence of mass society, leaders in education and business increasingly viewed methods of selection – be it for higher education, governmental bureaucracies or industrial jobs – that had previously relied on personal familiarity, family status, community connections or craft guild hierarchies, as antiquated and out of place.

As a consequence, space opened for newer approaches to selection, inflected less by the older Victorian language of character than by seemingly more *au courant* Progressive formulations steeped in the idiom of science and engineering. Civil service reform, advocated by Progressives as a way of replacing the regime of politics and spoils with one of "ability", was typical of turn-of-the-century moves to redefine merit. Reformers extolled transparency, objective measures and equal opportunities for all, seeking to replace backroom patronage and subjective assessments that to them were symbols of corruption (Ingraham 1995; Shepard 1884). In addition, there were a number of significant changes in the nature of education. Higher education expanded enormously, spurred by the Morrill Act (1862) for land-grant colleges and by the philanthropy of Gilded Age robber barons such as Rockefeller, Carnegie and Stanford for private universities (Reuben 1996; Rudolph 1962; Veysey 1965). At the same time, publicly funded systems of secondary education in urban and suburban areas grew even more rapidly, meaning that the number of Americans, both men and women, with post-primary educations soared, with the result that such qualifications seemed less selective than they once had seemed. Finally, the piecemeal nature of the American education system, characterized by local control of public schools and universities and the existence of a wide variety of private institutions, meant that no approach to classification or selection based on uniform curricular standards or a singular ideal of public service was likely to develop. Within this cultural/social context, so different in important ways from France, psychologists and administrators met the arrival of the Binet-Simon scale not with indifference, but with enthusiasm, touching off a vogue for testing that had powerful and far-reaching consequences.

Building an American intelligence: a techno-scientific solution

The 1905 Binet-Simon scale arrived in the United States in 1908, one of the spoils of a research junket to Europe undertaken by American psychologist Henry H. Goddard of the New Jersey Training School for Feebleminded Girls and Boys in Vineland (Goddard 1908; Zenderland 1998). Goddard commenced experimenting with the scale soon after his return, but found it of limited value. When Binet published the 1908 revised Binet-Simon, Goddard at first hesitated to use it, recalling later that it had "seemed impossible to grade intelligence in that way. It was too easy, too simple" (Goddard 1916: 5). Intrigued by the possibility, however, Goddard finally administered the revised instrument to residents at his school, and reported himself to be amazed by the results. The scale, he declared, provided accurate diagnoses of the mental levels of all of the children he had examined (Goddard 1910: 389). What had taken Goddard and the staff months to determine through long exposure to the subjects, the Binet-Simon was able to reveal in a single testing session. It would soon be clear that Goddard's experience was by no means unique. By 1916, when Lewis Terman completed the Stanford-Binet, his version of the Binet-Simon intelligence scale, intelligence was already something of an industry in American psychology. Articles either about the Binet-Simon scale or research data generated by the scale filled professional journals; numerous rival versions of the scale competed for clientele and professional dominance; and a great deal of hand-wringing was in evidence about the improper use of the technology by those deemed "ill trained" to apply it appropriately (Goddard 1916; Terman 1913; Zenderland 1998). American psychologists were infatuated with the test; they adopted with few reservations what their French counterparts found either uninteresting or problematic (Schneider 1992; Wolf 1973). In the process, however, they adopted wholesale the version of intelligence – singular, hierarchical, unidimensional – built into the Binet-Simon instrument, as well as a vision of how the scale might best be deployed (Kitson 1916).

When American psychologists confronted the new psychological instrument, it appeared to them to fit the prescriptions of psychological science for objectively produced quantitative data, and as well to have application to a number of areas of fundamental concern to American culture. At first, however, in the prewar years, the response of psychologists in the US to the potentials of the scale was not so entirely different from that of their French colleagues. Although far more enthusiastic about its possibilities, the first generation of mental testers often started out by assuming that the range of direct applications would be relatively limited, involving mostly the detection of pathological conditions associated with feeblemindedness or failure in school. Goddard, a psychologist at an institution for the feebleminded, was in this sense typical of the American psychologists who initially experimented with intelligence testing; almost all worked either with school children or those deemed of limited cognitive capacity.

Had intelligence and its tests remained tied to psychological research projects and a limited set of clinical applications, it is difficult to imagine that they would have had any broad impact on American culture, for all of their resonance with Progressive ideology and middle-class social anxieties (Lunbeck 1994). However, in the latter part of the 1910s two events propelled intelligence and its tests into national prominence. First, in 1916 Lewis Terman completed his Stanford-Binet Intelligence Scale, the articulation of intelligence that would quickly come to dominate the growing field of mental testing research and practice (Chapman 1988; Gould 1996; Minton 1988). Standardized on almost 1,000 California school children, the Stanford-Binet constituted the most complete revision of the Binet-Simon scale for an American population then undertaken, and was deemed technically superior in every sense, at least for white middle-class children. One of Terman's most important innovations was to introduce the concept of the "intelligence quotient" (IQ), a ratio of mental age to chronological age originally proposed by the German psychologist William Stern in 1912 and designed to produce a measure of intelligence that was independent of the examinee's age (Stern 1914: 80; Terman 1919: 8–9). This quantity, Terman asserted, "has been found in the large majority of cases to remain fairly constant", an opinion he used to buttress his conclusion that "[t]here is nothing in one's equipment, with the exception of character, which rivals IQ in importance" (Terman *et al.* 1917: 10). With IQ, Terman had fully transformed intelligence into a standardized, quantifiable characteristic applicable to the entire range of human minds. Whatever variation individual intellects of the same IQ might manifest, and even whatever growth they might sustain, were rendered invisible in the process of producing a Stanford-Binet intelligence quotient. Its primary function was to create a linear index of relative brightness that could encompass the idiot, the genius and, most notably, everyone in between, whether child or adult, male or female, white or black. Especially with Terman's packaging, which emphasized the innate hereditary nature of intelligence and its overwhelming significance in determining an individual's life course, IQ became a characteristic of potentially immense significance, relevant to social and personal decisionmaking well beyond the confines of the psychological clinic.

Second, the advent of World War I afforded American psychologists the opportunity to demonstrate the relevance of intelligence measures to more mainstream arenas than the asylum or programs for the educationally lagging. Harvard psychologist Robert M. Yerkes assembled a group of mental testers – including Terman and Goddard – to aid the war effort by providing the Army with an efficient way of classifying the millions of new recruits it would need to mobilize for the war. These psychologists developed a new method of administering mental tests by groups, in the form of Army Alpha (for literates) and Army Beta (for English-language illiterates), and examined over 1.75 million soldiers. The results were then used as one means of sorting recruits into various categories of military usefulness – ranging from officer candidates to those deemed unfit for frontline duty – and of justifying those decisions (Carson 1993; Kevles 1968). The enormous legitimacy given to intelligence testing by this program, along with the publicity focused on the finding that the average American soldier had a mental age of thirteen and thus that a large percentage were "feebleminded" or worse, transformed an endeavor that had existed mainly on the margins of American culture to one that seemed right in the center. Confronted with scientific evidence that seemed to confirm their worst fears about the declining quality of the American population, leaders in many sectors of American society – education, industry, government – turned to tests of "intelligence" to aid their personnel processes.

By the end of the war, the version of intelligence and its instruments promulgated by the military testers had emerged victorious. New multiple-choice tests began to supplant the Stanford-Binet as the most common technology of intelligence assessment, and became commercialized commodities sold by a number of publishing houses or newly founded companies such as Psychological Corporation (Sokal 1981). At the same time, the greatest growth in the new intelligence industry occurred in applications to school and business, where leaders turned to intelligence testing as an objective, efficient and credible means of differentiating students, workers, and applicants for employment or admissions. The nature of intelligence reified in Army Alpha and these postwar measures perpetuated the Stanford-Binet model: a unitary, global entity, biological in origin and hereditary, that allowed all human beings to be ranked on a single scale, and presumed that intelligence was a prime factor in success in virtually all human endeavors. Intelligence in this form could explain, in almost Darwinian terms, why some individuals were at the top of the social/occupational hierarchy, and others were at the bottom.

This was not the only conception of intelligence jockeying for position in early twentieth-century American culture. But its embodiment in an easily commodified and disseminated technology of display, the mental test, that fit the needs of the efficiency-seeking bureaucracies of Progressive-era America, provided an enormous advantage to the unitary understanding of the human mind. By making visible fine grades of intellectual difference – whether revealed or created – tying those distinctions to particular social consequences – class and occupation – both of which were represented as linear gradations, and promising that profits could be made from psychological assessments, the intelligence instrument produced a reality that proved difficult to dispute, especially in a political culture preoccupied with balancing demands for merit and equality. In addition, because intelligence was translated into technologies – forms and mental tests – from which first army personnel and then large segments of the civilian population simply could not escape, both the examinees and those using the testing information were encouraged to think in concrete terms about intelligence, what it might mean, what its importance might be, and how it might be used. In reaction to this insertion of intelligence and its tests into the social landscape, and to the broader claims advanced by social scientists to reorganize the polity according to similar objective methods and rationalized procedures, questions began to emerge about the nature of democratic citizenship.[7]

Grand ambitions or monumental hubris?

Scarcely six months after the armistice ending World War I, Joseph Kinmont Hart of Reed College used the pages of the education journal *School and Society* to wonder about the fate of democracy (Hart 1919). It was a rather unlikely question to ponder at the end of America's triumphal success in Europe, where the nation, with a minimum loss of American lives, had seemingly made good on its claim to make the world safe for democracy. Hart was writing during the first moments of the "Red Scare" of 1919–1920, in which a wave of strikes and a rash of bombings ignited a wholesale crusade against Bolsheviks, socialists, anarchists, labor organizers, foreigners, blacks, and anyone else who could be painted sufficiently "red" or "other" to be deemed a threat to the American way of life (Painter 1987). But this internal menace was not the immediate source of Hart's anxieties. Rather, he worried about the lesson of the war itself, and specifically about how the spectacular successes of science in wartime would translate into an America at peace. Spurred on by the experience of the war, with its vast marshalling of material and manpower and its heady application of expertise to the management of the economy, Hart imagined a social/political order not just open to the authority of science, but subservient to and transformed by it (Camfield 1969; Kevles 1995; Yerkes 1920). In Hart's new, postwar America, science was to be the final arbiter, dispassionately settling social questions and finally dispelling local prejudices by bringing objectivity and impartial reason to what had previously been hidden behind custom and corruption.[8] Democracy itself required such a move in Hart's view, for only science, and particularly social science, could legitimately establish the boundaries within which a true democracy could operate:[9]

> Without science there can be no democracy, but only old prejudicial social forms, degenerating into autocracy, again....In the future, all crucial action of a social nature must be determined by scientific investigation, rather than by customs, and men must be brave enough to fight for these things, even to the losing of their – jobs!
>
> (Hart 1919: 256–257)

Although Hart's rather hyperbolic plea that scientists risk even their careers to extend the authority of their findings to every aspect of social life may have fallen on deaf ears, his overall ambitions for the social sciences certainly did not. In the postwar period, the social sciences in America flourished as never before, and in no field was this more true than psychology, where many psychologists, having made the Army safe for intelligence, returned from their military duties at the end of World War I determined to carry the gospel of science and mental testing to the public at large.[10] As Yerkes remarked in a letter to Abraham Flexner, president of the General Education Board (GEB) of the Rockefeller Foundation, in 1919, "[a]lready we are bombarded by requests from public school men for our army mental tests in order that they may be used in school systems" (Yerkes 1919b).

Psychologists' first serious foray into bringing science to the service of postwar democracy was the creation of the National Intelligence Tests (NIT) in 1919, a joint product of two one-time rivals but wartime colleagues, Terman and Yerkes (along with Melvin E. Haggerty, Edward L. Thorndike and Guy M. Whipple). With funding from the General Education Board of the Rockefeller Foundation in place, Yerkes *et al.* met over the course of 1919 to design a new test, the NIT, modeled on the military's Army Alpha examination, but modified to fit the capabilities of a school-age population (Yerkes and Terman 1919). Completed by the winter, the NIT was a collection of group-administered, multiple-choice instruments designed to rank the entire American school population on a single scale. Once adopted, its creators contended, a wholesale transformation could be wrought in the nature of American education. No longer need students of varying abilities be grouped in the same classroom; no longer need all students be subjected to the same curriculum; and no longer need every student be prepared for the same future. Rather, as B. R. Buckingham put it in 1921 in an editorial in the *Journal of Educational Research*:

Our educational and intelligence tests permit us to ascertain the capacities of pupils far more accurately than ever before. Thus, the teacher becomes a guide and director. He is still a trainer of youth but he selects one to be trained in this way and another in that. ... Instead of prescribing the same treatment for all, he will become the expert diagnostician. On the basis of mental ability he will reclassify children, and because of their special abilities, he will further subdivide them.

(Buckingham 1921: 139)

Where once the single-room schoolhouse had stood as an icon of the commitment to primary education for all, now American psychologists proposed a new, more modern substitute: the multi-tracked high school, in which the results produced by impersonal mechanisms of assessment could be translated into objective systems of classification and separate educational destinies, all justified as a form of equal treatment by representing children as more different than the same, and less susceptible to molding than to sieving.[11] In an article entitled "The mental rating of school children", in fact, Yerkes went so far as to suggest that children be seen as different and grouped separately according to their level of intelligence as early as kindergarten, and after fifth grade be sent off onto distinct educational tracks: professional, for the high intelligence group A children; industrial, for the medium intelligence group B children; and manual, for the low intelligence group C children (Yerkes 1919a).

The demands of educational efficiency and the ideals of democracy themselves required, these psychologists believed, that the schools be transformed according to the dictates of science. "I believe that the real meaning of democracy", University of Michigan psychologist Guy M. Whipple noted in 1922, "is properly safeguarded in the notion of 'equity of opportunity,' and if any nation is destined to perish it is that one which fails to provide the best possible educational training for those of its rising generation that show promise of educational leadership" (Whipple 1922: 602). Yerkes contended as well that equality of opportunity was the sole true form of democratic education, suggesting that only ability grouping would allow "the free intermingling of children of the various [class] strata in any given intelligence section" (Yerkes 1919a). Though few noticed the parallel, in many respects Whipple, Yerkes, *et al.* championed a version of education and democracy not far different from that institutionalized in France. Where the French used competitive examinations and exclusion of most from the upper echelons to create a system that was elite-dominated but technically open to all, these American psychologists proposed an approach that remained inclusive, but could still identify and sanction an elite. Both proclaimed the democratic bases of their educational visions on the grounds of equality of opportunity, and both justified the differential provisioning of educational resources on the belief that all people were decidedly *not* created equal, and that social progress demanded that these differences be acknowledged and acted upon.

Needless to say, this was not a vision shared by everyone in postwar America. Some more traditionally minded Americans simply rejected it out of hand, skeptical about the pretensions of "experts" and more comfortable with traditional educational structures and well established pedagogical approaches. For them, the common school was a potent symbol of American democracy and its commitment to equality as uniform treatment of all, and any attempt to restructure it in the name of science and human difference posed a threat to basic values that had few offsetting compensations. Others, more self-consciously modern, however, could not slough off the claims of science nor the cult of opportunity so easily. Walter Lippmann, John Dewey, William C. Bagley, and other Progressive intellectuals and educators were as committed as the psychologists to objective methods and the reform of democratic institutions according to the dictates of empirical fact, and shared as well the belief that opportunity and access lay at the heart of the American concept of equality. While they were troubled by various features of the vision put forward by Terman, Yerkes, *et al.*, of a new educational system, and by implication a refashioned democratic citizenry, they could not simply reject it out of hand. Rather, in the pages of magazines and journals ranging from the *Saturday Evening Post* and the *Atlantic Monthly* to *School and Society* and the *Journal of Educational Research*, they formulated challenges to specific factual claims and interpretations, so that the findings of psychological science might be domesticated within their own conceptions of democracy and scientific objectivity.

"The sky is falling": race, democracy, and the IQ

Although the United States had survived World War I largely unscathed, in the immediate postwar period many Americans remained concerned about the nation's future. Troubled by the enormous influx of new immigrants and uneasy about the social/cultural transformations that had accelerated with the century's end, members of the old elite, especially, feared that the war marked not the triumph of civilization, but another moment in its precipitous decline (Lears 1981). When the news broke about the average mental age of the American soldier, many were not so much shocked as confirmed in the worst of their suspicions, and seized on this "fact" as a golden opportunity to ring the alarm and publicly decry the state of the American republic. Echoing worries about national degeneration and decline that had been prevalent for the preceding three decades, for example, Cornelia James Cannon, wife of noted Harvard physiologist Walter B. Cannon, opined in the pages of the *Atlantic Monthly* that "the lower grade man is material unusable in a democracy" (Cannon 1922: 154). George B. Cutten, president of Colgate University, followed suit, suggesting in *School and Society* that "we have never had a true democracy, and the low level of the intelligence of the people will not permit of our having one" (Cutten 1922: 479). Perhaps most inflammatory were the claims put forth by Harvard-educated Boston lawyer Lothrop Stoddard in *The Revolt Against Civilization* (1922), in which he marshaled the testing data as part of a eugenicist and frankly racist portrait of civilization under siege:

Against these assaults of inferiority; against the cleverly led legions of the degenerate and the backward; where can civilization look for its champions? Where but in the slender ranks of the racially superior – those "A" and "B" stocks which, in America for example, we know to-day [because of the World War I Army testing data] constitute barely 13½ per cent of the population? It is this "thin red line" of rich, untainted blood which stands between us and barbarism and chaos. There alone lies our hope. Let us not deceive ourselves by prating about "government", "education", "democracy": our laws, our constitutions, our very sacred books, are in the last analysis mere paper barriers, which will hold only so long as there stands behind them men and women with the intelligence to understand and the character to maintain them.

(Stoddard 1925: 106)

Like his friend and fellow Ivy League graduate Madison Grant, whose own racial call to arms *The Passing of the Great Race* (1916) had been a best seller, Stoddard easily wove together fears of degeneracy, horrors of miscegenation, visions of corporeal and racial purity, nightmares of race war, images of primitive savagery, social Darwinist renderings of evolution, and skepticism about education and democracy, all to render vivid the image of a beleaguered aristocracy of red-blooded intellect – "A" and "B" men – upon whose powers to repress and procreate rested the future of civilization (Bederman 1995). Florid though the account surely was, its core drew on the popular pronouncements of much more distinguished and professional scholars. In fact, one of Stoddard's chief sources was Scottish-born Harvard psychology professor William McDougall, whose *Is America Safe for Democracy?* (1921) also seized on the Army testing data to buttress dire conclusions about the biological warrant for democratic politics.

McDougall laced his tract with much of the new psychological knowledge – especially the latest findings from mental testing and eugenics research – in order to establish (along the lines of Herbert Spencer) that civilization in the form of modern industrial urban life was growing ever more complex. As a result, he argued, "the demand for A and B men steadily increases", while the supply inexorably diminished (McDougall 1921: 168). Promoted as an investigation into "the influence of anthropological constitution on the destinies of nations", McDougall's account was concerned above all with race, understood in ethnonational terms as much as in broad color-based distinctions. McDougall's goal was to preserve the presumed apex of humanity, Nordic stock, from the deleterious effects of degeneration from within, symbolized by the procreative menace of the feebleminded, and degradation from without, symbolized above all by the specter of black/white miscegenation. Indeed, throughout his text, data on white/"colored" differences in IQ and other racial characteristics – derived from at times tortured interpretations of the Army testing results – loomed large, serving as the touchstone for his arguments about the inferiority of non-Nordic Europeans, and anchoring his conclusion that only vigorously enforced policies of positive and negative eugenics could halt America's decline and make it again ready for robust, white-dominated democracy (McDougall 1921: 51–58).

McDougall's, and for that matter Stoddard's, intertwining of what they took to be the perils and potentials of modernity around the notions of the fragility of "civilization" and the preservation of the "race" (through careful tending of its most meritorious biological specimens), as historian Daniel J. Kevles has pointed out, articulated a set of hopes and worries common among segments of the middle-class white population in the US at the turn of the century (Kevles 1986: 72, 76; Bederman 1995; Newman 1999; Pernick 1996). Nonetheless, for all of the cultural resonance of these positions, more critical responses by prominent public intellectuals were not long in coming. In his address before the Society of College Teachers of Education on 27 February 1922, William Bagley of Teachers College Columbia led the charge, by providing an impassioned rebuttal of a number of these arguments, especially as they applied to education (Ravitch 2000). Rejecting what he termed belief in "educational determinism", or the primacy of innate mental ability, and the theory of aristocracy which it implied, Bagley instead celebrated the power of education to expand the intelligence of the common man and championed the provisioning of the same basic education for all. "If education is to save civilization", Bagley declared, "it must lift the common man to new levels, *and not so much to new levels of industrial efficiency as to new levels of thinking and feeling*" (Bagley 1922: 380). In Bagley's view, education was at least as important a contributor to an individual's overall intelligence as all other factors combined, and its relationship to the achievement of a just and peaceful society overwhelming (Bagley 1925). While he did not reject the concept of general intelligence, nor the value of intelligence testing for partic- ular purposes, he did strongly denounce the vision of a society ruled by an intellectual elite chosen virtually from birth. Only mass education, American- style, Bagley contended, could truly enable the maintenance of a society open to the voices of all (Bagley 1925).

A few months later Bagley's cause was joined by Walter Lippmann, who in a series of six articles in the *New Republic* took Stoddard and the mental testing community to task for what he argued were their shoddy procedures in gener- ating and interpreting the Army test results (Lippmann 1922b). Lippmann argued that the figure of thirteen years for the average mental age was on the face of it absurd; IQ tests were mechanisms for classifying not instruments for measuring; predictions about school performance had little relevance to success in life; intelligence itself was an ill-defined concept within psychology; and there was little evidence that intelligence tests measured an innate heritable trait. He then concluded that however useful IQ examinations might be to accomplish specific classifications in specific settings, they failed to measure anything like pure intelligence, while according mental testers inordinate social power. "If the intelligence test", he proposed, "really measured the unchangeable hereditary capacity of human beings, as so many assert, it would inevitably evolve from an administrative convenience into a basis for hereditary caste" (Lippmann 1922b). The following year, developing his arguments further in an article in the *Century*

Magazine, Lippmann turned to the Army testing data relied on by McDougall to establish the intellectual inferiority of "coloreds", and by pointing out the extreme regional variations in IQ regardless of race and their correspondence to the quality of the local school systems, made an impassioned defense of education and the possibilities of a democracy open to all.[12] In one of his salvos at Terman, Lippmann revealed clearly the emotional basis of his reaction to the testers:

> I hate the impudence of a claim that in fifty minutes you can judge and classify a human being's predestined fitness in life. I hate the pretentiousness of that claim. I hate the abuse of scientific method which it involves. I hate the sense of superiority which it imposes.
>
> (Lippmann 1923b)

Observations such as these struck a nerve with a number of *New Republic* readers, among them John Dewey, who responded to Lippmann's articles by questioning not so much the existence of individual differences but rather their limitation to any single construct such as intelligence (Dewey 1922a; 1922b). In his own reflections in the *New Republic*, Dewey contended that the essence of democracy was radical individuality, the belief that each person encompassed a unique set of attributes and that the duty of education was to allow those talents to flourish. "Democracy will not be democracy", Dewey observed, "until education makes its chief concern to release distinctive aptitudes in art, thought and companionship. At present the intellectual obstacle in the way is the habit of classification and quantitative comparisons" (Dewey 1922b: 63). Mental testing was ill conceived, he continued along lines that French psychologists had argued, because it tried to hammer complicated human beings into simple administrative boxes, thus producing a society at odds with the goals of true "civilization". The fetish for numbers, statistics and quantitative categories, Dewey argued, was an artifact of "[o]ur mechanical, industrialized civilization" and produced a "reverence for mediocrity, for submergence of individuality in mass ideals and creeds" that was inimical to both true education and true democracy (Dewey 1922b: 61). Dewey rejected notions of superiority and inferiority, whether applied to races or individuals, on the grounds that, while morally equal, human beings were otherwise incommensurable; each had to be appreciated in his or her own unique way.

These attacks by Bagley, Lippmann and Dewey on the testing community and its instruments did not go unchallenged; sarcastic responses from Terman and more considered replies from a number of other psychologists soon filled the pages of popular and professional journals. Terman turned first to Bagley. In the pages of the *Journal of Educational Research* he argued that Bagley's refusal to concede the significance of differences in individual native mental endowment was in essence a denial of the truths of science and a return to superstition, and that Bagley was actually imperiling rather than protecting democracy (Terman 1922–3). Terman preached the need to adapt the curriculum to the individual needs of the child, and not vice-versa, as most efficient for both child and society. He then went on to lambaste Bagley for failing to understand how intelligence testing could aid in producing a truly egalitarian democracy, one in which opportunity could flourish through identification of the most able, regardless of their class backgrounds, who would then receive the education most fitted to their abilities.

Terman was, if anything, even more dismissive of Lippmann, suggesting in his *New Republic* rejoinder that Lippmann lacked the expertise to judge the psychologists' work and that Lippmann's own understanding of intelligence was laughably naive (Terman 1922–3; Minton 1988). Characterizing (or was it caricaturing?) Lippmann as asserting that "the essential thing about a democracy is not equality of opportunity, as some foolish persons think, but equality of mental endowment", Terman again celebrated the use of mental tests to "sift the schools for superior talent in order to give it a chance to make the most of itself, in whatever stratum of society it may be found" (Terman 1922–3: 117). Terman simply swept aside most of Lippmann's technical criticisms of the Army testing procedures and results, although he did allow himself to "explain" the controversial thirteen-year figure for the average mental age of the Army recruits by conceding that there was some disagreement within the professional community over the exact age where adult intelligence began. Most significantly, where Lippmann had argued passionately that the number of high-grade "A" and "B" men was a function of the time allotted to complete the test, and that more than the 13½ per cent that Stoddard had made famous would have scored in those ranges if they had been given sufficient opportunity to complete each task, Terman countered that timing had little effect on a person's overall ranking, and that more time would simply have shifted the scale, without changing its meaning. In essence, Terman saw the proportion of most intelligent as fixed, and used relative test performance to identify them; Lippmann, on the other hand, considered the absolute level of performance itself as critical, and so contended that the most intelligent were all those who exhibited proficiency to a certain level, and not simply the top n per cent. Both conceded that mental tests could reveal a kind of merit, but understood that merit in decidedly different ways.

For the next two or three years, insults continued to fly and a variety of positions continued to be debated, with each commentator in one way or another wrestling with the implications of the possible existence of innate differences in mental ability for American society as a whole. In the end, the debate did not so much get resolved as drop from a boil to a simmer. While the frequency of articles in the popular and semi-professional press about intelligence and its tests remained high throughout the 1920s, after 1925 few authors accorded particular attention to the issue of intelligence and democracy.[13] Rather, articles about the use, or misuse, of intelligence tests in particular (most typically educational) situations predominated, with the appropriateness of intelligence testing itself largely assumed. In this, the press reflected the American cultural landscape writ large. By the mid-1920s, a range of social decisionmaking systems routinely made recourse to assessments of intelligence, using them as aids in determining whether or not an individual should be hired by a firm, placed in an asylum for the feebleminded, declared by the courts to be of diminished capacity, or assigned to the academic track in the public high school.

A tempest in a teapot? Domesticating the natural order

The furor over intelligence and democracy in the early 1920s makes visible a critical moment at which the issues of merit, intelligence and its tests were transforming aspects of American democracy, and American democracy was defining and shaping features of intelligence and its implications. To turn first to one of the most obvious aspects of this transformation, whatever position the major contributors to the conversation about intelligence and democracy took, by its conclusion all admitted that intelligence mattered. They might not have agreed on what it was, whether IQ tests measured it, whether it could be acquired or improved, or even whether it was the most significant human attribute, but for the most part each conceded that it was something important and worth arguing about (Carson 1994; Danziger 1997).

For many Americans, the significance of intelligence lay first and foremost in its place in discussions of race, and specifically as a means of describing how various racial and ethnic groups differed from one another. Part and parcel of the development of scientific racism, intelligence in this usage became so well entrenched that even those most assiduously attempting to dismantle the prejudices surrounding their particular group – be it women or African Americans or Irish Americans – were much less likely to argue that differentiation according to intelligence was inherently wrong than to contend that, given adequate opportunities, their group would prove equal in intellectual capacity to that of white middle-class males.[14] In addition, the host of transformations, from urbanization to the rise of industrial corporate capitalism, that produced elements of a mass society in the United States concomitantly opened space for new methods to regulate, administer and make sense of what was becoming, in the eyes of many, a nation of immigrants and strangers. Following World War I, for example, the new urban high schools and expanding corporate bureaucracies saw in ability grouping a means of sorting quickly the flood of new students and job applicants and of organizing large-scale education or industry according to one of the buzzwords of the era, efficiency.[15] This move was facilitated by the creation of new positions for educational psychologists in the rapidly growing school systems and industrial psychologists in expanding corporate America. When combined with the commodification of intelligence itself as an object packaged into standardized tests sold by a variety of private companies, such changes allowed intelligence to permeate large sectors of the culture and to become part of the everyday experience of millions of Americans, from World War I veterans, to children given the Stanford-Binet by their school psychologists, to job applicants assessed as part of the hiring process. Under such conditions the importance of intelligence was proclaimed by the very pervasiveness of its measurement technology.

If all participants agreed that intelligence mattered, most were equally certain that science was significant as well. However much controversy the new mental tests engendered, few critics chose to reject their use entirely. Neither Bagley nor Lippmann, for example, suggested that mental testing lacked value or that its use in schools should simply be precluded. Indeed, Lippmann was careful to specify a number of ways in which he thought intelligence tests could contribute usefully to school and society, and even Dewey conceded that there were certain practical situations where classification was appropriate and the tests might prove helpful (Dewey 1922b). Whatever else was in dispute, the relevance of scientific findings and pronouncements to issues of public policy and even to the nature of American democracy was largely accepted. Bagley and Lippmann may have strongly disagreed with the conclusions that Terman and Whipple drew about how education should be organized and democracy should be understood, but they did not claim that drawing such conclusions and subjecting public institutions to the light of science were themselves inappropriate. Whether the public embraced or despised their work, once psychologists made credible the claim that testing might strengthen American commitments to equality and efficiency, simply ignoring it proved difficult at best. Rather, the task of sorting out rival claims and agendas as to the implications of such a project pushed both public institutions and the practices of psychologists themselves to make responses and concessions, restructuring important aspects of both.

Finally, it is important to underscore the limits to scientific authority that evolved in the course of the debate and thus to make clear how fully the resolution involved repositionings on all sides. Perhaps the best way to explore this issue is to ask, who won? Unlike the French situation, where the answer was clear cut – mental testing found little resonance among either psychologists or educationists/industrialists/political leaders – the American situation was more ambiguous. Lacking France's well institutionalized national educational system, relatively homogeneous population, and rather clearly demarcated and deeply entrenched class system, and embracing a more participatory model of democracy, American society responded to intelligence and its tests in a variety of at times contradictory ways. From the vantage point of the end of the 1920s, or even the end of the twentieth century, one would be hard pressed to say that either the testers or their critics had completely prevailed. Scientific authority did not simply triumph, or if it did, its triumph was not simple; rather, the two sides reached a fairly complicated set of accommodations. Psychologists gained extensive powers to categorize and manage those deemed marginal, especially the feebleminded, and institutions often carried out even terribly coercive practices such as sterilizations on the basis of test results. Administrators established the ability-grouped, multi-tracked high school throughout the United States, and the results of mental tests were often a key criterion determining who was placed where. At least during the 1920s a number of companies used intelligence tests as aids in deciding who to employ and where to place them, especially in the context of hiring entry-level white-collar workers. And many colleges and universities turned to intelligence testing as part of their process of admitting students and advising them on possible academic majors.

The critics of testing, however, also achieved some important results: no state or private agency ever put into place a system of testing, classifying, and then preparing children for particular career trajectories based solely on the results of intelligence measures. No university ever used mental tests alone to decide admissions. Public officials never turned to intelligence tests as important gate keepers even for immigration or access to voting, where some were actively constructing systems of restriction. And many Americans — from recruits making snide remarks about the Army testing, to fundamentalists celebrating Christian over secular values, to Deweyites committed to radical individuality — continued to embrace more complicated understandings of merit than those put forward by Terman, Yerkes and Whipple, including ones that celebrated characteristics other than brains (Ryan 1997). In addition, Lippmann, Dewey, Bagley, *et al.* created a rhetoric of doubt about psychological instruments that facilitated the raising of questions in any particular instance of their use, especially around the issue of the meaning of statistical findings for individual cases. Moreover, numerous Americans — including such intellectuals as Randolph Bourne or Franz Boas and most leaders of America's racial and ethnic minority communities — remained ambivalent or skeptical about claims for the innate and heritable nature of intelligence and its implications for racial or ethnic groups, with many more abandoning such beliefs by the end of the decade. More generally, while intelligence testing did have important effects in a number of areas at the level of administrative practice, the broader social vision of the "determinists" was largely rejected. Their highly rationalized and hyper-efficient "brave new world" — in which each citizen would be slotted into his or her occupation through the objective determinations of psychological experts – found few takers (Ryan 1997).

The partialness of this outcome must be emphasized. Viewed from a distance, what is most striking about the controversy over intelligence and democracy in the United States is that the testers and their opponents produced a space for debate, one in which notions of democracy, equality and merit were contested and re-formed. While scientific expertise was an important constituent of the conversations, its claims were as much open to dispute and revision as those from any other source. As such, this settlement thwarted the grand ambitions, if not the monumental hubris, of the American intelligence testers, who imagined a social world shorn of debate and strife through the certainties and efficiencies of their science.

Conclusion: intelligence, democracy, and co-productions of merit

The dispute over the place of intelligence and its tests in American culture was closely linked with analyses of the nature of American democracy and how notions such as equality, citizenship and merit should be understood in light of the findings of the tests. Why? Why should a new scientific procedure, intelligence testing, and the data that it generated have initiated such extensive soul-searching about the nature and future of democracy among members of the American intellectual elite? How did the scientific and political come to be so intimately linked? And, to return to the comparative aspects of the story, why did a similar conversation over the proper representation of democracy fail to erupt in France? What was it about these cultures that made their settlements of the tensions between democracy and merit so different, both in terms of the realities they created and the relative robustness of their particular solutions?

To its promoters in the United States, measurements of intelligence promised simultaneously to reveal one of the fundamental characteristics of an individual's nature and to allow social decisions about that person to be made according to seemingly objective and neutral criteria. It was a social technology that, in their rendering, could provide both equal treatment and accountability, and one perfectly suited to the new Progressive demands for a coordinated response to America's rapidly changing social landscape (Campbell 1995; Keller 1994; Skocpol 1992). The supporters touted a democracy founded on belief in human differences as fundamental, in equality of opportunity and in the primacy of demands for social efficiency. To its critics, however, the vogue of intelligence threatened to undercut the very premise of American democracy by naturalizing a social hierarchy and substituting the norms of a particular group, the mental testers, for those of the nation as a whole. They too celebrated democracy and the importance of equality and accountability, but their democracy was one emphasizing the malleability of human nature, a common cultural heritage and a thoroughgoing commitment to social mobility. Their critiques of the tests were in part technical, that the instruments failed to provide the degree of legitimation that they proclaimed, and in part more fundamental, that any technology that threatened the American ideal of the liberal, self-directing citizen capable of personal growth and transformation was intrinsically problematic.

The clash over the claims of the mental testers, examined from this perspective, was largely a struggle over who should have the power to define what was and was not equal, democratic and fair. It was a political argument, and an argument as well over exactly how politics should be done in an age of human science.[16] What gave this argument such purchase was that, by promising to provide a technology able to determine merit objectively and to organize the polity according to "natural" criteria, psychologists readily connected their new instruments with long-standing concerns about how to structure a republic along lines that maintained both democracy and efficient allocation of social resources. If successfully established, mental testing would almost invisibly naturalize particular definitions of merit and particular determinations of who should have access to what social goods, producing results little more controversial than those provided by the French system of competitive examinations, the *concours*.

These "obvious" connections between intelligence and merit that the American mental testers both fashioned and traded on and that even most critics broadly accepted, appear in a much different guise when developments in the

United States are contrasted with those in other cultures. French psychologists and public officials, as we have seen, did not conceive of intelligence and its tests in the same way as their American counterparts, and the relevance of these objects to questions of merit was simply not admitted within French intellectual and administrative culture. Even to French psychologists, measurements of intelligence were at most one part of assessing and understanding the capabilities and deficits of particular individuals. No less obsessed with merit than their American counterparts, and much more entranced by the possibility of technocratic solutions to social problems, republicans in France nonetheless felt little need to stabilize their ways of establishing merit by recourse to natural objects such as intelligence. Rather, given a republican vision in which the active intervention of the state was deemed critical to the maintenance of the nation and its citizens, French republicans by and large looked to the government to actively select and mold the next generation of elite leaders. The free play of "natural" talents, for them, was much less significant an ideal than meeting the needs of the nation and its citizens through a system of training open to all.

The differences in how intelligence and merit were constituted within these two political cultures clearly reveals the complex and local nature of the interrelations of science, politics and society. Although the intelligence test itself moved relatively frictionlessly from one culture to another, the meanings of intelligence and the worries it engendered certainly did not.[17] Rather, they were intertwined with particular cultural needs and made possible particular ways of shaping aspects of both the natural and social orders. France, with its heritage of absolutism and centralization, created a national system of education, pyramidal in structure, to ensure that the "best" reached the top of the administrative and educational hierarchies. A national curriculum, competitive examinations, and the eventual commitment to universal primary education, all insured that equality and merit would emerge as the seemingly natural results of a properly operating system. The United States, on the other hand, while also committed to equality and merit, has to this day eschewed such a centrally driven, systematic approach to the making of an elite. Deep skepticism about an interventionist state, especially in the realm of directly molding the citizenry, coupled with a pervasive ideology of personal liberty and radical individualism and a decentralized political structure, have all combined to make the French approach to sorting and grading people untenable at best. Preferring to provide equal opportunity and to let "natural" endowments flower as they will, Americans have turned instead to other methods, including recourse to naturalized objects such as intelligence and its tests, in order to understand and assess human beings. Quantified, unidimensional and hierarchical — intelligence as developed by American mental testers was constructed so as to fulfill demands for accountability, equality and merit in an American context in which plurality could flourish, state intervention remain minimal, and coordination of diversity without centralized control be privileged. The merit of science, in the American case, did not fit the same needs in France; correspondingly, the science of merit flourished in the one context, and withered in the other.

Notes

1　I would like to thank Tom Broman, Ellen Herman, members of the University of Michigan History Department non-tenured faculty colloquium, and especially Sheila Jasanoff for their very helpful comments on this article.

2　Michel Callon, among others, has been examining the role of lay people in scientific debate and the constitution of scientific fact. He has seen this phenomenon as relatively recent in origin. However, in this article it will be clear that contestations by lay people of the "truths" of the human sciences are long standing, reflective, I believe, of their sense of having their own form of expertise in such matters.

3　Stephen Jay Gould points out that Binet, at numerous times, insisted that intelligence was "not a single, scalable thing like height", and that the scale was only intended to be used with possibly backward children. Theta H. Wolf and Read D. Tuddenham also emphasize that Binet never committed to viewing intelligence as a single mental faculty, preferring to see what he was measuring as a complex of mental functions expressed in a set of externalized behaviors. Nevertheless, as constructed, the Binet-Simon scale *did* produce a singular measurement and was designed to be broadly administered.

4　Indeed, even the convulsive Dreyfus Affair (1898–1899) can be seen as, in part, a struggle between the claims of talent and prerogatives of tradition (Johnson 1966; Mayeur and Rebérioux 1987; Nord 1995).

5　Schneider makes much this same point (1992: 128). A recent example of the French connection between merit and the pyramidal educational system is the current controversy over introducing a form of affirmative action into the selection process for one of the *grandes écoles*, the Institut d'Etudes Politiques (Sciences Po) (Daley 2001).

6　For a sample of the large literature on the social/cultural transformations of the late nineteenth century, see Bannister 1979; Bederman 1995; Hawkins 1997; Higham 1970: 73–102; 1994; Painter 1987; Wiebe 1967.

7　On psychological testing and Progressive culture, see Brown 1992; Chapman 1988; Church 1971; Cravens 1978; Karier 1972; Minton 1987; Morawski and Hornstein 1991; Samelson 1979.

8　For a related approach from the vantage point of biology, see Wiggam 1922.

9　For a strikingly similar post-World War II argument, see Popper 1950.

10　It was also in the immediate postwar period that another approach to the psychological, Freudianism, spread widely, especially among the intellectual and upper middle classes in the United States. On this phenomenon, see Buhle 1998; Burnham 1967; 1968; Caplan 1998; Hale 1995.

11　On the modern American high school, see Angus and Mirel 1999; Cremin 1988; Nasaw 1979; Tyack 1974. On mental testing in the school system, see Chapman 1988; Fass 1980; Resnick 1982; Williams 1986.

12　However, for a more jaundiced appreciation of mass democracy produced at almost the same time, see Lippmann 1922a.

13　On publication rates in the popular press about intelligence and its tests, see Hart's analysis of articles indexed in the *Reader's Guide to Periodical Literature* for the period 1905–1930, Table 3 in Hart 1933.

14　From this perspective, W. E. B. Du Bois' famous 1903 essay extolling the importance of the "talented tenth" was only one instance among many in which an author more or less took for granted distinctions in individual intelligence, while resoundingly rejecting claims about group inferiority (Du Bois 1903).

15　As Elizabeth Frazer succinctly put it in an article in the *Saturday Evening Post* about the new kinds of jobs available for sectors of the working and lower middle classes, "Sheer brawn, youth, quickness no longer count all. It needs something else to get by. And that something is gray matter. Brains" (Frazer 1923: 133). On the rise of white-collar work in America, see Chandler 1977; Trachtenberg 1982; Zunz 1990.

16 For an excellent examination of politics and the human sciences in the post-World War II era, see Herman 1995. And for an interesting case study of the tangle of science and politics, see Jasanoff 1992.

17 This somewhat challenges Bruno Latour's emphasis on the immutability of his immutable mobiles (Latour 1987).

11 Mysteries of state, mysteries of nature

Authority, knowledge and expertise in the seventeenth century

Peter Dear

Order and experience

As this volume amply demonstrates, the relationship between science and the state is not a given. It depends on both the kind of science and the kind of state; it also exists on a number of different levels of interaction. The processes by which the state is daily realized in countless human actions and those by which scientific activity is carried forward have, of course, characteristically different products.[1] The former constitute civil order, whereas the latter supposedly generate knowledge. But one of the fundamental relations between the two realms is revealed by recasting the product of scientific activity as another kind of *order*, not social but natural. This is the main implication of the arguments in Shapin and Schaffer's *Leviathan and the Air-pump*.[2] The ways of producing social and natural order do not belong to mutually exclusive universes, because sanctioned social and political procedures often go into making up proper scientific practice,[3] while science is routinely used to facilitate and legitimate political arrangements or decisions. But perhaps the most obvious connection may be seen in the role of *authority* in each realm. Doing the required thing and believing the right thing are seldom to be cleanly disentangled in either of these overlapping arenas.[4]

In work focused on the seventeenth century, I have previously considered issues relating to differences in the constitution of "experience" in different disciplinary domains. At the root of this work is the idea that our only access to "experience" is through the accounts of it provided by the experiencers as well as by their related, non-linguistic actions. Scientific experience is a construal of sense-data mediated and augmented by countless arrays of socio-cognitive conventions, and it is those conventions that concern the historian and social analyst.[5]

The notion of "experience" is inseparable from the notion of *expertise*. It is not irrelevant to note that, in the seventeenth century, one said in Latin *expertus sum* to mean "I have experienced", generally meaning in the sense of having experienced something frequently and as a matter of routine. One who is experienced is an expert, and an expert knows things by virtue of being experienced in the relevant ways of the world. A farmer is experienced in the ways of crop growing or cattle; a banker in the ways of finance; or an auto mechanic in the ways of car engines, all by virtue of having experienced such things often and routinely.[6]

However, this situation only effectively obtains when there are many such experts. If an individual claims a unique expertise possessed by no one else, the *a priori* credibility of that claim is inevitably much less (all other things being equal) than would be the case if many people were already believed to possess that trait. An expert, in other words, is someone who is reckoned to be *likely* to be experienced in the relevant matters. In this sense, expertise has to be generic; it cannot be truly unique. If it were, it would be no better than a kind of private language. On this reading, then, experience as expertise translates into a question about the culturally sanctioned techniques whereby credibility for experiential assertions is established. In effect, shared experience relies on the ability to recognize a kind of attribute or property that people ("experts") can be said to possess. Expertise thus resembles "tacit knowledge", as understood by scholars in science studies.

In this chapter, I want to examine some features of the relationship between the ideas of "tacit knowledge", "skill" and "expertise" as a way of understanding legitimate authority and its constitution in the seventeenth century.

Expertise and common knowledge in the seventeenth century.

Although the modern English word "expertise" did not itself exist in the seventeenth century, the notion of authority certainly did.[7] I thus use "expertise" to designate the particular kind of authority that was associated specifically with claims to personal experience, a word perhaps most closely translated in early modern Europe by the Latin word *peritia*, with *peritus* as its adjectival form meaning "skilled" or "experienced". In the Europe of the seventeenth century, a successful presentation of oneself as possessing expertise in knowledge concerning the natural world was especially difficult, because the pre-eminent form of such knowledge was "natural philosophy". Natural philosophy, in its conventionally accepted guise in the learned world of the universities, had trouble dealing with novelty. An expert would automatically have trouble in natural philosophy because, as an academic endeavor based on the teachings of Aristotle, it was typically concerned with *common knowledge* – it was a matter of coming up with explanations for generally known and accepted phenomena. Claims to specialized experiential knowledge of a sort that most people did not possess found no real place in such an endeavor; it was very difficult to make philosophy out of private experience, because asserting a personal experiential claim was quite different from making a philosophical demonstration in Aristotle's strict sense of necessary causal proof. The establishment of an experiential claim as credible therefore required some independent fulcrum on which to rest, one that did not require a simple, brute reliance on an uncorroborated assertion.

A number of models existed in the seventeenth century by which justification in the sciences of nature could proceed. The most famous example is that of citation of authorities. When orthodox, university-based scholastic philosophy of nature was criticized by its opponents in this period, a standard complaint was that it relied on authority — especially that of Aristotle himself — rather than on first-hand examination of nature. Citation of authority to underwrite empirical assertions was indeed a usual practice, and may be seen as a way of establishing an experience as common: an experiential claim that resided in a commonly accepted, authoritative textual source such as Aristotle's *Physics* was automatically a common possession. Why the source was authoritative was from this perspective beside the point: given that it was accepted, for whatever reason, as a common repository, the establishment of a common store of experience about which to philosophize had been achieved. The mere use of the repository (the authority) presupposed its acceptability.[8]

Natural philosophers working within the conventional scholastic structure of Aristotelianism[9] were fairly secure in using Aristotelian writings as authorities of this kind, because their primary audience had been taught from the outset to accept the privileged status of Aristotelian authority as an integral part of the very structure of what philosophy was.[10] For those working outside the confines of that structure, however, such expectations were more problematic.

In practice, natural-philosophical and mathematical-scientific arguments in the seventeenth century created credibility for their empirical claims by means that were essentially textual. Experiences that were attested in authoritative texts like Aristotle's, or in common wisdom, like the idea that the bodies of murder victims bleed on the approach of the murderer, routinely stood in for the reader's own experience.[11] The creation of credibility thus relied on the existence of well formed expectations and habits of cognition among the relevant readership. But when experiences did not reside in either of those convenient storehouses, other means were needed to render them convincing — means that worked by establishing the competence of the speaker to make experiential claims.[12]

Two famous examples illustrate the point. The first is Galileo's account of fall along inclined planes, published in his *Discourses and Demonstrations Concerning Two New Sciences* in 1638. What this account does not do is provide an experimental narrative approximating the modern norm: there is no description of a specific experimental event, or set of events, carried out at a particular time, and with a detailed quantitative record of the outcomes. Instead, Galileo merely says that, with apparatus of a certain sort, he had found that the results he got agreed exactly with his theoretical assumptions — and he says that he repeated the trials "a full hundred times", always with the same result. Such expressions were ways of saying "again and again until there was no longer any doubt":[13] Galileo is establishing the authenticity of his experience that falling bodies do behave as he says by basing it on a multiplicity of unspecified instances that add up to his claimed expertise, the property that qualifies him to make this claim about how falling bodies behave.

The second example shows how Galileo's sensibilities about scientific experience were quite unremarkable. In his *Dialogue Concerning the Two Chief World Systems* of 1632, Galileo allows Simplicio, the Aristotelian straw man character in the dialogue, to talk in precisely this approved way. In the course of a famous exchange about the dropping of weights from the mast of a moving ship, Salviati, Galileo's mouthpiece, says that the outcome can be known even without resort to experience. To this Simplicio retorts: "So you have not made a hundred tests, or even one? And yet you so freely declare it to be certain?". Galileo is perfectly content to use the figure of "a hundred times" even in the construal of proper scientific experience by a notional opponent; there is no sense here that he is using an unusual kind of argument. Shortly after this exchange, Salviati himself refers to the determination of the rate of acceleration of an iron ball by tests "many times repeated". This is just what experience *was*; the matter was not controversial.[14]

Thus the trick to using experience in the establishment of a demonstrative science of nature lay in finding means, generally discursive, to make that experience commonplace. The point was to present it as if it were known independent of any specific instance, such that everyone else could know it too. Analogously, when I assert that Mt Everest is the highest mountain in the world, I cannot reply in a way satisfactory to an empiricist if challenged as to how I know it. If you do not share my worldview such that it is simply known to you too, your only immediate recourse is to accept or reject the claim on the grounds of my authority – or, less immediately, through other authorities. Notice that the previous examples from Galileo implicitly rely on the presumed authority of his own spokesman, Salviati, in the dialogue itself.

Furthermore, there is no way in such matters of eliminating the role of brute authority entirely. This is especially evident in the case of those sorts of experiential claims that refer to specific occurrences, such as experimental trials. In an absolute sense, it is always possible that the reporter of experimental trials is lying, or was mistaken in construing the results. To be quite sure of the validity of claimed results one might, rather than simply accepting other people's word on the matter, try the experiments oneself. But even that would not suffice, because of the ambiguities and circularities associated with experimental replication nowadays well known from the sociological work of Harry Collins.[15] Collins points out that determining the correct outcome of an experiment necessarily involves knowing whether the experiment was performed competently; but the ultimate criterion by which the competence of the experimental performance is judged is whether or not it gives the correct result. This experimental-scientific version of the hermeneutic circle indicates why believing empirical claims in the seventeenth century had finally to come down to an unanalyzable residue of brute credibility. The experimenter was believed simply because that person was credible. Expertise cannot be analyzed all the way down without its ceasing to appear as expertise. An irreducible and unanalyzable core must always remain at the center; if it is unveiled or explicated, its efficacy vanishes.[16]

Tacit knowledge and skill

The theme of "tacit knowledge" in science studies is canonically traced back to the work of Michael Polanyi in the 1950s, but it has more recently taken on a new twist with its use as an underpinning for examinations of "skill". In effect, the tacitness of tacit knowledge has been used to underwrite an irreducible notion of skill in scientific work: tacit knowledge by definition cannot be spelled out, and by representing a "skill" (say, in experimental manipulation) as a kind of tacit knowledge, it too becomes unanalyzable, a brute motor of scientific accomplishment.[17] A crucial ambiguity lurks in some considerations of this matter, wherein "skill" as an *attributed* property of a practitioner is conflated with "skill" as an effective attribute, genuinely inhering in the subject, to which appeal can be made in the framing of explanations.[18]

One reason to be wary of the "tacit knowledge" approach to expertise and skill is that it seems to transcend the empirically accessible realm of social conventions; it appears to require the attribution by the analyst of additional, hidden properties possessed by the people who are credited by others with a particular skill or expertise. In 1993, Kathy Olesko published an article in which she questioned the overeager use of the category "tacit knowledge" in the specific domain of the study of scientific research schools in the nineteenth century.[19] Her lack of sympathy for the invocation of "tacit knowledge" as an explanatory category evidently stems, not from a total rejection of the notion, but from a concern that it is too easily resorted to, and thereby dissuades historians from searching for less transcendent, more specific (and testable) explanations for the dissemination of knowledge-practices.

Olesko's particular point of focus is that of formal instruction, as represented in texts and lectures. She argues that these media successfully disseminated much of the know-how associated with certain experimental techniques in physics, the romantic concept of tacit knowledge and its spread by first-hand apprenticeship being largely unnecessary for her account. Of course, one should immediately qualify her argument by observing that these textbook techniques would themselves have relied on taken-for-granted practical manipulative and other abilities found routinely in other laboratories far from the place of origin of the specific procedures being detailed: that is, much of the "tacit knowledge" required to conduct the work successfully would already have been in place, much as in the case of advanced cookery books, which do not detail every step in a recipe or assist in such things as the skill-laden determination of "dropping consistency". Olesko's arguments are an appropriate caution, however: "tacit knowledge" as an explanatory category should be a last resort, not a first. It is also worth noting that the kind of tacit knowledge involved here seems to relate to an ascription by the historian of a genuine skill, rather than simply an observed attribution of skillfulness by relevant contemporaries. But this is not necessarily the case; Olesko's argument could apply equally well to the latter situation too. In both cases we have to do with a supposed (and brute, irreducible) property possessed by a person: "expertise".

In part, these considerations involve a version of Steven Shapin's emphasis on trust in the making of natural knowledge; in Shapin's treatment, trust appears as a similarly primitive concept.[20] As a kind of order, trust-relationships have to be established and conducted according to relevant social conventions. We therefore need to examine how accepting, or trusting, the expertise of another in seventeenth-century experimental practice was accomplished, and what models for trusting behavior were available. This examination will in turn speak to the practical and, so to speak, political character of shared – scientific – experience.

Experiment and the authority of Otto von Guericke

Otto von Guericke, in his *Experimenta Nova* of 1672, makes the following distinction regarding competing astronomical systems, such as the Ptolemaic and the Copernican:

> Truly, because there is a difference between believing and knowing *(for to believe is to agree with some speaker on account of authority: however, to know is to understand something through its cause)*…it is easy to determine as true that system which is known causally, and which is to be preferred over that which is offered on the authority of the speaker: "Why do you tell me to believe if I am able to know?" says Augustine.[21]

As a general rule to follow, this is perhaps unexceptionable, but its utility would appear to be severely limited. One of the claims of which Guericke was particularly proud was that his weather barometer (which indicated by means of a little wooden manikin) could tell you if there was a great storm a hundred, or even two hundred, miles away. As he tells a correspondent, the manikin would sometimes descend to a much greater degree than usual, and when that happened, "experience afterwards taught through written accounts that at the same time, by storms whether at sea or on land, there had been great calamities, although where I was, the wind had not then been so violent". He does not know the cause of this phenomenon, but by its means he can tell the occurrence of large storms far away, their locations subsequently becoming known from news reports (*ex novellis*).[22]

Guericke thus indicated in his own work the occasional necessity of relying on "authority" to make knowledge: he could not have made his discovery without reliance on news reports from elsewhere with which to correlate his observations. In this case, he had no other recourse, on his own account. He did not know the precise cause of the barometric drop, only that it appeared to be a sign of distant storms. Causal knowledge, he had said, was to be preferred over "authority"; but the latter was here essential because there was no alternative. The same lesson may be seen in other areas of Guericke's work: one of the more celebrated cases of disseminated scientific experience in the seventeenth century concerns Guericke's own air-pump experiments. These were publicly displayed and widely publicized in the 1650s and early 1660s, chiefly through writings by the German Jesuit Gaspar Schott. The ways in which Guericke created his public experiences, Schott disseminated them, and others (like Robert Boyle) took them up present the emerging social meaning of a particular sort of experience concerning nature. They also show how "new" experiments, as Guericke called them, tended to escape the bounds of his favored "causal" knowledge and leave him relying, once again, on "authority".

Our chief windows on Guericke's experiments are the reports made by Schott, together with Guericke's own considerably later account in his *Experimenta Nova*. Certain features are clear, however: in particular, the celebrated trials of the "Magdeburg hemispheres" seem to have been deliberately designed and staged as spectacle (in 1657) some time after Guericke's invention of the basic air pump. The protocol for these displays was as follows: a pair of copper hemispheres, fitting closely together, had the air in their enclosed interior pumped out. The immense force required to separate them, owing to the pressure of the circumambient air, could then be shown – most spectacularly by using teams of horses straining in opposite directions on ropes attached to the respective hemispheres.[23] Furthermore, this was spectacle before men of civic and imperial consequence.

Schott was responsible for the wide publicity of Guericke's work in the republic of letters, with his accounts given first in the *Mechanica Hydraulico-pneumatica* of 1657. Indeed, it was Schott who dubbed Guericke's air-pump work the "Magdeburg experiment". Schott's account appears in the form of a short treatise appended to the *Mechanica*, bearing on its equivalent of a title-page the legend: "Experimentum novum Magdeburgicum, quo vacuum aliqui stabilire, alij evertere conantur" (i.e. the new Magdeburg experiment, by which some strive to establish the vacuum, others to overturn it). The "experiment" is lavishly attributed to Guericke; attendant discussions by Schott and others of its possible implications are also prominently advertised.[24] Schott describes how Guericke had come up with a new machine, which he showed off to

> the most eminent prince John Philip, archbishop of Mainz and bishop of Würzburg, who observed it in his seat at Würzburg; where, in the presence of the same eminent prince, I have seen the whole set-up more than once, I have examined it, I have entrusted it to writing, I have communicated it to men of letters at Rome and elsewhere and have sought their judgement; nor is there anyone who doesn't praise the ingenuity of its author.[25]

Schott goes on to provide accounts of various experiments and their apparatus, and quotes some letters to him from Guericke, including material on the Magdeburg hemispheres.[26] The conflation or mutual enfolding of civil and experimental authority together with personal testimony is striking.

One of Schott's colleagues who was quoted at length on these experiments and their meaning was Melchior Cornaeus, the professor of theology at Würzburg (where Schott was professor of mathematics). Cornaeus had seen and examined the "experiment" with Schott on several occasions (unnumbered repetition once again), and nearly twenty pages of Schott's treatise are given over to reprinting the material from Cornaeus's *Physicorum Disputationes* that discussed the question of the vacuum in light of these demonstrations.[27]

Guericke's experiments are discussed at greater length, with full illustrations, in one of Schott's later publications, the *Technica Curiosa* of 1664. By this time the experiments were well known, having already spawned the famous work on air-pumps of Robert Boyle in England.[28] Once again, Guericke's letters to Schott are quoted at length. In the letter (dated 30 December 1661) that concerns the hemispheres and horses, Guericke boasts that "I have often exhibited this experiment in the presence of eminent men".[29]

Schott subsequently includes much more detailed accounts of Guericke's experiments than those given in the quoted letters, based on fuller information deliberately acquired from Guericke.[30] Schott is, however, less concerned there to provide circumstantial detail of specific trials than he is to detail the structure of the apparatus and its proper use, presented in the common quasi-geometrical form found in the mathematical sciences.[31] The problem that the geometrical approach attempted to solve was that empirical claims regarding individual, specific occurrences were not philosophical knowledge. They were merely historical particulars, apparently failing to engage with the universally true statements required for the making of natural philosophical demonstration. To deal with this difficulty, therefore, Schott needed to be able to rely on techniques by which such an event might be worked up into a true scientific experience of the universal (Aristotelian) kind that could be used in deriving philosophical consequences; an experimental narrative that did not possess obvious scientific implications would have been neither worth making nor worth contesting. Schott's concern in both the 1657 and 1664 accounts of the "Magdeburg experiment" was therefore to focus on discussion of the experiment's implications for ideas about the possibility of voids in nature.[32] The ascription of expertise, in the guise of Guericke's lauded ingeniousness in these experiments, was itself a kind of argument from authority (an expert whom no one recognizes as such is not an expert).

Recently some scholars have suggested that the characteristically early-modern form of authority exercised by the absolutist state might have played some role in determining the means and form of the establishment of empirical fact in natural philosophy, perhaps by shaping the characteristic ways in which philosophers made appeal to the certifying capacity of the king or other nobles acting as his surrogates.[33] Guericke's concern to stress the "eminence" of those before whom he had shown his experiments illustrates this point to some degree. But the connection may also apply at a more fundamental level. Consider once more the demonstration involving the hemispheres and the horses: it calls to mind the episode that begins Foucault's *Discipline and Punish*.[34] In comparing early-modern French penal practices with those of the nineteenth century, Foucault first presents a contemporary description of the execution of a would-be regicide in 1757. Among other horrors, the penitent criminal was to be quartered – torn asunder by four horses, each attached by rope to one of his limbs. Like Guericke's hemispheres, this procedure proved more difficult than the onlookers expected; indeed, more difficult even than the executioners expected, so that the man's limbs had at last to be cut with a knife before the horses could tear them from the trunk. The elaborate ceremony of this public punishment is then contrasted with a document from the mid-nineteenth century, a set of rules to govern the days of young prison inmates, from dawn till dusk.[35] Foucault wishes to emphasize the disparity between the spectacular vengeance of the king and the hidden, apparently inevitable workings of the prison. Just so might we try to understand the disparity between the early-modern showpiece experiment, which focused truth on public demonstration, and the nineteenth-century (modern) laboratory protocol. As with the disciplined activity of the ideal modern prison, laboratory procedures too have their authorizing protocols and their sequestered enactments, which lend their knowledge-pronouncements the air of inevitable, bureaucratic truth – the truth of the nineteenth-century liberal state. Thus, as we focus on the early-modern experiment, using Guericke's Magdeburg hemispheres as its emblem, we can at the same time examine the ways in which an absolutist regime in early-modern Europe attempted to establish its own political authority – because the one is not in reality distinct from the other. By showing the crucial *groundlessness* of that authority, we also see the fundamental groundlessness of expertise when understood as a translation of absolutist political authority.

Mystery of state and the demonstrative regress: the invisible core

The doctrine of the "divine right of kings", promoted in its various ways most famously in England by the Stuarts and (more successfully) in France by Louis XIV, traded on the notion of "mysteries of state" (*arcana imperii*). Kingship, and the decisions that the monarch was called upon to make, supposedly involved considerations and judgments that would sometimes be unfathomable to outsiders. Not surprisingly, contemporaries (and not only opponents) often conflated the idea with Machiavelli's ideas about "*reason* of state". The main difference between "mystery of state" and "reason of state" was that "mystery" stressed some element of transcendence, such that royal edicts would be based on considerations that went beyond articulable rationality; whereas reason of state could be codified in terms of the various, even deceitful, stratagems that the prince might sometimes be obliged to adopt in order to preserve and apply his power effectively.[36] Many in the sixteenth and seventeenth centuries found Machiavelli's doctrines wicked, of course, because they implied that properly conducted kingship was something other than the product of noble enlightenment. The notion of "mystery" of state, on the other hand, elevated kingly decisions, and in fact typically sanctified them, with the notion of the ruler as the Lord's anointed, attended by the consequent holy status of kingship and of the edicts that emerged from it. That move too was one that Machiavelli had analyzed, but this analysis was not always seen as merely debunking. It was possible to see the prince as having been freed from the usual moral constraints precisely through divine sanction. Hence Jean Bodin claimed, in his *Six livres de la république*, that Machiavelli had "profaned" what Bodin called the "sacred mysteries of political philosophy" because he had not represented matters in this reverential way.[37]

In practice, of course, a view of kingship and government as divinely ordained, as set-apart, required a great deal of acceptance by subjects of the legitimacy of government actions. This was especially important in the large number of cases where the justifying grounds for actions were obscure or even potentially suspicious; implied divine sanction was a useful monarchical prop in such circumstances. Natural philosophers in the seventeenth century who wanted to convince people of an empirical assertion therefore had available as a possible model the following strategy: if the assertion could be made in such a way as to suggest that there was an unanalyzable, primitive, ineffable quality investing the philosopher's qualifications to speak – that is, justifying an ascription of expertise – then perhaps that claim could be made as unquestioningly acceptable as the edict of an absolute prince. In the case of the prince's authority, if all subjects do as a matter of fact acknowledge it, then its legitimacy will not itself need to be justified, because the acceptance in practice constitutes the legitimacy. The real work is therefore hidden in the ways in which that acceptance has already been ensured. In the case of the philosopher, the analogous move translates into ensuring the acceptance of one's expertise.[38]

The mutual relevance of these parallel systems can be illustrated more concretely by looking at specific cases of their inter-relation. In particular, Thomas Hobbes, especially given his prominent role in recent historiography concerning seventeenth-century experimentalism, usefully maps out precisely this territory. Hobbes, of course, was a great champion of absolutist government, seeing it as the necessary form of government towards which a society ought inevitably to develop. Shapin and Schaffer have argued that, for Hobbes, the state is the ultimate guarantor of generally shared, public knowledge, of which demonstrative knowledge is itself the most powerful form. Hobbes needed to appeal to such transcendent authority in practically all areas of knowledge, including natural philosophy, because without it agreement could not be forced, and dissension would be the result.[39] In his conception of the relationship between the polity and the practice of natural philosophy, notions of expertise are essentially collapsed into notions of state authority; they are not really distinct.

In setting out his position, Hobbes stressed the importance of a determinate method in making knowledge. At the beginning of *De Corpore* (1655) he wrote: "Every man brought philosophy, that is, natural reason, into the world with him; for all men can reason to some degree, and concerning some things: but...most men wander out of the way, and fall into error for want of method".[40] Much like Galileo, Hobbes adhered to a strict demonstrative (hence also methodical) ideal in philosophy that had geometry as its model. But unlike Galileo, Hobbes explicitly denied the adequacy of this model for natural philosophy. Hence the following famous passage:

> [T]he Science of every Subject is derived from a praecognition of the Causes, Generation, and Construction of the same; and consequently where the Causes are known, there is place for Demonstration, but not where the

Causes are to seek for. Geometry therefore is demonstrable; for the Lines and
Figures from which we reason are drawn and described by our selves; and
Civill Philosophy is demonstrable because, we make the Commonwealth our
selves. But because of Naturall Bodies we know not the Construction, but
seek it from the Effects, there lyes no demonstration of what the Causes be
we seek for, but onely of what they may be.[41]

Thus Hobbes argues that deductive synthesis from underlying principles to
their consequences, as in geometry, is the right way to proceed even in the case
of natural philosophy – just as in "civil philosophy". But, as the passage shows,
when applied to natural philosophy this approach would not result in a proper
demonstration of the classical Aristotelian kind – one derived from necessary,
true causes. Analysis, or resolution, could usually arrive at potential physical
causes that were capable – once accepted – of explaining the original effects
with the force of necessary demonstration. But unless the causes themselves were
somehow known to be the true ones, as opposed to being mere suppositions that
yielded the right consequences, no true physical demonstrations in the strict
Aristotelian or mathematical sense could be achieved. Deduction from those
causes, for Hobbes, would simply confirm that the effects would follow *if* those
particular causes were predicated.

Hobbes' conception of the formal structure of a science was a standard one
in contemporary considerations of method. It closely resembles the influential
account of the so-called "demonstrative regress" that had been given by Jacopo
Zabarella in the late sixteenth century.[42] The theory of the demonstrative regress
has the advantage of showing precisely where the irreducible authority requisite
in Hobbes' account resides. The basic procedure of the demonstrative regress
took the following form: commencing with a phenomenon to be explained, a
process of "resolution", or logical analysis, discovers a candidate cause for the
phenomenon. There follows a stage of "composition", or synthesis, whereby the
phenomenon is logically deduced from that supposed cause, so as to explain it in
the proper Aristotelian scientific way. The difficulty lies in the movement from
the resolutive stage to the compositive stage: analyzing a phenomenon to locate
fundamental principles apparently underlying it does not guarantee that those
principles will function as causes from which the phenomenon can be deduced.

The resolution aims at displaying some factor in the situation that is, analytically, necessarily associated with the phenomenon. But in itself, such a resolution
provides no warrant for using that factor as the basis for a subsequent deductive
causal explanation. This is because the resolution serves only to show that the
factor is a constant concomitant of the phenomenon. Logically, it is unable to
show that the factor is the phenomenon's cause. Consider the phenomenon of
cold weather in winter. One of astronomical winter's constant concomitants is
the prominence (in the northern hemisphere) of the constellation Orion in the
evening sky, in contrast to the situation in the summer. We need not, however,
conclude that Orion's visibility was the cause of coldness in winter.[43] We might
find more plausible the proposition that another constant concomitant, the much

lower elevation of the sun in the sky during the winter, is the true cause. In order, that is, to decide whether any particular constant concomitant is a true causal factor,[44] an independent determination must be made in between the resolutive and the subsequent compositive stages. By its very nature, this determination cannot be thoroughly formalized in the same manner as resolution or composition; each instance would rely crucially on particularities of the situation. Zabarella labelled this process *negotiatio*, an imprecise process of "thinking things over" that was aimed at creating conviction in the mind that there was indeed a necessary causal relation between the phenomenon and a particular constant concomitant. Just as Descartes had difficulty in giving formal criteria for determining whether an idea was truly "clear and distinct" – or, indeed, just as in logical reasoning one is sometimes reduced to saying that something "just follows" – Zabarella would have the inquirer mull things over until persuaded.[45]

The possibility of *negotiatio* relied on the notion that the mind can grasp metaphysically real universals, since the sought causes would be such universals. Zabarella's idea, that is, involves the possibility of grasping intuitively a universal that has some kind of extra-mental reality out in the world itself. It now becomes relevant to consider that Hobbes, notoriously, was a nominalist. Hobbes held that meaningful talk of universals could only refer to concepts (human concepts only, insofar as God's mind is inaccessible to us).[46] True physical causes would therefore remain unknowable, because if real universals were inaccessible, then Zabarellan *negotiatio* would have no possibility of gaining a toe-hold; there would remain an unbridgeable gulf between resolution and composition. Causes in geometry, or in human society, were immune from such nescience simply because they were human constructions. In their cases, the universal concepts in the mind of the inquirer were literally the same as the ones generating the effects to be explained: the gap between resolution and composition that *negotiatio* was needed to fill is already closed.

Hobbes' denial of a truly demonstrative natural philosophy did not prevent him from developing his own accounts of the physical world, but those accounts held the status of being the "most rational" explanations rather than being necessarily true. They had the civic advantage of being shared by everyone in an ideal Hobbesian society. In such a society, furthermore, there would be no philosophical experts. The only "expert" is the king, the central authority who disciplines all reasoning, by use of the sword if necessary. Hence the argument in *Leviathan and the Air-pump* that Hobbes maintained that even mathematics relied on authority.[47] Shapin and Schaffer base their claim on Hobbes' remark that if people had interests invested in mathematical propositions, those propositions would be as controversial as those of theology or politics. Theirs seems an implausible inference, given the way in which Hobbes routinely treated mathematical demonstration as a privileged form of knowledge that, unlike most other forms, was capable of producing certain rather than merely conjectural deductive demonstrations. Hobbes in fact had a high regard for geometry precisely because its demonstrations could not, he thought, be doubted by any rational and attentive person: just so, the authority of the king, having been granted to him, cannot, Hobbes thought, properly be questioned.[48] Mathematics, of course, was not physics; that is, the switch from resolution to composition at the crucial Zabarellan switch-point does not present the same difficulties, because physical causes are not involved. But Hobbes did recognize the difficulties that still attended mathematical reasoning, and mathematical controversy, and he emphasized the role of a central authority in a discussion concerning arithmetic. Arithmetic, representing reckoning in general, was a field in which

> the ablest, most attentive, and most practised men, may deceive themselves, and inferre false Conclusions; Not but that Reason it selfe is always Right Reason, as well as Arithmetique is a certain and infallible Art: But no one mans Reason, nor the Reason of any one number of men, makes the certaintie; no more than an account is therefore well cast up, because a great many men have unanimously approved it. And therfore, as when there is a controversy in an account, the parties must by their own accord, set up for right Reason, the Reason of some Arbitrator, or Judge, to whose sentence they will both stand, or their controversie must either come to blowes, or be undecided, for want of a right Reason constituted by Nature; so is it also in all debates of what kind soever.[49]

So even in the cases of such topics as "geometry and the commonwealth", absolute central authority was important in Hobbes' view of things, because it properly directed everyone's reasoning past such indeterminacies.

In a Hobbesian society, therefore, there could not be a multiplicity of experts: that would too much resemble enthusiasm, with many competing sources of authority.[50] Consequently, the production of novelty (as with air-pump experiments) was not central to Hobbes' views on proper knowledge-making: novelty required experts in order for it to become properly certified; novelties were not things that everyone already knows. In effect, Hobbes' ideal society has its central mysteries of irreducible expertise in exactly the same place as its "mysteries of state" – both are lodged in the prince. The famous seventeenth-century English treason of envisaging (or "intending") the king's death was, we might say, tantamount to contemplating the disappearance of both social and cognitive order: "the king is dead; long live the king" was the only thinkable way to deal with it.[51]

Hobbes' apparent nominalism makes sense in this regard, too, precisely as an *epistemological* nominalism. Rather than simply denying that there are such things as true universals (although he often ridiculed the idea), his point is, more fundamentally, that we could not come to know them unless we had made them ourselves.[52] The nearest equivalent to expertise regarding some aspect of the natural world, for Hobbes, really amounts to having familiarity with officially sanctioned ways of thinking about things; officially sanctioned linguistic conventions. There is no self-sufficient, independent expert save the king. Many irreducible sources of authority have collapsed into one.

Mathematics, kings and experts: who knows?

The success of mathematical sciences such as mechanics, astronomy and optics in the seventeenth century has long been a dominant theme in our understanding of the period. But the kinds of experience that attached to them can be better understood once we examine their structuring of expertise. The Aristotelian-style qualitative physics of the schools had relied on widely distributed, and in principle common, experience as its empirical underpinning. The mathematical sciences imported by contrast a more specialized form of experience into formal knowledge-making. The methodological self-consciousness attending it, expressed by many mathematical scientists in the course of the century, involved attempts to validate long-standing ways of managing particular experience so as to make it universal,[53] as we saw above in the case of Schott's handling of Guericke's work. The Hobbesian model provides a sort of paradigm case of this issue, or perhaps its *reductio ad absurdum*: the central, authoritative prince makes his singular, private experience communal simply by virtue of his own authority. Thus the individual astronomer or optician needed to acquire some semblance of a comparable civic authority in order to achieve the same thing. Schott in effect did this, when he advertised and discussed Guericke's work, by calling on the social/institutional sanction of his network of Jesuit colleagues and correspondents, just as Guericke took care to speak of presenting his experiments before the archbishop. These institutional sites and the philosophers' places within them were the arks that contained the mystery of Schott's and Guericke's claimed expertise.

Mathematical sciences also had a further advantage: they did not, by the usual definitions, concern themselves with physical causes or with the essences of things. Much like Hobbes' conventionalized natural philosophy, mathematics constituted a knowledge-system that was developed out of authoritatively established axioms, postulates and definitions, which had to be accepted without proof at the outset.

The Cartesian approach to natural philosophy serves to underscore the point. Descartes tried to obviate the problem (of accrediting a claim to expertise) by means of methodological solipsism: the metaphysical grounding of his natural philosophy was meant to convince each individual of certain unquestionable truths through what was in effect a process of turning everyone into Descartes. In his *Meditations*, Descartes presents himself like Hamlet, bounded in a nutshell and counting himself a king of infinite space: he extrudes a universe from the workings of his own mind. It was easy to be both king *and* expert when there was only the one of you. Sources of authority, whether they were many or few, had ultimately to reside in a mystery. Descartes' mystery was the free gift of God, and that was what enabled him to know anything at all. Other mysteries were often less clear-cut, but there was always one somewhere.

Experts are assumed to know more than they can say – the classic authority of the teacher. In that sense we have returned to the realm of "tacit knowledge", knowledge that cannot be spelled out. Olesko's argument warns us to restrict severely the arena within which we resort to the notion of tacit knowledge; nonetheless, it always lurks inside any system of knowledge, if no more than as a singularity at the centre. Expert witnesses in the modern courtroom are there precisely because their credibility is reckoned to go beyond what they can justify on the witness stand. If they tried too hard to justify everything they said with explicit appeals to evidence and the grounds of their reasoning, that credibility would be damaged; in the US legal system at least, the role of cross-examination is often to achieve precisely that. Justifying everything (even if it were possible) would leave no core of mysterious competence — it would leave nothing. Similarly, modern democratic governments, which nowadays, fashionably, purport often to strive for "transparency" in their procedures,[54] cannot in reality achieve any such thing without at the same time utterly abrogating their *authority*. Just so, a "mystery of state" in the seventeenth century could never be justified by marshaling all the reasons for a government action. It had to remain a mystery, a divinely sanctioned version of the Machiavellian "reason of state". Expertise, the bedrock of most shared experience (whether a prince's or a natural philosopher's), was either ineffable, or else toothless.

Epilogue

The moral justification of claims to expertise rests on similar ambiguities. A much later example, a passage from Claude Bernard's *Introduction à l'étude de la médecine expérimentale* (1865), serves as a striking illustration. Bernard says:

> in science, ideas are what give facts their value and meaning. It is the same in morals, it is everywhere the same. Facts materially alike may have opposite scientific meanings, according to the ideas with which they are connected. A cowardly assassin, a hero and a warrior each plunges a dagger into the breast of his fellow. What differentiates them, unless it be the ideas that guide their hands? A surgeon, a physiologist and Nero give themselves up alike to mutilation of living beings. What differentiates them also, if not ideas?[55]

This interesting view of the matter attempts to displace potential moral criticism by appealing to a higher realm of existence, the world of ideas, which will underpin the physiologist's claim to an expertise that is morally justifying. Expertise implies rights, foremost among them the right to be believed in one's area of competence. Bernard's remarks involve an expert's right to perform otherwise questionable actions. He speaks of that right as springing from the ideas moving the individual concerned rather than resulting from some kind of social sanction. Much like the traitor who intends the death of the king, Nero's actions are condemned by Bernard on the basis of the intentions that motivate them, not on the material character of the actions. By contrast, when Hobbes had written of the impossibility of commanding a person's beliefs (since only outward actions can be disciplined), he had taken almost exactly the opposite view: only the visible actions mattered.[56] And Hobbes was widely held to be wicked. Ideas and personal experience are routinely held aloof from the socio-culturally structured, as if they possessed an independent existence. But seeing the world through collective eyes, like sharing a language, requires that we share minds. The sociology (and hence experience) found in the real world is much more complicated than that discussed by Descartes, and credibility is not just a matter of inner states of belief. In the polity of the United Kingdom in 1876, not long after Bernard wrote the words quoted above, Parliament was to place physiological vivisection under strict legal controls.[57] Absolutism was not the only context of political/scientific co-production.

Notes

1 For a perspective on the "state" that stresses its everyday realization, see Philip Corrigan and Derek Sayer, *The Great Arch: English State Formation as Cultural Revolution* (Oxford: Blackwell, 1985).

2 Steven Shapin and Simon Schaffer, *Leviathan and the Air-pump: Hobbes, Boyle, and the Experimental Life* (Princeton: Princeton University Press, 1985). See "Introduction" to the present volume for discussion of their approach.

3 For an unusually blatant case, see Daniel J. Kevles, *The Baltimore Case: A Trial of Politics, Science, and Character* (New York: Norton, 1998).

4 It should be said that the kind of "science" under consideration here is concerned with theoretical understanding of nature rather than practical control of nature, as difficult as a sharp distinction is to make between them. The ongoing practical signifi-cance of the distinction, however, while clear in the seventeenth century (with the label "natural philosophy"), remains important today: see James C. Scott, *Seeing Like a State: How Certain Schemes to Improve the Human Condition Have Failed* (New Haven: Yale University Press, 1998), where the state projects that the author associates with "high modernism" are held to disregard practical agricultural knowledge rooted in local experience.

5 Peter Dear, *Discipline and Experience: The Mathematical Way in the Scientific Revolution* (Chicago: University of Chicago Press, 1995).

6 In general on such present-day issues, see Sheila S. Jasanoff, *Science at the Bar: Law, Science, and Technology in America* (Cambridge MA: Harvard University Press, 1995).

7 The earliest use of the English word "expertise" listed in the *Oxford English Dictionary* dates from 1869.

8 This absolutely commonplace practice provoked much criticism in the seventeenth century: see, for one influential study of the backlash, the classic Richard Foster Jones, *Ancients and Moderns: A Study of the Scientific Movement in Seventeenth-century England* (St Louis: Washington University Press, 1961) ch. 6. The matter is discussed more generally in Peter Dear, *"Totius in verba*: Rhetoric and Authority in the Early Royal Society", *Isis* 76(1985): 145–161.

9 In the sense of an organization around the works of Aristotle, independent of partic-ular doctrinal details.

10 See, for a detailed account focused on France, L. W. B. Brockliss, *French Higher Education in the Seventeenth and Eighteenth Centuries: A Cultural History* (Oxford: Clarendon Press, 1987).

11 Dear, *Discipline and Experience*, p. 75.

12 Cf. Stephen Turner, "What is the Problem with Experts?", *Social Studies of Science* 31(2001): 123–149.

13 Dear, *Discipline and Experience*, p. 126; on the commonplace character of such expres-sions, chs 3, 5.

14 See *ibid.*, pp. 126–127.

15 H. M. Collins, *Changing Order: Replication and Induction in Scientific Practice* (London: Sage, 1985).

16 Sheila Jasanoff, "Science, Politics, and the Renegotiation of Expertise at EPA", *Osiris* 7(1992): 195–217, examines just such problems in attempts made by a modern American governmental agency to display political "transparency" as a means of justifying its decisions.

17 But for a close empirical examination of the negotiated complexity even of routine "tacit skills", see Kathleen Jordan and Michael Lynch, "The Sociology of a Genetic Engineering Technique: Ritual and Rationality in the Performance of the 'Plasmid Prep'", in Adele E. Clark and Joan H. Fujimura (eds) *The Right Tools for the Job: At Work in Twentieth-Century Life Sciences* (Princeton: Princeton University Press, 1992) pp. 77–114.

18 Trevor Pinch, H. M. Collins and Larry Carbone, "Inside Knowledge: Second Order Measures of Skill", *Sociological Review* 44(1996): 163–186. Michael Polanyi, *Personal Knowledge: Towards a Post-Critical Philosophy of Science* (Chicago: University of Chicago Press, 1962) pp.195–202, exemplifies a rather "mystical" approach to such matters that appears to involve a similar (creative?) conflation.

19 Kathryn M. Olesko, "Tacit Knowledge and School Formation", *Osiris* n.s. 8(1993): 16–29. This special volume of *Osiris* is dedicated to historical work on localized scientific research schools in the recent Anglo-American scholarly tradition rather than the somewhat different German work that looks at more geographically distributed entities. For a recent discussion of similar issues, see also Myles Jackson, *Spectrum of Belief: Joseph von Fraunhofer and the Craft of Precision Optics* (Cambridge MA: MIT Press, 2000) esp. pp. 10–13.

20 Steven Shapin, *A Social History of Truth: Science and Civility in Seventeenth-Century England* (Chicago: University of Chicago Press, 1994).

21 Otto von Guericke, *Experimenta Nova (ut Vocantur) Magdeburgica de Vacuo Spatio* (Amsterdam, 1672; facs. rpt. Aalen: Otto Zeller, 1962) p. 218a. All translations from this book are my own; there is also a rather poor English translation by Margaret Glover Foley Ames (Dordrecht: Kluwer, 1994).

22 Guericke, *Experimenta Nova*, letter to Stanislaus Lubienietzki dated 2 April 1666, pp. 195b–196a; see also *ibid.*, pp. 100a–b (quoting from a letter to Schott of 1661), 115b.

23 Guericke is quoted on the hemispheres and horses in Gaspar Schott, *Mechanica Hydraulico-pneumatica* (Würzburg, 1657) pp. 460–461; Schott, *Technica Curiosa, Sive de Mirabilia Artis* (Würzberg, 1664), presents a formal account of it on pp. 38–39 (with a handsome fold-out plate, Iconismus III), and quotes a letter from Guericke of 1661, p. 48. The procedure is also described in Guericke, *Experimenta Nova*, p. 104, complete with another large illustration ("Iconismus XI").

24 Schott, *Mechanica Hydraulico-pneumatica*, p. 441.

25 *Ibid.*, p. 444.

26 *Ibid.*, pp. 445–449.

27 *Ibid.*, p. 451; Cornaeus material pp. 466–484. See for further discussion of Jesuit ideas on the void Michael John Gorman, "Jesuit Explorations of the Torricellian Space: Carp-bladders and Sulphurous Fumes", *Mélanges de l'Ecole Française de Rome. Italie et Méditerranée*, tome 106, fasc. 1 (1994) pp. 7–32.

28 Schott, *Technica Curiosa*, comprises twelve books, of which the first concerns "Mirabilia Magdeburgica", while the second is on "Mirabilia Anglicana", meaning Boyle's work.

29 *Ibid.*, p. 48.

30 See remarks in *ibid.*, p. 38.

31 Cf. Dear, *Discipline and Experience*, ch. 2, sect. III.

32 For further discussion of Schott's use of a Jesuit network to focus on the philosophical implications of Guericke's work, see Michael John Gorman, "The Scientific Counter-

Revolution: Mathematics, Natural Philosophy and Experimentalism in Jesuit Culture, 1580–c.1670" (Ph.D. dissertation, Florence: European University Institute, 1998) ch. 6, "Experiment, Expertise and Centralized Authority: The Vacuum Debate", pp. 160–197.

33 Christian Licoppe, *La Formation de la pratique scientifique: Le Discours de l'expérience en France et en Angleterre (1630–1820)* (Paris: Éditions La Découverte, 1996) esp. ch. 2; Mario Biagioli, *Galileo, Courtier: The Practice of Science in the Culture of Absolutism* (Chicago: University of Chicago Press, 1993); Mario Biagioli, "Scientific Revolution, Social Bricolage, and Etiquette", in Roy Porter and Mikulás Teich (eds) *The Scientific Revolution in National Context* (Cambridge: Cambridge University Press, 1992) pp. 11–54. For a valuable historiographical overview and discussion of early-modern absolutism, see Gerhard Oestreich, *Neostoicism and the Early Modern State* (Cambridge: Cambridge University Press, 1982) ch. 15, "The Structure of the Absolute State". That absolutism in practice was significantly mediated by local power structures, and hence differed significantly from its theoretical expositions, is classically shown by William Beik, *Absolutism and Society in Seventeenth-century France: State Power and Provincial Aristocracy in Languedoc* (Cambridge: Cambridge University Press, 1985).

34 Michel Foucault, *Discipline and Punish: The Birth of the Prison*, trans. Alan Sheridan (New York: Vintage Books, 1995). I am grateful to a member of the audience at my presentation to the Notre Dame Department of History and Philosophy of Science (October 1998) for having encouraged me to focus on this comparison.

35 *Ibid.*, pp. 3–7.

36 See Peter S. Donaldson, *Machiavelli and Mystery of State* (Cambridge: Cambridge University Press, 1988) esp. ch. 4; Maurizio Viroli, *From Politics to Reason of State: The Acquisition and Transformation of the Language of Politics 1250–1600* (Cambridge: Cambridge University Press, 1992) esp. ch. 6; also J. G. A. Pocock, *The Machiavellian Moment: Florentine Political Thought and the Atlantic Republican Tradition* (Princeton: Princeton University Press, 1975). See also Biagioli, *Galileo, Courtier*, pp. 51–52, on the untouchability (and hence unchallengeability) of the "mystery" associated with the prince.

37 Quoted in Donaldson, *Machiavelli*, p. 115 (my translation).

38 Thus the speaker needs to be granted a degree of personal expertise, rather than simply having particular claims accepted on the basis of their official sanction – even if the "expert" might be seen as a vicar of the monarch.

39 Shapin and Schaffer, *Leviathan and the Air-pump*, pp. 152–154; see below for a slight qualification of their argument.

40 Quoted in John Watkins, *Hobbes's System of Ideas: A Study in the Political Significance of Philosophical Theories* (London: Hutchinson, 1965) p. 48.

41 Thomas Hobbes, *The English Works of Thomas Hobbes of Malmesbury, now first collected and edited by Sir William Molesworth*, 11 vols (London, 1839), vol. 7, p. 184; see also Tom Sorell, *Hobbes [The Arguments of the Philosophers]* (London: Routledge and Kegan Paul, 1986) pp. 137–139. A useful overview of Hobbes' views on scientific demonstration is Douglas Jesseph, "Hobbes and the Method of Natural Science", in Tom Sorrell (ed.) *The Cambridge Companion to Hobbes* (Cambridge: Cambridge University Press, 1996) pp. 86–107.

42 For details, see Peter Dear, "Method and the Study of Nature", in Daniel Garber and Michael Ayers (eds) *The Cambridge History of Seventeenth-Century Philosophy*, 2 vols, (Cambridge: Cambridge University Press, 1998) vol.1, pp. 147–177, esp. p. 152.

43 Note that this is my own example, not Zabarella's.

44 The Aristotelian doctrine of monocausality is actually involved here, but may for present purposes be disregarded. In general see Nicholas Jardine, "Epistemology of the Sciences", in Quentin Skinner, Charles Schmitt, Eckhard Kessler and Jill Kraye (eds), *The Cambridge History of Renaissance Philosophy* (Cambridge: Cambridge University Press, 1988) pp. 685–711.

45 Cf. for example David Bloor, *Knowledge and Social Imagery*, 2nd edn (Chicago: University of Chicago Press, 1991) on formal logic.

46 For a useful recent discussion of the nuances of Hobbes' nominalism, see Douglas M. Jesseph, *Squaring the Circle: The War Between Hobbes and Wallis* (Chicago: University of Chicago Press, 1999) pp. 205–211.

47 Shapin and Schaffer, *Leviathan and the Air-pump*, p. 153. Their point holds, however, for a weaker claim concerning control over the authorized *teaching* of mathematics.

48 The ambiguity in Hobbes' arguments here is discussed in Sorell, *Hobbes*, pp. 45–50. Quentin Skinner, *Reason and Rhetoric in the Philosophy of Hobbes* (Cambridge: Cambridge University Press, 1997) ch. 8, details the importance to Hobbes of necessary demonstration in the science of politics.

49 Thomas Hobbes, *Leviathan* (London: Dent, Everyman's Library, 1914 [1651]) p. 19.

50 On "enthusiasm" as a political bugbear in England, see Michael Heyd, *Be Sober and Reasonable: The Critique of Enthusiasm in the Seventeenth and Early Eighteenth Centuries* (Leiden: E. J. Brill, 1995).

51 Ernst H. Kantorowicz, *The King's Two Bodies: A Study in Mediaeval Political Theology* (Princeton: Princeton University Press, 1957) is the classic study on this theme; see esp. p. 15. See also Simon Werrett, "Healing the Nation's Wounds: Royal Ritual and Experimental Philosophy in Restoration England", *History of Science* 38 (2000): 377–399.

52 Cf. Jesseph, *Squaring the Circle*, pp. 208–209.

53 This is a basic argument of Dear, *Discipline and Experience*.

54 See especially Yaron Ezrahi, *The Descent of Icarus: Science and the Transformation of Contemporary Democracy* (Cambridge MA: Harvard University Press, 1990); Jasanoff, "Science, Politics".

55 Claude Bernard, *Introduction to the Study of Experimental Medicine*, trans. Henry Copley Greene (Dover, 1957), p. 103.

56 See e.g. Hobbes, *Leviathan*, p. 240.

57 Richard D. French, *Antivivisection and Medical Science in Victorian Society* (Princeton: Princeton University Press, 1975) is the standard study.

12 Reconstructing sociotechnical order

Vannevar Bush and US science policy

Michael Aaron Dennis

Introduction

In July 1945, Vannevar Bush, head of the wartime Office of Scientific Research and Development (OSRD) presented to President Harry S. Truman a report entitled *Science: The Endless Frontier* (*SEF*). Long viewed as the origin of American science policy, both the report and its author are mythic figures in the history of American science and technology. No government document with respect to science and technology possesses such talismanic value. By comparison, Henry Smyth's *Atomic Energy for Military Purposes*, released after the use of the atomic bomb and containing a far more sober understanding of the political problems posed by wartime research, vanished into libraries and used bookstores.[1] After fifty years, reporters, politicians and science policy analysts speak of the "Bush report" as if its meaning and consequences remain self-evident and significant. As the late Donald Stokes observed, part of the problem lay in the success with which the report's language, especially the concept of "basic research", effectively colonized the organization of postwar scientific research and technological development.[2] Supplementing, but not entirely replacing the language of pure and applied science – a language implicitly equating application with corruption – Bush's report and its novel intellectual taxonomy made government funding of academic research in the physical and biomedical sciences essential for national security and long-term economic growth.

Linguistic success had no organizational counterpart; the National Science Foundation (NSF) of 1950 bore little resemblance to Bush's National Research Foundation. The difference between the foundation of the report and the one of the ultimate enabling legislation represented a profound defeat for Bush in the struggles over the postwar organization of American research and development. In a path-breaking article, Daniel J. Kevles located the Bush report in divergent understandings of the relationship between science and society.[3] For Kevles, Bush's foundation was the American scientific elite's response to West Virginia Senator Harley S. Kilgore's plans for socially responsible science along with the geographical distribution of research funds. The prospect of non-scientists, especially politicians, directing research was anathema to Bush and other members of the wartime administrative elite. Other scholars, most notably Nathan Reingold, have followed the main lines of Kevles' "political reading", although disagreement remains over the details deserving emphasis. For Kevles and others it has been unproblematic that Bush's report was a potent piece of science policy, in some sense responsible for the establishment of the NSF, perhaps even what Larry Owens called the "constitution" for civil-technical relations in the postwar era.[4] Certainly this was a view that Bush encouraged, particularly in the work of his most authorized reader, Don Price, the founder of the Charles River School in science policy and author of several influential works, including *The Scientific Estate* (1965).[5] However, restricting Bush's report to the ghetto of science policy diminishes both the report and its author's complex motivations. Rather than read Bush as an architect of science policy, we should read him as an architect of American politics, actively attempting to steer the ship of state towards a future quite different from the one he would inhabit.

Questioning Bush's paternity with respect to the NSF is not new; examine Figure 12.1, a cartoon from the April 1950 *Chemical and Engineering News*. Science, the love child with four arms has a proud, if not defiant mother in the Mommy Congress. Bush is pictured posing the proverbial question – "Is this my child?". In addition to the generic scientists and the little sister (the NAS), there are two peeping toms. One, who may be the "ordinary" citizen, is unable to decide whether the mutant offspring is a bird or a beast; the other is a sinister-looking fellow watching in silence. Perhaps he was the enemy agent, waiting to carry off the scientists' secrets. Our interest in this image is twofold. First, it makes clear that contemporaries were

Figure 12.1   The New Arrival

Source: *Chemical and Engineering News*

unconvinced that Bush was responsible for the National Science Foundation. Second, such a claim makes possible a different question: what was Vannevar Bush doing in his famous report if he was not establishing the NSF?

At what price a state?

Writing to Harvard University president and fellow wartime research administrator James Bryant Conant, Bush explained that the problems were much more significant than the issues discussed in *SEF*:

> This broad question is whether we are bound down the path of France, or better of Australia or New Zealand. The parallelism with France is not exact and neither is the parallelism with Australia or New Zealand, but there are certainly common features and something of common trends.
>
> I can state, and in fact I have already stated, my belief that a democracy which temporarily girds itself with rigid controls is the most effective way to fight a modern war if it is not caught napping. But in order for this to be fully true the democracy must be sound. France was not sound, it had a great Army, there is no doubt about the valor of its people, it was behind on military techniques, but more important it promptly fell to pieces because its democracy had gotten into a terrible tangle, and it had been undermined from within by forces of disintegration put into effect from outside for that very purpose.[6]

Soundness was the issue; that is, was American democracy capable of withstanding the long war to come with the Soviet Union? Bush went on to make the point even more explicit:

> [t]he great question in my mind is whether this country is going down some similar path. There are plenty of indications about that…perhaps it is. In the 90s when great industrial combinations in this country came very close to taking over the United States Government and perpetuating some sort of oligarchy, we finally rose about it and that issue was settled rather conclusively. Today, however, we have a labor government and we have had one for twelve years, and there is a good deal of question whether we are not going to proceed under the control of labor, not exercised through a party of its own, but in diverse forms, some of them insidious. Government by the activities of pressure groups, whatever they may be, may be inevitable, but it is going to work only if there is a sufficient body of the citizenry that sees the point, preserves the balance, and maintains the government in a position above that of merely a tool or an adjunct to the group that happens to have the ascendancy at the moment. There is nothing anti-labor in my point of view, although it would promptly be interpreted as such. I would have been just as completely anti-capital in the same sense if I had been arguing a generation earlier.[7]

There is much here that we might unpack, but let us make clear its relevance for our work. We are interested in understanding what Bush was doing in *SEF*; this letter, written as he worked on a draft of the OSRD's final report to the president on its wartime affairs, expressed Bush's fears about the nation's future and was not restricted to our own narrow definition of science policy. Instead, Bush conceptualized science as part of a larger problem: the nature of the postwar American state.

Bush raises the central issue of this volume – co-production, the simultaneous production of technical and social order – in *SEF*. What the letter makes clear is the interconnectedness, for Bush, of politics, science and social order. Far from being theoretical or academic, Bush saw the soundness of the postwar American state as a matter of acute urgency and interest. He was not alone. Despite the success of the wartime alliance in defeating the Axis powers, the Soviet Union loomed on the horizon as the nation's next great threat. The question of survival was very much on the minds of Washington policymakers; central to this issue was the question of national identity. Would the prospect of a long, twilight struggle with the Soviet Union transform the United States into the very kind of state that it sought to defeat? Or to use the term coined by American political scientist Harold Lasswell, would the US become a "garrison state", a political entity in which the military, wedded to science and technology as the source of ever more powerful munitions, would become the dominant domestic power? Might the US, in standing against the Soviet Union, become more like its enemy than the nation inscribed within its own constitution?[8] Bush's letter makes it clear that he feared a transformation of the nation along just such unpleasant lines.

Bush's letter to Conant also raises a fundamental problem in the history of science, that of the relation of science and democracy. For practitioners of science and technology studies, Robert K. Merton's 1942 essay, "The normative structure of science", is the problem's *locus classicus*. As David Hollinger has persuasively argued, Merton's essay was part of a wider cultural project to defend democracy against the rivals which had emerged since World War I, especially various forms of fascism and Soviet communism.[9] We might easily dismiss the problem as discussed by Merton; the Cold War demonstrated that science might flourish under a variety of political systems – political loyalty trumped scientific internationalism. However, we need to understand how conceptions of science and technology operated as problems in politics. That is, we need to move the problem of science and democracy from the seminar room into the domain where actors' texts are instruments of practical political action. For example, Frederic Delano, head of the National Resources Planning Board, explained in August 1940, that while the US faced "the arrogant threat of military annihilation and the elimination of democratic institutions from the face of the earth", the "most revolutionary factor in modern life" was not "Nazism or Fascism", but the "unparalleled growth of science, invention and technology".[10] Whatever happened, "new means [were] emerging for the attainment of old ends, whether democratic or autocratic". We might dismiss Delano's text as another example of technological determinism where science and technology served as sources of novelty to which politicians responded, but such a reading would ignore his insight that "the old assumptions of democracy are still good, but its programs and practices must be adapted to a new world". Science and technology for men like Bush and Delano were problems in politics; we must read and understand their practical texts in the same ways we read works in our disciplinary history. For Merton, his students and countless followers, the problems were always the ones that politics posed for science; for Delano, Lasswell, and Bush, the focus would increasingly be on the problems posed by technical knowledge and its producers to established political order. Or more bluntly, the problem was one of scientists in society, not society or politics in science.

Written in the spring and early summer of 1945, *SEF* addressed the central political problem confronting Bush and others – what role would the US military play in the postwar American state and how would American scientists and engineers play a role in this new political configuration? In particular, *SEF* sought to organize federal patronage of the sciences so as to prevent the military from dominating the sciences, while insulating researchers from their enthusiasm for powerful technologies. Bush's solution to this problem in politics involved the creation of a new type of knowledge, "basic research", and the simultaneous construction of a new institutional mechanism for the public support of science, a National Research Foundation. The co-production of basic research and the NRF had as it upshot a new kind of state, one that relied upon the products of science and technology for both power and wealth. Supporting such a claim requires a recasting of the story of science and World War II.

In what follows, I revisit the history of wartime science from the perspective of the practical political problems that Bush and other producers and consumers of technical knowledge faced and resolved. After re-examining the horizon of possibilities available to Bush and contemporaries during the interwar era, we re-open the organization of science for war and the management of science during the war. Although Bush won the battle over the organization of wartime research, other judgments made by Bush, especially his conviction about the temporary character of the wartime research institutions, severely restricted the role he played in the organization of postwar research and development. Three wartime problems forced Bush to address postwar concerns: first, problems relating to the production and use of novel weapons developed in OSRD laboratories; second, the American military's fascination with the German cruise and ballistic missiles; and third, the military's impressive and unrelenting planning for the organization of postwar research. Central to this last point was one of the war's great unanticipated consequences: the seductive power of weapons technology on American researchers. It was in this complicated political context that Bush crafted *SEF*, and it would be in this arena where Bush's vision would lose. Co-production in this chapter is a story of engineering failure, of an inability to successfully define and defend a new form of knowledge as well as the mechanisms for its establishment and use. Perhaps most poignantly, Bush realized just what he had lost.

The land that time forgot

Vannevar Bush arrived in Washington DC in early 1939 as the new director of the Carnegie Institution of Washington (CIW), one of the nation's first private research institutions, and as the new chairman of the National Advisory Committee for Aeronautics (NACA).[11] Bush had left his post as Dean of Engineering and Professor of Electrical Engineering at MIT, in part to pursue administrative challenges unavailable while his friend Karl T. Compton remained MIT president. Bush was a creature of the interwar political economy of science. He had successfully negotiated with both industry and private philanthropies for the support of MIT research; he had been largely unsuccessful, as Larry Owens has shown, in forging a relationship between the federal government and the Institute for the support of technical investigations that might benefit both the government and the university. Bush's sensibilities developed during a period when the federal government played little role in academic research. Although university-based researchers made various efforts, such as the short-lived Science Advisory Board (SAB), it proved difficult, if not impossible, to find a way for universities to fund research with federal dollars save for the research conducted in the nation's agricultural experiment stations.[12] We might summarize the problem in the following table (Table 12.1), divided along the axis of dispute over whether the university's or the state's structure should change.

Interwar researchers and government officials possessed a restricted range of models for instituting federal funding of research. For members of the US scientific community, the abortive SAB was the mechanism of choice. Under Karl T. Compton's leadership, the two-year experiment paid for by the Rockefeller Foundation and located within the National Academy of Sciences, attempted to produce an agenda that would interest the Roosevelt administration in sponsoring academic research in areas of interest to the government. Compton, Bush and other physical scientists believed that universities would and could set up interdisciplinary research centers to serve

Table 12.1 Possible university–government relations in the 1930s

	State Structure	
University Structure	Change both	Change state, not university [NRPB]
	Change university, not state [SAB]	Both unchanged [OSRD]

the legislative branch in resolving the nation's economic crisis. The Science Advisory Board operated under the belief that the crisis of the thirties demanded a restructuring the university around specific technical problems transcending disciplinary boundaries. In turn the structure and character of the American state need not change. A very different view of university–government relations operated in the other major attempt at generating federal patronage for academic research, the National Resources Planning Board (NRPB), under the direction of the American president's favorite uncle, Frederic Delano. Established as part of the Department of Interior under Harold Ickes, the NRPB sought to use the university's existing disciplinary structure to legitimize an expansion of the executive branch's powers through the addition of scientific expertise. Traditional academic structures would justify administrative expansion and innovation. That the NRPB was the darling of American social scientists only increased the unease of natural scientists and engineers like Bush and Compton, who saw the social sciences as the academic wing of the Roosevelt administration. Of importance for what follows was the inability of any of the participants, even Bush, to imagine a set of circumstances in which the structure of both the university and the state would change.

In case of war...

Vannevar Bush's role in organizing American science for war is legendary, but the story omits the challenges posed by the task, as well as the competition that Bush bested in one of his few bureaucratic victories. In May 1940, as the phony war exploded, Arthur Holly Compton, the famous cosmic ray physicist, nominated Bush as the new Secretary of the Navy, explaining in clipped telegraphic prose:

> Demonstrated effectiveness new weapons makes vital that nations [*sic.*] defense be head by men familiar with application scientific technique. Therefore urge appointment such person as Vannevar Bush to key position Secretary of Navy rather than anyone bound by military tradition. Prompt effective concentration of technical men and facilities on military problems essential to nations [*sic.*] defense.[13]

Compton's message captured the urgency and novelty of the new war; it was a war in which Bush had already articulated a role for science as early as April 1939, explaining to the chief, Herbert Hoover, that "the whole world situation would be much altered if there were an effective defense against bombing by aircraft".[14] Bush wrote to Hoover to secure advice on how the Carnegie might support research on the use of radio waves to detect aircraft at both Stanford and MIT; it was knowledge that Bush had acquired through his contacts at the Institute as well as through his new Washington connections at the National Academy and the NACA. It was personal and informal knowledge that made it possible for Bush to approach FDR through contacts with Harry Hopkins and Delano and establish the National Defense Research Committee (NDRC) in June 1940.[15] However, the strengths that Bush brought to this new organization were also potential weaknesses.

Challengers quickly emerged for the new organization. In August 1940, Secretary of the Interior Ickes approached FDR with a plan for the establishment of an Office of Scientific Liaison that would coordinate American science through a distinctive sociology of knowledge. Arguing that cutting-edge knowledge lay untouched in researchers' minds and filing cabinets, Ickes urged FDR to have American scientists send their filing cabinets to Washington DC, where unemployed scientists and graduate students would mine the files for useful inventions and discoveries. For Ickes, such an approach would vastly increase the scale and scope of the government research effort; even with the addition of the NDRC, Ickes argued that only five to six hundred researchers were advising the government, leaving the remaining 99,500 without a way of participating in the war effort.[16] An operational Office of Scientific Liaison located in a permanent Cabinet office would offer a whole new meaning for the Department of the Interior. Ickes' plan found its way to Bush's office; FDR explained to Ickes that the existing arrangements were satisfactory for the coming conflict, since there were "serious limitations to having a single agency of the Federal Government maintain direct and complete liaison with 'science' as a general and broad field."[17] Later, in August 1941, Ickes launched another salvo in an attempt to gain control of wartime science, only to lose once more.

Bush's new agency also prompted fears within the military.[18] Harold Bowen, director of the Naval Research Laboratory and an ardent Bush critic, welcomed the establishment of the NDRC, but warned his superiors that when the "present emergency" ended the NDRC would "*supplant* instead of *supplement* the research activities of the Army and Navy".[19] Jealous of the funds that Bush had raised for the development of radar, a sum greater than all the money ever spent by NRL on the same technology, Bowen saw only a single potential benefit in the NDRC – at war's end the armed services would acquire a significant set of research programs. Such a move would happen because of the temporary character of Bush's organizations, a feature that both Bush and Bowen saw as significant, albeit for quite different reasons.

The temporary status of the wartime research agencies, the NDRC, and after July 1941, the Office of Scientific Research and Development (OSRD) was a crucial feature in Bush's early bureaucratic success. According to Bush, the wartime agencies were to exist for the duration of the emergency and then dissolve. Hence, the OSRD would not create new permanent laboratories, but contract with universities for research and development.[20] Possessing the virtue of a finite duration subject to re-negotiation, contractual terms embodied a particular political perspective clearly articulated in the new agency's overhead policies. In 1940, overhead had not yet become the lifeblood of the American research university; instead, university administrators, like the wartime research leaders, were concerned that they should not be seen as taking advantage of the emergency to line their own pockets. To avoid such appearances, the NDRC and OSRD adopted a policy in which "the educational institution shall not be the gainer, all things considered, and shall have contributed to the work that part of its facilities which can be contributed without current budgetary loss".[21] Often abbreviated as "no-gain-no-loss" or "no-profit-no-loss", this contractual formulation, coupled to the temporary character of the OSRD, cut to the heart of the wartime administrators' understanding of the political economy of science. To return to the chart above, Bush originally believed that the US might fight the war and organize within a temporal bubble; at war's end the bubble would deflate and the prewar institutional assemblage would flow back into place. The new organizations would exist in a social space bounded on one side by the university-based research facilities, on another by the corporations that would build the weapons developed in the university laboratories, and by the armed services that would pay for and use the new technologies. If one believed that the wartime organizations were to exist for the duration of the emergency and no longer, then preserving the boundaries among neighboring institutions was among the highest priorities, as was the regulation of the traffic crossing those same divides. How members of the interwar elite came to realize that they were incapable of policing and maintaining these borders as the war continued is our next concern.

Stasis as a political project

Maintaining an organization's static position in a dynamic world is an engineering feat. Success demands the control of the organization's internal dynamics, as well as its relations with outside actors. Bush's attempt to generate political stasis rested upon the control of the OSRD's relations with industry and the military, the military's understanding of new weapons, and a resolute desire to ignore various attempts to plan for the organization of postwar research and development. All this social engineering had a single goal – to allow for the easy restoration of the prewar political economy of science. Just as many feared a return to the Great Depression once the hostilities ended, so did Bush, Conant and others believe that the military support of research and development would quickly evaporate after victory. Three developments undermined Bush's efforts to restore the world of the thirties: problems related to the production and use of new weapons; military enthusiasms for weapons developed by the enemy, but not by the US; and the military's desire to organize research and development after the cessation of hostilities. Individually, Bush believed that he might deal with each problem successfully; together they dragged him to the recognition that the war would forever change American science.

Problems of production

Moving innovations from the laboratory to the factory was a problem in both institutional relations and political theory. In turn, moving items into production demanded that the armed services use the new weapons on the battlefield.

Without orders and the inherent possibility of battlefield use, production was both irrelevant and impossible. Production demanded the translation of the laboratory prototype into a mass-produced artifact that the military would use. Even before Pearl Harbor, the OSRD understood that some inventions might require special effort and handling to fill military needs.[22] How to do this consonant with the OSRD's founding beliefs was the problem. For example, radar sets were technologically complex devices that might work on a laboratory bench and nowhere else without a great deal of tinkering and moral suasion. Mass-producing such instruments was nearly impossible; however, the presence of a few such sets might affect the course of a particular battle. Bush observed that it might prove necessary to custom-make apparatus before it could be produced in mass quantities. Indeed, Bush was a critic of American industry's desire to engage only in mass production, rather than the limited production sometimes required by the actual circumstances of combat.[23] Bush's attempt to solve this problem managerially worked in two distinct directions. First, he established the "few quick program" and the engineering transition office. The former institutionalized the custom manufacture of a limited number of devices if all other production mechanisms failed; the latter attempted to insure that an adequate supply of components existed for new weapons so that shortages would not hamper production.[24] Second, in early 1942 Bush pushed for the creation of the Joint New Weapons Committee of the Joint Chiefs of Staff, his personal attempt to influence the war's grand strategy. The JNW was to make clear to military leaders the power of the new technologies. For our purposes, what is important is that Bush sought to separate issues related to supply (production) and demand (use) of new weapons. Others developed alternative mechanisms, effectively erasing the very boundaries that Bush sought to maintain.

First, Merle Tuve, the leader of the wartime effort to develop a proximity fuze for anti-aircraft shells, advocated a far more radical solution.[25] Arguing that the researcher's responsibility extended from the laboratory to the factory and onto the battlefield, Tuve sent his group into private factories to supervise production of the complicated and technologically demanding fuze. He also sent lab members, usually single men, into the Navy to serve as evangelists for the fuze, convincing officers to use the new device by demonstrating its effectiveness in combat. Tuve obliterated the very boundaries that Bush sought to erect and maintain separating the OSRD from its corporate and military partners.

In another assault on OSRD autonomy, Ed Bowles, Bush's first doctoral student and fellow MIT electrical engineering professor, created the Radiation Laboratory Model Shop in early 1942.[26] The Rad Lab had been the origin of Bush's own "few-quick" policy, but Bowles' model shop was not solely dedicated to putting prototypes into the military's hands. Instead, the model shop was an attempt to integrate industrial design and production concerns into the weapons development process. Devices developed in the Rad Lab were retooled in the Model Shop so that firms might actually produce them in quantity. It was a form of industrial education that linked the lab closely to the factory and moved the lab bench that much closer to the assembly line. Once again, wartime exigencies erased Bush's organizational boundaries.

Guided missile fever

No weapon is as powerful as the one possessed only by the enemy. In 1943 the German army began using radio-controlled missiles against Allied shipping in the Mediterranean. These were large bombs ranging from 500 to 4000 pounds with wings dropped from aircraft and guided to their target with remote controls. Although Allied troops quickly developed countermeasures against these weapons, the US military found their potential intoxicating. The slipperiness of the phrase "guided missile" is important to remember; today we would label the German munitions as distant ancestors of the "smart bomb" since gravity was their primary propulsive force. US researchers, especially in the armed services and the NDRC, worked on the development of various "glide bombs" as early as 1941. Bush sought to use the military's interest in the enemy's weapons to raise the status of the JNW; arguing that an "extraordinary range of effort" needed knitting together to "produce rather striking results". Although it was unlikely that Germany could develop non-jammable weapons, Bush found it disturbing that the potential importance of such weapons was "in no sense grasped by the people who are responsible for our war effort".[27] Once again, Bush sought to control both the supply and the demand of new weapons by organizing research on the new technologies and by playing a role in developing the tactical and strategic contexts in which such devices would be used. Events quickly conspired against him.

An unjammable device, the German V-1, materialized in the skies above England in summer 1944. As one correspondent wrote to Washington:

> [t]he flying bomb has made quite an impact on many of us over here. Ever since Luis [Alvarez] and I first saw them crossing the South Coast flying straight and level at two to three thousand feet immune to flak and almost to fighters, we have been captivated by the potentialities of such a weapon.[28]

We cannot underestimate the importance of the German rocket weapons in accelerating the American military's interest in this technology. Whether viewed as a "bad weather air force" or "all weather artillery", the pilot-less buzz bomb soon appeared as the "most important weapon" of a war littered with advances in destructive technology.[29] For Bush, the military's interest in the new technology expressed itself in his desire to organize the nation's missile effort; as early as August 1941, Bush explained that "we ought to forget the rocket affair, or else go at it hard. At the present time in this country it is a side issue receiving somewhat casual attention".[30] Organization and management were responses to the far more ominous threat expressed by the new weapon's enthusiasts:

If we are to use this weapon in this war, it is most important that the inventors be kept away from it. We must take it over completely from the enemy and produce it with no changes except those dictated by our manufacturing processes.[31]

(emphasis in original)

"Muddling along for years with misguided missiles", the armed services had now been handed a vehicle on a "silver platter" ; the Germans had done what the US "failed to do". The truth was that this weapon fell out of the sky; critics might use its very existence to devalue the need for a research and development establishment separated from the armed services and industry. In turn Bush lost control of the US effort to build a copy of the V-1; further missile research by the armed services could not be contained, but Bush could survey the situation. By 1944, the US had spent roughly $394 million on various missile projects, with none ready for combat; Bush reported that he was "appalled". The US missile program was the upshot of "any group of enthusiasts, having available funds, and receiving approval from one of a conceivable number of places". "Enthusiasts" referred here not only to military officers intoxicated by a new weapon, but to the researchers, such as those at CalTech who wanted to design and build such technologies.[32] Furthermore, there was no single authority capable of canceling projects incapable of aiding the war effort.[33] What Bush learned from the guided missile frenzy was that the armed services found $394 million a small amount of money and that they were all for committees to coordinate their missile programs, as long as such committees did not interfere with their research efforts. Ironically, Bush's call for coordination produced a report calling for the establishment of a panel to set national guided missile priorities and coordinate the various programs.[34]

Postwar planning

Seeing Bush, Kilgore, and to a lesser extent the Research Board for National Security (RBNS) as the loci for planning postwar research and development, leads us to ignore two key facts about such plans. First, such documents emerged in many contexts as early as 1943, especially among active duty military officers and their academic colleagues. Second, active scientists and engineers as well as administrators authored such plans. The second set of authors is important, for it takes us to a major problem confronting Bush as the war continued. Put simply, none of the members of the wartime scientific elite ever believed that American academic researchers would want to continue working on weapons after the cessation of hostilities. Early OSRD demobilization plans rested upon such an assumption. In fact, while the military would clamor for postwar planning of research and development, researchers were powerful allies in such plans. Writing in December 1942, the Navy's Coordinator of Research and Development could declare that the "personnel of this office are so fully occupied with war work that they are not undertaking any post-war planning".[35]

Nonetheless, the author argued that the sudden end of the war, without adequate planning, would be a disaster. A warehouse full of "woolen underwear" would survive the loss of all available shopkeepers, so long as one guard and a can of mothballs remained on duty. Scientific knowledge did not possess a similar shelf life, in part because its storage was so bound up with the individuals who produced and consumed such knowledge. Mimeographs of the latest findings circulated among those with a need to know, but reconstructing new knowledge from these new literary forms would prove a difficult, if not impossible task, especially after the original authors and their audience scattered to their prewar homes. Even at this early stage of postwar planning, the Navy recognized a difference between technical knowledge and other goods; in particular the necessity of binding bodies and knowledge together to yield a product of postwar value.

By 29 December 1943, Bush's postwar planning file contained nine different memoranda written by OSRD contractors, military officers, and other OSRD administrators, including James Conant. All the plans shared several assumptions. First, that the prewar and postwar worlds would resemble each other unless a vast effort were undertaken to effect change. Stasis was a given; all the writers agreed that without effort the armed services would quickly return to their interwar nadir. As one writer observed, "no one would think of continuing to devote such a large part of our scientific resources to military ends as we are doing today".[36] Second, writers were concerned with preparations for a future war, as well as creating some successor to the OSRD. Third, each author had a set of ideas on how to preserve working relations between high-ranking military officers and civilian researchers interested in weapons work.[37] An important corollary to this last point was the assumption that the existing civil service system would never produce or allow talented individuals to work on important military products. It was a given that civil service scientists and their military counterparts were not as capable as researchers working in universities or industry.[38] Talent was an issue, as was the underlying belief that weapons research was not of interest to academic scientists save for the exigencies of war.

Early 1944 saw a steady reiteration by Bush of the claim that the "OSRD should not continue into the peace period, for its structure is adapted entirely for emergency actions in times of war". However, by March 1944 Bush could not resist the demand by the Army and Navy to begin discussions of postwar military research and development.[39] Even Congressional friends like James Wadsworth and Judge Woodrum, members of the House Committee on Postwar Military Policy, reiterated the importance of postwar military research and development policy, observing that officers involved in procuring OSRD weapons "live[d] in fear that when the war is over we shall abandon our scientific research and development activities".[40] Soon the agenda for an April meeting began circulating, complete with assumptions and discussion points. In addition to the belief that no new laboratories were needed for military research and development, the key assumption was the following:

[s]cientists of the highest level will not in peacetime be interested in sufficient numbers in full-time government employment to give the country the
best that science has to offer in the way of research and development of
instrumentalities of war. Some way should therefore be found to keep the
best scientific minds in the country interested in national defense research
and available for consultation and part-time service for the Army and Navy
during peacetime.[41]

We are lucky to have a transcript of the April conference. What is striking
about the transcript is that Bush ran the conference while actually saying very little;
instead he allowed the military officers and Frank Jewett, president of the National
Academy to seize the floor. In turn, the participants agreed with Bush's agenda,
especially on the lack of interest by top researchers in government jobs or military
research. However, what brought great consensus was the recognition that money
could make anything possible; "there has never been any trouble in getting [this]
cooperation from industry or universities if you had the money to get it".[42] One
theme to emerge from the conference was the belief that if the armed services
failed to provide a means for the organization of postwar research and development, then someone else would. It was for this reason that the meeting ended with
a call for the secretaries of the Navy and War to appoint a committee to study the
problem and provide an official solution – the Wilson Committee.

Named for its chair, Charles Wilson, head of the War Production Board and
General Electric, the Committee investigated the organization of postwar military research and development during the summer of 1944.[43] Several things
stand out in the Committee's deliberations. First, almost immediately two very
different alternatives emerged for the organization of defense research. The first,
proposed by Merle Tuve, postulated a new independent agency, a Research
Board for National Security (RBNS) that would let contracts with universities
and industry for studies of advanced weaponry. Independence in two important
senses was the crucial feature for Tuve and the other Committee members who
supported this plan. An independent agency with its own congressional appropriation would be capable of resisting pressures from the armed services and
others for ineffective weapons. Furthermore, an independent agency might fund
multiple contracts attempting to produce the same ends through different means.
Independence would allow for parallel development to proceed despite claims
that such work was simply costly duplication. In turn, an independent agency
would allow the civilian scientists and military officers to work together as equals,
since neither would be dependent upon the other. Only by working together as
equals did Tuve believe that first-class researchers would accept their responsibility for national security.

The Committee's other plan, introduced and promoted by Frank Jewett, called
for a new institution within the National Academy of Sciences that would draw
upon funds contributed by the armed services to coordinate military research and
development. For Tuve and his allies on the Committee, especially the representatives selected by the Secretary of the Navy, Jewett's plan begged many questions,

but none so fundamental as the obvious. If this was such a great idea, why had it not been implemented for the war now underway? Jewett's plan was predicated on the dissolution of the OSRD and a return to the prewar institutional ecology. Jewett argued that the need for a quick solution made Tuve's idea of an independent agency unrealistic; legislation often had unexpected consequences and such organizations were "long-lived beasties" that were "almost impossible to kill or alter" once they had been legislated into existence. The Academy plan possessed flexibility and required no legislation; all that was required was for the Secretaries of the Army and Navy to turn funds over to the Academy. Such a plan could be implemented quickly without going through Congress, and provide an opportunity for crafting legislation far from the world of "war hysteria". If one had to operate in a "world of stark realism and starkly realistic men", as Jewett argued, then the Academy-based Research Board for National Security was the most promising solution.[44] Writing in disgust after the Committee's second meeting, Tuve argued that the Committee and the future had been "pretty thoroughly torpedoed"; by September it was apparent that the Academy-based RBNS would succeed. Ironically, it was Bush, sitting on the sidelines observing the Wilson Committee's deliberations, who forced a change in plans.

In September Bush announced that the OSRD should begin planning for its own termination as soon as the war in Europe ended. According to Bush, unfinished contracts would be turned over to the armed services or closed out; only research essential for the war against Japan would continue.[45] For Bush, demobilization was necessary to return researchers to their prewar roles in industry and academia. It was a last, bold attempt to return to the prewar world, before enthusiasts could consolidate a hold upon OSRD resources and personnel. It was also a bureaucratic bombshell. Observing the aftermath, Air Force General Henry "Hap" Arnold wrote: "these long haired scientists have a hard time getting together. They are about as jealous as Brigham Young's seventeenth and eighteenth wives were, so that there is a lot of throat cutting going on between the scientists".[46] Arnold, like so many in Washington, and in laboratories across the nation, read Bush's announcement as a call to cut their own deals. For example, Arnold contacted CalTech aeronautical wizard Theodore Von Karman to conduct a study of the Air Force's postwar research and development needs. Furthermore, Arnold had been working with Ed Bowles on designing a new form of industrial-military cooperation to strip the B-29 of excess weight so that the plane might carry bombs and fuel from the newly acquired bases in the Marianas islands in the Pacific.[47] This work would lay the foundations for Project RAND, itself a scheme of organizing postwar research and development. Others, like Merle Tuve, began the process of moving their organizations from OSRD to Navy sponsorship. By January 1945 Tuve would be in charge of the Navy Bureau of Ordnance's guided missile project, Bumblebee. Potential OSRD demobilization scattered the various players like leaves in the wind. As if that were not enough, Niels Bohr arrived in Washington DC in September 1944 attempting to preclude a nuclear arms race, just as Bush and Conant began to understand how a successful Manhattan Project would affect both military and diplomatic affairs.[48]

Amidst the chaos of fall 1944, Bush received FDR's letter asking the OSRD director to translate wartime organizational success into postwar science policy. As Bush's aide, Caroll Wilson noted, "Bush did not write it nor did he ask for it, but he had the opportunity to see it before it was sent and made some suggestions which were incorporated".[49] The letter arrived just as Bush testified before the House Postwar Military Affairs Committee on Research and Development. Furthermore, Bush had realized in September that FDR planned on welding science and technology to the long-term survival of the nation through the development and use of nuclear weapons. Stasis had evaporated as a possible goal. In August, Bush had told the young radar historian Henry Guerlac that "he was not damn fool enough" to think he could enforce his vision on others.[50] FDR's letter provided him with one more opportunity to try.

Science policy: endless frustration

Roosevelt's letter of 17 November asked Bush four questions:

- How, consistent with military security, might the world become aware of the contributions made to the advancement of science during the war;
- How might "the war of science against disease" continue during the peace;
- "What can the Government do now and in the future to aid research activities by public and private organizations? The proper roles of public and private research, and their interrelation, should be carefully considered";
- Could a program be developed to find and develop American scientific talent to assure that such research would continue on a level comparable to that of the war?[51]

Bush quickly organized four committees to address the president's questions. The committee reports became appendices to the report; it is striking that despite his solicitation of these inputs, Bush crafted *SEF* as his own report. Question three on the role of the government in support of research quickly became the largest and most important. Under the direction of Isaiah Bowman, president of Johns Hopkins University, historians and economists, including Henry Guerlac, I. B. Cohen and Paul Samuelson, provided extensive documentation and discussion of the government's role in American science. That group's final report is the source for the often quoted quip that "applied research invariably drives out pure". Most striking about this committee report is that it makes clear how much American researchers were distrustful of federal monies. It is possible to read the Bowman Committee report as the writings of men who fear they are recommending the least palatable alternative – federal funding of university-based research. Given this background it is clear that *SEF* was Bush's own report.

SEF is a very simple, yet in many respects a rhetorically powerful text. In the course of the report, the author attempts to paint a picture of the history and future of science in the US. Put simply, the report postulates a form of knowledge, basic research, which is the essential tonic for economic growth and national security. Until World War II, the US had been a net importer of such knowledge; to the extent that Americans sponsored basic research in US universities, support came from the private foundations and to a much lesser extent, industry. Save for agricultural research, the government supported very little that might count as basic research. Given that the war had destroyed the previous sources of academic research – Western Europe – it was now incumbent upon the government to support such research in American universities.

For our purposes, there are two points to make about *SEF*. First, at no point in his letter did FDR suggest that Bush craft an organizational response to the questions. Proposing a new government agency was the upshot of deciding that the government needed to fund academic science, as well as a belief that the proper organization of such support could not be left to legislators alone or to pre-existing government organizations, including the National Academy. Second, the dramatic difference between the instrumentality proposed by Bush lay in the organization's structure and function. In particular, while the Bowman Committee had considered an organization that would draw upon the National Academy for prestige, personnel and political shelter, Bush proposed an independent agency to provide for basic research. What remains striking about Bush's National Research Foundation was not so much the mechanisms for insulating the director from presidential authority, as Kevles originally argued, as the presence of a Division of National Defense alongside Divisions of Medical Research, Natural Science, Scientific Personnel and Education, and Publications and Scientific Collaboration. Bush explicitly argued that the Wilson Committee's interim Research Board for National Security was only a temporary measure; whereas the Foundation's National Defense Division would "be primarily to conduct long-range scientific research on military problems – leaving to the Services research on the improvement of existing weapons".[52]

Bush's proposed National Defense Division was to perform several important political functions. First, it clearly took control of research related to future weapons away from the armed services and placed it within civilian control. Just as industrial corporations had learned earlier in the century to separate research from production, so Bush believed that the military, the consumers of basic research, needed to be separated from the production of such knowledge.[53] Second, such research would have to undergo scrutiny by those who were not necessarily enthusiasts for such investigations. In other words, supporters of various guided missile schemes would have to justify and coordinate their efforts. Not only was Bush preventing the military from controlling research and development, he was attempting to control the access of researchers to the military's pet projects. Yet, during the Bowman Committee deliberations, I. I. Rabi had casually observed that at least 75 per cent of the 600 workers at the MIT Radiation Laboratory would welcome an opportunity to continue their radar

242 Michael Aaron Dennis

researches after the cessation of hostilities.[54] The very assumption that Bush and others made about the desirability of military research and development was therefore profoundly mistaken.

Of course, by July 1945, the Research Board for National Security was on its way to the historical dustbin. Neither the armed services nor the National Academy were able to successfully structure a contract or other arrangements for the organization to exist.[55] President Truman informed Jewett in June that "the OSRD should not be liquidated at an early date", and that the RBNS should be reconstituted as an advisory board for the OSRD. Bush responded with great alacrity to Truman's new suggestion, arguing that such a move would reverse Bush's understanding with Roosevelt over the temporary status of the OSRD; plus, Bush explained he had written a report (*SEF*) arguing for a separate agency for civilian research on military matters. The Academy-based RBNS would serve as a bridge to this future. If Truman disagreed, Bush proposed "that it would be better to have no civilian post-war military research program at all for an interval, leaving this to the services".[56] Sweeping the pieces off the chessboard, Bush prepared to leave the table; it was petulant, but it was the act of a man who realized that he had vastly underestimated the power of all the parties in play. By the end of July the armed services were prepared to support legislation to establish Bush's National Research Foundation, so long as the Foundation guaranteed that at least 20 per cent of its funding would go to the National Defense Division, and that military men would figure on the organization's board.[57]

Truman confided to his diary after the Trinity test that the Japanese would surrender when "Manhattan appears over their homeland"; he could not have imagined what it would do in Washington DC to scramble Bush's plans for organizing postwar research and development.[58] News of the weapon precipitated not only an arms race between the US and the Soviet Union, but an arms race between the Army and the Navy. On 7 August, the Navy Office of Research and Inventions established a Nuclear Physics Division, and on 9 August those who established the division declared "the state of ignorance in the Navy Department is nothing less than shocking in this field".[59] In late September, the Air Force, working with Ed Bowles, began discussions of atomic powered missiles and atomic warheads, talks that would lead to the first official RAND contract.[60] Finally, in October, the armed services explained to Jewett that the use of the Atomic Bomb demanded a "thorough resurvey" of military research and development; in turn, the Army and the Navy would contract directly for whatever research and development they required until the establishment of a postwar research organization.[61] The RBNS was dead, the National Science Foundation was not yet born, and the armed services had become the most ferocious consumers of science and technology. In September 1944, Bush declared that "when this war is over I want to be a private citizen, able to say what I think"; in September 1945, Bush watched as the military and their researchers took over the future of American science and technology.[62]

Once more into the breach: the JRDB and the breaking of Vannevar Bush

October 1945 saw Bush still in harness, writing the OSRD final report and watching the armed services "running wild" with their research and development requests.[63] Legislation to establish a postwar research foundation remained mired in controversy; Truman initially vetoed legislation calling for a Bush-style foundation because the director of the foundation was appointed by, and accountable to, an independent board, rather than the president. We need to read this organizational struggle in light of the letter with which this essay began. Institutional insulation would have prevented American science from becoming simply another interest group with a claim on the treasury. Herein lay the ultimate articulation of Bush's desire for some connection with the prewar world, a position most clearly articulated in the Bowman Committee's description of the individuals who should sit on the Foundation's board:

> confidence must be reposed in the integrity, character, and qualifications of the individuals comprising the board of directors. No curbs, restrictions or limitations on their powers would provide adequate safeguards or take the place of character and ability.[64]

Bush echoed such thoughts in *SEF* when he asked for limitations on the funds that researchers could accept in compensation for doing the foundation's business.[65] In other words, the Division members would not be for sale and would act in the nation's interest rather than their own or in the interest of the armed services. We might see this as a remarkably quaint as well as simplistic belief, but it was rooted in that most basic assumption – that work on weapons or government research in general would never appeal to first-rate minds. Equally important was the corollary that such minds were also profoundly moral and proper individuals, who would shun such weapons work. What is remarkable is just how obdurate and resilient this belief remained for Bush.

If Bush's NRF was not to come into existence, what was Bush to do? First, he did not go quietly. The OSRD official history project was nothing less than a massive attempt both to record the history of science at war and to influence public discussion of postwar plans for science and technology.[66] Bush's ideas on the unification of the military services, a cause he championed during and after the war, came to the fore in the war's immediate aftermath as legislative discussions on this topic and the establishment of a separate air force emerged. For Bush, the establishment of a single department of defense offered an opportunity to establish a unitary organization of research and development within the armed services. In June 1946 the Secretaries of the Army and Navy offered Bush a new job, chair of a new committee on military research and development, the Joint Research and Development Board (JRDB).

In existing histories of American science, the JRDB is often pointed to as a failure.[67] Insofar as the Board failed in its goal to create a unitary military research and development policy in the US, we might read it as a failure; but doing so would seriously misread the Board's methods and goals. The JRDB was Bush's last attempt to control military research and development; it was an institution born of the failure of Congress and administration to agree on a national research foundation, and Bush's own fears about the military's plans for American science. On more than one occasion Bush acknowledged that the armed services had stepped into the breach formed by the failure to establish federal support of basic research. However, Bush believed that the public and the universities would never accept the military as the dominant patron of American science.[68] It was a poor prediction, but it served as one legitimization of his attempt to create a new kind of organization in the as yet dis-united national military establishment.

Nothing about the JRDB was simple. Even the language Bush used to discuss it with the Secretaries of War and Navy proved endlessly frustrating. Put simply, Bush agreed to chair an organization that would coordinate military research and development already underway in each service. The Board would replace the Joint New Weapons Committee, and while it would have no power to alter or initiate research within either service, it would have the authority to "allocate responsibility" in research areas of joint interest. In his correspondence with the Secretaries over the Board's powers, Bush used the guided missile as an example. If the Board determined that a particular type of missile was best pursued by the Army, then the Navy would not perform research on such a weapon. In turn, the Army would decide internally whether the Ordnance Department or the Air Force should fund and manage the work. Central for the success of the Board was the development of a wide-ranging information gathering apparatus, an instrument taking the form of committees and sub-committees devoted to such topics as electronics, guided missiles, basic physical science, aeronautics and armaments. Using the guided missile was not arbitrary; it was a statement of just what was at stake in the new Board's deliberations. Far from fading, guided missile fever had grown even more intense in the postwar period. Bush's attitude towards the armed services found itself further reflected in his understanding of the Board's powers; he explained to Secretary Patterson that the Board was "a court for the arbitration and determination of a specific class of over-lapping interests", complete with a mechanism for enforcement and an "equivalent of a district attorney".[69] The legal metaphor is crucial to understanding Bush's attitude here. While the power of the Committee flowed from the authority conferred by the Secretaries of War and Navy, the "district attorney" was the Committee's secretariat who reported directly to Bush. What is striking is that Bush drew upon criminal rather than civil law for his metaphor. Corralling and containing the armed services would take the equivalent of the powers the state used to arrest and sentence criminals. It was the clearest statement of the fundamentally adversarial thinking that had come to inform Bush's own views of the armed services and their relations to the production of new knowledge and weapons.

Suffice it to say Bush's experiences with the Board were far from pleasant. Ostensibly, the JRDB's goal was the production of a unitary plan of military research and development; in practice the JRDB was an incredibly successful domestic intelligence gathering apparatus that compiled an inventory of US research and development. Were we able to run the IBM punch cards littering the JRDB archive through their ancient tabulators, we might be stunned by the staggering display of US wealth and power invested in weapons. At the same time, the Board would possess a Policy Council, later succeeded by the Weapons Systems Evaluation Group, that attempted to fulfill Bush's other long-held dream of integrating the nation's research effort into strategic thinking at the highest levels.[70] The passage of the 1947 National Security Act led to the dropping of "Joint" from the Board's name; Bush agreed to remain as chair for another year. However, it became increasingly clear that while the armed services might pay lip service to the Board's goals, they were intent upon fashioning their own research empires. As Ed Bowles explained to Hap Arnold, "Bush would like to tackle such problems as those which would lead him to make recommendations as to what our relative forces should be"; in turn, this would leave the armed services with no "real responsibility".[71]

Arnold's brief response underscored the problems faced by Bush's desire to organize military research and development and integrate science and technology into the construction of military strategy:

> There has always been the possibility of the civilian scientists' extending their sphere of action, grasping for more power, – ever since they were finally, and quite enthusiastically, boosted to top flight status in World War II. Under control, they will be wonderful; but if allowed to run wild; to endeavor to capitalize on too all-inclusive ambitions, it may be catastrophic for the Armed Services.[72]

Arnold articulated a not uncommon feeling among the military about Bush, one whose origins lay in Bush's contentious relationship with Admiral King, but it was also a statement about how unification was not going to solve any of the military's organization or political problems. Upon leaving the RDB in October 1948, Bush wrote to Secretary Forrestal once again to argue for the importance of the newly formed Weapons System Evaluation Group as part of an improved and coordinated Joint Chiefs of Staff. It was part of a larger set of observations that Bush offered to the Secretary. The National Research Foundation did not merit even a mention; instead, Bush concluded his last RDB memo by observing that "if war comes, in spite of our best efforts, in the days of atom bombs and long range bombers, we can win that war and preserve our way of life".[73] Of course, such a last line begged the question just what was "our way of life".

Modern arms and free men: can a democracy have both?

In the aftermath of the RDB, Bush returned to the presidency of the Carnegie Institution of Washington; he had failed to engineer a world in which basic research and an institution dedicated to its production would flourish, just as he had failed to engineer a single unitary plan for military research and development. In his final public act, Bush addressed the educated layperson as well as the government policymaker and his peers in *Modern Arms and Free Men: A Discussion of the Role of Science in Preserving Democracy* (*MAFM*). The book performed two basic tasks. First, Bush believed that much of the information available to the public about the revolution in warfare was over-wrought. Were war to come it would be destructive, but not the end of civilization. Worse was the possibility that fear "might force our system into a form where genuine liberty no longer exists".[74] This was the fear of the garrison state, but *MAFM* was more than a polemic about the possibility that America might become more like its enemy than itself. Instead, Bush argued that the difference between the US and the USSR lay in different approaches to the past. It was easy to argue that because the past contained horror and war, so must the future. Bush identified this belief with the Soviet system and its ideology of world domination. In turn, the Soviet system rested upon a false understanding that science was all there was to know. Unlike the totalitarian state, Bush argued that the democratic polity drew a different lesson from the past, one about the limits of scientific reasoning and the need to believe in the possibility of change. Central to Bush's argument was that the democratic state recognized that science was not the only way of knowing nor the scientist necessarily the best qualified to understand all dimensions of the world.

Here we can see another meaning of Bush's new concept, basic research; it was the source of a new faith that would produce novelty — novelties that might find use in weapons or defenses, but also novelties that might break the "pattern of sordid strife". What was new under the sun was that researchers might not recognize this "truth". Hence Bush's obsession with organizational form — proper structures would provide the institutional spaces in which genuine novelty might emerge and be developed. We also see a connection to Bush's other famous text, "The builders", his metaphorical take on historical time and the growth of knowledge.[75] In that text, itself a modern retelling of the riddle of the sphinx, Bush expressed the transgenerational problem of social order as the task of building a structure complete with the development of the infrastructure to support the builders. Understanding construction was more than recognizing the importance of materials or the building trades, it was essential that people understood the social world that made building any structure possible. Making social order was at one with building the institutions to preserve freedom. Fear, whether of nuclear destruction or totalitarian inevitability, which much of *MAFM* sought to dispel, would only make building a just and democratic polity that much more difficult. Far from being a technocratic manifesto, *MAFM* ended by arguing that the salvation of the US lay in the skills of politicians and their ability to determine who was trustworthy. Politicians, acting with the consent of the governed and well informed by experts, might design institutions that would allow democracy to flourish, even under the threat posed by the Soviet Union. It was a vision of the future that put its faith in the wisdom of individuals – military officer, politician or scientist. It was a vision utterly out of step with its present.

MAFM was not intended for a mass audience. Bush translated much of the book's contents into a heavily illustrated two-part essay in *Life* magazine as well as a brief, heavily animated film, *If Moscow Strikes*. Both projects sought to ease the nation's fears about the future of warfare; the latter was especially striking in seeking to diffuse the anxiety triggered by the detonation of the first Soviet atomic bomb in August 1949. The film was a box office failure, but what remains striking is a photograph made to promote the film. It is a photograph of Bush's head, floating in clouds, surrounded by a mushroom cloud, a radar antennae and circular display, and supersonic missiles. It is an image that accurately captures how irrelevant Bush had become to the world he helped make. Showing him floating above the surface, disembodied, and without the hands that might fashion change, either textually or materially, it captures Bush's frustrating inability to get anything he wanted done in the postwar era. Bush had written of faith, but surely he could not have welcomed this image of a head, wrapped in a crown of thorns, over which he had no control.

Fade to black?

Asking what researchers actually did opens up a new way to write the history of postwar American science, just as the very idea of co-production allows us to understand why we need a new history of postwar science and technology. Bush's project in co-production failed, in part, because he could not successfully imagine how both the military and the researcher had transformed each other during and after World War II. Nor could he successfully design a new taxonomy of knowledge and the institutional mechanisms necessary for its survival and growth. The insulation Bush sought to achieve for American science, first in the NRF and later in the RDB, rested upon a vision of the researcher made untenable by the war and the research vistas opened by the atomic bomb and the guided missile. Yet Bush was right to fear this development and attempt to manage it; Lasswell had argued in his garrison state essay that such a state could only emerge with the willing cooperation of technical and scientific researchers. Bush didn't believe that officers or researchers could contain their enthusiasms; hence, he believed that institutions rather than individuals acting alone would prevent the emergence of an American garrison state. Perhaps the clearest demonstration of just how different the postwar state was lay in a simple observation by one of Bush's protégés, CalTech president and Rad Lab director Lee DuBridge. Writing as Korea heated up and many feared that the Soviet Union would dominate the globe, he claimed: "what we need now is a 1950 version of Van Bush and apparently he has not yet been found".[76] Nor would he appear. Even Bush did not want to reveal the extent of his failure at war's end:

[t]he few years just after the war were not pleasant ones for me. I was chairman of the Joint New Weapons Committee, had no backing whatever

from Forrestal, and accomplished very little. I should have had the good sense to keep out of it. But I don't think there is need to get any of this into the record.[77]

Unpleasant, painful, and awkwardly necessary to understanding our present, our past and our possible futures, the story told here might also make us realize that the postwar American state's history is first and foremost the history of a state of knowledge.

Notes

1 Henry De Wolf Smyth, *Atomic Energy for Military Purposes* (Washington DC, 1945; Stanford: Stanford University Press, 1989).
2 Donald E. Stokes, *Pasteur's Quadrant: Basic Science and Technological Innovation* (Washington DC: Brookings Institution, 1997).
3 Kevles, Daniel J. "The National Science Foundation and the Debate over Postwar Research Policy, 1942–1945", *Isis* 68(1977): 5–26. Despite claims to significant differences, much analysis follows Kevles' lead: see Nathan Reingold's "Vannevar Bush's New Deal for Research; or, The Triumph of the Old Order", in *Science, American Style*, ed. Nathan Reingold, 284–333 (New Brunswick: Rutgers University Press, 1991; 1987); Kleinman, Daniel J., *Politics on the Endless Frontier: Postwar Research Policy in the United States* (Durham NC: Duke University Press, 1995); and Zachary, G. Pascal, *Endless Frontier: Vannevar Bush, Engineer of the American Century* (New York: Free Press, 1997). Also influential was Dupree, A. H., "The Great Instauration of 1940: The Organization of Scientific Research in War", in *The Twentieth Century Sciences*, ed. G. W. Holton (New York, Norton, 1972).
4 Owens, L. (1990) "MIT and the Federal 'Angel': Academic R&D and Federal-Private Cooperation before WWII", *Isis* 81: 188–213.
5 Price, Don K., *Government and Science: Their Dynamic Relation in American Democracy* (New York: New York University Press, 1954); Price, Don K., *The Scientific Estate* (Cambridge MA: Harvard University Press, 1965). I owe the phrase as well as the idea of the "Charles River school of science policy" to Sheila Jasanoff.
6 20 October 1945, VB to J. B. Conant, Box 27, Folder: 614 (Conant '39–'46), Vannevar Bush Papers, LC.
7 20 October 1945, VB to J.B. Conant, Box 27, Folder: 614 (Conant '39–'46), Vannevar Bush Papers, LC.
8 Lasswell, H. (1941) "The Garrison State", *American Journal of Sociology* 46: 455–468; for an attempt to understand this concept in postwar America, see Hogan, M. J., *A Cross of Iron: Harry S. Truman and the Origins of the National Security State* (New York: Cambridge University Press, 1998). Also addressing this issue is Friedberg, A. L. (1992) "Why Didn't the United States Become a Garrison State?", *International Security* 16(4): 109–142; and Friedberg, A. L., *In the Shadow of the Garrison State: America's Anti-Statism and Its Cold War Grand Strategy* (Princeton: Princeton University Press, 2000).
9 Hollinger, David A., "The Defence of Democracy and Robert K. Merton's Formulation of the Scientific Ethos", in *Knowledge and Society*, eds Robert Alun Jones and Henrika Kuklick (Greenwich CT: JAI Press, 1983) 1–15.
10 See 2 August 1940, Frederic Delano to FDR plus attachment "Memorandum on Democracy and Planning in Crisis", President's Secretary File, Department Files, Interior, 1940–1944, Box 54, Franklin D. Roosevelt Library, Hyde Park, New York. Quotes from attachment, pages 1–2.
11 On Bush's biography we are now fortunate to have Zachary, G. P., *Endless Frontier: Vannevar Bush, Engineer of the American Century* (New York: Free Press, 1997).

12 On the Science Advisory Board and NRPB, see Genuth, J. (1987) "Groping Towards Science Policy in the 1930s", *Minerva* 25: 238–268.

13 See 23 May 1940, A. H. Compton to Frederic Delano, OF 4010, FDR Library, telegram attached.

14 10 April 1939, V. Bush to H. Hoover, Box 51, File 1261, V. Bush Papers, LC.

15 The classic NDRC origin story is Baxter, J. P., *Scientists Against Time* (Boston MA: Little, Brown, 1946) pp. 3–26; and more recently, Kevles, D. J., *The Physicists: The History of a Scientific Community in Modern America* (New York: Knopf, 1977) pp. 287–301.

16 See 19 August 1940, Ickes to FDR, OF 4010, FDR Library; and 16 September 1944, Bush to J. P. Baxter, RG227, History Office, Box 7, "Organization NDRC-OSRD" USNA.

17 See note attached to 19 August 1940, Ickes to FDR, OF 4010, FDR Library. Bush's views on the state of defense research circa January–February 1941 are found in Bush, "Organization of Defense Research", which can be found in OF 2240, FDRL or Box 51, Folder 1269, VBPLC. On FDR's reasons for agreeing to the creation of the OSRD to subsume the NDRC, see 20 May 1941, FDR to Wayne Coy [Director, Bureau of Budget], OF 4482, FDRL.

18 More on this can be found in Pursell, C., "Science Agencies in World War II: The OSRD and its Challengers", in *The Sciences in the American Context: New Perspectives*, ed. N. Reingold (Washington DC: Smithsonian Institution Press, 1979).

19 See 29 January 1941, H. G. Bowen to Chief of Naval Operations, RG 298, Box 3, "Policy". USNA.

20 On the contractual organization of wartime research and development management see Owens, L. (1994) "The Counterproductive Management of Science in the Second World War: Vannevar Bush and the Office of Scientific Research and Development", *Business History Review* 68: 515–576.

21 On overhead policies, see 29 August 1940, "Memorandum to the Members of the NDRC", RG 227, Box 21, "Contracts, Overhead, 1940–1942"; Stewart, I., *Organizing Scientific Research for War* (Boston MA: Little, Brown, 1948) p. 208; and Compton, K. T., R. W. Trullinger *et al.*, *Scientists Face the World of 1942* (New Brunswick: Rutgers University Press, 1942) p. 22.

22 See 19 November 1941, Vannevar Bush to Members OSRD Advisory Council, "Production of the New Devices", RG 298, Box 11, "Notice of Meetings", USNA.

23 See 26 January 1943, Vannevar Bush, "Research and the War Effort", An Address delivered at the AIEE National Technical Meeting, RG 227, Box 49b, "V. Bush, 1944", MIT Rad Lab History Office Files, Waltham, MA.

24 A particularly good discussion of the "few quick" program is found in 24 January 1942, F. S. Gordon to K. T. Compton, RG 227, Division 7 Files, Office Files of Harold Hazen, Box 70, "Transition Office".

25 On the proximity fuze, see Dennis, M. A. (1994). " 'Our First Line of Defense': Two University Laboratories in the Postwar American State", *Isis* 85(3): 427–455; on the recognition of the novelty of the production scheme, also see 3 January 1942, Lt. T. C. Wilson to Files, RG 298, Box 60, "T.C. Wilson", USNA.

26 See 29 January 1942, Edward L. Bowles to Karl T. Compton, Box 21, "Correspondence 5/40–8/42", Bowles Papers, Manuscripts Division, LC. On Bowles, see Pang, A. S.-K. (1990) "Edward Bowles and Radio Engineering at MIT, 1920–1940", *Historical Studies in the Physical and Biological Sciences* 20: 313–337.

27 See 1 October 1943, Bush to Bundy, and attached report, "Guided Missiles", RG 218, Joint New Weapons Committee, Box 4, "Guided Missiles, 7/43–10–43", USNA. Bush's own ideas about guided missiles, or controlled glide bombs, are found in 4 October 1943, Bush to Dean Moreland, also in this same archival location.

28 See 27 June 1944, David Griggs to Edward L. Bowles, Box 32, "Correspondence 4/44–6/44", Edward L. Bowles Papers, Manuscripts Division, Library of Congress.

29 See 27 July 1944, Journal Entry, Henry Guerlac Papers, Box 30, Manuscripts Collection, Kroch Library, Cornell University. Guerlac's journal is a record of his time as the Radiation Laboratory's historian.

30 12 August 1941, Bush to Bundy and Hunsaker, RG 298, Box 56, "Rockets–Jet Propellants".

31 See Griggs to Bowles, *op cit.* note 28. The "no change" design was also labeled a "Chinese copy", see Guerlac Journal, *op cit.*

32 Koppes, C. R., *JPL and the American Space Program: A history of the Jet Propulsion Laboratory* (New Haven: Yale University Press, 1982).

33 For the cost estimates, see 24 October 1944, C. L. Wilson to E. L. Moreland, RG 227, Box 8A, "Missile, Guided-Program"; on Bush's criticisms see 25 October 1944, Bush to JNW Members, RG 218, JNW Records, Box 4, "Guided Missiles, 10/43/ to 12/44". On the fate and production of the US copy of the V-1, see 5 February 1945 D. T. Griggs to Lt General Carl Spaatz, Edward L. Bowles Papers, Box 33, "2/45 Correspondence".

34 See the report on guided missiles attached to 27 December 1944, Joseph Boyce to C. L. Wilson, RG 227, Box 8A, "Guided Missile Study Group".

35 See 19 December 1942, Chief of Research and Development to Vice Chief of Naval Operations, RG 227, Box 12, "Postwar Planning".

36 A useful discussion of the multiple plans is found in 29 December 1943, Lyman Chalkley to V. Bush, RG 227 Box 12 General Records, Postwar Planning, (1942–1943). Chalkley had first emerged as a critic of the wartime mobilization whom Bush co-opted with a job in the OSRD administration. He subsequently became one of Bush's most trusted aides.

37 A particularly clear example of this is found in 20 September 1943, M. A. Tuve to Captain C. L. Tyler, RG 227, Box 12 General Records, Postwar Planning (1942–1943), p. 2.

38 For example, "[t]he frustration of bureaucracy and the dry-rot of civil service prevent Government research laboratories from obtaining and holding the most competent men", in 11 June 1943, David Luke Hopkins, "The National Institute for Research and Development, NIRD(?)", in RG 227 Box 12, General Records, Postwar Planning, 1942–1943.

39 Quote from 3 February 1944, Bush to D. Luke Hopkins, RG 227, OSRD, Box 12 "Postwar Planning"; on giving in to demands to begin discussions of postwar military research and development, see 6 March 1944, Bush to J. A. Furer, RG 227, Box 12, "Postwar Planning, 1944".

40 14 April 1944, James W. Wadsworth to Bush, RG 227, Box 12, Postwar Planning.

41 See "Agenda for Conference to Consider Needs for Postwar Research and Development for the Army and Navy", RG 298, Box 52, "Postwar Research".

42 See "Proceedings of the Conference to Consider Needs for Post-War Research and Development for the Army and Navy", Box 86, MATP; quote page 9.

43 The standard sources on the Wilson Committee remain Kevles, D. J. (1975) "Scientists, the Military, and the Control of Postwar Defense Research: The Case of the Research Board for National Security, 1944–46", *Technology and Culture* 16: 20–47; and Sherry, M. S., *Preparing for the Next War: American Plans for Postwar Defense, 1941–1945* (New Haven: Yale University Press, 1977) pp. 134–159; also of interest is Reingold, N. (1991; 1987) "Vannevar Bush's New Deal for Research: Or, The Triumph of the Old Order", in *Science, American Style* (New Brunswick: Rutgers University Press, 1991 [1987]) pp. 284–333. The following Tuve documents allow one to trace the Committee's deliberations: 22 June 1944, "Notes for First Meeting of Committee on Planning for Army and Navy Research", Box 114, "Bush Report and National Research Foundation", MATP; 22 June 1944, "Addendum to Minutes of Meeting, June 22, 1944", Box 87, Envelope, MATP; 4 July 1944, "Notes for Second

Meeting, July 6, 1944", Box 85, "Tuve", MATP; and 10 July 1945, Tuve to Charles E. Wilson, Box 85, "Tuve", MATP.

44 Quotes from 17 August 1944, Jewett to K. T. Compton, RG 298, Box 52, "Postwar Research Volume 2".

45 For a copy of Bush's long and undated demobilization memo, see September 1944, Bush to OSRD, RG 227, Division 7, (Getting) Technical Subject Files, Box 194, "Demobilization, NDRC".

46 12 September 1944, H. H. Arnold to Carl Spaatz, Box 33, "September 1944, E. L. Bowles Papers, LC.

47 On Von Karman and Arnold, see 7 November 1944, Arnold to Von Karman, Box 33, "Nov-December 1944", Bowles Papers. On the origins of Project RAND, see the following documents, all located in Box 32, E. L. Bowles Papers: 28 August 1944, Bowles to Arnold; 7 October 1944, A. E. Raymond [of Douglas Aircraft] to E. L. Bowles, Box 32; on the possibility that RAND refers to the stripper, Sally Rand, see 29 November 1944, Lt General M. F. Harmon to Bowles, who writes in reference to the stripped-down B-29 bomber: "In the event that our daylight strikes in the near future do not encounter any more serious fighter threat involving the employment of the turret guns than they have on missions so far conducted, I will be ripe for conviction that we should go for the Gypsy Rose Lee model". RAND might mean "research and development" or "research and no development", but more than likely it was an acronym of many meanings, one that inevitably recollected the project's origins in transforming the B-29 "into a bomber instead of a gasoline tanker in operating from bases in the Marianas". For more on RAND's history, see Kaplan, F., *The Wizards of Armageddon* (New York: Simon and Schuster, 1983); Hounshell, D. (1997) "The Cold War, RAND, and the Generation of Knowledge, 1946–1962", *Historical Studies in the Physical and Biological Sciences* 27: 237–267; and Jardini, D. R., *Out of the Blue Yonder: The RAND Corporation's Diversification into Social Welfare Research, 1946–1968. History* (Pittsburgh: Carnegie Mellon University, 1997).

48 For an excellent discussion of US nuclear policy at this time, see Hershberg, J. G., *James B. Conant: Harvard to Hiroshima and the Making of the Nuclear Age* (New York: Alfred A. Knopf, 1993) pp. 194–207; on Bohr's own views, also see 7 September 1944, Bohr to FDR, OF2240, FDRL.

49 See 12 December 1944, Wilson to P.C. Putnam, RG 227, Box 11A, "Postwar Military Policy Committee".

50 See 20 August 1944, Henry E. Guerlac, "Interview with Dr. Vannevar Bush", RG 277, OSRD Files, Radiation Laboratory Papers, Box 49b, History Office, "V. Bush, 1944". Quote from page 5; of Bush, Guerlac wrote: "the man is positively magnetic: friendly, shrewd, frank and made of steel springs".

51 Any copy of the report has the letter of 17 November as either front matter or as an appendix. See Bush, V., *Science–The Endless Frontier* (Washington DC: Office of Scientific Research and Development, 1945).

52 *SEF*, 34.

53 On separating research and production, see *SEF*, 32:

> Industry learned many years ago that basic research cannot often be fruitfully conducted as an adjunct to or a subdivision of an operating agency or department....It [research] should not be conducted in an atmosphere where it is gauged and tested by operating or production standards.

On the historical dimensions of the introduction of research in to industry and the complex relations of research and production, see Leslie, S. W., *Boss Kettering* (New York: Columbia University Press, 1983); Reich, L. S., *The Making of American Industrial Research: Science and Business at GE and Bell, 1876–1926* (New York: Cambridge University Press, 1985); Wise, G., *Willis R. Whitney, General Electric, and the Origins of*

U.S. Industrial Research (New York: Columbia University Press, 1985); and Dennis, M. A. (1987) "Accounting for Research: New Histories of Corporate Laboratories and the Social History of American Science ", *Social Studies of Science* 17: 479–518.

54 Dr. Rabi gave as the opinion of the chiefs of division in his laboratory of 600 people that at least 75 per cent would like to stay on in a similar set-up after the war.

>   These men have learned the value of adequate financial support and the intellectual pleasures of working together. As long as cooperative effort does not involve centralized dictation it is unobjectionable.

See "Minutes of the Meeting of the Bowman Committee held on March 26 and 27, 1945 at the Johns Hopkins University", Box 32, Folder 9, p. 4, I.I. Rabi Papers, LC. The minutes also have several pithy statements about the value of the work done by the historians on the committee's secretariat.

55 See 2 June 1945, K. T. Compton to Clark S. Robinson, "NAS Organization 1945, NAS RBNS General", National Academy of Sciences Archives: "At the moment the Research Board for National Security is held up by the fact that the Army and the Navy have not yet succeeded in working out a method acceptable to the Bureau of the Budget for making available the funds necessary for us to proceed".

56 On Truman's views on the RBNS, see 11 June 1945, Truman to Jewett; Bush's response to this letter, of which he had been sent a copy, 12 June 1945, both are located in "Organization 1945, NAS RBNS General", NAS Archives. Perhaps the greatest irony here is that Truman's letter to Jewett was typed on RBNS letterhead which had the Academy's address and telephone number, along with the following statement printed under RESEARCH BOARD FOR NATIONAL SECURITY: "Established in 1945 by the National Academy of Sciences at the request of the Secretary of War and the Secretary of the Navy". Reams of unused stationary in the NAS Archives are the RBNS' greatest legacy. Truman's views are also recorded in the papers of Harold Smith, the Director of the Bureau of the Budget, who records that on 8 June 1945, Truman declared of the Academy-based RBNS: "We cannot let this outfit run the Government". Harold Smith Papers, Box 3, "Conferences with the President, 1945 (Truman)", FDRL.

57 On the military support's of Bush's NRF over Kilgore's NSF, see 28 July 1945, R. D. Conrad to Chief of Office of Research and Inventions (Navy), RG 298, Box 8, "Legislation":

>   Congress will almost certainly pass some "Public Welfare" sort of research bill. The Magnuson [Bush] version is far superior to the Kilgore one, but the socialistic nature of the Kilgore bill will put it across unless it meets more unified opposition than is now apparent, or (what comes to the same thing) unless the Magnuson…gets greater backing.

58 Truman quoted in Rhodes, R., *The Making of the Atomic Bomb* (New York: Simon and Schuster, 1986) p. 688.

59 See 7 August 1945 and 9 August 1945, R. D. Conrad to Chief of Research and Inventions, RG 298, Box 80, Nuclear Physics. Of course, this gives the lie to the golden age views on the origins of the Office of Naval Research. Put simply, ONR sponsored nuclear physics to "catch-up" to a perceived Army advantage in atomic weapons. For an Air Force perspective on the Navy's new research effort, see 31 August 1945, St. Clair Street to Commanding General, Army Air Forces, Box 34, "Correspondence August–Ocotober 1945", E. L. Bowles Papers.

60 See 4 October 1945, Bowles to Robert Patterson, Box 34, "August–October 1945", ELB.

61 See 18 October 1945, Robert Patterson, Secretary of War and James Forrestal, Secretary of the Navy, to Frank Jewett, "Organization 1945, NAS: RBNS General", NAS Archives.

62 13 September 1944, Bush to Maj. General C. C. Williams, RG 227, OSRD, Box 11A, "Postwar Military Policy Committee".

63 1 October 1945, Bush to Conant, Box 27, Folder 614, VBPLC.

64 See Bowman Committee Report, *SEF*, 117. Readers should note the similarities between these words and Steven Shapin's *The Social History of Truth* with its emphasis upon gentlemanly status and credibility. Certainly there are similarities, but it is unlikely that Bush or any of his colleagues perceived themselves as gentlemen; that was a status reserved for someone like Secretary of War Stimson and very few others. Instead, I prefer to think of this as explicated by Donald T. Regan, former Reagan White House chief of staff. When Nancy Reagan orchestrated his firing, Regan replied that he had plenty of "f–ck you money"; that is, he could tell Nancy Reagan off and walk away. It is far coarser than gentlemanly behavior, but it is the world Bush lived in as well as our own.

65 See Bush, *SEF*, 36. Bush suggested that Division members receive a $50 per diem and earn no more than $10,000 annually while working for the Foundation.

66 I have addressed this issue elsewhere, see Dennis, M. A., "Echoes of the Past: Henry Guerlac and Radar's Historiographic Problem", in O. Blumtritt (ed.) *Tracking the History of Radar* (Piscataway NJ: IEEE, 1994); and Dennis, M. A., "Historiography of Science: An American Perspective", in J. Krige and D. Pestre (eds) *Science in the Twentieth Century* (Amsterdam: Harwood Academic Publishers, 1997) pp. 1–26.

67 For example, see Price, D. K., *Government and Science: Their Dynamic Relation in American Democracy* (New York: New York University Press, 1954) pp. 144–159; Friedberg, A. L., *In the Shadow of the Garrison State: America's Anti-statism and its Cold War Grand Strategy* (Princeton: Princeton University Press, 2000) pp. 296–340. Unfortunately, the JRDB's massive archive remains the best way to learn about the organization.

68 For an example of this, see 4 November 1946, Bush to Conant, Box 27, "Conant '39–'46", where Bush addresses the possibility that a foundation may not be established. On the Navy's support of university research, Bush explained that "certainly they support second-rate people in third-rate institutions". For Bush and Conant such support was another reason to get the military out of the business of funding university science; implicit was the idea that military officers, no matter how benevolent, were incapable of judging quality research.

69 This letter is available in several collections; the copy quoted from here is 21 May 1946, Bush to Patterson, RG 330, RDB Files, Box 186, "2/1–2/6 on GM Agenda".

70 On the Policy Council, see 18 July 1947, Bush to Patterson, RG 330, Entry 341 Box 56, RDB-117–1947. This letter also includes a useful discussion of the Board's first year.

71 13 May 1948, Bowles to Arnold, Box 36, "May–November 1948", Bowles Papers.

72 19 May 1948, Arnold to Bowles, Box 36, "May–November 1948", Bowles Papers.

73 13 October 1948, Bush to Forrestal, RG 330, RDB Files.

74 Bush, V., *Modern Arms and Free Men: A Discussion of the Role of Science in Preserving Democracy* (New York: Simon and Schuster, 1949) p. 212.

75 Originally published in 1945, and reprinted in Bush, V., *Science is not Enough* (New York: William Morrow and Company, 1967) pp. 11–14.

76 20 December 1950, Lee DuBridge to Gregory Breit, Folder 108.8, Lee DuBridge Papers, CalTech Archives.

77 11 December 1970, Bush to Conant, MC 78, Box 2, "Correspondence – Last name begins with *C*", MIT Archives.

13 Science and the political imagination in contemporary democracies

Yaron Ezrahi

In Chorus I of his poem *The Rock*, T. S. Eliot asks

> Where is the wisdom we have lost in knowledge?
> Where is the knowledge we have lost in information?
>
> (Eliot 1960)

The poet captures here one of the principal themes of modernity, the shifts from wisdom to knowledge and from knowledge to information as ways or means of knowing. If Eliot were writing today perhaps he would have added another line in which he wonders about the latest and perhaps the most dramatic shift, from information transmitted by means of words and numbers to images, to visual cinematic representations of reality transmitted mostly by the mass electronic media. While "in-formation" is a term which still preserves the association of knowing with the inner person, with the mind, we need a term which will reflect the increasing reliance on outside, external flow of images, the particular association between sight and distance. T. S. Eliot might have wondered today not only where is the wisdom we have lost in knowledge and the knowledge we have lost in information, but also "where is the in-formation we have lost in 'out-formations'?". Following the informational mode of knowing or representing the world, what I call here "outformations" suggests still another stage in the direction of the alienation of the means of knowing from personality, perhaps even a certain return to aspects of the collective imaginary construction of experience by myth.

Introduction

As I have suggested elsewhere, the principal characteristics of the impact of scientific culture on modern (especially democratic) politics include, among other things:

(a) the growing deployment of professional-instrumental and technical vocabularies in fields of political discourse formerly regulated by religious, moral and legal ones;

(b) the deployment of the machine as a metaphor in discussions of the state and the market;

(c) trust in the transparency of political realities to the public and therefore in the possibility of public political accountability;

(d) faith in the compatibility between individual autonomy, the advancement and diffusion of certified knowledge and representations of political reality, and the possibility of rational consensus among citizens (Ezrahi 1990; 1996).

In the following I shall focus on recent implications of the decline of the Enlightenment's synthesis of knowledge and politics and the rise of new configurations of knowing and doing politics which are connected with the shifts from knowledge to information, and from information to outformations as characteristic (although by no means unchallenged) means of knowing and guiding politics.

From wisdom to knowledge

Wisdom as a form of knowing or communicating knowledge (I use the term "knowledge" also as a generic term for all forms of knowing) is characteristically unformalized and even unformalizable. It comes as very contextually rich in meanings, links, associations and references; it is frequently possessed by unique individuals: saints, sages, wise men and women, rabbis, priests, mystics, old people and the like. Very often, it is a form of knowledge transmitted orally and sometimes by texts which may or may not be esoteric. As a form of knowing or teaching, wisdom is not usually easily acquired or teachable, nor accessible through the mastery of technical skills. It is often associated with faith in the privileged access of the wise to supernatural sources of knowledge or to unique revelatory experiences. There are variants of wisdom which are more closely associated with experience than with inspiration or extraordinary mental powers. "Words of wisdom" are characteristically polysemous mixtures of cognitive, moral, emotional, social, philosophical and practical references. The wise usually enjoy a privileged status within a community of followers. It is an hierarchical form of knowing and teaching. Sometimes "wisdom" is transmitted by simple statements or narratives. In these forms, wisdom can be detached from particular agents and travel widely in culture. The gems of wisdom found in *Ecclesiastes* or Montaigne's *Essays* are well known examples. All such expressions of wisdom invite endless reflections and interpretations, especially those which are supposed to have layers of esoteric, hidden meanings.

By comparison with wisdom, *knowledge* in the scientific sense is perceived as much more systematically organized and formalized – especially due to its logical and mathematical components. François Jullien observed that whereas wisdom as a form of knowledge is characteristic to Chinese culture, philosophy and science are particularly Western. He ties these difference to a host of wider cultural values and traits, some of which relate to characteristic Western configurations of politics. Thus knowledge as it emerged in the West relates to values such as clarity, logical rigor, a sharp distinction between truth and error, conflicts of opinions and the urge for their rational resolution. Wisdom by comparison is inclusive of truth and its opposites, irenic rather than polemic, allusive rather than explicit or public, and often expressed in silence (Jullien 2002). No one can deny, of course, the omnipresence of informal layers of "tacit knowledge" in science (Polanyi 1974 Routledge; Latour 1987). But the production, certification and communication of scientific knowledge engages a host of methodologies and tools, whose intended or unintended import has the effect of decontextualizing and depersonalizing claims of knowledge, thus rendering them particularly useful in the production of the modern democratic order. Inasmuch as science, much more explicitly, is a socially cooperative enterprise, scientists, as Robert K. Merton insists, produce and possess their knowledge "together" (Merton 1957). Moreover, by contrast to wisdom, scientific knowledge and skills are presumed teachable. They involve the mastery of technical mental or material operations and are, therefore, more independent of unique personal experiences, inspiration or unusual personality traits. Hence, although scientific knowledge, especially in its formal mathematical embodiments, may in fact be restricted to specialists, the fact that it can be learned renders it more accessible in principle and therefore, at least apparently, more democratic. Inasmuch as the public perceives science as knowledge produced by means of a social process and possessed by a group, the authority of the individual scientist seems to be less personalized than that of the sage.

The impersonal nature of scientific authority relates also to the commitment, expressed in the ethos of science and the norms of scientific practice, to separate the content of scientific knowledge from the emotional, ethical, religious or political dispositions of the scientists, both as individuals and as groups. For a considerable part of the history of the relations between science and politics, the idea of a context-free knowledge was instrumental for the protection of scientists and scientific institutions from direct political interventions, and ironically facilitated the evolution of the distinct politically useful social authority of science (Porter 1995; Scott 1998). The need to belittle the input of personality, politics and context into the process of knowledge production, and the tendency to present knowledge in terms of the mirror metaphor as a reflection of the objective properties of the world, made science and scientific authority into invaluable political resources for the construction of the democratic political order. But this universe, a product of an early Enlightenment genre of the modern political and cultural imagination, has been gradually replaced by another. In contemporary socio-political and cultural contexts the idea of context-free knowledge is anachronistic, abstract, barely believable and therefore less compelling.

In the course of the twentieth century, the visible impact of science on public affairs has revealed and dramatized the political uses of knowledge, encouraging the view that scientists and technologists take sides in political and military conflicts. The politicization of the public image of science appeared compatible with new historical and sociological studies of science, whose intended or unintended import was to support a trend to recontextualize scientific knowledge, to highlight the fact that it has been much more context-responsive than many scientists would have us believe.

From knowledge to information

In some respects, the transition from knowledge to information as a more socially inclusive means of knowing facts or accounting for, and guiding, action, has been a response to the need to keep knowledge objective or technically valid in, not independent of, context. The way to achieve that was to localize objectivity and contextualize technicality in relation to specific goals or tasks, rather than treat them as general properties of a mode of knowing. While information evolved as a category of knowledge more contextually relevant to specific areas of discourse and action, by comparison with knowledge it has been usually more detached from the theoretical context in which it was produced, systematically conceptualized, and justified. Information is characteristically more restricted to the technical practical surface of knowledge. It is knowledge stripped of its theoretical, formal, logical and mathematical layers and made to fit quick, often "do-it-yourself" tasks and operations. Information is often but thin knowledge, a shortcut approach to the need to have operational guidelines for decisions and actions without getting into the scientific accounts, the knowledge base or the metaphysical foundations that ground these guidelines. Matching drugs with symptoms without getting into the deeper structure of disease and the chemical processes which particular drugs induce is, for example, a matter of information, not knowledge, so are reports of the fluctuations in the cost of living index, or inflation rates, or an instruction book for producing an atomic bomb.

The language with which we talk about information suggests that by comparison with knowledge the former is perceived as more socially transportable, that it travels more freely in "channels of information" and is more easily storable in "data banks". Because it tends to be more mechanical, information seems more accessible, less dependent upon the mediation of "men of knowledge". As a socio-cultural configuration, information tends to conceal the interpretive layers and normative commitments underlying its structures and uses. When users discover that being informed is not sufficient to solve a problem or to act effectively, they may need to go back to the knowledge base of the information they possess in order to discover why their operations or expectations were thwarted, what is missing in their guidelines, or what other options, not contained in the information they used, are actually available.

When it is represented by information rather than by knowledge, "reality" can be flattened and simplified and hence also in some sense democratized as a reference for discourse or action. When T. S. Eliot writes about the losses we incur in shifting from wisdom through knowledge to information, he may be thinking of this very process as a thinning out of layers of meanings, references and associations, a process of impoverishing human understanding and experience. Eliot, no doubt, misses the poetical, philosophical, religious and ethical dimensions of knowledge and experience which were part of earlier configurations of culture, the polysemicity of language, the complexity, the depth and, perhaps more than anything else, the wholeness and the all-encompassing coherence of our life and our world-view. In this view the move from wisdom through knowledge to information not only tends to diminish the source of knowledge as an agency, but also the agency of the recipient (Eliot 1960). Still, this process should be viewed more dialectically as also making the informed individual less dependent upon other people. Because information is more mechanically organized and communicable, it can often replace agencies by machines. The culture of information which diminishes the presence of the knower involves more abstract and impersonal relations between agents and between them and the world. Unlike the wise man, the informed person need not be sagacious and his personality may be standardized for the purposes of packing and transmitting information. Unlike the knowledgeable, the merely informed need not make heavy investment in learning. One need not be judicious, wise, inspired or technically sophisticated. Still one must be able to process information. Information is often specifically designed or directed to be used for a purpose.

From information to outformations

Even this usually minimal requirement is removed, however, in the case of outformations. There is no outformations processing which is parallel to information processing. Outformations constitute a much more diffused configuration of pictures, sounds, narratives, frames, etc. Moreover, even more than information, outformations appear to be out there without specific relations to any visible agents. By comparison with knowledge and information, outformations, however, are more like wisdom in combining cognitive, emotional, aesthetic and other dimensions of experience. They are rich and frequently intense like wisdom, but unlike it, they are largely disconnected templets of stimuli. Whereas in the case of wisdom the sage functions as the organizer and the source of a rich multidimensional understanding, in the case of outformations similarly dense configurations of meanings and associations are characteristically more eclectic and directly accessible.

Against the expectations built up by the cultures of knowledge and information, outformations, as a constant flow of inanimate or animated images, problematize the claims of the electronic media to provide us with reliable representations of reality. Like the scientists or the experts also the producers of outformations and their diffusers actually mediate between the "world" and the public. But the camera, or rather lay cultural orientations towards photographs and moving pictures, allow the agents of outformations to even more effectively erase their fingerprints. The camera has a unique power to both appear as an accessible instrument of creative works and generate imaginary worlds which deny their own contrived creative production process. Because of this ambiguity, producers of political outformations persistently worry that viewers may lose faith in what they see and discover the degree to which the world they represent on the screen is made up. News programs and documentaries especially depend on viewers' willingness to overlook the techniques and fictions used to create and augment "objective" reality effects. CNN has been trying to overcome this ambiguity between fiction and reality by running commercials in which it shows faces in various expressive states accompanied by a voice saying "real anger", "real fear", "real hope", etc., thus trying to reinforce spectators' trust in the communicative and representational efficacy of the medium. During the war on Saddam's Iraq (spring 2003) direct reports relayed by journalists embedded with the fighting troops gave viewers a sense of "touching" reality, although unlike those embedded in "reality", these television viewers can exit or enter "reality" at will like audiences in the movie theatre. In the latter case viewers have the attractive option of regulating the scope and length of their exposure to reality. In the absence of correct or incorrect ways to process outformations, the mediators try "to train" the viewers' imagination by clustering and repetitions. In the case of outformations it is more difficult to use criteria such as relevance, logic, systematicity, quantitative computations, conceptual genealogy and the like to ground reality constructs. This is partly due to the fact that outformations tend to aim at much wider and more diverse audiences or spectators and be influenced by a complex set of goals including entertainment, marketing, persuasion, etc. It is also partly due to the fact that whereas the languages of knowledge and information, and particularly logic and mathematics, discipline the import of their employment, outformations produce messages and communications whose import is more diffused and unruly. Outformations mix the transmission of information with affective, aesthetic, entertaining effects in ways which have already been anticipated in the earlier versions of the culture of mass media news. The production of news programs in which music, drama and visual beauty were deliberately used to attract spectators, has been aptly called "infotainment" combining norms of entertainment taken from the performing and the visual arts with norms of accurate accounts of reality whose origins are traceable to the culture of science. The television screen itself, as the site of moving pictures, is like a window into the real. But at the same time the very frame of the screen, like the boundaries of the canvas, already organizes and aestheticizes the visual experience of the viewers, making it also more painterly.

Not surprisingly, with the development of this trend it has become widely evident that the idea of reality which arises out of outformations, the welding of the real with the painterly or the theatrical, more than the idea of reality which arises out of knowledge or information, openly invites the viewer's imagination to appreciate, and participate in, the various creative contrivances which enter its productions. Hence as means for the construction or representation of reality, and we are concerned here particularly with political reality, outformations often make spectators more conscious and more reflexive of the fact that some parts of what our culture treats as reality are made of fictions and some fictions are even more informative than supposedly direct representations. In addition, as Luc Boltansky has shown, the relations between the new mass media environment and viewers' emotional and political responses involve profoundly different and, in many respects, novel causal patterns (Boltansky 1999). The fact that outformations mediate the contemporary experience of the politically real, that it is via the small screen that we observe the agents, events and other features of the political game, relates, of course, to their extraordinary accessibility. Moreover, modern interactive media technology has enormously enlarged the options for shifting from passive to active engagement, introducing the element of play into the engagement with politics by means of the mass media. Along the move from knowledge to information, the move from information to outformations often represents the sacrifice of depth and perhaps also accuracy to accessibility. Universal accessibility is apparently more important for the legitimation of contemporary constructions of reality than accuracy, impersonality, "rationality" and other such criteria that relate to the culture of scientific representations. They do not seem to be disciplined by the scientific commitment to repress affective, emotional, aesthetic or psychological elements as disruptions or distortions of the cool, rational, even boring representations of the world. In the new culture of outformations even news and documentary movies often function just as genres integrated into fictional worlds of entertainment to produce "reality effects".

Despite the successful attempts to erase the traces of their production process, perhaps more than any antecedent forms of knowing, outformations make contemporary humanity aware of the role of the imagination and of creativity in the production of notions of reality which travel in our culture and politics. Like literature, poetry and the arts, but unlike science, outformations directly engage our emotional, aesthetic and more generally our sensual selves. They more deliberately and directly mix references to the "external" world with appeals or references to our inner worlds. Despite the diminished intellectual groundedness of these concepts of the real, their radical inclusiveness or accessibility gives them the required legitimation and fixes them as shared references in the context of public discourse and action. This fact may indicate that even during earlier periods where concepts of the real were mediated by knowledge and subordinated to the norms of the culture of science, what actually certified them, or their simplified versions, for public currency was not so much their cognitive groundedness in observations, experiments and logic as their presumed advantages as involving more public rather than private or elite forms of knowing. In this respect like the earlier moves from wisdom to knowledge and from knowledge to information, the move from information to outformations represents another stage in the very process by which more inclusive, more publicly accessible definitions of reality assume greater social validity, currency and political relivance than former more restricted ones. Moreover, the role of outformations in our culture and politics may indicate a cultural, perhaps a postmodern, shift from foundational to non-foundational and dynamic conceptions of reality, a growing move from reason to the imagination as the faculty which consciously mediates the making and the unmaking of political worlds in our time. Among other things, this shift may reflect the intuition that *collective imagining is a more participatory medium for constructing the political universe than public reason*. It does not require, for instance, the special role of the Kantian public intellectual as a model to laypersons for the correct employment of reason in the context of public affairs. It may actually represent instead a postmodern version of the social contract idea, an actual, ongoing participation of, at least parts of, the public in the construction and deconstruction of the political order as a continual spectacle in which actors and producers try to anticipate viewers tastes, choices, and behaviors which directly or indirectly decide how long the political world constructed, and its main protagonists, can stay on and, therefore, also outside the screen. As such it may constitute a deeper expression of Hobbes' and Vico's idea of knowledge in politics, the idea that as humans we can know only what we make. The state is our artificial creation and therefore we can both know and be free in politics. If the collective political imagination can be seen as constantly producing and reproducing the political world, if the public can sense its powers to imagine particular political agents, authorities or institutions into (or out of) being, then political reality is no longer experienced as alien and pre-imposed, any more than are the laws which are made in democratic states with the (symbolic rather than actual) participation of the public and its representatives.

This change raises a host of questions, some new but all in a radically novel technological and socio-cultural context. The principal query is what are the important shifts in the genres of the political imagination of the relations between power, order and reality, which underlie the ways we organize our political lives?

Low- and high-cost realities

In order to explore some aspects of this question I would like to suggest that we distinguish between what may be called low- and high-cost realities, between constructs of the world, or parts of the world, which require heavy investment of resources such as time, money, effort and skills, and those which engage less resources on the part of those who consume these realities. We have actually been prepared to recognize such differences in the transition from knowledge to information. Scientific knowledge constructs high-cost realities. It combines systematic descriptions of the world with tested, arduously worked-out explanations which may beget technologies for the manipulation of nature. High-cost or high-investment realities tend to be specialized and be demanded by particular professional communities and institutions. Medical researchers produce high-investment accounts of biological realities for the use of medical experts, hospitals, food and drug control agencies, etc. Physicists produce such high-cost accounts of the physical world which are used by engineers for instance in the space program or in the field of atomic energy. Economists work out high-cost scientific accounts of the economy which require high investments by their clients, although they are often translated by different agents into information which enters the currency of low-cost representations of economic realities used by policymakers, investors and the wider public. In some sense, of course, all scientists are both producers and consumers of high-cost reality, because knowledge is both a product and a means of production of more knowledge. High-cost reality is usually a very densely organized system of concepts, facts, clues, rules, interpretive codes, working metaphors, methodological skills, operations, evidence, claims and rhetoric. As such, they cannot be accessible to laymen and are in fact esoteric. Historically, science-based technologies have often served to mitigate the inaccessibility of scientific knowledge by providing lay publics with sensual embodiments of its validity or instrumentality. The spectacular balloon flight in Metz, France, in October 1773, validated to a huge lay public claims of scientists they could not read or understand in the *Journal de Physique* (Darenton 1968). So in a sense even professionally complex knowledge could have sometimes been made to appear democratically accountable by means of the visual rhetoric of pre-electronic outformations. Machines and visible operations could function in such cases as eloquent rhetorical devices of more esoteric forms of knowledge claims. The shift from relying on knowledge to relying on information has often served a similar purpose, translating high-cost realities to low-cost realities and furnishing more publicly accessible references to the more esoteric claims of knowledge. To be informed is, then, a more minimal state of knowing, or of being qualified to act in a particular situation. So along with wisdom, knowledge and information too can be regarded as elements in distinct genres of the political imagination, modes of relating power, order and reality which differ with respect to the degree of their implicit commitments to hierarchy or equality, constancy or fluidity, holism or individualism, specificity or generality, the zones of high- and low-cost representations of reality, and other such values.

Beyond information, the most prevalent form of low-cost reality consists of outformations, that is of general, not very elaborate, eclectic images or representations which become temporarily fixed as public terms of political and other realities. "Low-cost" refers here mostly to consumers (while being cheap to the viewers as consumers, outformations may be very costly to produce). The "producers" of the modern presidency have become experts in the choreography of political outformations. One of these experts interviewed by the *New York Times* (16 May 2003), referred to George W. Bush's "Top Gun" landing on the deck of the carrier *Abraham Lincoln* as "one of the most audacious moments of presidential theatre in American history". Another expert stressed the attention the White House pays not only to what the president says but also to what the "American people see. Americans are leading busy lives...If they can have an instant understanding of what the president is talking about by seeing 60 seconds of television, you accomplish your goal as communicators". Such low-cost realities depend on the immediate experience of the flow of pictures and sounds in the electronic media. They become the shared means by which contemporary men and women conceive, imagine, remember, think, relate or act in politics (as well as in the market and other socio-cultural sites). Outformations are powerful enough, in our time, to mediate much of the historical memory or the sense of the past, as the impact of Zapruder's film of the Kennedy assassination may testify. Outformations allow huge publics to rely on their eyes, and simulate the sense of witnessing real events without the trouble of actually being there (Katz and Dayan 1985). Low-cost reality is a very successful commercial product in our culture which constantly enjoys spectacular demand by modern mass publics. Unlike knowledge, outformations and the low-cost representations of reality which they produce are characteristically unspecialized and usually not designed to fit particular narrow audiences. The tendency of producers and editors working in the electronic media is usually to appeal to as wide an audience as possible. Still, of course, the flow of outformations on the small screen is often edited and adapted to various types of programs stressing different needs and values. But TV icons, personalities, places and events are projected with sufficient repetitiveness over spans of time to create the experience of a stable, shared, and therefore *familiar* world to produce in audiences the sense of reality. The most important characteristics of outformations as a principal component of the predominant current genre of the (liberal) democratic political imagination are their fast pace and their capacity to produce the sense of immediacy. Electronically mediated public *visibility* and *immediacy* are the two principal parameters which have come to largely control what can be represented as political agencies and facts to mass audience in our universe. Visibility is widely perceived as providing a degree of protection to claims of factuality from subjective bias, whereas immediacy reinforces the sense of reality with respect to objects such as war or politics which are in a state of continual flux.

Given the extensive commercialization of the contemporary mass media, the supply and demand of low-cost, low entry-threshold realities, has become perhaps the most important feature of our culture and politics. Particularly in the sphere of politics, representations or productions of political realities which are cheap for consumers constitute a profound break with the Enlightenment vision of democratic politics or of self-government by educated and knowledgeable citizens. Condorcet insisted that only citizens who know the truth can actually control or diminish the power of the government. The point is not, of course, that this Enlightenment conception of politics was ever realized and has only recently collapsed. It is rather that the ethos of enlightened politics which supported such developments as universal education, and the institutionalization of public accountability in many, especially Western, societies, has increasingly appeared to be irrelevant to politics mediated and shaped by what we have called outformations. My point is that this shift represents a change between alternative cultures of democratic legitimation. We can perhaps discern a shift from legitimation of the type which derives from beliefs and expectations that uphold the notion that decisions and actions are not arbitrary when they are grounded, at least in part, in knowledge or accurate information, to legitimation of the type which derives more from certain constellations of outformations. The replacement of high-cost by low-cost political reality reflects the diminished propensity of contemporary publics to invest personal or group resources in understanding and shaping politics and the management of public affairs (Putnam 1995; Jasanoff 2001). In the sphere of politics, the behavior of contemporary publics often suggests that they regard familiarity with what goes on in the political world by means of low-cost, thin and quick outformations as good enough, or sufficient for their needs. In our time, politics, as one observer put it, is "just another window". In most countries, it is not even a full television channel. One of the most intriguing questions raised by this state of affairs is why do contemporary publics have such a reduced willingness to invest in understanding and influencing politics?

Modes of knowing and doing politics

Although there is a historical dimension to shifts between our four states or modes of knowing, especially their dependence on different values and technologies, we are describing here neither a linear nor an all-encompassing, or totally irreversible, process. It would be instructive, therefore, to examine, along the axes of time and place, which of the prototypes of knowing or representing reality on our list, or which combination of them, governs which sphere of social discourse or action, and which is dominant in society at large. For our purposes the most intriguing question is why politics has come to be mediated in most contemporary democracies by outformations and their reality constructs. I have already noted that outformations, as the fabric of "cheap", "low-entry" reality constructs, seem particularly compatible with politics, which is characteristically inclusive, high-speed and sustainable with minimal citizens' attention. The latent political functions of the shift from the centrality of linguistically and numerically organized information to that of outformations, can be illuminated by comparison with the implications of the earlier shifts from traditional to modern scientific knowledge and later to information.

Historically observers have tended to regard wisdom, in its many varieties, as associated with traditional society, and knowledge or information with modernized societies. As we have indicated above, when compared with the former, the latter two forms have usually suggested more participatory modes of knowing and also more objective and impersonal ones (Ezrahi 1980). Historically, the ethos and practice of popular political participation was connected with the delegitimation of the personalized heirarchical authority structures of monarchic and aristocratic regimes. Moreover, just as the scientific enterprise was based on the belief that discrete individual scientists can evolve a coherent and objective body of knowledge, the modern liberal democratic presumption that individuals are the ultimate source of political power and authority does not appear to have foreclosed the possibility that individuals as discrete starting points for the construction of the political order can generate coherent, whole political systems. Among the emerging liberal and democratic circles in Europe and other Western societies, the legal fiction of the social contract, the institutions of representative government, and the modern free press were expected to bridge individualism and legitimate order. The idea of objective public knowledge was a central element in this new modern model of a polity, the product of a new genre of the political imagination in which order rests on the capacity of discrete individuals to reach consensus or generate working majorities. The demand for traditional forms of personalized individual knowledge – which like wisdom are distinct by contextual richness, attachment to unique individuals and often also by esoteric meaning, the demand for wisdom in the wider sense which may include poetry, art and various esoteric practices – has not altogether disappeared from the political arena. But it has been much more pronounced in the non-political spheres of culture, personal life and health. As I suggested above, the central elements of a traditional political imagination which involves wisdom, hierarchy and secrecy are not compatible with the modern political order. In politics, democratization came to the world with an increasing cultivation of the ideals of a transparent universe and knowledgeable or, at least, informed citizens. Many of the projects of the Enlightenment, like a universal language, demonstrative encyclopedias, museums of science, public instruction and the like, were meant to enhance the role of knowledge and information in building up, and managing, the political world without relying on hierarchical authorities. Lavoisier's deliberate exclusion of the alchemists from the scientific discourse in chemistry over which he presided in his journal, and his insistence on replacing their allegorical language by a language which would force chemists to subject themselves to the public tests of "nature", reflected that turn towards the more public culture of knowledge more consistent with the Enlightenment vision of open participatory politics. As anticipated by figures such as Hobbes, Priestley, Paine, Jefferson, Condorcet and Kant, the norms of clarity, publicity and impersonality which were cultivated in relation to scientific discourse had profound effects on political rhetoric. Public knowledge was supposed to be a principal means of disciplining political speech as part of the general attempt to control arbitrary political authority and power (Skinner 1996).

Given these close connections between the evolution of the culture of scientific discourse and practices and modern forms of authoritative political discourse and action, the shift of emphasis from knowledge to information as a reference for public discourse and action, or as a popular image of knowing and representing reality, could not be without political implications. Such shifts usually indicate important changes in the co-production of knowledge and the socio-political order. Like the transition from wisdom to knowledge, the transition from knowledge to information reinforced modes of knowing or representing reality which appeared more impersonal, accessible, instrumental and, insofar as they are less mediated by an elite group of scientists, also more individually accessible. As such this transition can be seen as a shift between two close yet distinct genres of the democratic political imagination. By and large, as a form or means of knowing, information implied a further removal of individual personality, individual intention and group privilege in the authoritative construction and representation of reality. Universal availability and friendliness to users made the informational mode of knowing appear as an adequate solution to the anxiety of trusting, or depending on, the authority of men of knowledge. This development was often symbolized, as I indicated above, in the fact that the communication of information could take place among machines, and by the tendency to facilitate its communication among persons by standardizing the steps of information processing. As we shall see below, the move from information to outformations has been widely perceived as implying even more publicly accessible concepts of "reality", more participatory modes of knowing the world.

If knowledge is usually perceived as something possessed by scientists and other experts, information and outformations appear more external and independent representations of the world. The features of information as a means of knowing and describing the world, its impersonality, technicality, standardization, universal accessibility, in many cases also its materiality (Blondheim 1994), and the features of outformations especially as machine-mediated visual communications, may appear as particularly effective for concealing biases and tendentious editing. In this sense even more than knowledge, and precisely by virtue of their more elusive associations with specific sources and agents, information and outformations could exemplify Foucault's point about "regimes of truth" as products of hidden power relations and hidden purposes. Particularly in the context of modern commercial culture, experts on marketing have developed and refined strategies for making consumers "informed" such that they "voluntarily" choose the "desired" product. These techniques have been transferred and extensively applied to the marketing of political candidates and policies in contemporary democracies. The latent ritualistic functions of "informed choices" or "informed consent" in contemporary politics, the ways individuals can be made to feel as autonomous decisionmakers while actually acting against their own values and interests, can be illustrated in the way "informed consent" often works in medical practice. It was introduced into medical practice in some countries in the 1970s, in order to guide doctors in providing their patients with the medical information relevant to the choice of treatment. The idea was that patients should participate in such choices in order to reflect their personal values and judgment. The point of this change was that health can no longer be regarded by doctors as something definable with reference to a uniform fixed value order which places, for instance, the value of the length of the individual's life at the top. Different individuals would tend, for instance, to order or balance the value of extending their lives against the value of the quality of life in various ways, and accordingly might prefer different treatments. But as many reports indicate, while many patients participate in choosing their treatment, their decisions are often based on inadequate information processing by medical standards, leading to choices and results often inconsistent with their stated values. But even in these cases clearly informed consent by reducing the power of doctors to influence the choices of medical treatments, added legitimacy to the decisions taken. The working of "informed consent" in medical practice can illustrate the ways in which making laypersons, or for that matter the public at large, "informed" can actually generate decisions or actions which, while being more legally, morally and also politically acceptable, are at the same time less rational, instrumental or beneficial to lay people in the strict sense of the word. The autonomy and dignity of patients, as well as of voters and consumers, are preserved while their interests, even by their own standards, are not advanced as they should be. The working of "informed consent" in the medical context can illustrate then how information may function as a means in rituals of legitimation, authorizing decisions or actions without actually making them more rational or technically instrumental or effective in relation to desired goals. In the political context, such rituals of legitimation may be either manipulated by feeding the public with biased information, or arise spontaneously from public ignorance and inadequate information processing. The availability of information could thus be used to voluntarize public assent within actually hierarchical power and action structures, and without controlling the arbitrary uses of power and authority. From the perspective of political realism, which discards the possibility of truly democratically decentralized forms of self-government, information is even better than knowledge as a means of legitimating the inevitable working of hierarchies in politics and making them appear accountable. While in the case of scientific knowledge the professional scientific community can still act as a guardian of the correct and warranted use of knowledge, in the case of information the presence of such guardians is diminished, although not altogether eliminated. As a resource of democratic political rhetoric and authority information is, in other words, more politically effective for sustaining a system of political legitimation based on the Enlightenment myth of democracy in which power is checked by public knowledge. While such a state of affairs falls short of basic democratic ideas, this practice may still sustain important democratic values such as a sense of individual dignity and autonomy, decentralization, publicity, etc.

The transition from information to outformations in fact represents, as I have indicated above, another step in this direction going further than information in producing low-cost political realities for currency in public discourse and action, and in inducing in the public a sense of participation in the political process. It is also more detached from the foundational strata of knowledge and, therefore, less congenial for professional intellectual criticism and accountabilities. If it is still possible in some cases for educated laymen and skilled experts to work their way back from information to knowledge, to retrace the steps and return to the theoretically denser and more explicit conceptual frames in which information is embedded, this is not a likely possibility in the case of outformations. Because the outformations which generate such a diffuse spectrum of stimuli are not produced by any agreed-upon or transparent methodologies, because the processing of outformations largely depends upon unconscious inferences, projections and conclusions, and because their pace and alternations are so fast, they do not present their consumers with the possibility or the requirement of discovering the clues as to how they are made, how they work, how they can be interpreted, and how their origins or effects can be traced and assessed. They apparently have enormous powers to produce in viewers the illusion of knowing something real. So while enhanced accessibility constitutes a democratic gain, the erosion of discernible grounds and methodologies of criticisms constitutes a democratic loss. Accessibility seems, however, much more salient than the gradual erosion of the culture of criticism. In 1869, for instance, the number of people who could feel that they were, or be regarded as, speaking authoritatively on a presidential candidate like Ulysses Grant, was probably very limited. But by 2001, probably any American including your grandmother or your uncle could speak about their "direct" impressions of George W. Bush, and you would listen to them very carefully, knowing that their opinions might be indicative of a multitude of other laypersons who felt confident they knew the candidate and could decide how to vote.

Moreover, since, unlike knowledge and information, outformations provide a weaker basis for criticism and distancing; because in politics the culture of outformations does not rest to the same degree on the idea of independent reality against which claims of accurate or valid accounts can be checked and criticized, the very distinctions between the world and its representatives are much more ambiguous. This ambiguity may have diminished the force of the demand that speakers or actors should know the "real facts" of the situation, a demand so central to the scientifically inspired Enlightenment notion of politics. This development is related, in part, to the increasing role of both public utterances and actions as political gestures rather than as directed to state valid facts or bring about substantive results. While there is a near-universal agreement that what I have called outformations, the flow of inanimate and animated vocal images in our electronic media, have enormous impact on spectators and on the shape and nature of politics and culture, the diffused and diverse nature of their effects across individuals and groups makes it difficult to discern the specific casual relations and mechanisms that connect specific outformations with specific effects. Contemporary communications scholars and other social scientists do not have a satisfactory theoretical basis for explaining, accounting for or predicting the specific impact of the flow of outformations on behavior, although there have been a few relatively successful attempts.

Considering this state of affairs, Foucault's suspicion that culture, and especially modes of knowing, are instruments of hidden powers, may be both partly supported and partly repudiated. It would be supported because in our mostly commercialized mass electronic media the actual power of capital may be invisible, concealed by the professional frames introduced by producers, editors, reporters and artists. It may be particularly difficult to trace the ways in which entertaining TV programs function as hidden means for influencing consumers' choices, or how the power of capital and its transactions with politics may influence news reporting by means of self-censorship exercised by reporters aware of the interests of their employers. But on the other hand, the absence of tested and reliable knowledge of how to produce or use specific outformations in order to bring about specific behaviors raises serious doubts about the validity of suspicions of the kind advanced by Foucault. The wish to manipulate consciousness and behavior may not be matched by the capacity to actually carry out such a scheme.

The camera and the political uncanny

It is interesting to note that despite their break with the cultures of knowledge and information, outformations derive a large part of their powers from their roots in the cultural traditions and habits cultivated by the association of the sense of sight with science, technology and the modern experience of the real. This is a cultural and psychological fact with enormous political implications. While the transition from "natural" sight to "artificial" mechanically mediated sight by means of the camera poses important questions about the meaning of visual experience, this technological change enables sight, or more particularly pictures, to play a crucial role in mediating modern mass democratic politics. The photographic culture of our time has cultivated in us the belief "that we can hold the whole world in our heads as an anthology of images" (Sontag 1977; Scheuer 2000). More than being engaged in arguments and counter-arguments, we tend to collect images of political personalities and events. The repetition of these images due to their presence over time in the public electronic arena, or due to the recycling of their film record, for example of the Kennedy assassination, or of the embrace between Bill Clinton and Monica Lewinsky, tends to stabilize such images, make them familiar and instantly recognizable, thus lending them some of the qualities of our common sense reality.

In addition, the extraordinary force of the camera and its products in our society derives from its unique status as a bridge between the cultures of science and the arts, between its central function as a means of mechanically recording the external world, and as a creative artistic tool; from its ability to serve simultaneously impressions and expressions, its association in our mind with objective documentation, with facts as well as with aesthetic values and the subjective gaze. Because of this dualism, the capacity of the camera to weld together elements of the trust in external facts and elements of the emotional-sensual desire for the imaginary composition of the world, to marry the external references of knowledge and the creative faculty of the imagination, allows modern mass media to generate images which can be experienced as real facts and represent facts which can be experienced as suasive images. The power of outformations in our culture lies precisely in this fusion of reality and fantasy and the constant unresolvable flip-flop fluctuations between them (Sontag 1977). This puzzle and this fascination are augmented by the fact that the fusion of the real and the fantastic, the sincere and the posed or the theatrical, allows the mass media to enlist the uncanny, the constant unresolvable shifts, for instance, between experiencing persons on the screen as face/mask/face/mask, as a regular magnet for viewers. Every viewer is constantly either consciously or unconsciously haunted by the question: Is it real or not? What is a fiction and what is a fact? Which fact will suddenly be exposed as mere fiction and which fiction will amazingly turn out to be a fact? When will the mask on the face of a political celebrity unexpectedly drop sufficiently to reveal a part of the hidden face? These processes often evolve from the accumulation of many exposures and bits and pieces of information over time. Think of how the meaning of the Clinton-Lewinsky casual hug on the television screen changed with each of its many reruns as the affair unfolded. The boundaries between facts and fictions are increasingly blurred, even in genres of television show which explicitly and directly declare themselves to be committed to reliable representations of reality, like news or documentaries. Contemporary publics are generally more aware that even these supposed representations of reality are actually compositions which often adopt as props elements of artistically produced fictive worlds. In the context of this new culture of outformations it has become increasingly evident to image producers that contemporary television viewers are more fascinated by the desire to experience the fantastic as real and the real as fantastic than by the desire for accurate, reliable, dry representations of the conventionally real. From the point of view of modern democratic political theory, such developments may suggest the possibility that the often intuitive, and sometimes even the deliberate, role of the imagination, together with the disciplined recording gaze, in the individual and social co-production of contemporary notions of reality, is more compatible with the sense of freedom in our culture, with our deep irreverence towards authority, than concepts of factual reality presented to us with the decisive voice of scientific or expert authority. The more plastic notions of reality associated with outformations seem to give more leverage to the "consumers" of reality or facts than do notions of reality associated with knowledge or information. They are less confined by formal frames and interpretive codes. The unique adequacy of realities mediated by outformations to democratic sensibilities, lies largely in the fact that if in the cases of knowledge and information there are distinctions between correct and incorrect ways of knowing or information processing, the absence of clearly correct or incorrect procedures for processing outformations seems more compatible with their users' sense of autonomy, dignity and efficacy. In other words, at least at the level of common experience, realities constructed with the fabric of outformations appear less mediated, more plastic and more engaging. The eerie awareness of the capacity of the camera to serve realism and fantasy, the fact that, as Clifford Geertz put it, "The real is just as imagined as the imaginary" (Geertz 1980) must on the one hand satisfy deep desires to realize, or at least momentarily experience, our fantasies as real, and on the other hand to experience at least parts of our reality as fantastic. In the context of politics, the ability of mass electronic media to serve as an instrument of collective imagining and translate images on the screen into such things as a real president, or real groups, upholds such desires and expectations. The difference between individual and collective political imagining is in fact the difference between fantasies, allegorized by Cervantes in *Don Quixote*, which tend to remain fantasies or influence only individual conduct, to fantasies and images which can not only produce reality effects but in fact, by means of the contemporary political process, legislate themselves into existence as real agencies, institutions, events and facts. The potential of the modern mass media to project socially and politically self-realizing images has, of course, boosted such developments as modern identity politics. Groups are being created and dismantled by processes in which the role played by the projection of their images in the mass media is often crucial. The mass media have become a means for the socio-political production and projection of novel identities, some of which have become politically animated as actual movements and groups. The role of imagination in shaping our conceptions of political power, authority and order, is of course, not new. Thinkers such as Machiavelli, Hobbes and Rousseau even treated it deliberately, designing the legal and moral fictions, the civic religions, and the strategies of stagecraft which along with those of statecraft were necessary in their opinion for the making and regulating of particular political worlds. They held on the whole more hierarchical models of the working of the political imagination, leaving a privileged role to intellectuals like themselves. The transition between hierarchical and more open and equal notions of the working of the political imagination and of representations of reality, is inseparable from the historicity of the very political imagination which generates and forms them. Such conceptions of political (and other types of) reality reflect, therefore, the imagination which is working at any one time in a particular society, with its particular technological, cultural and psychic underpinnings.

Four concepts of liberty

It may be useful for our purposes to distinguish four concepts of political freedom associated with four ways of relating to the political world. The first is the freedom of knowledgeable and informed citizens from being dependent on the opinions and authority of others. This kind of freedom (type A), corresponds to the classical Enlightenment notion of the role of knowledge in liberating citizens from depending on power and being vulnerable to deception. The second kind of freedom (type B), clearly unpopular among Enlightenment intellectuals, is the freedom to escape the constraints of factual reality, the freedom to live in worlds of fantasy created by poetry, literature, drama, metaphysics, mysticism and, more recently, drugs and the internet. The third type of freedom (type C) is the freedom of citizens to collectively imagine into existence a political world of their own making. By contrast to the subjective or the private imagination, a shared collective imagination has, as thinkers such as Vico and Rousseau appreciated, enormous powers to produce and sustain political orders. For some citizens, participation in the imaginative production of political reality may be at least partly conscious. Such reflexivity, however, is not likely to be shared by the public at large. Rousseau's concept of civil religion was meant as a program for socializing the public into a system of collective imaginings which he thought would produce modern democratic citizens, and the modern experience of freedom and equality. In the case of Hobbes, I think, we have a type-C freedom (the freedom to create particular forms of order) presented to us in the garments, the language, of freedom type A (the informed voluntary adherence to the requirements of action guided by objective truth). To present the imaginary as natural or as scientifically valid was a common Enlightenment rhetorical strategy. We can obtain a rare glimpse into Hobbes' awareness of the necessity of combining the two strategies in *Leviathan*, where he states that "If nature…has made men equal, that equality is to be acknowledged; or if nature made men unequal; yet because men that think themselves equal will not enter conditions of peace but upon equal terms, such equality must be admitted" (Hobbes 1962).

Here Hobbes clearly designs a role for the imagination in creating a political reality. The fourth type of political freedom (type D) consists of the ability to freely switch back and forth between freedom types A, B and C, between the freedom of the knowledgeable from depending on other people's opinions, the freedom of fantasy, and the freedom to produce, by participating in the shaping of the collective political imagination, self-realizing political worlds. I would like to suggest that contemporary mass electronic media culture actually facilitates the development of this inclusive type-D freedom, and that this is a principal cause of its extraordinary attraction. In some respects this freedom to shift at will between alternative modes of imagining the world and the self in relation to it, appeals to the human play impulse. Friedrich Schiller held that it is creative aesthetic play unconfined by necessity, the exercise of the "legislative faculty" of the imagination, that renders art the ultimate territory of human freedom (Schiller 1960). Once the modern interactive mass electronic media facilitated a partial convergence between playful aesthetic orientations and the experience of politics, the Schillerian concept of freedom could be partially extended to politics, with both its democratic and anti-democratic implications.

Postmodern politics: a degenerative shift?

In our time, the commercial economic basis of most of the electronic media encourages the exploitation and the accentuation of the benefits of the ambiguities between fiction and reality for magnifying the elements of entertainment and marketing. Entertainment is the means by which the owners of the mass media can keep viewers in front of their television sets and sell them as potential consumers to advertisers at high prices. But keeping viewers in front of television sets is also the interest of political agents, of the government and the opposition. This is partly why political commercials, or more generally such things as the presidency, Congress, even the Supreme Court are in many respects elaborate "productions". If politics mediated by outformations were not sufficiently visible and entertaining, viewers would switch to straight entertainment programs. As a matter of fact this has already happened in many countries, and may have also something to do with declining public participation in the political process (Putnam 2000). Another factor working here is apparently the sense many viewers of politics on television have, that their ability to contact and store in their mind what I have called above low-cost reality representations, amounts to a kind of participation. This kind of virtual participation recalls Rousseau's concern that the experience of theater-goers who get intensely engaged with the figures and their encounters on stage, may actually sap their emotional and moral energies and exhaust their capacity to act in the civic context. Still, television, like the theater, participates in shaping the political imagination which influences our behavior and therefore also the very structures and directions of politics. The fact that outformations flow constantly and that immediacy is such a salient feature of low-cost representations of political reality, makes the visual culture of our time a site of a very different kind of politics than that associated with the cultures of scientific knowledge and information (McChesney 1999). Does this kind of politics represent a necessarily degenerative shift in contemporary democracies? Following the traumas of modern fascism and totalitarianism which culminated in World War II and the Cold War, many liberal and democratic thinkers insisted that objective public knowledge and free, reliable information, constitute the best protection against the dangers of arbitrary political power and of mass passions and violence aroused by political imagination undisciplined by reason and enlightenment. The characteristics of the contemporary political imagination in democratic states, and of the culture of outformations which shapes it, seem to repudiate the strong version of this thesis, and call attention to the working of other no less significant factors in constructing the political order. These surely include the special dynamics and fragmentation of the contemporary political imagination, its symbiosis with commercial culture and light mass entertainment, spreading public distrust of public authorities and institutions, and the decline of mass political activism. If seen in terms of a political universe constructed with the materials of the Enlightenment political imagination and particularly of knowledge and information, the shift to outformations may be easily seen as degenerative. But from the perspective developed here, this change can be redescribed as a part of a deeper shift between distinct liberal democratic genres of politics. Such changes in the configurations of knowledge and power must be evaluated in terms of their overall consequences and their impact on a wide spectrum of political values, not just as cracks in an ongoing or a hegemonic political world.

The decline of science as a factor in contemporary mass democratic politics does not mean, of course, that the demand for high-cost scientifically constructed "realities" does not persist in other spheres. But the radical transformation of conceptions and images of reality in contemporary culture and politics also has consequences for science as an authority and a social institution. Science is no longer the resource it once was, with which policies and public choices could be legitimated as impersonal, objective and technical. It is no longer as important as it once was as a component of modern state authority. Consequently, scientists are much less in demand by politicians who seek to legitimate their positions and actions before an informed and skeptical public, and therefore politicians have on their part diminished incentives to "buy" the cooperation of scientists by large allocations of public money to, and by public (political) endorsement of, basic research and the general goal of the advancement and the diffusion of knowledge.

14 Afterword

Sheila Jasanoff

The idiom of co-production, as we have argued in this volume, represents a major synthesis of scholarship in science and technology studies (S&TS). At once capturing and helping to crystallize shared orientations from a broad cross-section of the field, this interpretive framework illuminates how cognitive understandings of the world we live in are tied at many points to social means of intervening in or coping with that world. The concept of co-production thus rejects the simplifications of both social determinism and scientific or technological determinism; it sees science neither as constituted by interests alone nor as an unmediated reflection of nature. On the contrary, it presumes that knowledge and its material embodiments are products of social work and, at the same time, constitutive of forms of social life. It acknowledges that lived "reality" is made up of complex linkages among the cognitive, the material, the normative and the social – and that understanding these links is indispensable to meaningful projects of social theory and prescriptive analysis. For all these reasons, co-production offers as much traction in explicating the social dimensions of scientific and technological change as in exploring the cognitive and material bases of other powerful political and cultural configurations.

We have seen that co-productionist literature in S&TS engages with questions that are broadly speaking both metaphysical and epistemological – that is, both about the way the world is and how we find out about it. I have called the former type of work *constitutive*, because it speaks to the creation of fundamental ordering devices and categories; I have called the latter type *interactional*, because it deals with the conflicts and accommodations that arise when competing natural and social orders are brought into confrontation. In either case, what distinguishes co-productionist analysis from conventional metaphysical or epistemological inquiry is its constant rejection of *a priori* demarcations. Indeed, co-production blurs the very distinction between metaphysics and epistemology, showing how our knowledge of things as they are relates to earlier choices about how we wish to know things in the first place. Neither the existence of things nor our knowledge of them can be taken for granted in this framework. Rather, the object is to illuminate how particular states of knowledge come into being, what makes them persist or disappear, and how they shape and are shaped by people's deeper political and cultural, as well as cognitive and material commitments.

In this concluding chapter, I pull together the volume's principal themes by highlighting again the four objectives we hope to serve by adding co-production to the conceptual repertoire of the social sciences. These are description, explanation, normative analysis, and prediction – this last as a possible spur to social action and change. Under each heading, the contributors to this volume have shown that the idiom of co-production usefully supplements the insights derived from traditional social science disciplines. It problematizes categories that have been taken as foundational in other analytic programs – such as macro and micro, structure and agency, state and society – but it also shows how questioning such categories can lead to systematic lines of inquiry rather than to conceptual confusion. In particular, the idiom of co-production can be usefully deployed, as we have seen, whenever knowledge is incorporated into identities, institutions, discourses and representations. These four terms are in some sense fundamental to all current social thought; co-production simply offers different, and generative, ways of characterizing their nature, structure, effects and boundaries.

Yet, expansive though this framework is, co-production remains only one possible way to account for the relations of science, technology and society. It aims neither to be a universal grand theory, nor to be univocal in the sense of commanding all who adopt this perspective to invoke it in precisely the same ways, using the same units of analysis, and with the same interpretive or critical intent. Working in the co-productionist idiom, in short, requires not only attention to its possibilities but also modesty about its limits.

Description: science in society, society in science

Like science itself, theories of scientific change once tended to extract their object of investigation from contamination by "the social". The resulting austere vision of science – as driven more by logic than interests and more by personal inspiration than political economy – has long since been set aside in favor of richer accounts that stress the multiple human commitments involved in the production and application of knowledge. Social histories of science and technology have become commonplace, as have, since the pathbreaking work of anthropologists and sociologists of science in the 1970s (Latour and Woolgar 1979; Bloor 1976), studies focusing on the construction of knowledge through human agency, instruments and will. The theme of co-production can be seen as a productive extension of this trend. If early sociologists of science were concerned principally with bringing the social back into knowledge-making, a new generation of S&TS scholars has acknowledged the need to explore, in a fully symmetrical move, the playing out of systems of knowledge and technology within society. The co-productionist framework, as elaborated in this volume, crucially furthers this move.

The birth of S&TS as a field is often dated to the publication of Thomas Kuhn's (1962) *The Structure of Scientific Revolutions* or, by the field's own cognoscenti, to the still earlier work of Ludwik Fleck (1979 [1935]), who, in attributing the development of the Wassermann test for syphilis to a "thought collective", provided a crucial precursor for Kuhn's notions of scientific paradigms and normal science. Yet Kuhn was not a co-productionist in the sense proposed by the contributors to this volume. As Ian Hacking has perceptively observed, Kuhn saw himself as an internalist historian of science, and for all that he "emphasized a disciplinary matrix of one hundred or so researchers, or the role of exemplars in science teaching, imitation, and practice, he had virtually nothing to say about social interaction" (Hacking 1999: 43). But like a river gathering flood from many tributaries on its way to the sea, a later generation of S&TS scholarship has acquired depth and force from fields that *do* take social interaction as their primary concern. Today, S&TS draws inspiration as much from ethnography, law, cultural studies and feminist theory as it does from intellectual history or studies of particular technoscientific systems. The emergence of co-production as a powerful analytic lens reflects this intersection and cross-fertilization of perspectives.

Co-production insists on contextualization. Since Clifford Geertz (1973: 5–10) introduced the term "thick description" into everyday academic discourse, it has become clear that attention to context is a prime methodological principle of interpretive work in the social sciences. Some fields, such as social and cultural history, never denied the need to understand phenomena in their contexts, but many areas of the social sciences – especially those centered on scientistic images of humans as predictable, calculating agents – have modeled behavior as obeying law-like regularities, independent of politics, culture, time or place. By contrast, work in the co-productionist idiom sees knowledge practices as firmly "situated" (Haraway 1991: 183–201) – yet with permeable boundaries that not only allow contextual factors to seep in and mold the production of science and technology, but also, and equally, enable scientific and technological achievements to loop back and reorder the organization and self-perception of society.

For all these reasons, there is considerable descriptive richness to be gained from the co-productionist approach, a claim amply supported by the chapters in this volume. Whether in the work of international bodies (Miller, Thompson, Storey, Waterton and Wynne) and specialist professional communities (Rabeharisoa and Callon, Hilgartner, Lynch), or in the political work of scientists or experts and the state (Carson, Dear, Dennis, Ezrahi), the co-productionist vision illuminates the thickness of connections between what we know and how we know it. Constitutive studies have sharpened our sensitivity to new and emergent sociotechnical phenomena, while work in the interactional mode has alerted us to subtle cognitive differences between and among competing social orders.

Co-productionist analysis, as repeatedly documented in the foregoing chapters, shifts our attention from *fact*-making (the traditional preserve of much work in science studies) to *sense*-making as a topic of overarching interest, with scientific sense-making as a particular, if highly significant, subcategory. It brings society's collective habits of interpreting and ordering experience within the perimeter of scholarly inquiry. As a result, our questions about the social world start changing: we ask how states see (Scott 1998), how institutions think (Douglas 1986), how the law knows (Jasanoff 1995), how cultures reason (Sahlins 1995), and how societies grapple with risk (Beck 1992). Significantly, questions like these promise to bring S&TS scholarship into more fruitful conversation with traditions in the disciplinary social sciences that have grappled with similar questions about institutionalized knowledge and its relations to power.

Explanation: against linearity

Co-productionist accounts advance the goal of explanation in several ways which the foregoing chapters have brought into sharper focus. First, even more than other S&TS concepts, co-production is starkly opposed to linear and mono-causal stories about scientific, technological or social progress. Constantly highlighting the contexts in which events occur, and which they in turn remake, these stories promote more complex forms of accounting in which causes and effects are braided together in strands that resist artificial separation into dependent and independent variables. Such narratives make simple explanations for most phenomena harder to sustain. In compensation, they open up questions, and offer at least partial enlightenment, in areas that could not readily be fitted to conventional understandings of cause and effect. Put differently, by rejecting linearity, co-production stories undoubtedly complicate the "why" questions that have formed the staple of much social science research; at the same time, they add to the agenda of the social sciences a series of "how" questions that either have eluded systematic inquiry or else were rendered invisible by existing disciplinary framings.

Further, the chapters in this volume demonstrate the fertility of the co-production framework in bringing new objects and developments before the S&TS analyst's gaze. As we have repeatedly observed, this approach is particularly useful in making sense of emergent phenomena. It shows how certain conceptual designs and cognitive formulations gain ground at the expense of others, and how, once adopted, these successful settlements come to be seen as natural, inevitable or determined in advance. Importantly, co-productionist accounts display the specific mechanisms by which such erasures occur, mechanisms that routinely involve the production or reconstitution of scientific and technical knowledge. Thus Carson explains how "intelligence" became a marker of American citizens, but not of their comparably endowed French counterparts, producing in consequence different "human kinds" (Hacking 1999) on the two sides of the Atlantic. That Americans measure this quality of intelligence with a test originally developed in France only makes the result the more piquant. National and supra-national identities – such as being European, African, global or imperial – take shape, in part, through the activities of knowledge-making bodies in chapters by Waterton and Wynne, Thompson, Miller, and Storey. These authors show the contingent and contested character of such emergent identities, and the impossibility of stabilizing them without recourse to institutionalized ways of knowing. On a different scale, Hilgartner shows how ideas of property, and associated norms of what counts as public or private, are unexpectedly, almost invisibly, renegotiated in the daily transactions of genome scientists.

Other chapters offer explanations for problems that arguably only come into distinct view through the lens of co-production. These are questions that arise when we explicitly inquire into the social arrangements that prop up particular natural orders or, in reverse, the epistemologies that help to sustain particular social orders. How, for example, did experimentally grounded knowledge acquire unchallenged authority in the seventeenth century, even though the personal testimony of the experimenter was always vulnerable to skeptical questioning (Dear)? How did a perception of the weather as consisting of local temperature and precipitation patterns yield to a view of the climate as a unified global phenomenon affecting the entire planet (Miller)? How have the identity of the "research subject" and related research practices changed as genetics-based biomedicine produces new kinds of relationships between investigators and patients (Rabeharisoa and Callon)? How do mundane aspects of legal procedure constitute, but also validate, the identity of experts and the nature of expertise (Lynch)? What work did the concept of "basic science" do in the postwar discourse of American science policy, and how did it help cement a new ordering of science and the state (Dennis)? And how has the pervasive influence of the mass media affected civic epistemologies, altering the perceptions and standards of reality by which democratic polities make their collective choices (Ezrahi)?

We note that nothing in the formulation of these questions renders them in principle inaccessible to historical, sociological or political inquiry. As a practical matter, however, questions like these only began to surface when S&TS scholars thought to look at social and scientific change from the standpoint of co-production, asking how each kind of transformation implicates and influences the other. For the most part, the disciplinary social sciences still unquestioningly accept the boundary between nature and society as given. Questions that assume the hybridity of these domains as a starting premise do not easily arise in such contexts. Once they are on the table, moreover, they may require a blending of concepts and methods that feels particularly comfortable to researchers in S&TS.

Normativity: erasures and alternatives

Co-productionist accounts, as already noted, permit us to regain access to the political and cultural histories of facts and artifacts; in this sense, they facilitate not only interpretation but also critique. The possibility of critical engagement is perhaps most apparent when a co-productionist eye is brought to the analysis of emerging orders. It is at the point of emergence, before things are completely stabilized or black-boxed, that one most easily observes the mutual uptake of the social and the natural. It is also at this moment of flux that processes of co-production are most influential in setting the stage for future human development. Important normative choices get made during the phase of emergence: in the resolution of conflicts; the classification of scientific and social objects; the standardization of technological practices; and the uptake of knowledge in different cultural contexts. Once the resulting settlements are normalized (social order) or naturalized (natural order), it becomes difficult to rediscover the contested assumptions that were freely in play before stability was effected.

Many of the preceding chapters set out in detail what is at stake in bringing new forms of cognitive and social life into being – and how, through institutional means, such conflicts are eventually resolved, or at least rendered unthreatening (see, in particular, Miller, Storey, Waterton and Wynne, Dennis). Working through one example may help to clarify the point. In their history of the European Environment Agency (EEA), Waterton and Wynne showed how practices of producing objective, policy-relevant information worked as surrogates for different models of European integration: first, a model of Europe as homogeneous, centralized, and capable of full-blown harmonization by official policy institutions; second, a much more chaotic and bottom-up Europe, in which information provision is more a matter of strategically highlighting ignorance, and thereby creating different, situated possibilities for citizen intervention. A strength of these authors' analysis is that they do not force closure on the imagination of Europe any more than the EEC, the chief actor in their story, is able to do. Rather, we are left with a sense of different, co-existing, normatively loaded *ideas* of Europe, whose institutions of knowledge-making emerge as important, and meaningful, sites of political identity-building. In short, Waterton and Wynne restore the most fundamental kind of politics – decisions about what kind of polity to be or to become – to a sphere of technical decisionmaking from which politics has tended to be leached away in most high-modern theorizing about expertise.

Co-production is also helpful as a framework within which to make sense of persistent differences in the way societies define or cope with "the same" phenomenon, be it human intelligence (Carson), endangered species (Thompson) or climate change (Miller). By accounting for the multiple ways in which knowledge becomes embedded in institutions, practices, norms and material objects, this way of looking at order demonstrates how cultural discrepancies in knowledge/power relations arise and can be sustained over long periods of time. Such divergent settlements in different cultural and political contexts can become a source of potentially serious conflicts and misunderstanding. In turn, illuminating the reasons for divergence holds out hope for cooperative behavior or, at the limit, deliberated cultural autonomy – as in Thompson's on the whole optimistic account of African elephant management, in which an undemocratic universalist regime of species protection was replaced by a more locally diversified, context-sensitive approach.

Most generally, co-productionist accounts add to existing theories of power, refining our understanding of what power means, and how it is formed and exercised. That knowledge is a form of power is not, of course, any longer a new idea in either social theory or S&TS; nor does it come as a shock that institutions exercise power through specific knowledge-making practices that form and constrain human subjectivities. Yet there are several ways in which the idiom of co-production inflects and accentuates these general propositions. First, it simply provides a constant reminder that, not only does knowledge constitute power, but equally power frames and organizes knowledge; hence, wherever power originates or is concentrated, one should also look for its expression through knowledge. As in Yeats' famous sonnet, *Leda and the Swan*,[1] power and knowledge come coupled, and one can therefore always ask how the exercise of the one relates to the formation and uptake of the other. Second, the concept of co-production alerts us to the fact that power is constituted as much through the elision of marginalized alternatives as through the positive adoption of dominant viewpoints. Strategic silences, no less than sites of explicit articulation, hence are grist for the mill of co-production. Third, co-productionist analysis is symmetrically concerned with both stability and instability: thus not only the radical paradigm shift (Kuhn 1962) but also the long-term persistence of cultural and political formations calls for intellectual engagement in this framework. In this respect, co-production sees the very taken-for-grantedness of entrenched power structures as a spur to further inquiry.

Prediction, prescription and action

Co-production, we have argued, sacrifices simplicity for richness and linearity for deeper contextualization. So conceived, this approach is more consistent with projects of interpretation than intervention. Co-productionist accounts may be historical or ethnographic or comparative; their ambition is rarely predictive or prescriptive on the model of the policy sciences or economics. Such studies are better suited to explaining how things came to be ordered in particular ways than at forecasting the future impacts of specific choices and decisions. And yet, as we have also suggested, co-production can yield predictive insights in some circumstances – for example, by pointing out deep cultural regularities in knowledge-making and use; by displaying the basis of institutionalized ways of knowing; by explaining what is likely to be at stake in particular identities or representations; or by showing how technical discourses may impose systematic frames of meaning on events that might otherwise seem random. In short, the co-productionist perspective is predictive in something like the way good history is predictive: it may not be a reliable guide to exactly how things will play out the next day or the next year; yet, without its benefits, societies may be doomed to repeating the same mistakes, using and reusing the same epistemological blinders.

There is, however, a different and more reflexive point to be made about the implications of the co-productionist framework for social action and change. For if, after all, this theoretical orientation makes sense today, then the very fact of inserting such a perspective into the world should loop back, in Hacking's (1999) terms, and reorganize to some degree the way we think about the relations of knowledge, power and culture. Are there signs that co-production – itself a constitutive, historically situated, cognitive frame — is having this kind of influence in the world? Is it only an analyst's category or is it also playing a role, in however limited a fashion, as an actor's category, and, if the latter, then for which types of actors? These questions are worth exploring in greater detail than is possible in this brief conclusion, but one or two straws in the wind may be cited from the earlier chapters.

Both Waterton and Wynne and Rabeharisoa and Callon offer case studies that can be seen as bridging the gap between co-production as an analytic approach and co-production as a strategic instrument in the hands of knowledgeable social actors. In the former case, it is the European Environment Agency that to some extent self-consciously directs its knowledge-making practices toward realizing a political vision of Europe. By interpreting notions of objectivity and policy-relevance in particular ways, the EEA has arguably opened the door to new forms of engagement between European citizens and the European policy apparatus. Though threatening to the authority of Brussels in the short run, this openness may prove beneficial for a vastly enlarged Europe whose politics may be increasingly resistant to strict homogenization and top-down, central control.

In the latter case, Rabeharisoa and Callon show how the French muscular dystrophy association has taken a variety of steps, from data gathering to creating a new discourse of patient engagement, in order to facilitate non-traditional relationships among patients, their families and the biomedical establishment. At stake is the very definition of the research subject, a role formerly seen as passive and inexpert, but redefined in this case to permit the possessors of subjective knowledge of a disease to participate on something like an equal footing with those possessing objective knowledge of their condition. "Lay" patients and "trained" experts thus find themselves on an epistemologically leveled playing field, each now recognized as a knowledge-bearer with the capacity to participate in new cooperative forms of medical research and development.

Under what conditions do such strategic uses of co-production become imaginable? Perhaps it takes a threat of life-and-death proportions. It may be no accident that the stakes for both the EEA and the muscular dystrophy association were exceptionally high — nothing less than existence itself. The EEA was struggling to establish itself as a relevant actor, with the autonomy to shape its mission independently of Brussels. The French patients and their families were coping with a debilitating disease for which there was no cure in sight. Under such extreme pressures, it may become easier to be more instrumental, if not more reflexive, about all of one's resources and faculties, including those of knowledge-making. For the rest, most of the actors in the foregoing chapters seem to perform the scripts of co-production without consciously taking on board their transformative potential. But let us be forewarned: this, too, may be only a passing state of knowledge. Careful readers of this book, at any rate, will surely come away thinking differently about the relations between knowledge and power, and of their own capacity to intervene strategically — and we can only hope for the good — in that ever more important relationship.

Note

1   Yeats ends the sonnet, which describes Leda's ravishing by the swan Zeus, with the couplet:

Did she put on his knowledge with his power
Before the indifferent beak could let her drop?

(Yeats 1956)

References

1 The idiom of co-production

Bowker, G. C. and Star, S. L. (1999) *Classification and Its Consequences*, Cambridge MA: MIT Press.

Branscomb, L. M. and Keller, J. H. (eds) (1998) *Investing in Innovation: Creating a Research and Innovation Policy that Works*, Cambridge MA: MIT Press.

Collins, H. M. (1985) *Changing Order: Replication and Induction in Scientific Practice*, London: Sage.

Daston, L. (ed.) (2000) *Biographies of Scientific Objects*, Chicago: University of Chicago Press.

Dear, P. (1995) *Discipline and Experience: The Mathematical Way in the Scientific Revolution*, Chicago: University of Chicago Press.

Ezrahi, Y. (1990) *The Descent of Icarus*, Cambridge MA: Harvard University Press.

Foucault, M. (1972) *The Archaeology of Knowledge*, New York: Pantheon.

Geertz, C. (1973) *The Interpretation of Cultures*, New York: Basic Books.

Gingrich, A. and Fox, R. G. (eds) (2002) *Anthropology, by Comparison*, London: Routledge.

Gross, P. R. and Levitt, N. (1994) *Higher Superstition: The Academic Left and Its Quarrels with Science*, Baltimore: Johns Hopkins University Press.

Hacking, I. (1992) "World-Making by Kind-Making: Child Abuse for Example", pp. 180–213 in Douglas, M. and Hull, D. (eds) *How Classification Works: Nelson Goodman Among the Social Sciences*, Edinburgh: Edinburgh University Press.

——(1999) *The Social Construction of What?*, Cambridge MA: Harvard University Press.

Jasanoff, S. (1995) *Science at the Bar: Law, Science, and Technology in America*, Cambridge MA: Harvard University Press.

Jasanoff, S., Markle, G. E., Petersen, J. C. and Pinch, T. (eds) (1995) *Handbook of Science and Technology Studies*, Thousand Oaks: Sage.

Knorr-Cetina, K. (1999) *Epistemic Cultures: How the Sciences Make Knowledge*, Cambridge MA: Harvard University Press.

Koertge, N. (1998) *A House Built on Sand: Exposing Postmodernist Myths about Science*, New York: Oxford University Press.

Kuhn, T. S. (1962) *The Structure of Scientific Revolutions*, Chicago: University of Chicago Press.

Latour, B. (1987) *Science in Action: How to Follow Scientists and Engineers through Society*, Cambridge MA: Harvard University Press.

——(1988a) "The Politics of Explanation: An Alternative", pp. 155–176 in Woolgar, S. (ed.) (1988) *Knowledge and Reflexivity: New Frontiers in the Sociology of Knowledge*, London: Sage.

——(1988b) *The Pasteurization of France*, Cambridge MA: Harvard University Press.

——(1993) *We Have Never Been Modern*, Cambridge MA: Harvard University Press.

Mowery, D. C. and Rosenberg, N. (1989) *Technology and the Pursuit of Economic Growth*, Cambridge: Cambridge University Press.

Pickering, A. (ed.) (1992) *Science as Practice and Culture*, Chicago: University of Chicago Press.

Pickering, A. (1995) *The Mangle of Practice: Time, Agency, and Science*, Chicago: University of Chicago Press.

Porter, T. M. (1992) "Objectivity as Standardization: The Rhetoric of Impersonality in Measurement, Statistics, and Cost-benefit Analysis", *Annals of Scholarship* 9: 19–59.

Rabinow, P. (1996) *Making PCR: A Story of Biotechnology*, Chicago: University of Chicago Press.

——(1999) *French DNA: Trouble in Purgatory*, Chicago: University of Chicago Press.

Richards, E. and Martin, B. (1995) "Scientific Knowledge, Controversy, and Public Decision Making," 1506–536 in Jasanoff, S., Markle, G. E., Petersen, J. C. and Pinch, T. (eds) (1995) *Handbook of Science and Technology Studies*, Thousand Oaks: Sage.

Rosenberg, N. (1994) *Exploring the Black Box: Technology, Economics and History*, Cambridge: Cambridge University Press.

Scott, P., Richards, E. and Martin, B. (1990) "Captives of Controversy: The Myth of the Neutral Social Researcher in Contemporary Scientific Controversies", *Science, Technology, and Human Values* 15: 474–494.

Shapin, S. (1994) *A Social History of Truth: Civility and Science in 17th Century England*, Chicago: University of Chicago Press.

Shapin, S. and Schaffer, S. (1985) *Leviathan and the Air-pump: Hobbes, Boyle, and the Experimental Life*, Princeton: Princeton University Press.

Sokal, A. and Bricmont, J. (1998) *Fashionable Nonsense: Postmodern Intellectuals' Abuse of Science*, New York: Picador.

Traweek, S. (1988) *Beamtimes and Lifetimes: The World of High Energy Physicists*, Cambridge MA: Harvard University Press.

Woodhouse, E., Hess, D., Breyman, S. and Martin, B. (2002) "Science Studies and Activism: Possibilities and Problems for Reconstructivist Agendas", *Social Studies of Science* 32(2): 297–319.

2 Ordering knowledge, ordering society

Anderson, B. (1991) *Imagined Communities*, 2nd edn, London: Verso.

Barber, B. R. (1995) *Jihad vs. McWorld*, New York: Times Books.

Barnes, B. (1977) *Interests and the Growth of Knowledge*, London: Routledge.

——(1988) *The Nature of Power*, Cambridge: Polity.

Barnes, B. and Edge, D. (eds) (1982) *Science in Context: Readings in the Sociology of Science*, Cambridge MA: MIT Press.

Bauman, Z. (1991) *Modernity and Ambivalence*, Ithaca NY: Cornell University Press.

Beck, U. (1992) *Risk Society: Towards a New Modernity*, London: Sage.

——(1998) "Politics of Risk Society", pp. 9–22 in Franklin, J. (ed.) *The Politics of Risk Society*, Cambridge: Polity.

Benedict, R. (1989) *The Chrysanthemum and the Sword*, Boston: Houghton Mifflin.

Biagioli, M. (1999) *The Science Studies Reader*, New York: Routledge.

Bijker, W. E. (1997) *Of Bicycles, Bakelites, and Bulbs: Toward a Theory of Sociotechnical Change*, Cambridge MA: MIT Press.

Bijker, W. E., Hughes T. and Pinch, T. (eds) (1987) *The Social Construction of Technological Systems: New Directions in the Sociology and History of Technology*, Cambridge MA: MIT Press.

Bloor, D. (1976) *Knowledge and Social Imagery*, London: Routledge and Kegan Paul.

Bourdieu, P. (1980) *The Logic of Practice*, Stanford: Stanford University Press.

Bowker, G. C. and Star, S. L. (1999) *Sorting Things Out: Classification and Its Consequences*, Cambridge MA: MIT Press.

Callon, M. and Latour, B. (1992) " 'Don't Throw the Baby Out with the Bath School', A Reply to Collins and Yearley", pp. 343–368 in Pickering, A. (ed.) *Science as Practice and Culture*, Chicago: University of Chicago Press.

Caro, R. A. (1974) *The Power Broker: Robert Moses and the Fall of New York*, New York: Knopf.

Carson, J. (1993) "Army Alpha, Army Brass, and the Search for Army Intelligence", *Isis* 84: 278–309.

Clarke, A. and Fujimura, J. (eds) (1992) *The Right Tools for the Job: At Work in the Twentieth-century Sciences*, Princeton: Princeton University Press.

Collins, H. M. (1985) *Changing Order: Replication and Induction in Scientific Practice*, London: Sage.

Collins, H. M. and Yearley, S. (1992) "Epistemological Chicken", pp. 301–326 in Pickering, A. (ed.) *Science as Practice and Culture*, Chicago: University of Chicago Press.

Collins, R. (1998) *The Sociology of Philosophies*, Cambridge MA: Harvard University Press.

Daston, L. (1988) *Classical Probability in the Enlightenment*, Princeton: Princeton University Press.

Daston, L. (ed.) (2000) *Biographies of Scientific Objects*, Chicago: University of Chicago Press.

Daston, L. and Galison, P. (1992) "The Image of Objectivity", *Representations* 40: 81–128.

Dear, P. (1995) *Discipline and Experience: The Mathematical Way in the Scientific Revolution*, Chicago: University of Chicago Press.

Dear, P. (ed.) (1991) *The Literary Structure of Scientific Argument: Historical Studies*, Philadelphia: University of Pennsylvania Press.

Douglas, M. (1986) *How Institutions Think*, Syracuse NY: Syracuse University Press.

Ellul, J. (1964) *The Technological Society*, New York: Vintage.

Epstein, S. (1996) *Impure Science: AIDS, Activism, and the Politics of Knowledge*, Berkeley: University of California Press.

Ezrahi, Y. (1990) *The Descent of Icarus*, Cambridge MA: Harvard University Press.

Foucault, M. (1971) *The Order of Things: An Archaeology of the Human Sciences*, New York: Pantheon Books.

——(1972) *The Archaeology of Knowledge*, New York: Pantheon.

——(1973) *Madness and Civilization: A History of Insanity in the Age of Reason*, New York: Vintage Books.

——(1978) *The History of Sexuality*, New York: Pantheon.

——(1979) *Discipline and Punish*, New York: Vintage Books.

——(1994) *The Birth of the Clinic: An Archaeology of Medical Perception*, New York: Vintage Books.

Galison, P. (1987) *How Experiments End*, Chicago: University of Chicago Press.

——(1996) *Image and Logic: A Material Culture of Microphysics*, Chicago: University of Chicago Press

Gibbons, M., Limoges, C., Nowotny, H., Schwartzman, S., Scott, P. and Trow, M. (1994) *The New Production of Knowledge*, London: Sage.

Gieryn, T. F. (1999) *Cultural Boundaries of Science: Credibility on the Line*, Chicago: University of Chicago Press.

Greenberg, D. S. (2001) *Science, Money, and Politics: Political Triumph and Ethical Erosion*, Chicago: University of Chicago Press.

Gross, P. R. and Levitt, N. (1994) *Higher Superstition: The Academic Left and Its Quarrels with Science*, Baltimore: Johns Hopkins University Press.

Guston, D. H. (2001) *Between Politics and Science: Assuring the Integrity and Productivity of Research*, Cambridge: Cambridge University Press.

Habermas, J. (1975) *Legitimation Crisis*, Boston MA: Beacon Press.

Hacking, I. (1990) *The Taming of Chance*, Cambridge: Cambridge University Press.

——(1992) "World-Making by Kind-Making: Child Abuse for Example", pp. 180–213 in Douglas, M. and Hull, D. (eds) *How Classification Works: Nelson Goodman Among the Social Sciences*, Edinburgh: Edinburgh University Press.

——(1995) *Rewriting the Soul: Multiple Personality and the Sciences of Memory*, Princeton: Princeton University Press.

——(1999) *The Social Construction of What?*, Cambridge MA: Harvard University Press.

Haraway, D. J. (1989) *Primate Visions: Gender, Race, and Nature in the World of Modern Science*, New York: Routledge.

——(1991) *Simians, Cyborgs, and Women: The Reinvention of Nature*, New York: Routledge.

——(2000) *Modest_Witness@Second_Millennium.FemaleMan©_Meets_Oncomouse™*, New York: Routledge.

Harwood, J. (1993) *Styles of Scientific Thought: The German Genetics Community, 1900–1933*, Chicago: University of Chicago Press.

Hilgartner, S. (2000) *Science on Stage: Expert Advice as Public Drama*, Stanford: Stanford University Press.

Irwin, A. and Wynne, B. (eds) (1994) *Misunderstanding Science? The Public Reconstruction of Science and Technology*, Cambridge: Cambridge University Press.

——(2001) "Ordering Life: Law and the Normalization of Biotechnology", *Politeia* XVII(62): 34–50.

Jasanoff, S. (1986) *Risk Management and Political Culture*, New York: Russell Sage Foundation.

——(1990) *The Fifth Branch: Science Advisers as Policymakers*, Cambridge MA: Harvard University Press.

——(1992) "Science, Politics, and the Renegotiation of Expertise at EPA", *Osiris* 7: 195–217.

——(1995) *Science at the Bar: Law, Science and Technology in America*, Cambridge MA: Harvard University Press.

——(2001) "Image and Imagination: The Emergence of Global Environmental Consciousness", in Miller, C.A. and Edwards, P.N. (eds) *Changing the Atmosphere: Expert Knowledge and Global Environmental Governance*, Cambridge MA: MIT Press.

——(forthcoming a) *Designs on Nature: Science and Democracy in Europe and the US*, Princeton: Princeton University Press.

——(forthcoming b) "What Inquiring Minds *Should* Want to Know", *Studies in the History and Philosophy of Science*.

Jasanoff, S. and Wynne, B. (1998) "Science and Decisionmaking", pp. 1–87 in Rayner, S. and Malone, E. L. (eds) *Human Choice and Climate Change*, Washington DC: Battelle Press.

Jasanoff, S., Markle, G. E., Petersen, J. C. and Pinch, T. (eds) (1995) *Handbook of Science and Technology Studies*, Thousand Oaks: Sage.

Joerges, B. (1999) "Do Politics Have Artifacts?", *Social Studies of Science* 19(3): 411–432.

Keller, E. F. (1985) *Reflections on Gender and Science*, New Haven: Yale University Press.

Kitcher, P. (2001) *Science, Truth, and Democracy*, Oxford: Oxford University Press.

Knorr-Cetina, K. (1999) *Epistemic Cultures: How the Sciences Make Knowledge*, Cambridge MA: Harvard University Press.

Koertge, N. (1998) *A House Built on Sand: Exposing Postmodernist Myths About Science*, New York: Oxford University Press.

Kuhn, T. S. (1962) *The Structure of Scientific Revolutions*, Chicago: University of Chicago Press.

Latour, B. (1987) *Science in Action: How to Follow Scientists and Engineers through Society*, Cambridge MA: Harvard University Press.

——(1988a) "The Politics of Explanation: An Alternative", pp. 155–176 in Woolgar, S. (ed.) (1988) *Knowledge and Reflexivity: New Frontiers in the Sociology of Knowledge*, London: Sage.

——(1988b) *The Pasteurization of France*, Cambridge MA: Harvard University Press.

——(1990) "Drawing Things Together", pp. 19–68 in Lynch, M. and Woolgar, S. (eds) (1990) *Representation in Scientific Practice*, Cambridge MA: MIT Press.

——(1992) "Where Are the Missing Masses? The Sociology of a Few Mundane Artifacts", pp. 225–258 in Bijker, W. E. and Law, J. (eds) *Shaping Technology/Building Society*, Cambridge MA: MIT Press.

——(1993) *We Have Never Been Modern*, Cambridge MA: Harvard University Press.

——(1996) *Aramis or the Love of Technology*, Cambridge MA: Harvard University Press.

——(1999) *Politiques de la nature: comment faire entrer les sciences en democratie*, Paris: Découverte.

Latour, B. and Woolgar, S. (1979) *Laboratory Life: The Social Construction of Scientific Facts*, Beverly Hills: Sage.

Law, J. (2002) *Aircraft Stories: Decentering the Object in Technoscience*, Durham NC: Duke University Press.

Lewontin, R. (2000) *The Triple Helix: Gene, Organism, and Environment*, Cambridge MA: Harvard University Press.

Lynch, M. (ed.) (2001) "Pandora's Ballot Box (Comments on the 2000 Presidential Election)", *Social Studies of Science* 31 (3): 425–67.

Lynch, M. and Woolgar, S. (eds) (1990) *Representation in Scientific Practice*, Cambridge MA: MIT Press.

Merton, R. K. (1973) "The Normative Structure of Science", pp. 267–278 in Merton, R.K., *The Sociology of Science: Theoretical and Empirical Investigations*, Chicago: University of Chicago Press.

Mol, A. and Law, J. (1994) "Regions, Networks and Fluids: Anaemia and Social Topology", *Social Studies of Science* 24: 641–671.

Mukerji, C. (1989) *A Fragile Power: Scientists and the State*, Princeton: Princeton University Press.

Mulkay, M. J. (1976) "Norms and Ideology in Science", *Social Science Information* 15: 637–656.

Nelkin, D. (ed.) (1992) *Controversy: Politics of Technical Decisions*, Newbury Park CA: Sage.

Noble, D. (1984) *Forces of Production*, New York: Knopf.

Nowotny, H. (1990) "Knowledge for Certainty: Poverty, Welfare Institutions and the Institutionalization of Social Science", pp. 23–41 in Wagner, P., Wittrock, B. and Whitley, R. (eds) *Discourses on Society: The Shaping of the Social Science Disciplines*, Sociology of the Sciences, vol. 15, Dordrecht: Kluwer.

Nowotny, H., Scott, P. and Gibbons, M. (2001) *Re-Thinking Science: Knowledge and the Public in an Age of Uncertainty*, Cambridge: Polity.

Pickering, A. (1995) *The Mangle of Practice: Time, Agency, and Science*, Chicago: University of Chicago Press.

Pickering, A. (ed.) (1992) *Science as Practice and Culture*, Chicago: University of Chicago Press.

Polanyi, M. (1962) "The Republic of Science", *Minerva* 1: 54–73.

Porter, T. M. (1992) "Objectivity as Standardization: The Rhetoric of Impersonality in Measurement, Statistics, and Cost-benefit Analysis", *Annals of Scholarship* 9: 19–59.

——(1995) *Trust in Numbers: The Pursuit of Objectivity in Science and Public Life*, Princeton: Princeton University Press.

Rabinow, P. (1996) *Making PCR: A Story of Biotechnology*, Chicago: University of Chicago Press.

——(1999) *French DNA: Trouble in Purgatory*, Chicago: University of Chicago Press.

Reardon, J. (2001) "The Human Genome Diversity Project: A Case Study in Coproduction", *Social Studies of Science* 31: 357–388.

Richards, E. and Martin, B. (1995) pp. 206–236 in Jasanoff, S., Markle, G. E., Petersen, J. C. and Pinch, T. (eds) (1995) *Handbook of Science and Technology Studies*, Thousand Oaks: Sage.

Rorty, R. (1989) "Science as Solidarity", in Lawson, H. and Appignanesi, L. (eds) *Dismantling Truth: Reality in the Post-Modern World*, London: Weidenfeld and Nicolson.

——(1991) *Objectivity, Relativism and Truth*, Cambridge: Cambridge University Press.

Sahlins, M. D. (1995) *How "Natives" Think: About Captain Cook, for example*, Chicago: University of Chicago Press.

Sclove, R. (1995) *Democracy and Technology*, New York: Guilford Publications.

Scott, J. C. (1985) *Weapons of the Weak: Everyday Forms of Peasant Resistance*, New Haven: Yale University Press.

——(1998) *Seeing like a State: How Certain Schemes to Improve the Human Condition Have Failed*, New Haven: Yale University Press.

Scott, P., Richards, E. and Martin, B. (1990) "Captives of Controversy: The Myth of the Neutral Social Researcher in Contemporary Scientific Controversies", *Science, Technology, and Human Values* 15: 474–494.

Shapin, S. (1994) *A Social History of Truth: Civility and Science in 17th Century England*, Chicago: University of Chicago Press.

——(1996) *The Scientific Revolution*, Chicago: University of Chicago Press.

Shapin, S. and Schaffer, S. (1985) *Leviathan and the Air-pump: Hobbes, Boyle, and the Experimental Life*, Princeton: Princeton University Press.

Smith, M. R. and Marx, L. (eds) (1994) *Does Technology Drive History?*, Cambridge MA: MIT Press.

Sokal, A. and Bricmont, J. (1998) *Fashionable Nonsense: Postmodern Intellectuals' Abuse of Science*, New York: Picador.

Stepan, N. (1982) *The Idea of Race in Science: Great Britain, 1800–1960*, Hamden: Archon Books.

Storey, W. K. (1997) *Science and Power in Colonial Mauritius*, Rochester: University of Rochester Press.

Traweek, S. (1988) *Beamtimes and Lifetimes: The World of High Energy Physicists*, Cambridge MA: Harvard University Press.

Wagner, P., Wittrock, B. and Whitley, R. (eds) (1991) *Discourses on Society: The Shaping of the Social Science Disciplines*, Sociology of the Sciences, vol. 15, Dordrecht: Kluwer.

Wilmut, I, Schnieke, A. E., McWhir, J., Kind, A. J. and Campbell, K. H. S. (1997) "Viable offspring derived from fetal and adult mammalian cells", *Nature* 385: 810–813.

Winner, L. (1986) "Do Artifacts Have Politics?", pp. 19–39 in *The Whale and the Reactor*, Chicago: University of Chicago Press.

Woolgar, S. (ed.) (1988) *Knowledge and Reflexivity: New Frontiers in the Sociology of Knowledge*, London: Sage.

Wynne, B. (1989) "Frameworks of Rationality in Risk Management: Towards the Testing of Naive Sociology", pp. 33–45 in Brown, J. (ed.) *Environmental Threats: Social Sciences Approaches to Public Risk Perceptions*, London: Belhaven.

3 Climate science and the making of a global political order

Agarwal, A. and Narain, S. (1991) *Global Warming in an Unequal World*, Delhi: Centre for Science and Environment.

Agrawala, S. (1997) "Explaining the Evolution of the IPCC Structure and Process", ENRP Discussion Paper E-97–05, Kennedy School of Government, Harvard University, August.

Anderson, B. (1983) *Imagined Communities*, London: Verso.

Brickman, R., Jasanoff, S. and Ilgen, T. (1985) *Controlling Chemicals: The Politics of Regulation in Europe and the United States*, Ithaca NY: Cornell University Press.

Camilleri, J. (1996) "Impoverishment and the National State", in F. O. Hampson and J. Reppy (eds) *Earthly Goods: Environmental Change and Social Justice*, Ithaca NY: Cornell University Press.

Chayes, A., and Chayes, A. H. (1995) *The New Sovereignty: Compliance with International Regulatory Agreements*, Cambridge MA: Harvard University Press.

Choucri, N. (1993) *Global Accord: Environmental Challenges and International Relations*, Cambridge MA: MIT Press.

Collins, H. M. and Pinch, T. J. (1982) *Frames of Meaning: The Social Construction of Extraordinary Science*, London: Routledge and Kegan Paul.

Cronon, W. (1992) "A Place for Stories: Nature, History, and Narrative", *Journal of American History* March: 1347–1376.

Edwards, P. (2001) "Representing the Global Atmosphere", pp. 31–65 in C. A. Miller and P. N. Edwards (eds) *Changing the Atmosphere: Expert Knowledge and Global Environmental Governance*, Cambridge MA: MIT Press.

Edwards, P., and Schneider, S. (2001) "Self-Governance and Peer Review in Science-for-Policy", pp. 219–246 in C. A. Miller and P. N. Edwards (eds) *Changing the Atmosphere: Expert Knowledge and Global Environmental Governance*, Cambridge MA: MIT Press.

Ezrahi, Y. (1984) "Science and Utopia in Late 20th Century Pluralist Democracy: With Special Reference to the USA", in E. Mendelsohn and H. Nowotny (eds) *Nineteen Eighty-Four: Science Between Utopia and Dystopia, Sociology of the Sciences*, vol. 8, Dordrecht: Reidel.

——(1990) *The Descent of Icarus: Science and the Transformation of Contemporary Democracy*, Cambridge MA: Harvard University Press.

Foucault, M. (1979) *Discipline and Punish*, New York: Vintage.

Gieryn, T. F. (1996) "Boundaries of Science", pp. 393–443 in S. Jasanoff, G. E. Markle, J. C. Petersen and T. Pinch (eds) *The Handbook of Science and Technology Studies*, Thousand Oaks: Sage.

Haas, P. (1990) *Saving the Mediterranean: The Politics of International Environmental Cooperation*, New York: Columbia University Press.

Haas, P. (ed.) (1992) "Knowledge, Power, and International Policy Coordination", *International Organization* 46(1).

Haas, P., Keohane, R. and Levy, M. (eds) (1993) *Institutions for the Earth: Sources of Effective International Environmental Protection*, Cambridge MA: MIT Press.

Hambidge, G. (1941) "Climate and Man: A Summary", in G. Hambidge, M. J. Drown, F. W. Reichelderfer, L. H. Bean, J. B. Kincer, L. F. Page, C. G. Rossby, C. F. Sarle, C. W. Thornthwaite and E. W. Woolard (eds) *Climate and Man*, Washington DC: US Government Printing Office.

Hampson, F. O. and Reppy, J. (eds) (1996) *Earthly Goods: Environmental Change and Social Justice*, Ithaca NY: Cornell University Press.

Hardt, M. and Negri, A. (2000) *Empire*, Cambridge MA: Harvard University Press.

Houghton, J. T. and Bolin, B. (1992) "Preface", in J. T. Houghton, B. A. Callander and S. K. Varney (eds) *Climate Change 1992: The Supplementary Report to the IPCC Scientific Assessment*, Cambridge: Cambridge University Press.

Houghton, J. T., Meiro Filho, L. G., Callander, B. A., Harris, N., Kattenberg, A. and Maskell, K. (eds) (1996) *Climate Change 1995: The Science of Climate Change*, Cambridge: Cambridge University Press.

Jasanoff, S. (1986) *Risk Management and Political Culture*, New York: Russell Sage Foundation.

——(1990) *The Fifth Branch: Science Advisers as Policymakers*, Cambridge MA: Harvard University Press.

——(1996a) *Science at the Bar: Law, Science, and Technology in America*, Cambridge MA: Harvard University Press.

——(1996b) "Science and Norms in Global Environmental Regimes", pp. 173–197 in F. O. Hampson and J. Reppy (eds) *Earthly Goods: Environmental Change and Social Justice*, Ithaca NY: Cornell University Press.

——(1997) "Compelling Knowledge in Public Decisions", pp. 229–252 in L. A. Brooks and S. VanDeveer (eds) *Saving the Seas: Values, Scientists, and International Governance*, Silver Springs: University of Maryland Press.

——(2001) "Image and Imagination: The Emergence of Global Environmental Conciousness", pp. 309–337 in C. A. Miller and P. N. Edwards (eds) *Changing the Atmosphere: Expert Knowledge and Global Environmental Governance*, Cambridge MA: MIT Press.

Jasanoff, S. and Wynne, B. (1998) "Science and Decisionmaking", pp. 1–87 in S. Rayner and E. Malone (eds) *Human Choice and Climate Change: The Societal Framework*, Columbus: Battelle Press.

Kandlikar, M. and Sagar, A. (1997) "Climate Change Science and Policy: Lessons from India", ENRP Discussion Paper, E-97–08, Kennedy School of Government, Harvard University, August.

Keohane, R., and Nye, J. (2001) *Power and Interdependence*, 3rd edn, New York: Longman.

Keohane, R. and Levy, M. (eds) (1996) *Institutions for Environmental Aid: Pitfalls and Promise*, Cambridge MA: MIT Press.

Litfin, K. (ed.) (1998) *The Greening of Sovereignty in World Politics*, Cambridge MA: MIT Press.

Miller, C. A. (2000) "The Dynamics of Framing Environmental Values and Policy: Four Models of Societal Processes", *Environmental Values* 9: 211–233.

——(2001a) "Challenges to the Application of Science to Global Affairs: Contingency, Trust, and Moral Order", pp. 247–285 in C. A. Miller and P. N. Edwards (eds) *Changing the Atmosphere: Expert Knowledge and Global Environmental Governance*, Cambridge MA: MIT Press.

——(2001b) "Hybrid Management: Boundary Organizations, Science Policy, and Environmental Governance in the Climate Regime", *Science, Technology and Human Values* 26(4): 478–500.

Miller, C. A. and Edwards, P. N. (2001) "Introduction: The Globalization of Climate Science and Climate Politics", pp. 1–30 in C. A. Miller and P. N. Edwards (eds) *Changing the Atmosphere: Expert Knowledge and Global Environmental Governance*, Cambridge MA: MIT Press.

National Research Council (NRC) (1966) *Weather and Climate Modification: Problems and Prospects*, Washington DC: National Academy Press.

——(1979) *Carbon Dioxide and Climate: A Scientific Assessment*, Washington DC: National Academy Press.

——(1982) *Carbon Dioxide and Climate: A Second Assessment*, Washington DC: National Academy Press.

——(1983) *Changing Climate: Report of the Carbon Dioxide Assessment Committee*, Washington DC: National Academy Press.

Ripert, J. (1991) "Report of the IPCC Special Task Force on Developing Countries", in Jaeger, J. and Ferguson, H. L. (eds) *Climate Change: Science, Impacts and Policy. Proceedings of the Second World Climate Conference*, Cambridge: Cambridge University Press.

Rosenau, J. N. (1992) "The Relocation of Authority in a Shrinking World", *Comparative Politics* 24(3): 253–272.

Rueschemeyer, D. and Skocpol, T. (eds) (1995) *States, Social Knowledge, and the Origins of Modern Social Policies*, Princeton: Princeton University Press.

Scientific Committee on Problems of the Environment (SCOPE) (1986) *The Greenhouse Effect, Climatic Change, and Ecosystems*, New York: Wiley.

Scott, J. (1998) *Seeing like a State: How Certain Schemes to Improve the Human Condition Have Failed*, New Haven: Yale University Press.

Shapin, S. (1994) *A Social History of Truth: Civility and Science in Seventeenth Century England*, Chicago: University of Chicago Press.

Slaughter, A.-M. (1997) "The Real New World Order", *Foreign Affairs* 76(5): 183–197.

Takacs, D. (1996) *The Idea of Biodiversity: Philosophies of Paradise*, Baltimore: Johns Hopkins University Press.

Tolba, M. (1991) "Address by Dr. Mostafa K. Tolba", in J. Jaeger and H. L. Ferguson (eds) *Climate Change: Science, Impacts and Policy. Proceedings of the Second World Climate Conference*, Cambridge: Cambridge University Press.

White, R. M. (1978) "Climate and Public Policy", in National Academy of Sciences, *The National Research Council in 1978: Current Issues and Trends*, Washington DC: National Academy Press.

World Commission on Environment and Development (WCED) (1987) *Our Common Future*, Oxford: Oxford University Press.

World Meteorological Organization (WMO) (1979) *World Climate Conference: Geneva, February, 1979*, Geneva: World Meteorological Organization.

Young, O. (ed.) (1998) *Global Governance: Drawing Insights from the Environmental Experience*, Cambridge: MIT Press.

4 Co-producing CITES and the African elephant

De Waal, A. (1989) *Famine that Kills: Darfur, Sudan, 1984–5*, Oxford: Clarendon Press.

Escobar, A. (1995) *Encountering Development: The Making and Unmaking of the Third World*, Princeton: Princeton University Press.

Guha, R. (1998) "Radical Environmentalism and Wilderness Preservation: A Third World Critique", pp. 270–275 in Pojman, L. (ed.) *Environmental Ethics: Readings in Theory and Application*, Belmont CA: Wadsworth.

Hemley, G. (ed.) (1994) *International Wildlife Trade: A CITES Sourcebook*, Washington DC: WWF Island Press.

Hutton, J. and Dickson, B. (eds) (2000) *Endangered Species, Threatened Convention: The Past, Present and Future of CITES*, London: WWF-UK Earthscan.

Jasanoff, S. and Martello, M. L. (2004) *Earthly Politics: Local and global in Environmental Governance*, Cambridge MA: MIT Press.

Kenya Wildlife Service (1997) *Kenya's Position on the Proposal to Downlist the African Elephant to Appendix 2 of CITES to Allow Trade in Ivory and Other Products: Executive Summary*, Nairobi: Kenya Wildlife Service.

Kiss, A. (ed.) (1990) *Living with Wildlife: Wildlife Resource Management with Local Participation in Africa*, Washington DC: World Bank.

Lewis, D. and Carter, N. (1993) *Voices from Africa: Local Perspectives on Conservation*, Washington DC: World Wildlife Fund.

Mann, D. E. (1991) "Environmental Learning in a Decentralised World", *Journal of International Affairs* 44: 301–337.

Norgaard, R. (1994) *Development Betrayed: The End of Progress and a Coevolutionary Revisioning of the Future*, London and New York: Routledge.

Ole Parkipuny, M. S. and Berger, D. J. (1993) "Maasai Rangelands: Links between Social Justice and Wildlife Conservation" in Lewis, D. and Carter, N. (eds) *Voices from Africa: Local Perspectives on Conservation*, Washington DC: World Wildlife Fund, 1993: 113–31.

Overseas Development Administration (1994) *Whose Eden?: An Overview of Community Approaches to Wildlife Management, A Report to the Overseas Development Administration of the British Government*, London: International Institute for Environment and Development.

Parker, I. and Amin, M. (1983) *Ivory Crisis*, London: Chatto and Windus.

Poole, J. (1996) *Coming of Age with Elephants*, London: Hodder and Stoughton.

Tackacs, D. (1996) *The Idea of Biodiversity: Philosophies of Paradise*, Baltimore: Johns Hopkins University Press.

Thompson, C. (2001) "When Elephants Stand for Competing Philosophies of Nature: Amboseli National Park, Kenya", pp. 166–190 in Law, J. and Mol, A. (eds) *Complexities: Social Studies of Knowledge Practices*, Durham NC: Duke University Press.

Waithaka, J. (1997) *Events that Led to the Downlisting of Elephants to Appendix 2 of CITES During the Tenth Meeting of the Conference of Parties (COP) Held in Harare, Zimbabwe, 9th–20th June, 1997*, Nairobi: Kenya Wildlife Service.

Western, D. (1997a) *In the Dust of Kilimanjaro*, Washington DC: Island Press.

——(1997b) *Report on the CITES Convention, Harare 1997*, Nairobi: Kenya Wildlife Service.

Western, D., Wright, M. and Strum, S. (eds) (1994) *Natural Connections: Perspectives in Community-based Conservation*, Washington DC: Island Press.

5 Knowledge and political order in the European Environment Agency

Anderson, B. (1991) *Imagined Communities*, 2nd edn., London: Verso.

Commission of the European Communities (1990) "Council Regulation 1210/90 on the establishment of the European Environment Agency and the European environment information and observation network", OJ L120, 11 May.

Douglas, M. (1966) *Purity and Danger: An analysis of Concepts of Pollution and Taboo*, London: Routledge and Kegan Paul.

——(1975) *Implicit Meanings: Essays in Anthropology*, London: Routledge and Kegan Paul.

European Environment Agency (1996) "The EEA Information Strategy", Doc.EEA/025/96/Rev 1.

——(1999) *Europe's Environment at the Turn of the Century*, Copenhagen: EEA.

EEC (1990) Council Directive on the Deliberate Release to the Environment of Genetically Modified Organisms, Official Journal of the European Communities, L 117, 8 May, 15–27.

Etzkowitz, H. and Leydesdorff, L. (2000) "The Dynamics of Innovation: From National Sysems and 'Mode 2' to a Triple Helix of University-Industry-Government Relations", *Research Policy* 29: 109–123.

Gibbons, M., Limoges, C., Nowotny, H., Schwartzman, S., Scott, P. and Trow, M. (1994) *The New Production of Knowledge: The Dynamics of Science and Research in Contemporary Societies*, London: Sage.

Harremous, P., Gee, D., Vas, S., Stirling, A. and Wynne, B. (2001) *Late Lessons from Early Warnings*, Copenhagen: EEA (London: Earthscan, 2002) .

Horton, R. (1971) "African Traditional Thought and Western Science", pp. 208–266 in Young, M. F. D. (ed.) *Knowledge and Control: New Directions for the Sociology of Eduction*, London: Collier-Macmillan.

Kreher, A. (1997) "Agencies in the European Community – a step towards administrative integration in Europe", *Journal of European Public Policy* 4(2): 225–45.

Levidow, L. and Carr, S. (2002) "Precautionary Regulation: GM Crops in the European Union", Special Issue, *Journal of Risk Research* 3(3): 187–285.

Latour, B. (1999) [1992, abridged 1998] "One More Turn After the Social Turn", pp. 276–289 in Biagioli, M. (ed.) *The Science Studies Reader*, London: Routledge.

Nowotny, H., Scott, P. and Gibbons, M. (2001) *Rethinking Science: Knowledge and the Public in an Age of Uncertainty*, London: Polity.

Porter, T. (1995) *Trust in Numbers: The Pursuit of Objectivity in Science and Public Life*, Princeton: Princeton University Press.

Starr, S. L. and Greismer, J. (1989) "Institutional Ecology, 'Translations', and Boundary Objects: Amateurs and professionals in Berkeley's Museum of Vertebrate Zoology, 1907–39", *Social Studies of Science* 19: 387–420.

Traweek, S. (1988) *Beamtimes and Lifetimes: The World of High Energy Physicists*, Cambridge MA: Harvard University Press.

von Schomberg, R. (1996) "The Laborious Transition to a Discursive Policy Process on the Release of GMOs", in van Dommeln, A. (ed.) *The Limits of Risk Assessment: Coping with Deliberate Release*, Tilburg, Buenos Aires: International Centre for Human and Public Affairs.

Waterton, C. and Wynne, B. (1996) "Building the European Union: Science and the Cultural Dimensions of Environmental Policy", *Journal of European Public Policy*, 3(3): 421–440.

Wynne, B. (1992) "Uncertainty and Environmental Learning: reconceiving science and policy in the preventive paradigm", *Global Environmental Change* 2(2): 111–127.

Wynne, B. and Lawrence, D. (1989) "Transporting Waste in the European Community: a free market?", *Environment*, 31(6): 12–17.

Wynne, B. and Waterton, C. (1998) "Public Information and the Environment: The Role of the European Environment Agency", in Lowe, P. and Ward, S. (eds) *British Environmental Policy and Europe: Politics and Policy in Transition*, London: Routledge.

7 Mapping systems and moral order: constituting property in genome laboratories

Biagioli, M. (1998) "The Instability of Authorship", *FASEB Journal* 12: 3–16.

Boyle, J. (1996) *Shamans, Software, and Spleens: Law and the Construction of the Information Society*, Cambridge MA: Harvard University Press.

Callon, M. (1994) "Is Science a Public Good?", *Science, Technology, and Human Values* 19: 395–424.

Cambrosio, A. and Keating, P. (1995) *Exquisite Specificity: The Monoclonal Antibody Revolution*, New York: Oxford University Press.

Fortun, M. (1998) "The Human Genome Project and the Acceleration of Biotechnology", in Thackray, A. (ed.) *Private Science: Biotechnology and the Rise of the Molecular Sciences*, Philadelphia: University of Pennsylvania Press.

Foucault, M. (1977) "What Is an Author?", in Bouchard, D. F. and Simon, S. (eds) *Language, Counter-Memory, Practice*, Ithaca NY: Cornell University Press.

Hagstrom, W. O. (1966) *The Scientific Community*, New York: Basic Books.

Heller, M. A. and Eisenberg, R. S. (1998) "Can Patents Deter Innovation? The Anticommons in Biomedical Research", *Science* 280: 698–701.

Hilgartner, S. (1995) "The Human Genome Project", in Jasanoff, S., Markle, G. E., Petersen, J. C. and Pinch, T. J. (eds) *Handbook of Science and Technology Studies*, Thousand Oaks: Sage.

——(1998) "Data Access Policy in Genome Research", in Thackray, A. (ed.) *Private Science: Biotechnology and the Rise of the Molecular Sciences*, Philadelphia: University of Pennsylvania Press.

——(in press) "Making Maps and Making Social Order: Governing American Genome Centers, 1988–1993", in Rheinberger, H.-J. and Gaudillière, J-P. (eds) *From Molecular Genetics to Genomics: The Mapping Cultures of Twentieth Century Genetics*, New York: Routledge.

Hilgartner, S. and Brandt-Rauf, S. (1994a) "Data Access, Ownership, and Control: Toward Empirical Studies of Access Practices", *Knowledge: Creation, Diffusion, Utilization* 15: 355–372.

——(1994b) "Controlling Data and Resources: Access Strategies in Molecular Genetics", presented at a conference on "University Goals, Institutional Mechanisms, and the Industrial Transferability of Research", Stanford University, March 1994. Available at http://www.sts.cornell.edu/hilgartner_files/controlling data.html.

Jasanoff, S. (1995) *Science at the Bar*, Cambridge MA: Harvard University Press.

——(2003) "In a Constitutional Moment: Science and Social Order at the Millennium", pp. 155–180 in Joerges, B. and Nowotny, H. (eds) *Looking Back, Ahead: The 2002 Yearbook of the Sociology of the Sciences*, Dordrecht: Kluwer.

Jordan, B. (1993) *Travelling Around the Human Genome: An In Situ Investigation*, Mountrouge, France: INSERM John Libbey Eurotexte.

Kitcher, P. (2001) *Science, Truth, and Democracy*, Oxford: Oxford University Press.

Knorr-Cetina, K. (1999) *Epistemic Cultures: How the Sciences Make Knowledge*, Cambridge MA: Harvard University Press.

Kohler, R. E. (1994) *Lords of the Fly: Drosophila Genetics and the Experimental Life*, Chicago: University of Chicago Press.

Latour, B. (1987) *Science in Action*, Cambridge MA: Harvard University Press.

——(1993) *We Have Never Been Modern*, Cambridge MA: Harvard University Press.

Maier, E., Hoheisel, J. D., McCarthy, L., Mott, R., Grigoriev, A. V., Monaco, A. P., Larin, Z. and Lehrach, H. (1992) "Complete Coverage of the Schizosaccharomyces Pombe Genome in Yeast Artificial Chromosomes", *Nature Genetics* 1: 273–277.

McCain, K. (1991) "Communication, Competition, and Secrecy: The Production and Dissemination of Research-related Information in Genetics", *Science, Technology, and Human Values* 16: 491–516.

Rabinow, P. (1999) *French DNA: Trouble in Purgatory*, Chicago: University of Chicago Press.

Stemerding, D. and Hilgartner, S. (1998) "Means of Co-ordination in the Making of Biological Science: On the Mapping of Plants, Animals, and Genes", in Disco, C. and van der Meulen, B. J. R. (eds) *Getting New Technologies Together*, New York: De Gruyter.

Thackray, A. (1998) *Private Science: Biotechnology and the Rise of the Molecular Sciences*, Philadelphia: University of Pennsylvania Press.

8 Patients and scientists in French muscular dystrophy research

Bailey, P., Yearley, S. and Forrester, J. (1999) "Involving the Public in Local Air Pollution Assessment: A Citizen Participation Case Study", *International Journal of Environment and Pollution* 11(3): 290–303.

Barataud, B. (1992) *Au nom de nos enfants*, Paris: J'ai Lu.

Barbot, J. (2002) *Les malades en mouvements. La médecine et la science à l'épreuve du sida*, Paris: Balland.

Barral, C., Gobatto, I., Maffioli, B. and Spaak, I. (1991) *Naissance et développement du mouvement de lutte contre les maladies neuromusculaires en France (1958–1982)*, Rapport AFM (Association Française contre les Myopathies)/CTNERHI (Centre Technique National d'Etudes et de Recherches sur les Handicaps et les Inadaptations).

Barthe, Y. (2000) "La mise en politique des déchets nucléaires. L'action publique aux prises avec les irréversibilités techniques", unpublished thesis, Ecole des Mines de Paris.

Brown, P. (1992) "Popular Epidemiology and Toxic Waste Contamination: Lay and Professional Ways of Knowing", *Journal of Health and Social Behaviour* 33: 267–281.

Callon, M., Lascoumes, P. and Barthe, Y. (2001) *Agir dans un monde incertain. Essai sur la démocratie technique*, Paris: Seuil.

Callon, M. and Rip, A. (1992) "Humains et non-humains. Morale d'une co-existence", pp. 140–56 in Theys, J. and Kalaora, B. (eds) *La terre outragé. Les experts sont formels autrement*, Paris: Autrement.

Carricaburu, D. (1993) "L'Association Française des Hémophiles face au danger de contamination par le virus du SIDA: stratégie de normalisation de la maladie et définition collective du risque", *Sciences Sociales et Santé* XI(3–4): 55–82.

Collins, H. and Evans, R. (2002) "The Third Wave of Science Studies: Studies of Expertise and Experience", *Social Studies of Science* 32(2): 235–296.

Dasgupta, P. and David, P. (1994) "Towards a New Economics of Science", *Research Policy* 23(5): 487–522.

Dresser, R. (2001) *When Science Offers Salvation: Patient Advocacy and Ethics*, Oxford: Oxford University Press.

Epstein, S. (1995) "The Construction of Lay Expertise: AIDS Activism and the Forging of Credibility in the Reform of Clinical Trials", *Science, Techology and Human Values* 20(4): 408–437.

Kaufmann, A. (forthcoming) "Mapping the Human Genome at Généthon Laboratory: The French Muscular Dystrophy Association and the Politics of the Gene", in Rheinberger, H. J. and Gaudillière, J. P. (eds) *The Mapping Cultures of Twentieth-century Genetics*, London: Routledge.

Kepper, Y. de (1988) *Les enfants myopathes. Un pari sur l'espérance*, Paris: Fayard.

Kerr, A., Cunningham-Burley, S. and Amos, A. (1997) "The New Genetics: Professionals' Discursive Boundaries", *The Sociological Review* 45(2): 254–278.

——(1998) "Drawing the Line: An Analysis of Lay People's Discussions about the New Human Genetics", *Public Understanding of Science* 7(2): 113–133.

Knorr-Cetina, K. (1996) "Le 'souci de soi' ou les 'tâtônnements': ethnographie de l'empirie dans deux disciplines scientifiques", *Sociologie du Travail* XXXVIII(3): 311–330.

Latour, B. (1995) *La science en action*, Paris: Gallimard Folio.

Paterson, F. and Barral, C. (1994) "L'Association Française contre les Myopathies: trajectoire d'une association d'usagers et construction associative d'une maladie", *Sciences Sociales et Santé* XII(2): 79–111.

Rabeharisoa, V. and Callon, M. (1999) *Le pouvoir des malades. L'Association Française contre les Myopathies et la recherche*, Paris: Les Presses de l'Ecole des Mines.

——(2002) "The Involvement of Patients' Associations in Research", *International Social Science Journal* 17: 57–65.

Rabeharisoa, V. (2003) "The Struggle Against Neuromuscular Diseases in France and the Emergence of the 'Partnership Model' of Patient Organization", *Social Science and Medicine* 57(11): 2127–2136.

Rangnekar, D. (2002) "Shaping the Landscape of Biomedical Research: Are Patients Groups Influential?", unpublished paper, University of York.

Rip, A. (forthcoming) "Spaces of Indigeneous Knowledge in Western Science and Science Policy", *Science, Technology and Human Values*.

Wynne, B. (1996) "May the Sheep Safely Graze? A Reflexive View of the Expert-lay Knowledge Divide", pp. 44–83 in Lash, S., Szerszynski, B. and Wynne, B. (eds) *Risk, Environment and Modernity. Towards a New Ecology*, London: Sage.

9 Circumscribing expertise: membership categories in courtroom testimony

Anderson, W. (1992) "The Reasoning of the Strongest: The Polemics of Skill and Science in Medical Diagnosis", *Social Studies of Science* 22: 653–684.

Bar-Hillel, Y. (1954) "Indexical Expressions", *Mind* 63: 359–379.

Bruce, S. and Wallis, R. (1983) "Rescuing Motives", *British Journal of Sociology* 34(1): 61–71.

——(1985) " 'Rescuing Motives' Rescued: A Reply to Sharrock and Watson", *British Journal of Sociology* 36(3): 467–470.

Collins, H. M. (1988) "Public Experiments and Displays of Virtuosity: The Core-set Revisited", *Social Studies of Science* 18: 725–748.

Coulter, J. (1982) "Remarks on the Conceptualization of Social Structure", *Philosophy of the Social Sciences* 12: 33–46.

——(1996) "Human Practices and the Observability of the 'Macrosocial'", *Zeitschrift für Soziologie* 25: 337–345, reprinted pp. 29–41 in Schatzki, T. R., Knorr-Cetina, K. and von Savigny, E. (eds) *The Practice Turn in Contemporary Theory*, London: Routledge.

Dear, P. (2001) "Science Studies as Epistemography", pp. 128–141 in Labinger, J. and Collins, H. (eds) *The One Culture*, Chicago: University of Chicago Press.

Doing, Park (2002) "Lab Hands and 'The Scarlet O'", unpublished paper, Department of Science and Technology Studies, Cornell University (under review for *Social Studies of Science*).

Durkheim, Emile (1982) [1895] *The Rules of Sociological Method*, New York: Free Press.

Edmond, G. (2001) "The Law Set: The Production of Medical Propriety", *Science, Technology and Human Values* 26: 191–236.

———(2002) "Legal Engineering: Contested Representations of Law, Science (and Non-science) and Society", *Social Studies of Science* 32: 371–412.

Foucault, M. (1980) "Two Lectures", pp. 37–54 in Gordon, C. (ed.) *Power/Knowledge: Selected Interviews and Other Writings 1972–1977*, New York: Pantheon Books.

Garfinkel, H. (1967) *Studies in Ethnomethodology*, Englewood Cliffs: Prentice Hall.

———(1991) "Respecification: Evidence for Locally Produced, Naturally Accountable Phenomena of Order, Logic, Reason, Meaning, Method, etc. in and as of the Essential Haecceity of Immortal Ordinary Society (I): An Announcement of Studies", pp. 10–19 in Button, G. (ed.) *Ethnomethodology and the Human Sciences*, Cambridge: Cambridge University Press.

———(2002) *Ethnomethodology's Program: Working out Durkheim's Aphorism*, Lanham MD: Rowman and Littlefield.

Garfinkel, H. and Sacks, H. (1970) "On Formal Structures of Practical Actions", pp. 337–366 in McKinney, J. C. and Tiryakian, E. A. (eds) *Theoretical Sociology: Perspectives and Development*, New York: Appleton-Century Crofts.

Gieryn, T. (1999) *Cultural Boundaries of Science: Credibility on the Line*, Chicago: University of Chicago Press.

Gieryn, T., Bevins, G. and Zehr, S. (1985) "Professionalization of American Scientists: Public Science in the Creation/Evolution Trials", *American Sociological Review* 50: 392–409.

Goffman, E. (1959) *The Presentation of Self in Everyday Life*, New York: Anchor Books.

Goodwin, C. (1994) "Professional Vision", *American Anthropologist* 96: 606–633.

Hester, S. and Eglin, P. (eds) (1997) *Culture in Action: Studies in Membership Categorization Analysis*, Washington DC: International Institute for Ethnomethodology and Conversation Analysis, and University Press of America.

Huber, P. (1991) *Galileo's Revenge: Junk Science in the Courtroom*, New York: Basic Books.

Jasanoff, S. (1990) *The Fifth Branch: Science Advisers as Policymakers*, Cambridge MA: Harvard University Press.

———(1995) *Science at the Bar: Law, Science, and Technology in America*, Cambridge MA: Harvard University Press.

———(1998) "The Eye of Everyman: Witnessing DNA in the Simpson Trial", *Social Studies of Science* 28: 713–740.

Jayyusi, L. (1984) *Categorization and the Moral Order*, London: Routlege and Kegan Paul.

Jordan, K. (1995) "Sociological Investigations into the Mainstreaming of the Polymerase Chain Reaction", unpublished doctoral dissertation, Department of Sociology, Boston University.

Latour, B. (1987) *Science in Action: How to Follow Scientists and Engineers through Society*, Cambridge MA: Harvard University Press.

Lawrence, C. (1985) "Incommunicable Knowledge: Science, Technology and the Clinical Art in Britain 1850–1914", *Journal of Contemporary History* 20: 503–520.

Lynch, M. (1993) *Scientific Practice and Ordinary Action*, New York: Cambridge University Press.

——(1995) "Springs of Action or Vocabularies of Motive?", pp. 94–110 in Gouk, P. (ed.) *Wellsprings of Achievement: Cultural and Economic Dynamics in Early Modern England and Japan*, Aldershot: Valarium.

Lynch, M. and Bogen, D. (1996) *The Spectacle of History: Speech, Text, and Memory at the Iran-Contra Hearings*, Durham NC: Duke University Press.

Lynch, M. and McNally, R. (2003) "'Science', 'Common Sense', and DNA Evidence: A Legal Controversy about the Public Understanding of Science", *Public Understanding of Science* 12(1): 83–103.

McHoul, A. (1987) "Why There Are no Guarantees for Interrogators", *Journal of Pragmatics* 11: 455–471.

Merton, R. K. (1973) "The Normative Structure of Science", pp. 267–278 in Merton, R. K., *The Sociology of Science: Theoretical and Empirical Investigations*, Chicago: University of Chicago Press.

Mills, C. W. (1940) "Situated Actions and Vocabularies of Motive", *American Sociological Review* 5: 904–913.

Nelkin, D. (1982) *The Creation Controversy: Science or Scripture in the Schools*, New York: Norton.

Peters, R. S. (1958) *The Concept of Motivation*, London: Routledge and Kegan Paul.

Pollner, M. (1987) *Mundane Reason*, Cambridge: Cambridge University Press.

Quinn, P. (1984) "The Philosopher of Science as Expert Witness", in Cushing, J., Delaney, C. F. and Gutting, G. M. (eds) *Science and Reality: Recent Work in the Philosophy of Science*, Notre Dame: University of Notre Dame Press.

Ruse, M. (1986) "Commentary: The Academic as Expert Witness", *Science, Technology, and Human Values* 11: 68–73.

Sacks, H. (1972) "An Initial Investigation of the Usability of Conversational Data for Doing Sociology", pp. 31–74 in Sudnow, D. (ed.) *Studies in Social Interaction*, New York: Free Press.

——(1979) "Hotrodder: A Revolutionary Category", pp. 7–14 in Psathas, G. (ed.) *Everyday Language: Studies in Ethnomethodology*, New York: Irvington.

Schegloff, E. A. (1968) "Sequencing in Conversational Openings", *American Anthropologist* 70: 1075–1095.

——(1984) "On Some Questions and Ambiguities in Conversation", pp. 28–52 in Atkinson, J. M. and Heritage, J. C. (eds) *Structures of Social Action: Studies in Conversation Analysis*, Cambridge: Cambridge University Press.

Shapin, S. (1989) "The Invisible Technician", *American Scientist* 77: 554–563.

Sharrock, W. W. and Watson, D. R. (1984) "What's the Point of 'Rescuing Motives'?", *British Journal of Sociology* 34: 435–451.

——(1986) "Re-locating Motives", *British Journal of Sociology* 36: 581–583.

Suchman, L. (1994) "Do Categories Have Politics? The Language/Action Perspective Reconsidered", *Computer Supported Cooperative Work* 2: 177–190.

Sudnow, D. (1965) "Normal Crimes: Sociological Features of the Penal Code in a Public Defender Office", *Social Problems* 12: 255–276.

Watson, D. R. (1978) "Categorization, Authorization and Blame-negotiation in Conversation", *Sociology* 12: 105–113.

Winch, P. (1958) *The Idea of a Social Science and its Relation to Philosophy*, London: Routledge and Kegan Paul.

10 The science of merit and the merit of science: mental order and social order in early twentieth-century France and America

Angus, David L. and Mirel, Jeffrey E. (1999) *The Failed Promise of the American High School, 1890–1995*, New York: Teachers College Press.

Bagley, William C. (1922) "Educational Determinism: Or Democracy and the IQ", *School and Society* 15: 373–384.

——(1925) *Determinism in Education: A Series of Papers on the Relative Influence of Inherited and Acquired Traits in Determining Intelligence, Achievement, and Character*, Baltimore: Warwick and York.

Bannister, Robert C. (1979) *Social Darwinism: Science and Myth in Anglo-American Thought*, Philadelphia: Temple University Press.

Bederman, Gail (1995) *Manliness and Civilization: A Cultural History of Gender and Race in the United States, 1880–1917*, Chicago: University of Chicago Press.

Binet, Alfred (1903) *L'Etude expérimentale de l'intelligence*, Paris: Schleicher Frères et Cie.

——(1908) "Préface", *L'Année psychologique* 14: v–vi.

——(1911) "Le bilan de psychologie en 1910", *L'Année psychologique* 17: v–xi.

Binet, Alfred and Simon, Théodore (1905a) "Méthodes nouvelles pour diagnostiquer l'idiotie, l'imbécilité et la débilité mentale", *Atti del V Congresso internazionale di psicologia*, Rome: Foranzi.

——(1905b) "Sur la necessité d'établir un diagnostic scientifique des états inférieurs de l'intelligence", "Méthodes nouvelles pour le diagnostic du niveau intellectual des anormaux", and "Application des méthodes nouvelles au diagnostic du niveau intellectuel chez des enfants normaux et anormaux d'hospice et d'école primaire", *L'Année psychologique* 11: 163–336.

——(1916) *The Development of Intelligence in School Children*, trans. Elizabeth S. Kite, Baltimore: Williams and Wilkins.

Bourdon, Benjamin (1926) *L'Intelligence*, Paris: Alcan.

Brooks, John I. (1993) "Philosophy and Psychology at the Sorbonne, 1885–1913", *Journal of the History of the Behavioral Sciences* 29: 123–145.

Brown, JoAnne (1992) *The Definition of a Profession: The Authority of Metaphor in the History of Intelligence Testing, 1890–1930*, Princeton: Princeton University Press.

Buckingham, B. R. (1921) "The School as a Selective Agency", *Journal of Educational Research* 3: 139.

Buhle, Mari Jo (1998) *Feminism and Its Discontents: A Century of Struggle with Psychoanalysis*, Cambridge MA: Harvard University Press.

Burnham, John C. (1967) *Psychoanalysis and American Medicine, 1894–1918: Medicine, Science, and Culture*, New York: International Universities Press.

——(1968) "The New Psychology: From Narcissism to Social Control", in Braeman, J., Bremner, R. and Brody, D. (eds) *Change and Continuity in Twentieth-Century America: The 1920s*, Columbus: Ohio State University Press.

Callon, Michel (forthcoming) "The Increasing Involvement of Concerned Groups in R&D Policies: What Lessons for Public Powers?", in Geuna, A., Salter, A. and Steinmueller, W. E. (eds) *Science and Innovation: Rethinking the Rationales for Funding and Governance*.

Camfield, Thomas M. (1969) "Psychologists at War: The History of American Psychology and the First World War", unpublished Ph.D. dissertation, University of Texas.

Campbell, Ballard C. (1995) *The Growth of American Government: Governance from the Cleveland Era to the Present*, Bloomington: Indiana University Press.

Cannon, Cornelia James (1922) "American Misgivings", *The Atlantic Monthly*, February, 145–157.

Caplan, Eric (1998) *Mind Games: American Culture and the Birth of Psychotherapy*, Berkeley: University of California Press.

Carroy, Jacqueline and Plas, Régine (1996) "The Origins of French Experimental Psychology: Experiment and Experimentalism", *History of the Human Sciences* 9: 73–84.

Carson, John (1993) "Army Alpha, Army Brass, and the Search for Army Intelligence", *Isis* 84: 278–309.

——(1994) "Talents, Intelligence, and the Constructions of Human Difference in France and America, 1750–1920", unpublished Ph.D. dissertation, Princeton University.

Chandler, Alfred D. (1977) *The Visible Hand: The Managerial Revolution in American Business*, Cambridge MA: Harvard University Press.

Chapman, Paul D. (1988) *Schools as Sorters: Lewis M. Terman, Applied Psychology, and the Intelligence Testing Movement, 1890–1930*, New York: New York University Press.

Church, Robert L. (1971) "Educational Psychology and Social Reform in the Progressive Era", *History of Education Quarterly* 11: 390–405.

Clark, Terry N. (1973) *Prophets and Patrons: The French University and the Emergence of the Social Sciences*, Cambridge MA: Harvard University Press.

Cravens, Hamilton (1978) *The Triumph of Evolution: American Scientists and the Heredity-Environment Controversy, 1900–1941*, Philadelphia: University of Pennsylvania Press.

Cremin, Lawrence A. (1988) *American Education: The Metropolitan Experience, 1876–1980*, New York: Harper and Row.

Cutten, George B. (1922) "The Reconstruction of Democracy", *School and Society* 16: 479.

Daley, Suzanne (2001) "Elite French College Tackles Affirmative Action", *New York Times*, 4 May.

Danziger, Kurt (1985) "The Origins of the Psychological Experiment as a Social Institution", *American Psychologist* 40: 133–140.

——(1990) *Constructing the Subject: Historical Origins of Psychological Research*, Cambridge: Cambridge University Press.

——(1997) *Naming the Mind: How Psychology Found Its Language*, London: Sage.

Degler, Carl N. (1991) *In Search of Human Nature: The Decline and Revival of Darwinism in American Social Thought*, New York: Oxford University Press.

Dewey, John (1922a) "Individuality Equality and Superiority", *New Republic* 33: 61–63.

——(1922b) "Mediocrity and Individuality", *The New Republic* 33: 35–37.

Du Bois, W. E. B. (1986) [1903] "The Talented Tenth", in *Writings*, New York: Library of America.

Fass, Paula S. (1980) "The IQ: A Cultural and Historical Framework", *American Journal of Education* 88: 431–458.

Flexner, Abraham (1919) Letter to Robert M. Yerkes, Surgeon General's Office. March 1. File 697: Mental Measurements, 1917–1942, box 328, R.G. 1.2. General Education Board Collection, Rockefeller Archive Center, N. Tarrytown NY.

Frazer, Elizabeth (1923) "On the Job: The White-Collar World", *Saturday Evening Post* 195: 27, 132–137.

Goddard, Henry H. (1908) *European Diary*, folder AA4(1) box M33.1, Henry Herbert Goddard Papers, Archives of the History of American Psychology, University of Akron, Akron OH.

——(1910) "Four Hundred Feeble-Minded Children Classified by the Binet Method", *Pedagogical Seminary* 17: 387–397.

——(1916) "Introduction", in *The Development of Intelligence in School Children*, trans. Elizabeth S. Kite, Baltimore: Williams and Wilkins.

Gould, Stephen Jay (1996) *The Mismeasure of Man*, revised edn, New York: Norton.

Hale, Matthew G. Jr (1995) *The Rise and Crisis of Psychoanalysis in the United States: Freud and the Americans, 1917–1985*, New York: Oxford University Press.

Hart, Hornell (1933) "Changing Social Attitudes and Interests", in *Recent Social Trends in the United States*, vol. 1, New York: McGraw-Hill.

Hart, Joseph Kinmont (1919) "The Progress of Science and the Fate of Democracy", *School and Society* 9: 249–259.

Hawkins, Mike (1997) *Social Darwinism in European and American Thought, 1860–1945: Nature as Model and Nature as Threat*, Cambridge: Cambridge University Press.

Herman, Ellen (1995) *The Romance of American Psychology: Political Culture in the Age of Experts*, Berkeley: University of California Press.

Higham, John (1970) "The Reorientation of American Culture in the 1890s", in *Writing American History: Essays on Modern Scholarship*, Bloomington: Indiana University Press.

——(1994) *Strangers in the Land: Patterns of American Nativism, 1860–1925*, 2nd edn, New Brunswick: Rutgers University Press.

Ingraham, Patricia W. (1995) *The Foundation of Merit: Public Service in American Democracy*, Baltimore: Johns Hopkins University Press.

Jasanoff, Sheila (1987) "Biology and the Bill of Rights: Can Science Reframe the Constitution?", *American Journal of Law and Medicine* 13: 249–289.

——(1990) *The Fifth Branch: Science Advisers as Policymakers*, Cambridge MA: Harvard University Press.

——(1992) "Science, Politics, and the Renegotiation of Expertise at EPA", *Osiris* 7: 195–217.

——(1999) "The Songlines of Risk", *Environmental Values* 8: 135–152.

Johnson, Douglas (1966) *France and the Dreyfus Affair*, London: Blandford Press.

Karier, Clarence J. (1972) "Testing for Order and Control in the Corporate Liberal State", *Educational Theory* 22: 154–180.

Keller, Morton (1994) *Regulating a New Society: Public Policy and Social Change in America, 1900–1933*, Cambridge MA: Harvard University Press.

Kevles, Daniel J. (1968) "Testing the Army's Intelligence: Psychologists and the Military in World War I", *Journal of American History* 55: 565–580.

——(1986) *In the Name of Eugenics: Genetics and the Uses of Human Heredity*, Berkeley: University of California Press.

——(1995) *The Physicists: The History of a Scientific Community in Modern America*, 2nd edn, Cambridge MA: Harvard University Press.

Kitson, Harry D. (1916) Contribution to "Mentality Tests: A Symposium", *Journal of Educational Psychology* 7: 278–286.

Latour, Bruno (1987) *Science in Action: How to Follow Scientists and Engineers Through Society*, Cambridge MA: Harvard University Press.

Lears, T. J. Jackson (1981) *No Place of Grace: Antimodernism and the Transformation of American Culture, 1880–1920*, New York: Pantheon Books.

Lemann, Nicholas (1999) *The Big Test: The Secret History of the American Meritocracy*, New York: Farrar, Straus and Giroux.

Lippmann, Walter (1922a) *Public Opinion*, New York: Harcourt, Brace.

——(1922b) "The Mental Age of Americans", "The Mystery of the 'A' Men", "The Reliability of Intelligence Tests", "The Abuse of the Tests", "Tests of Hereditary Intelligence", "A Future for the Tests", *New Republic* 32: 213–215, 246–248, 275–277, 297–298, 328–330; and 33: 9–11.

——(1923a) "A Defense of Education", *The Century Magazine* 106: 95–103.

——(1923b) "The Great Confusion: A Reply to Mr. Terman", *The New Republic* 33: 146.

Lunbeck, Elizabeth (1994) *The Psychiatric Persuasion: Knowledge, Gender, and Power in Modern America*, Princeton: Princeton University Press.

Mayeur, Françoise (1981) *Histoire générale de l'enseignement et de l'éducation en France, tome III: de la Révolution à l'Ecole républicaine*, Paris: Nouvelle Librairie de France.

Mayeur, Jean-Marie and Madeleine Rebérioux (1987) *The Third Republic from Its Origins to the Great War, 1871–1914*, Cambridge: Cambridge University Press,

McDougall, William (1921) *Is America Safe for Democracy?*, New York: Charles Scribner's Sons.

Minton, Henry L. (1987) "Lewis M. Terman and Mental Testing: In Search of the Democratic Ideal", in Sokal, Michael M. (ed.) *Psychological Testing and American Society, 1890–1930*, New Brunswick: Rutgers University Press.

——(1988) *Lewis M. Terman: Pioneer in Psychological Testing*, New York: New York University Press.

Morawski, Jill G. and Hornstein, Gail A. (1991) "Quandary of the Quacks: The Struggle for Expert Knowledge in American Psychology, 1890–1940", in Brown, JoAnne and van Keuran, David K. (eds) *The Estate of Social Knowledge*, Baltimore: Johns Hopkins University Press.

Nasaw, David (1979) *Schooled to Order: A Social History of Public Schooling in the United States*, New York: Oxford University Press.

Newman, Louise Michele (1999) *White Women's Rights: The Racial Origins of Feminism in the United States*, New York: Oxford University Press.

Nord, Philip (1995) *The Republican Moment: Struggles for Democracy in Nineteenth-Century France*, Cambridge MA: Harvard University Press.

O'Donnell, John M. (1985) *The Origins of Behaviorism: American Psychology, 1870–1920*, New York: New York University Press.

Painter, Nell I. (1987) *Standing at Armageddon: The United States, 1877–1919*, New York: Norton.

Pernick, Martin S. (1996) *The Black Stork: Eugenics and the Death of "Defective" Babies in American Medicine and Motion Pictures Since 1915*, New York: Oxford University Press.

Piéron, Henri (1929) *Principles of Experimental Psychology*, trans. J. B. Miner, New York: Harcourt, Brace.

——(1939) "Le laboratoire de psychologie de la Sorbonne", in *Centennaire de Th. Ribot: Jubilé de la psychologie scientifique française 1839–1889–1939*, Agen: Imprimerie Moderne.

——(1965) "Discours d'Henri Piéron pour le 75e anniversaire du laboratoire de psychologie de la Sorbonne", *L'Année psychologique* 65: 6–15.

Popper, Karl R. (1950) *The Open Society and Its Enemies*, Princeton: Princeton University Press.

Ravitch, Diane (2000) *Left Back: A Century of Failed School Reform*, New York: Simon and Schuster.

Resnick, Daniel P. (1982) "History of Educational Testing", in Wigdor, Alexandra K. and Garner, Wendell R. (eds) *Ability Testing: Uses, Consequences, and Controversies*, Washington DC: National Academy Press.

Reuben, Julie A. (1996) *Making of the Modern University: Intellectual Transformation and the Marginalization of Morality*, Chicago: University of Chicago Press.

Reuchlin, Maurice (1968) "La psychologie différentielle au XIXe siècle et au début du XXe: Métrique statistique et comparaison ordinale", *Revue de synthèse* 3rd series, 89: 383–400.

——(1978) *Histoire de la psychologie*, Paris: Presses Universitaires de France.

Richards, Barry (1988) "Lightner Witmer and the Project of Psychotechnology", *History of the Human Sciences* 1: 201–219.

Rodgers, Daniel T. (1987) *Contested Truths: Keywords in American Politics Since Independence*, New York: Basic Books.

Rudolph, Fredrick (1962) *The American College and University: A History*, New York: Vintage.

Ryan, Patrick J. (1997) "Unnatural Selection: Intelligence Testing, Eugenics, and American Political Cultures", *Journal of Social History* 30: 669–685.

Samelson, Franz (1979) "Putting Psychology on the Map: Ideology and Intelligence Testing", in Buss, Allan R. (ed.) *Psychology in Social Context*, New York: Irvington Publishers.

Schemo, Diana J. (2001) "Head of U. of California Seeks To End SAT Use in Admissions", *New York Times*, 17 February, national section.

Schneider, William H. (1989) "Henri Laugier, the Science of Work and the Workings of Science in France, 1920–1940", *Cahiers pour l'Histoire du CNRS* 5: 7–34.

——(1992) "After Binet: French Intelligence Testing, 1900–1950", *Journal of the History of the Behavioral Sciences* 28: 111–132.

Shepard, Edward Morse (1884) *The Competitive Test and the Civil Service of States and Cities*, New York: The Society for Political Education.

Shinn, Terry (1980) *L'Ecole polytechnique: 1794–1914*, Paris: Presses de la Fondation Nationale des Sciences Politiques.

Skocpol, Theda (1992) *Protecting Soldiers and Mothers: The Political Origins of Social Policy in the United States*, Cambridge MA: Harvard University Press.

Smith, Robert J. (1982) *The Ecole Normale Supérieure and the Third Republic*, Albany: SUNY Press.

Sokal, Michael M. (1981) "The Origins of the Psychological Corporation", *Journal of the History of the Behavioral Sciences* 17: 54–67.

Stern, William (1914) *The Psychological Methods of Testing Intelligence*, trans. Guy M. Whipple, Baltimore: Warwick and York.

Stoddard, Lothrop (1925) *The Revolt Against Civilization: The Menace of the Under Man*, New York: Charles Scribner's Sons.

Terman, Lewis M. (1913) "A Report of the Buffalo Conference on the Binet-Simon Tests of Intelligence", *Pedagogical Seminary* 20: 549–554.

——(1919) *The Intelligence of School Children*, Boston: Houghton Mifflin.

——(1922) "The Psychological Determinist; or Democracy and the IQ", *Journal of Educational Research* 6: 57–62.

——(1922–3) "The Great Conspiracy, or The Impulse Imperious of Intelligence Testers, Psychoanalyzed and Exposed by Mr. Lippmann", *The New Republic* 33: 116–120.

Terman, Lewis M., Lyman, Grace, Ordahl, George, Ordahl, Louise Ellison, Galbreath, Neva and Talbert, Wilford (1917) *The Stanford Revision and Extension of the Binet-Simon Scale for Measuring Intelligence*, Baltimore: Warwick and York.

Trachtenberg, Alan (1982) *The Incorporation of America: Culture and Society in the Gilded Age*, New York: Hill and Wang.

Tuddenham, Read D. (1963) "The Nature and Measurement of Intelligence", in Postman, Leo (ed.) *Psychology in the Making*, New York: Knopf.

Tyack, David B. (1974) *The One Best System: A History of American Urban Education*, Cambridge MA: Harvard University Press.

Veysey, Laurence R. (1965) *The Emergence of the American University*, Chicago: University of Chicago Press.

Weisz, George (1983) *The Emergence of the Modern University in France, 1863–1914*, Princeton: Princeton University Press.

Whipple, Guy M. (1922) "Educational Determinism: A Discussion of Professor Bagley's Address at Chicago", *School and Society* 15: 602.

Wiebe, Robert H. (1967) *The Search for Order, 1877–1920*, New York: Hill and Wang.

Wiggam, Albert E. (1922) "The New Decalogue of Science: An Open Letter from the Biologist to the Statesman", *The Century Magazine* 103: 643–650.

Williams, Stephen S. (1986) "From Polemics to Practice: IQ Testing and Tracking in the Detroit Public Schools and Their Relationship to the National Debate", unpublished Ph.D. dissertation, University of Michigan.

Wise, M. Norton (1988) "Mediating Machines", *Science in Context* 2: 77–113.

Wolf, Theta H. (1969) "The Emergence of Binet's Conception and Measurement of Intelligence: A Case History of the Creative Process", *Journal of the History of the Behavioral Sciences* 5: 113–134, 207–237.

Wolf, Theta H. (1973) *Alfred Binet*, Chicago: University of Chicago Press.

Yerkes, Robert M. (1919a) "The Mental Rating of School Children", typescript attached to letter Yerkes to Abraham Flexner; 29 January 1919, folder 3223, box 308, General Education Board Collection, Rockefeller Archive Center, N. Tarrytown NY.

——(1919b) Letter to Abraham Flexner, 17 January 1919, folder 3223, box 308, General Education Board Collection, Rockefeller Archive Center, N. Tarrytown NY.

——(1920) *The New World of Science: Its Development During the War*, New York: The Century Co.

Yerkes, Robert M. and Terman, Lewis M., Office of the Surgeon General (1919) Letter to General Education Board, 23 January 1919, General Education Board Documents of Record, vol. VIII, 1919, box 21; General Education Board Collection, Rockefeller Archive Center, N. Tarrytown NY.

Zenderland, Leila (1987) "The Debate Over Diagnosis: Henry Herbert Goddard and the Medical Acceptance of Intelligence Testing", in Sokal, M. M. (ed.) *Psychological Testing and American Society, 1890–1930*, New Brunswick: Rutgers University Press.

——(1998) *Measuring Minds: Henry Herbert Goddard and the Origins of American Intelligence Testing*, Cambridge: Cambridge University Press.

Zunz, Olivier (1990) *Making America Corporate, 1870–1920*, Chicago: University of Chicago Press.

13 Science and the political imagination in contemporary democracies

Blondheim, M. (1994) *News Over The Wires*, Cambridge MA: Harvard University Press.

Boltansky, L. (1999) *Distant Suffering, Morality, Media and Politics*, Cambridge: Cambridge University Press.

Bumiller, E. (2003) "Keepers of Bush Image Lift Stagecraft to New Heights", *New York Times*, 16 May, 1.

Darenton, R. (1968) *Mesmerism and the End of the Enlightenment in France*, Cambridge MA: Harvard University Press.

Eliot, T. S. (1960) "Two Choruses From 'The Rock'", in *The Waste Land and Other Poems*, New York: Harcourt, Brace.

Ezrahi, Y. (1980) "Science and the Problem of Authority in Democracy", pp. 43–60 in Gieryn, T. F. (ed.) *Science and Social Structure: A Festschrift for Robert K. Merton*, Transactions of the New York Academy of Sciences Series II, vol. 39.

——(1990) *The Descent of Icarus, Science and the Transformation of Contemporary Democracy*, Cambridge MA: Harvard University Press.

——(1996) "Modes of Reasoning and the Politics of Authority in the Modern State" pp. 72–89 in Olson, D. R. and Torrance, N. (eds) *Modes of Thought, Explorations in Culture and Cognition*, New York: Cambridge University Press.

Geertz, C. (1980) *Negara: The Theatre State in Nineteenth Century Bali*, Princeton: Princeton University Press.

Hobbes, T. (1962) [1651] *Leviathan*, Oxford: Blackwell.

Jasanoff, S. (2001) "Election 2000: Mechanical Error or System Failure", *Social Studies of Science* 31: 461–67.

Jullien, F. (2002) "Did Philosophers Have to Become Fixated in Truth?", *Critical Inquiry* 28: 803–824.

Katz, E. and Dayan, D. (1985) "Media Events: On the Experience of Not Being There", *Religion* 15: 306.

Latour, B. (1987) *Science in Action: How to Follow Scientists and Engineers through Society*, Cambridge MA: Harvard University Press.

McChesney, R. M. (1999) *Rich Media Poor Democracy*, Urbana: University of Illinois Press.

Merton, Robert K. (1957) "The Normative Structure of Science", in Storer, Norman W. (ed.) *The Sociology of Science: Theoretical and Empirical Investigations*, Chicago: University of Chicago Press.

Polanyi, M. (1974) *Personal Knowledge*, Chicago: University of Chicago Press.

Porter, T. M. (1995) *Trust in Numbers: The Pursuit of Objectivity in Science and Public Life*, Princeton: Princeton University Press.

Putnam, R. (1995) "Tuning In, Tuning Out: The Strange Disappearance of Social Capital in America", The 1995 Ithiel de Sola Pool Lecture, *Political Science and Politics*, 27: 664–682.

——(2000) *Bowling Alone: the Collapse and Revival of American Community*, New York: Simon and Schuster.

Scheuer, J. (2000) *The Sound Bite Society: Television and the American Mind*, New York: Four Walls Eight Windows.

Schiller, F. (1960) *On the Aesthetic Education of Man*, New York: Frederick Unger Publishing.

Scott, J. C. (1998) *Seeing like a State: How certain Schemes to Improve the Human Condition Have Failed*, New Haven: Yale University Press.

Skinner, Q. (1996) *Reason and Rhetoric in the Philosophy of Hobbes*, Cambridge: Cambridge University Press.

Sontag, S. (1977) *On Photography*, New York: Delta Books.

14 Afterword

Beck, U. (1992) *Risk Society: Towards a New Modernity*, London: Sage.

Bloor, D. (1976) *Knowledge and Social Imagery*, London: Routledge and Kegan Paul.

Douglas, M. (1986) *How Institutions Think*, Syracuse NY: Syracuse University Press.

Fleck, L. (1979) [1935] *Genesis and Development of a Scientific Fact*, Chicago: University of Chicago Press.

Geertz, C. (1973) *The Interpretation of Cultures*, New York: Basic Books.

Hacking, I. (1999) *The Social Construction of What?*, Cambridge MA: Harvard University Press.

Haraway, D. J. (1991) *Simians, Cyborgs and Women: The Reinvention of Nature*, New York: Routledge.

Jasanoff, S. (1995) *Science at the Bar: Law, Science, and Technology in America*, Cambridge MA: Harvard University Press.

Kuhn, T. (1962) *The Structure of Scientific Revolutions*, Chicago: University of Chicago Press.

Latour, B. and Woolgar, S. (1979) *Laboratory Life: The Social Construction of Scientific Facts*, Beverly Hills: Sage.

Sahlins, M. (1995) *How "Natives" Think: About Captain Cook, For Example*, Chicago: University of Chicago Press.

Scott, J. C. (1998) *Seeing like a State: How Certain Schemes to Improve the Human Condition Have Failed*, New Haven: Yale University Press.

Yeats, W. B. (1956) *The Collected Poems of W. B. Yeats*, New York: Macmillan, 212.

Index

316   *Index*

surveys, in muscular dystrophy research
147
sustainable development 8, 68, 79

tacit knowledge 207, 209–10, 219–20, 256
Takacs, D. 47, 71
Taliban regime 26
Tavenga, T. 82
Technica Curiosa (Schott) 212
television 258–9, 262–4, 268, 269–70, 272
Tempany, H. 126
Terman, L. M. 182, 189–90, 192, 197–8,
201
terrorism 1, 13–14, 16, 48, 49
textuality 4
thick description 2, 276
Thiselton-Dyer, Sir W. 112, 113, 115, 122
Thompson, C. 6–7, 41, 67–86, 277, 279
Thorndike, E. L. 192
Tolba, M. 46, 50, 60
tourism, wildlife 64–5 n.7, 71
toxic waste policies 97
Trade Record Analysis of Flora and Fauna
in Commerce (TRAFFIC) 70, 77, 78
transportation 48
Traweek, S. 6, 36, 93
Trinidad 111, 120, 121, 126
Truman, H. S. 242, 243
trust 20, 29, 56, 210–11
Tuddenham, R. D. 184, 204 n.3
Tuve, M. 234, 238, 239

uncertainty 8, 33–4, 97, 104
United Nations 46, 63
United Nations Conference on
Environment and Development (1992)
50–1
United Nations Conference on the Human
Environment (1972) 79
United Nations Environment Programme
(UNEP) 53, 56, 59
United Nations Framework Convention on
Climate Change 46, 51, 54, 59, 61
United Nations General Assembly 50, 56,
59
United States: educational system 10, 188,
192–4, 200–1; intelligence testing 10,
181, 182–3, 187–94, 196–7, 198–9,
200–1, 202–3, 277; and
Intergovernmental Panel on Climate
Change (IPCC) 56, 62–3; military
research and development 11, 225–53
universalism 95, 98, 104
universities 230–1, 232–3

utility 100

value 100
values 4, 38
Veysey, L. R. 188
Vico, G. 261, 271
visibility 263
visualization 28, 146–7
Von Karman, T. 239
von Schomberg, R. 96, 97
vulnerability science 34

Wadsworth, J. 237
Wagner, P. 33
Waithaka, J. 76
war 1, 14; management of science during
229, 231–6
Washington Convention *see* Convention on
International Trade in Endangered
Species of Fauna and Flora (CITES)
Waterton, C. 8, 41, 87–108, 277, 279, 281
Watts, F. 126
Weapons Systems Evaluation Group 245
weapons technology 229, 231–6, 244, 245
Weisz, G. 187
West India Royal Commission (Norman
Commission) (1897) 118–20, 122–3,
126–7
West Indian Bulletin 123, 127
West Indies 8, 109–30
Western, D. 76, 85 n.10
Whipple, G. M. 182, 192, 193, 201
White, R. M. 52
Wilde, O. 119
Wildlife Conservation Society 77
wildlife protection 6–7, 67–86, 279
Wildlife Trade Monitoring Unit (WTMU)
70
Wilmut, I. 15
Wilson, Caroll 240
Wilson, Charles 238
Wilson Committee 238–9
Windward Islands 119
Winner, L. 31, 33, 36
wisdom 254, 256, 258, 262, 264, 265
Wise, M. N. 185
Wolf, T. H. 184, 189, 204 n.3
Woodhouse, E. 4
Woodrum, J. 237
Woolgar, S. 19, 20, 40, 275
World Commission on Environment and
Development (WCED) 55, 64, 79
World Conservation Monitoring Unit
(WCMC) 70

Printed in Great Britain
by Amazon.co.uk, Ltd.,
Marston Gate.